Editors/Advisory Board

Members of the Advisory Board are instrumental in the final selection of articles for each edition of ANNUAL EDITIONS. Their review of articles for content, level, currentness, and appropriateness provides critical direction to the editor and staff. We think that you will find their careful consideration well reflected in this volume.

EDITOR

Fred H. Maidment
Western Connecticut State University

ADVISORY BOARD

Suhail Abboushi
Duquesne University

Lloyd L. Byars
Georgia Tech

Art Camburn
Buena Vista College

Ronald L. Caplan
The Richard Stockton College of New Jersey

Jack R. Clarcq
Rochester Institute of Technology

Richard Clodfelter
University of South Carolina

Joseph J. Dobson
Western Illinois University

Thomas Duda
SUNY at Canton

W. Frances Emory
Northern Virginia Community College

James Evans
University of San Diego

Peter S. Goodrich
Providence College

Kenneth E. Hoffman
Emporia State University

Mary G. Klinger
SUNY Empire State College

James A. McCambridge
Colorado State University

Robert O. Nixon
Pima Community College - West Campus

Douglas G. Ohmer
Northern State University

Joseph A. Petrick
Wright State University

Richard F. Poist
Iowa State University

Robert Scott
Community College of Baltimore County, Essex

Roberta Snow
West Chester University

Louis Zivic
Fitchburg State College

Staff

Jeffrey L. Hahn, Vice President/Publisher

EDITORIAL STAFF

Theodore Knight, Ph.D., Managing Editor
Roberta Monaco, Managing Developmental Editor
Dorothy Fink, Associate Developmental Editor
Addie Raucci, Senior Administrative Editor
Robin Zarnetske, Permissions Editor
Marie Lazauskas, Permissions Assistant
Lisa Holmes-Doebrick, Senior Program Coordinator

TECHNOLOGY STAFF

Richard Tietjen, Senior Publishing Technologist
Marcuss Oslander, Sponsoring Editor of eContent
Christopher Santos, Senior eContent Developer
Janice Ward, Software Support Analyst
Angela Mule, eContent Developer
Ciro Parente, Technology Developmental Editor
Joe Offredi, Technology Developmental Editor

PRODUCTION STAFF

Brenda S. Filley, Director of Production
Charles Vitelli, Designer
Mike Campbell, Production Coordinator
Eldis Lima, Graphics
Nancy Norton, Graphics
Juliana Arbo, Typesetting Supervisor
Julie Marsh, Project Editor
Jocelyn Proto, Typesetter
Cynthia Powers, Typesetter

To the Reader

In publishing ANNUAL EDITIONS we recognize the enormous role played by the magazines, newspapers, and journals of the public press in providing current, first-rate educational information in a broad spectrum of interest areas. Many of these articles are appropriate for students, researchers, and professionals seeking accurate, current material to help bridge the gap between principles and theories and the real world. These articles, however, become more useful for study when those of lasting value are carefully collected, organized, indexed, and reproduced in a low-cost format, which provides easy and permanent access when the material is needed. That is the role played by ANNUAL EDITIONS.

It could be said that one era ended and another began on September 11, 2001. Washington, D.C., and New York City were brutally attacked by terrorists who killed about 3,000 people plus those people who died in an airplane crash in Pennsylvania. Organizations, led by the government of the United States, are continuing to respond to the need to defeat the terrorists. But, in order for the United States to achieve victory in this new kind of war, American organizations, including corporations, will have to utilize and manage their resources effectively. This means that managers in both the civilian and military sectors of the country will have to perform their tasks in an efficient manner. Directing the nation's resources against these terrorists will be a primary focus of this country's government for the foreseeable future. Victory will only be achieved through constant vigilance and attention to detail, and it will be managers who will have the primary responsibility for those functions.

Since managers are the people charged with getting things done in today's society—a society that has been molded by the success of the management profession—the many new challenges that the world faces will be met, at least in part, by managers.

Managers must respond to a changing environment by keeping informed on the developments in the field. The articles that have been chosen for *Annual Editions: Management 04/05* represent a cross section of the current writings on the subject along with a few selected classics. This collection addresses the various components of management with emphasis on the functions of planning, organizing, directing, controlling, and staffing. Readings have been chosen from a wide variety of publications, including *The Harvard Business Review, People Management, MIT Sloan Management Review, Organizational Dynamics*, and *Business Week*.

Annual Editions: Management 04/05 contains a number of features that are designed to make it useful for people interested in management. These features include a *table of contents* with *abstracts* that summarize each article and highlight key ideas in bold italics, and a *topic guide* for locating articles on a specific subject. Also, there are selected *World Wide Web* sites that can be used to further explore the topics.

This volume is organized into seven units that deal with specific interrelated topics in management. Each unit begins with an overview that provides the necessary background information that allows the reader to place the selections in the context of the book. Important topics are emphasized, and *key points to consider* address major themes. Also, at the end of each unit are short cases and exercises that are designed to implement and expand on the general topic of the unit easily and effectively.

This is the twelfth edition of *Annual Editions: Management,* one of a long line of books addressing the evolution of management. This collection, we believe, provides the reader with the most complete and current selection of readings available on the subject. We would like to know what you think. Please take a few minutes to complete and return the postage-paid *article rating form* at the back of the volume. Any book can be improved, and we need your help to improve *Annual Editions: Management*.

Fred Maidment
Editor

ANNUAL EDITIONS

Management

Twelfth Edition

04/05

EDITOR
Fred H. Maidment
Western Connecticut State University

Dr. Fred Maidment is associate professor of management at Western Connecticut State University in Danbury, Connecticut. He received his bachelor's degree from New York University and his master's degree from the Bernard M. Baruch College of the City University of New York. In 1983 Dr. Maidment received his doctorate from the University of South Carolina. He resides in Connecticut with his wife.

McGraw-Hill/Dushkin
530 Old Whitfield Street, Guilford, Connecticut 06437

Visit us on the Internet
http://www.dushkin.com

Credits

1. **Managers, Performance, and the Environment**
   Unit photo—© 2004 by Sweet By & By/Cindy Brown.
2. **Planning**
   Unit photo—© 2004 by PhotoDisc, Inc.
3. **Organizing**
   Unit photo—© 2004 by PhotoDisc, Inc.
4. **Directing**
   Unit photo—TRW, Inc. photo.
5. **Controlling**
   Unit photo—© 2004 by PhotoDisc, Inc.
6. **Staffing and Human Resources**
   Unit photo—© 2004 by PhotoDisc, Inc.
7. **Perspectives and Trends**
   Unit photo—© 2004 by PhotoDisc, Inc.

Copyright

Cataloging in Publication Data
Main entry under title: Annual Editions: Management. 2004/2005.
1. Management—Periodicals. I. Maidment, Fred, *comp.* II. Title: Management.
ISBN 0–07–287441–4   658'.05   ISSN 1092–4876

© 2004 by McGraw-Hill/Dushkin, Guilford, CT 06437, A Division of The McGraw-Hill Companies.

Copyright law prohibits the reproduction, storage, or transmission in any form by any means of any portion of this publication without the express written permission of McGraw-Hill/Dushkin, and of the copyright holder (if different) of the part of the publication to be reproduced. The Guidelines for Classroom Copying endorsed by Congress explicitly state that unauthorized copying may not be used to create, to replace, or to substitute for anthologies, compilations, or collective works.

Annual Editions® is a Registered Trademark of McGraw-Hill/Dushkin, A Division of The McGraw-Hill Companies.

Twelfth Edition

Cover image © 2004 PhotoDisc, Inc.
Printed in the United States of America   1234567890BAHBAH54   Printed on Recycled Paper

Contents

To the Reader iv
Topic Guide xi
Selected World Wide Web Sites xvi

UNIT 1
Managers, Performance, and the Environment

The five articles in this section examine some of the dynamics of management in today's business environment.

Unit Overview xviii

Part A. Management

1. **The Manager's Job: Folklore and Fact,** Henry Mintzberg, *Harvard Business Review,* March/April 1990
   This classic essay by Henry Mintzberg replaces the traditional view of ***management functions***—to plan, to coordinate, to organize, and to control—with a look at what managers really do. 3

Part B. Management Skills, Roles, and Performance

2. **Why Companies Fail,** Ram Charan and Jerry Useem, *Fortune,* May 27, 2002
   Why do companies fail? The reason is not that the employees did not do their job adequately or that the market went against the company. The real reason is that the senior managers of the company did not do their jobs. 12

3. **If You Think You're Hard Enough,** Stefan Stern, *Management Today,* March 2003
   During the boom times of the 1990s, managers were encouraged to be more open. Now, with business more difficult than in the past, ***managers*** need to take a more guarded, ***tougher approach***. 19

Part C. The Environment

4. **Spotting Patterns on the Fly,** David Sibley and Julia Yoshida, *Harvard Business Review,* November 2002
   Patterns can be found in nature and learning to spot them can help managers to recognize ***patterns in business***. 23

5. **Restoring Public Confidence in American Business,** Murray Weidenbaum, *The Washington Quarterly,* Winter 2002–03
   During the past several years, ***American business*** has suffered a number of blows affecting the ***confidence*** that people have in it. Murray Weidenbaum has some ideas on what can be done to help restore people's faith. 29

Case I. Robin Hood; Exercise: Managerial Development 34

The concepts in bold italics are developed in the article. For further expansion, please refer to the Topic Guide and the Index.

v

UNIT 2
Planning

Five articles in this unit discuss the elements of decision making, strategic analysis, and strategic management.

Unit Overview   36

Part A. Management Classic

6. **A New Look at Managerial Decision Making,** Victor H. Vroom, from *Readings in Management,* South–Western, 1986
   There are many **ways to make decisions.** Selecting the most appropriate is the topic of this classic essay by Victor Vroom.   38

Part B. Decision Support Systems

7. **Management Accounting Master: Closing the Gap Between Managerial Accounting and External Reporting,** Soeren Dressler, *Journal of Cost Management,* January/February 2002
   Managers need effective and **accurate information to make decisions.** A globally harmonized **management accounting master** can integrate multiple accounting systems, serving as a blueprint for the organization.   48

Part C. Strategic Analysis

8. **Michael Porter: What Is Strategy?,** *Thinkers,* April 2002
   Michael Porter is one of the leading thinkers on management, especially **strategic management.** This article summarizes some of his ideas.   58

9. **Six Priorities That Make a Great Strategic Decision,** Mary Burner Lippitt, *Journal of Business Strategy,* January/February 2003
   In this article by Mary Burner Lippitt, read about the **six priorities for strategic thinking:** (1) state-of-the-art products/services; (2) market share; (3) building systems to maintain high performance; (4) process improvement; (5) developing a competent workforce; and (6) long-term positioning.   61

10. **The Americanization of Toyota,** *Business Week,* April 15, 2002
    There are few firms more identified with the Japanese automobile industry than Toyota. Yet, Toyota is changing as **the Japanese economy** remains in a recession and the American market takes on greater meaning.   65

Case II. The Fairfax County Social Welfare Agency; Exercise: NASA   68

UNIT 3
Organizing

In this section, four selections examine the impact of organization on the job of managing. Topics discussed include elements of organization, job design, and what is needed to fundamentally change a business.

Unit Overview   70

Part A. Management Classic

11. **Classifying the Elements of Work,** Frank B. Gilbreth and Lillian M. Gilbreth, from *Management Classics,* Goodyear, 1977
    Time and motion studies were among the earliest results of Frederick W. Taylor's work. In this selection, two of the pioneers in these studies discuss the ideas upon which time and motion studies are based.   72

The concepts in bold italics are developed in the article. For further expansion, please refer to the Topic Guide and the Index.

Part B. Elements of Organization

12. **Beyond Empowerment: Building a Company of Citizens,** Brook Manville and Josiah Ober, *Harvard Business Review,* January 2003
    There are **alternative forms of organization** to the traditional **bureaucratic forms** typically found in many **companies.** Some of them are as old as Western civilization itself. **81**

Part C. Designing and Changing the Organization

13. **Creating a Learning Organization,** Neal McChristy, *Office Solutions,* February 2002
    Successful organizations in the future are going to be those that allow their employees to grow and become more productive. **86**

14. **The Change-Capable Organization,** Patricia A. McLagan, *Training & Development,* January 2003
    Change is the only constant. Those **organizations** that are **able to change** are the ones that are going to be successful. **Mavericks** are often the key to change, and organizations must learn to embrace them. **89**

Case III. Resistance to Change; Exercise: Organizing **94**

UNIT 4
Directing

The five selections in this section examine how the elements of leadership, performance, and communication contribute to the art of directing a business organization.

Unit Overview **96**

Part A. Management Classic

15. **The Abilene Paradox: The Management of Agreement,** Jerry B. Harvey, *Organizational Dynamics,* Summer 1988
    Many **people in organizations** have found themselves in situations in which, because they did not say what they meant, they became caught in the web of the **Abilene paradox.** Jerry Harvey presents various aspects of this paradox. **98**

Part B. Leadership

16. **The Myth of Charismatic Leaders,** Joseph A. Raelin, *Training & Development,* March 2003
    Charismatic leaders do not always provide the best form of leadership for organizations. Some organizations, in fact, would be far better off without them. **108**

Part C. Performance

17. **Effective Performance Counseling,** *Leadership for the Front Lines,* February 15, 2002
    Evaluating employee performance is always a difficult task for managers. Here are some helpful hints on how to do a **performance appraisal** in an effective and humane manner. **111**

18. **The Myth of Synergy,** James Surowiecki, *MBA Jungle,* May 2002
    Synergy is at best an elusive concept. Often defined as 1+1=3, it is very difficult to attain. Often the rationale for mergers and acquisitions, synergy frequently fails to appear and the organization can end up with a synergy in which 1+1=1. **113**

Part D. Communication

19. **When You Disagree With the Boss's Order, Do You Tell Your Staff?,** Carol Hymowitz, *Wall Street Journal,* April 16, 2002
    How do you handle a situation **where you disagree with what the boss** has ordered? Do you let your employees know? Do you act as though you agree? **116**

The concepts in bold italics are developed in the article. For further expansion, please refer to the Topic Guide and the Index.

Case IV. Cub Scout Pack 81; Exercise: Listening 118

UNIT 5
Controlling

Four articles in this section consider what makes up effective control of the business organization.

Unit Overview 120

Part A. Management Classic

20. **An Uneasy Look at Performance Appraisal,** Douglas McGregor, *Harvard Business Review,* May/June 1957

    In this classic article, Douglas McGregor, who also wrote about the X and Y theories of management, looks at how *performance appraisals* can be effectively used to help management and to control the enterprise. 122

Part B. Financial Control

21. **The Cost of Failure,** Edward S. Robins, *Intelligent Enterprise,* March 1, 2003

    What happens when a firm fails, not slowly and gradually, but suddenly, when nobody is expecting it? To avoid this kind of financial catastrophe, Edward Robins suggests incorporating management and *analytic capabilities to assess risk.* 127

Part C. Security

22. **How Safe Is Your Job? The Threat of Workplace Violence,** Laurence Miller, *USA Today Magazine (Society for the Advancement of Education),* March 2002

    Violence in the workplace is a continuing problem that all companies must face. Doing something about it before it happens is the subject of this article. 132

Part D. Total Quality Management

23. **Mail Preparation Total Quality Management,** Richard W. Pavely, *Office Solutions,* April 2002

    The U.S. Postal Service is trying to improve its service while at the same time keeping costs under control. One of the techniques they are using is the *Mail Preparation Total Quality Management* (MPTQM) program. 135

Case V. Evaluation of Organizational Effectiveness; Exercise: Win as Much As You Can! 138

UNIT 6
Staffing and Human Resources

This section's four selections examine the elements necessarily considered when a workforce is developed.

Unit Overview 140

Part A. Management Classic

24. **Management Women and the New Facts of Life,** Felice N. Schwartz, *Harvard Business Review,* January/February 1989

    This is the article, first published in 1989, that started all the discussion of the *"Mommy Track"* and the *"Daddy Track"* for employees. 142

The concepts in bold italics are developed in the article. For further expansion, please refer to the Topic Guide and the Index.

viii

Part B.   Developing Human Resources

25. **Who Are You Really Hiring?,** Shari Caudron, *Workforce,* November 2002

    One of the necessary parts of any **hiring** process is a **background check.** This is especially true the higher one goes in the organization. Yet, some companies think they are saving money when they don't do these checks. Later they could find that they should have.   **149**

26. **Secrets of Finding and Keeping Good Employees,** Jim Sirbasku, *USA Today Magazine (Society for the Advancement of Education),* January 2002

    If you are going **to hire and keep good employees,** you must, after hiring them, make them feel that it is worth their while to stay. Remember, your competitors are always seeking your good employees, and it is up to you to keep them.   **153**

Part C.   Maintaining an Effective Workforce

27. **Pay It Forward,** Patricia K. Zingheim and Jay R. Schuster, *People Management,* February 7, 2002

    Modern and sophisticated **reward systems** not only reward at the individual level, but at the company, business unit, and team level. This article has some insights on how to do that.   **158**

Case VI. The "Homes" Is Where the Union Is; Exercise: Assumptions About People at Work   **160**

UNIT 7
Perspectives and Trends

These nine articles examine business challenges. Topics include multinational enterprise, corporate culture, and ethics.

Unit Overview   **162**

Part A.   Management Classic

28. **The Discipline of Innovation,** Peter F. Drucker, *Harvard Business Review,* August 2002

    Peter Drucker identifies several kinds of opportunities that can be used to help **develop innovation** in this classic article from the **Harvard Business Review.**   **165**

Part B.   The Multinational Corporation

29. **American Corporations: The New Sovereigns,** Lawrence E. Mitchell, *The Chronicle of Higher Education,* January 18, 2002

    Is there too much power in **multinational organizations**? At what point do corporations reach a condition where no single government or other entity has any jurisdiction over them? Would they effectively become sovereign states?   **171**

30. **The Need for a Corporate Global Mind-Set,** Thomas M. Begley and David P. Boyd, *MIT Sloan Management Review,* Winter 2003

    Corporations need to balance global consistency with local needs and the necessity to be able to respond to those needs. A **company-wide global mind-set** is necessary to do this successfully.   **174**

Part C.   Corporate Culture

31. **Helping Organizations Build Community,** Tracy Mauro, *Training & Development,* February 2002

    Using **corporate culture** to build and develop a firm is this article's subject.   **182**

The concepts in bold italics are developed in the article. For further expansion, please refer to the Topic Guide and the Index.

ix

Part D. Ethics and Social Responsibility

32. **Ensuring Ethical Effectiveness,** Randy Myers, *Journal of Accountancy,* February 2003

    Companies need a **code of ethics** if they are going to have a guide for behavior, and now the new **Sarbanes-Oxley Act** requires such a code.   **186**

33. **The Competitive Advantage of Corporate Philanthropy,** Michael E. Porter and Mark R. Kramer, *Harvard Business Review,* December 2002

    Companies have not used their **corporate giving** very effectively to advance their strategic agendas. This article by Michael Porter and Mark Kramer gives some guidance into how organizations might do a more effective job of using their philanthropy more to their **competitive advantage.**   **191**

34. **Who Cares Wins,** Stephen Cook, *Management Today,* January 2003

    Organizations that take an active role in addressing their **corporate social responsibility** tend to be more profitable. Investors, customers, and other stakeholders are beginning to recognize this, and those companies are reaping the benefits.   **203**

Part E. Small Business and Enterpreneurship

35. **Determining the Strategies and Tactics of Ownership Succession,** James Ahern, *National Underwriter Life and Health,* February 10, 2003

    Every entrepreneur will eventually have to make a plan for getting out of the business. **Retirement** includes many options, and every entrepreneur should consider **transition plan options** from the beginning.   **207**

Part F. The War on Terror

36. **Hearts, Minds, and the War Against Terror,** Joshua Muravchik, *Commentary,* May 2002

    The war on terror will not be won on the battlefield. The greater war on terror will be to capture the hearts and minds of the people in the Middle East and other parts of the world.   **209**

Case VII. The Trip to Denver; Exercise: The Resume—A Career Management Tool	**214**
Index	**216**
Test Your Knowledge Form	**219**
Article Rating Form	**220**

The concepts in bold italics are developed in the article. For further expansion, please refer to the Topic Guide and the Index.

Topic Guide

This topic guide suggests how the selections in this book relate to the subjects covered in your course. You may want to use the topics listed on these pages to search the Web more easily.

On the following pages a number of Web sites have been gathered specifically for this book. They are arranged to reflect the units of this *Annual Edition*. You can link to these sites by going to the DUSHKIN ONLINE support site at *http://www.dushkin.com/online/*.

ALL THE ARTICLES THAT RELATE TO EACH TOPIC ARE LISTED BELOW THE BOLD-FACED TERM.

Abilene paradox
15. The Abilene Paradox: The Management of Agreement

Accounting
2. Why Companies Fail
7. Management Accounting Master: Closing the Gap Between Managerial Accounting and External Reporting
14. The Change-Capable Organization
21. The Cost of Failure

Antitrust law
5. Restoring Public Confidence in American Business

Balanced scorecard
9. Six Priorities That Make a Great Strategic Decision
33. The Competitive Advantage of Corporate Philanthropy

Behavior
13. Creating a Learning Organization
17. Effective Performance Counseling

Benefits
12. Beyond Empowerment: Building a Company of Citizens
14. The Change-Capable Organization
20. An Uneasy Look at Performance Appraisal
24. Management Women and the New Facts of Life
26. Secrets of Finding and Keeping Good Employees
27. Pay It Forward
30. The Need for a Corporate Global Mind-Set

Blue-collar jobs
22. How Safe Is Your Job? The Threat of Workplace Violence

Business environment
2. Why Companies Fail
3. If You Think You're Hard Enough
4. Spotting Patterns on the Fly
8. Michael Porter: What Is Strategy?
14. The Change-Capable Organization
16. The Myth of Charismatic Leaders
18. The Myth of Synergy
22. How Safe Is Your Job? The Threat of Workplace Violence
24. Management Women and the New Facts of Life
26. Secrets of Finding and Keeping Good Employees
30. The Need for a Corporate Global Mind-Set
34. Who Cares Wins
36. Hearts, Minds, and the War Against Terror

Business ethics
12. Beyond Empowerment: Building a Company of Citizens
18. The Myth of Synergy
19. When You Disagree With the Boss's Order, Do You Tell Your Staff?
20. An Uneasy Look at Performance Appraisal
22. How Safe Is Your Job? The Threat of Workplace Violence
24. Management Women and the New Facts of Life
25. Who Are You Really Hiring?
32. Ensuring Ethical Effectiveness
33. The Competitive Advantage of Corporate Philanthropy
34. Who Cares Wins

Business law
5. Restoring Public Confidence in American Business

Business leadership
3. If You Think You're Hard Enough
4. Spotting Patterns on the Fly
12. Beyond Empowerment: Building a Company of Citizens
14. The Change-Capable Organization
16. The Myth of Charismatic Leaders
18. The Myth of Synergy
34. Who Cares Wins

Change
10. The Americanization of Toyota
13. Creating a Learning Organization
17. Effective Performance Counseling
29. American Corporations: The New Sovereigns

Codes of conduct
5. Restoring Public Confidence in American Business

Commercial law
5. Restoring Public Confidence in American Business

Communication
1. The Manager's Job: Folklore and Fact
6. A New Look at Managerial Decision Making
12. Beyond Empowerment: Building a Company of Citizens
13. Creating a Learning Organization
14. The Change-Capable Organization
15. The Abilene Paradox: The Management of Agreement
17. Effective Performance Counseling
19. When You Disagree With the Boss's Order, Do You Tell Your Staff?
20. An Uneasy Look at Performance Appraisal
22. How Safe Is Your Job? The Threat of Workplace Violence
24. Management Women and the New Facts of Life
25. Who Are You Really Hiring?
30. The Need for a Corporate Global Mind-Set
31. Helping Organizations Build Community
32. Ensuring Ethical Effectiveness
33. The Competitive Advantage of Corporate Philanthropy
34. Who Cares Wins

Competitive advantage
9. Six Priorities That Make a Great Strategic Decision
13. Creating a Learning Organization
17. Effective Performance Counseling
29. American Corporations: The New Sovereigns

Consumer power
9. Six Priorities That Make a Great Strategic Decision

Consumer protection
5. Restoring Public Confidence in American Business

xi

Controlling
1. The Manager's Job: Folklore and Fact
2. Why Companies Fail
6. A New Look at Managerial Decision Making
7. Management Accounting Master: Closing the Gap Between Managerial Accounting and External Reporting
8. Michael Porter: What Is Strategy?
11. Classifying the Elements of Work
19. When You Disagree With the Boss's Order, Do You Tell Your Staff?
20. An Uneasy Look at Performance Appraisal
21. The Cost of Failure
22. How Safe Is Your Job? The Threat of Workplace Violence
23. Mail Preparation Total Quality Management
25. Who Are You Really Hiring?
32. Ensuring Ethical Effectiveness

Copyright laws
5. Restoring Public Confidence in American Business

Corporate culture
2. Why Companies Fail
3. If You Think You're Hard Enough
10. The Americanization of Toyota
12. Beyond Empowerment: Building a Company of Citizens
14. The Change-Capable Organization
16. The Myth of Charismatic Leaders
18. The Myth of Synergy
20. An Uneasy Look at Performance Appraisal
22. How Safe Is Your Job? The Threat of Workplace Violence
27. Pay It Forward
28. The Discipline of Innovation
30. The Need for a Corporate Global Mind-Set
32. Ensuring Ethical Effectiveness
34. Who Cares Wins

Corporate law
5. Restoring Public Confidence in American Business

Corporate leadership
1. The Manager's Job: Folklore and Fact
2. Why Companies Fail
6. A New Look at Managerial Decision Making
8. Michael Porter: What Is Strategy?
9. Six Priorities That Make a Great Strategic Decision
13. Creating a Learning Organization
15. The Abilene Paradox: The Management of Agreement
19. When You Disagree With the Boss's Order, Do You Tell Your Staff?
20. An Uneasy Look at Performance Appraisal

Corporate organization
15. The Abilene Paradox: The Management of Agreement

Corporate performance
1. The Manager's Job: Folklore and Fact
2. Why Companies Fail
3. If You Think You're Hard Enough
6. A New Look at Managerial Decision Making
9. Six Priorities That Make a Great Strategic Decision
11. Classifying the Elements of Work
12. Beyond Empowerment: Building a Company of Citizens
14. The Change-Capable Organization
15. The Abilene Paradox: The Management of Agreement
16. The Myth of Charismatic Leaders
18. The Myth of Synergy
19. When You Disagree With the Boss's Order, Do You Tell Your Staff?
20. An Uneasy Look at Performance Appraisal
21. The Cost of Failure
23. Mail Preparation Total Quality Management
24. Management Women and the New Facts of Life

27. Pay It Forward
28. The Discipline of Innovation
34. Who Cares Wins

Corporate strategy
6. A New Look at Managerial Decision Making
9. Six Priorities That Make a Great Strategic Decision
11. Classifying the Elements of Work
15. The Abilene Paradox: The Management of Agreement
24. Management Women and the New Facts of Life
25. Who Are You Really Hiring?
33. The Competitive Advantage of Corporate Philanthropy

Costs-cost management
7. Management Accounting Master: Closing the Gap Between Managerial Accounting and External Reporting

Decision making in business
1. The Manager's Job: Folklore and Fact
2. Why Companies Fail
3. If You Think You're Hard Enough
6. A New Look at Managerial Decision Making
7. Management Accounting Master: Closing the Gap Between Managerial Accounting and External Reporting
8. Michael Porter: What Is Strategy?
9. Six Priorities That Make a Great Strategic Decision
11. Classifying the Elements of Work
15. The Abilene Paradox: The Management of Agreement
19. When You Disagree With the Boss's Order, Do You Tell Your Staff?
20. An Uneasy Look at Performance Appraisal
24. Management Women and the New Facts of Life
32. Ensuring Ethical Effectiveness
34. Who Cares Wins
36. Hearts, Minds, and the War Against Terror

Developing world
29. American Corporations: The New Sovereigns

Directing business
1. The Manager's Job: Folklore and Fact
5. Restoring Public Confidence in American Business
6. A New Look at Managerial Decision Making
8. Michael Porter: What Is Strategy?
11. Classifying the Elements of Work
14. The Change-Capable Organization
15. The Abilene Paradox: The Management of Agreement
16. The Myth of Charismatic Leaders
18. The Myth of Synergy
19. When You Disagree With the Boss's Order, Do You Tell Your Staff?
28. The Discipline of Innovation
30. The Need for a Corporate Global Mind-Set

Discipline
17. Effective Performance Counseling
22. How Safe Is Your Job? The Threat of Workplace Violence
31. Helping Organizations Build Community

E-business
18. The Myth of Synergy

Employee benefits
24. Management Women and the New Facts of Life

Employment law
5. Restoring Public Confidence in American Business

Enron
2. Why Companies Fail

Entrepreneurship
1. The Manager's Job: Folklore and Fact

Ethics
22. How Safe Is Your Job? The Threat of Workplace Violence

Feedback
13. Creating a Learning Organization
17. Effective Performance Counseling
31. Helping Organizations Build Community

Finance
2. Why Companies Fail
5. Restoring Public Confidence in American Business
7. Management Accounting Master: Closing the Gap Between Managerial Accounting and External Reporting
14. The Change-Capable Organization
21. The Cost of Failure
27. Pay It Forward

Financial statements
7. Management Accounting Master: Closing the Gap Between Managerial Accounting and External Reporting

Group dynamics
10. The Americanization of Toyota
13. Creating a Learning Organization
31. Helping Organizations Build Community

Hiring
25. Who Are You Really Hiring?

Human resources
6. A New Look at Managerial Decision Making
9. Six Priorities That Make a Great Strategic Decision
11. Classifying the Elements of Work
12. Beyond Empowerment: Building a Company of Citizens
13. Creating a Learning Organization
17. Effective Performance Counseling
20. An Uneasy Look at Performance Appraisal
22. How Safe Is Your Job? The Threat of Workplace Violence
24. Management Women and the New Facts of Life
25. Who Are You Really Hiring?
26. Secrets of Finding and Keeping Good Employees
27. Pay It Forward
30. The Need for a Corporate Global Mind-Set
35. Determining the Strategies and Tactics of Ownership Succession

Informal communication
13. Creating a Learning Organization
17. Effective Performance Counseling
31. Helping Organizations Build Community

International business
5. Restoring Public Confidence in American Business
7. Management Accounting Master: Closing the Gap Between Managerial Accounting and External Reporting
30. The Need for a Corporate Global Mind-Set

International organizations
29. American Corporations: The New Sovereigns

Job design
1. The Manager's Job: Folklore and Fact
6. A New Look at Managerial Decision Making
11. Classifying the Elements of Work
20. An Uneasy Look at Performance Appraisal
24. Management Women and the New Facts of Life

26. Secrets of Finding and Keeping Good Employees
27. Pay It Forward

Knowledge management
13. Creating a Learning Organization
17. Effective Performance Counseling

Labor relations
13. Creating a Learning Organization
17. Effective Performance Counseling
22. How Safe Is Your Job? The Threat of Workplace Violence
31. Helping Organizations Build Community

Management accountability
1. The Manager's Job: Folklore and Fact
3. If You Think You're Hard Enough
6. A New Look at Managerial Decision Making
12. Beyond Empowerment: Building a Company of Citizens
14. The Change-Capable Organization
15. The Abilene Paradox: The Management of Agreement
16. The Myth of Charismatic Leaders
21. The Cost of Failure
24. Management Women and the New Facts of Life
32. Ensuring Ethical Effectiveness
33. The Competitive Advantage of Corporate Philanthropy
34. Who Cares Wins

Management skills
2. Why Companies Fail
3. If You Think You're Hard Enough
4. Spotting Patterns on the Fly
6. A New Look at Managerial Decision Making
26. Secrets of Finding and Keeping Good Employees

Marketing
8. Michael Porter: What Is Strategy?
36. Hearts, Minds, and the War Against Terror

Morale
13. Creating a Learning Organization
17. Effective Performance Counseling
31. Helping Organizations Build Community

Motivating employees
9. Six Priorities That Make a Great Strategic Decision

Motivation
6. A New Look at Managerial Decision Making
9. Six Priorities That Make a Great Strategic Decision
10. The Americanization of Toyota
13. Creating a Learning Organization
15. The Abilene Paradox: The Management of Agreement
17. Effective Performance Counseling
24. Management Women and the New Facts of Life
31. Helping Organizations Build Community

Multinational corporations
7. Management Accounting Master: Closing the Gap Between Managerial Accounting and External Reporting
8. Michael Porter: What Is Strategy?
10. The Americanization of Toyota
29. American Corporations: The New Sovereigns
30. The Need for a Corporate Global Mind-Set

Nonverbal communication
17. Effective Performance Counseling
31. Helping Organizations Build Community

Not-for-profit organizations
34. Who Cares Wins

Organizational design
10. The Americanization of Toyota
29. American Corporations: The New Sovereigns
31. Helping Organizations Build Community

Organizational development
10. The Americanization of Toyota
29. American Corporations: The New Sovereigns
31. Helping Organizations Build Community

Organization change
2. Why Companies Fail
4. Spotting Patterns on the Fly
8. Michael Porter: What Is Strategy?
12. Beyond Empowerment: Building a Company of Citizens
14. The Change-Capable Organization
18. The Myth of Synergy
23. Mail Preparation Total Quality Management
28. The Discipline of Innovation
30. The Need for a Corporate Global Mind-Set
32. Ensuring Ethical Effectiveness
35. Determining the Strategies and Tactics of Ownership Succession

Organized labor
20. An Uneasy Look at Performance Appraisal
23. Mail Preparation Total Quality Management

Organizing
1. The Manager's Job: Folklore and Fact
2. Why Companies Fail
4. Spotting Patterns on the Fly
6. A New Look at Managerial Decision Making
8. Michael Porter: What Is Strategy?
10. The Americanization of Toyota
11. Classifying the Elements of Work
12. Beyond Empowerment: Building a Company of Citizens
14. The Change-Capable Organization
18. The Myth of Synergy
19. When You Disagree With the Boss's Order, Do You Tell Your Staff?
20. An Uneasy Look at Performance Appraisal
23. Mail Preparation Total Quality Management
24. Management Women and the New Facts of Life
28. The Discipline of Innovation

Planning
1. The Manager's Job: Folklore and Fact
2. Why Companies Fail
4. Spotting Patterns on the Fly
6. A New Look at Managerial Decision Making
7. Management Accounting Master: Closing the Gap Between Managerial Accounting and External Reporting
8. Michael Porter: What Is Strategy?
10. The Americanization of Toyota
20. An Uneasy Look at Performance Appraisal
25. Who Are You Really Hiring?
26. Secrets of Finding and Keeping Good Employees
27. Pay It Forward
28. The Discipline of Innovation
34. Who Cares Wins
35. Determining the Strategies and Tactics of Ownership Succession
36. Hearts, Minds, and the War Against Terror

Productivity
1. The Manager's Job: Folklore and Fact
2. Why Companies Fail
3. If You Think You're Hard Enough
6. A New Look at Managerial Decision Making
7. Management Accounting Master: Closing the Gap Between Managerial Accounting and External Reporting

9. Six Priorities That Make a Great Strategic Decision
11. Classifying the Elements of Work
12. Beyond Empowerment: Building a Company of Citizens
15. The Abilene Paradox: The Management of Agreement
16. The Myth of Charismatic Leaders
18. The Myth of Synergy
23. Mail Preparation Total Quality Management
24. Management Women and the New Facts of Life
26. Secrets of Finding and Keeping Good Employees
27. Pay It Forward
28. The Discipline of Innovation
34. Who Cares Wins

Rewards
17. Effective Performance Counseling
31. Helping Organizations Build Community

Safety
22. How Safe Is Your Job? The Threat of Workplace Violence

Security
25. Who Are You Really Hiring?

Social responsibility
29. American Corporations: The New Sovereigns
31. Helping Organizations Build Community
32. Ensuring Ethical Effectiveness
36. Hearts, Minds, and the War Against Terror

Sociocultural forces
29. American Corporations: The New Sovereigns

Staffing
11. Classifying the Elements of Work
12. Beyond Empowerment: Building a Company of Citizens
25. Who Are You Really Hiring?
26. Secrets of Finding and Keeping Good Employees
27. Pay It Forward

Strategic planning
7. Management Accounting Master: Closing the Gap Between Managerial Accounting and External Reporting
33. The Competitive Advantage of Corporate Philanthropy

Strategy
2. Why Companies Fail
4. Spotting Patterns on the Fly
6. A New Look at Managerial Decision Making
7. Management Accounting Master: Closing the Gap Between Managerial Accounting and External Reporting
8. Michael Porter: What Is Strategy?
10. The Americanization of Toyota
30. The Need for a Corporate Global Mind-Set
33. The Competitive Advantage of Corporate Philanthropy
36. Hearts, Minds, and the War Against Terror

Teams
13. Creating a Learning Organization

Technology
10. The Americanization of Toyota
23. Mail Preparation Total Quality Management
28. The Discipline of Innovation

TQM
23. Mail Preparation Total Quality Management

Trust
13. Creating a Learning Organization

17. Effective Performance Counseling

Verbal communication
31. Helping Organizations Build Community

War on terror
29. American Corporations: The New Sovereigns
36. Hearts, Minds, and the War Against Terror

Workforce development
1. The Manager's Job: Folklore and Fact
6. A New Look at Managerial Decision Making
11. Classifying the Elements of Work
12. Beyond Empowerment: Building a Company of Citizens
15. The Abilene Paradox: The Management of Agreement
18. The Myth of Synergy
19. When You Disagree With the Boss's Order, Do You Tell Your Staff?
20. An Uneasy Look at Performance Appraisal
24. Management Women and the New Facts of Life
25. Who Are You Really Hiring?
26. Secrets of Finding and Keeping Good Employees
27. Pay It Forward
35. Determining the Strategies and Tactics of Ownership Succession

Workplace health
22. How Safe Is Your Job? The Threat of Workplace Violence

World Wide Web Sites

The following World Wide Web sites have been carefully researched and selected to support the articles found in this reader. The easiest way to access these selected sites is to go to our DUSHKIN ONLINE support site at *http://www.dushkin.com/online/*.

AE: Management 04/05

The following sites were available at the time of publication. Visit our Web site—we update DUSHKIN ONLINE regularly to reflect any changes.

General Sources

HBS Educators & Research
http://www.hbs.edu/educators.html
Surf through the many valuable links attached to this Educators & Research News site and preview upcoming issues of the *Harvard Business Review*.

The New York Times
http://www.nytimes.com
Browsing through the extensive archives of the *New York Times* will provide you with a vast array of articles and information related to management issues.

STAT-USA
http://www.stat-usa.gov/stat-usa.html
This site, a service of the U.S. Department of Commerce, contains daily economic news, frequently requested statistical releases, information on export and international trade, domestic economic news, statistical series, and databases. Also try *http://www.fedstats.gov* for statistics produced by more than 70 U.S. federal government agencies.

The Wall Street Journal
http://interactive.wsj.com
This is an Internet edition of the *Wall Street Journal*, a newspaper that is used by managers the world over to put their business environments in context.

Workforce Online
http://www.workforceonline.com
This site, sponsored by *Workforce* magazine, discusses trends and resources, legal information, and fluctuating pay methods data, and it also offers a research center.

UNIT 1: Managers, Performance, and the Environment

Krislyn's Favorite Advertising & Marketing Sites
http://www.krislyn.com/sites/adv.htm
This extensive list of Web sites includes information on marketing research, marketing on the Internet, demographic sources, organizations, and associations. The site also features current books on business management and marketing.

Sheffield University Management School
http://www.shef.ac.uk/uni/academic/I-M/mgt/research/research.html
The Current Research page of this British school will lead you to information on real-world management issues. Links include the economics, finance, and management of technological change, labor economics, and industrial relations.

Two Scenarios for 21st Century Organizations
http://ccs.mit.edu/21c/21CWP001.html
The MIT Scenario Working Group here presents "Shifting Networks of Small Firms" and "All-Encompassing 'Virtual Countries'" that will be of interest to any company involved in organizing and structuring to meet the demands of the new business environment.

UNIT 2: Planning

American Civil Liberties Union (ACLU)
http://www.aclu.org/issues/worker/campaign.html
The ACLU provides this page on workplace rights in its "Campaign for Fairness in the Workplace." Briefing papers on workplace issues cover such privacy issues as lifestyle discrimination, drug testing, and electronic monitoring.

Benchmarking Network
http://www.well.com/user/benchmar/tbnhome.html
This Web site is an international resource guide to benchmarking as a method of corporate planning.

GBN Scenario Planning
http://www.gbn.com
Scenario planning is a fundamental tool for thinking strategically about the future. This site, which contains many scenarios, helps organizations to understand the external environment in relation to their own business ideas and competence.

UNIT 3: Organizing

From Foosball to Flextime: Dotcommers Are Growing Up
http://www.fastcompany.com/articles/2000/12/act_childcare.html
This article by Cecilia Rothenberger explains how dot.com companies are maturing and providing flextime, on-site day care, and other benefits that "grown-up" companies have provided for years.

Sympatico: Careers
http://www.ntl.sympatico.ca/Contents/Careers/
This Canadian media site provides an electronic network with a "GripeVine" for complaining about work and finding solutions to everyday career problems.

U.S. Department of Labor (DOL)
http://www.dol.gov
Browsing through this DOL site will lead you to a vast array of labor-related data and discussions of issues affecting managers, such as the minimum wage. It presents statutory and regulatory information, and more.

Work and Organizational Psychology, Stockholm University
http://www.psychology.su.se/units/ao/ao.html
Explore topics related to job design and other management organizational concerns through this site presented by Stockholm University's Department of Psychology, Division of Work and Organizational Psychology.

xvi

www.dushkin.com/online/

UNIT 4: Directing

ADR (Alternative Dispute Resolution): General
http://www.opm.gov/er/adrguide/
Essays on the subject of alternative dispute resolution can be found at this page, which includes an ADR glossary, a definition, techniques and evaluations, issues and problems facing judges, evaluation of ADR procedures, and much more information important to the area of conflict management.

Equity Compensation, Employee Ownership & Stock Options
http://www.fed.org
The Foundation for Enterprise Development is a nonprofit organization that suggests strategies to those who are making critical decisions to improve their companies' bottom lines. This site includes interactive resources and case studies.

Office.com: The Intranet for Small Business
http://www.individual.com
This site provides daily briefings and in-depth stories of interest to managers. These links relate to such major fields as computing and media, finance, and health care insurance.

UNIT 5: Controlling

Bill Lindsay's Home Page
http://www.nku.edu/~lindsay/
Professor William M. Lindsay's home page points to a variety of interesting Internet sources to aid in the study and application of Total Quality Management principles.

Computer and Network Security
http://www.vtcif.telstra.com.au/info/security.html
Telstra provides this index for those interested in technology/security issues. It provides links to Web sources, including commercial, educational, and government materials.

Internal Auditing World Wide Web
http://www.bitwise.net/iawww/
Valuable news, resources, events, and associations related to business auditing topics are provided here.

Office of Financial Management
http://www.doi.gov/
This site of the Office of Financial Management, in the U.S. Department of the Interior, describes its financial policy and procedures, financial reporting, management control program, accounting policy and systems, and auditing follow-up.

The Potential Downside of the National Information Infrastructure
http://www.annenberg.nwu.edu/pubs/downside/
Annenberg Senior Fellow Stephen Bates discusses the National Information Infrastructure (NII). View this page for discussions of NII, including issues regarding privacy rights in the workplace.

Total Quality Leadership (TQL) vs. Management by Results
http://deming.eng.clemson.edu/pub/den/files/tql.txt
Brian L. Joiner and Peter R. Scholtes describe the reasons why the TQL system of management should replace management by results for most companies, whether small or large. It addresses such concerns as to how TQL can improve customer service and return on investment, lead to higher productivity and more jobs, and affect utilization of information technology.

Workplace Violence
http://www.osha-slc.gov/SLTC/workplaceviolence/
The Occupational Safety & Health Administration (OSHA) maintains this site, which provides information and resources on workplace violence. OSHA has developed guidelines and recommendations to reduce worker exposure to this hazard.

UNIT 6: Staffing and Human Resources

Electronic Frontier Foundation "Privacy" Archive
http://www.eff.org
This civil liberties organization site provides links to articles, FAQs, and databases having to do with protection of privacy and free expression in the workplace. Drug testing and electronic communications privacy are explored.

School of Labor and Industrial Relations Hot Links
http://www.lir.msu.edu/hotlinks
This page links to government statistics, newspapers, libraries, and international intergovernmental organizations.

U.S. Equal Employment Opportunity Commission
http://www.eeoc.gov
Consult this site for small-business information, facts about employment discrimination, and enforcement and litigation.

UNIT 7: Perspectives and Trends

Institute for International Economics
http://www.iie.com
The site of this nonpartisan research institution, devoted to the study of international economics, contains views, reviews, working papers, publications, and press releases.

Small Business Management
http://management.tqn.com/msubs.htm
Information on how to start and effectively manage a small business is available on this site.

Terrorism Research Center
http://www.terrorism.com
The Terrorism Research Center features original research, counterterrorism documents, a comprehensive list of Web links, and monthly profiles of terrorist and counterterrorist groups.

World Trade Organization (WTO) Web Site
http://www.wto.org/index.htm
At the home page of the WTO, click on About the WTO, Site Map, Search, and Links to Related Organizations.

We highly recommend that you review our Web site for expanded information and our other product lines. We are continually updating and adding links to our Web site in order to offer you the most usable and useful information that will support and expand the value of your Annual Editions. You can reach us at: *http://www.dushkin.com/annualeditions/*.

UNIT 1
Managers, Performance, and the Environment

Unit Selections

1. **The Manager's Job: Folklore and Fact**, Henry Mintzberg
2. **Why Companies Fail**, Ram Charan and Jerry Useem
3. **If You Think You're Hard Enough**, Stefan Stern
4. **Spotting Patterns on the Fly**, David Sibley and Julia Yoshida
5. **Restoring Public Confidence in American Business**, Murray Weidenbaum
   CASE I. Robin Hood; Exercise: Managerial Development

Key Points to Consider

- What do you think of the manager's job? Do you think it is only to plan, direct, organize, control, and staff, or does he or she do other things? Explain.

- Do you think the manager's job is likely to change in the twenty-first century? In what ways?

- How do you think the environment is going to change for business and other organizations in the coming years? Do you think that change will increase or decrease in speed? Explain your answer.

Links: www.dushkin.com/online/
These sites are annotated in the World Wide Web pages.

Krislyn's Favorite Advertising & Marketing Sites
http://www.krislyn.com/sites/adv.htm

Sheffield University Management School
http://www.shef.ac.uk/uni/academic/I-M/mgt/research/research.html

Two Scenarios for 21st Century Organizations
http://ccs.mit.edu/21c/21CWP001.html

The need for management has been recognized since the early days of civilization. The concepts of leadership, administration, and management have existed since before the time of Plato. Some of the early modern writers in management include Frederick W. Taylor, Elton Mayo, and Mary Parker Follett. These people helped to establish the basis of modern management theory during the first part of the twentieth century.

Management has come a long way since the days of Taylor, Mayo, and Follett. The techniques and theories that they and their successors helped to develop have contributed to the establishment of industrialized countries as major forces in the world. These ideas helped American culture dominate the better part of the twentieth century, and the success of Western concepts is even now being seen in eastern Europe and the republics of the former Soviet Union. Management—the way people arrange their lives and businesses—is a major part of the success that capitalism is currently enjoying. The failure that the communist system experienced in the former Soviet bloc was not a failure of industrialism; rather, it was a failure of a system that unsuccessfully attempted to use that industrial base. This was not a failure of the machines or the workers that comprised the system, but of the way the system operated and managed the equipment and people. It was a situation that people of those countries would no longer tolerate as they rushed to embrace capitalism, democracy, pluralism, and finally management as keys to their future in the twenty-first century.

As a discipline, management faces new challenges. These challenges are mostly the result of management's success. They include the transformation of the American economy from one based upon industrialization to one based upon knowledge and the challenge of other economies, in particular, the newly integrated Europe. Another challenge is the new role of managers and management as more women, African Americans, Hispanic Americans, and other minorities, as well as more demanding groups of workers with different expectations, enter the workforce. Management is responding to these challenges in various ways. New ideas are constantly being projected in the midst of the chaos that is the legacy of the post–cold war world. Times

have indeed changed, and the tools necessary to meet those changes are only now being developed. Some of these tools and techniques will have lasting impact on the way managers perform their jobs, but others will be merely passing fads.

What do managers do? As Henry Mintzberg points out in the first article in this unit, even managers themselves do not always know. Mintzberg feels that it is important to separate fact from folklore, especially when it comes to managers' own time, which is the scarcest reserouce they have to allocate.

The new economy and the forms of management it will support will be very different from the environment of the past. "Why Companies Fail" must be analyzed to determine the reasons why many organizations crashed during the burst of the stock market bubble. The dominating strength of corporations will be based on brains, not brawn; the economic system will be international, not national, in scope; and competition will be even more fierce while an organization's competitive advantage in the marketplace will be even more fleeting. Only those organizations and managers that are strong will be able to meet the challenges of the future, as seen in "If You Think You're Hard Enough."

Organizations will need managers who can think clearly and are capable of "Spotting Patterns on the Fly," to deal with the changes in all kinds of environments. First, however, it will be necessary to restore the confidence that Americans have lost as a result of the recent scandals in industry, as Murray Weidenbaum discusses in "Restoring Public Confidence in American Business." Future organizations that think, create, and adapt to the changing conditions of an increasingly fluid environment are the ones that will survive and be successful.

America's new economy—and the managers who plan, direct, organize, control, and staff its businesses—must provide new, different, and creative approaches to meet the new competitive global environment. This will require better products and services, produced and marketed with improved, more efficient methods. Organizations no longer compete only domestically, as they did in the 1950s, when General Motors, Ford, and Chrysler dominated an American auto industry that also included such names as Studebaker, Packard, Hudson, Desoto, and Nash. Today, Ford and GM must compete on an international basis with Daimler-Chrysler and names like Nissan, Toyota, Honda, Volkswagen, and BMW. Corporations the world over must meet these new conditions or accept the fate of past organizations and follow Studebaker in its drive into oblivion.

Article 1

The Manager's Job: Folklore and Fact

The classical view says that the manager organizes, coordinates, plans, and controls; the facts suggest otherwise.

Henry Mintzberg

Henry Mintzberg is the Bronfman Professor of Management at McGill University. His latest book is Mintzberg on Management: Inside Our Strange World of Organizations *(Free Press, 1989). This article appeared originally in HBR July–August 1975. It won the McKinsey Award for excellence.*

If you ask managers what they do, they will most likely tell you that they plan, organize, coordinate, and control. Then watch what they do. Don't be surprised if you can't relate what you see to these words.

When a manager is told that a factory has just burned down and then advises the caller to see whether temporary arrangements can be made to supply customers through a foreign subsidiary, is that manager planning, organizing, coordinating, or controlling? How about when he or she presents a gold watch to a retiring employee? Or attends a conference to meet people in the trade and returns with an interesting new product idea for employees to consider?

What do managers do? Even managers themselves don't always know.

These four words, which have dominated management vocabulary since the French industrialist Henri Fayol first introduced them in 1916, tell us little about what managers actually do. At best, they indicate some vague objectives managers have when they work.

The field of management, so devoted to progress and change, has for more than half a century not seriously addressed *the* basic question: What do managers do? Without a proper answer, how can we teach management? How can we design planning or information systems for managers? How can we improve the practice of management at all?

Our ignorance of the nature of managerial work shows up in various ways in the modern organization—in boasts by successful managers who never spent a single day in a management training program; in the turnover of corporate planners who never quite understood what it was the manager wanted; in the computer consoles gathering dust in the back room because the managers never used the fancy on-line MIS some analyst thought they needed. Perhaps most important, our ignorance shows up in the inability of our large public organizations to come to grips with some of their most serious policy problems.

Somehow, in the rush to automate production, to use management science in the functional areas of marketing and finance, and to apply the skills of the behavioral scientist to the problem of worker motivation, the manager—the person in charge of the organization or one of its subunits—has been forgotten.

I intend to break the reader away from Fayol's words and introduce a more supportable and useful description of managerial work. This description derives from my review and synthesis of research on how various managers have spent their time.

In some studies, managers were observed intensively; in a number of others, they kept detailed diaries; in a few studies, their records were analyzed. All kinds of managers were studied—foreman, factory supervisors, staff managers, field sales managers, hospital administrators, presidents of companies and nations, and even street gang leaders. These "managers" worked in the United States, Canada, Sweden, and Great Britain.

A synthesis of these findings paints an interesting picture, one as different from Fayol's classical view as a cubist abstract is from a Renaissance painting. In a sense, this picture will be obvious to anyone who has ever spent a day in a manager's office, either in front of the desk or behind it. Yet, at the same time, this picture throws into doubt much of the folklore that we have accepted about the manager's work.

Folklore and Facts About Managerial Work

There are four myths about the manager's job that do not bear up under careful scrutiny of the facts.

Folklore: The manager is a reflective, systematic planner. The evidence of this issue is overwhelming, but not a shred of it supports this statement.

Fact: Study after study has shown that managers work at a unrelenting pace, that their activities are characterized by brevity, variety, and discontinuity, and that they are strongly oriented to action and dislike reflective activities. Consider this evidence:

Half the activities engaged in by the five chief executives of my study lasted less than nine minutes, and only 10% exceeded one hour.[1] A study of 56 U.S. foremen found that they averaged 583 activities per eight-hour shift, an average of 1 every 48 seconds.[2] The work pace for both chief executives and foremen was unrelenting. The chief executives met a steady stream of callers and mail from the moment they arrived in the morning until they left in the evening. Coffee breaks and lunches were inevitably work related, and ever-present subordinates seemed to usurp any free moment.

How often can you work for a half an hour without interruption?

A diary study of 160 British middle and top managers found that they worked without interruption for a half hour or more only about once every two days.[3]

Of the verbal contacts the chief executives in my study engaged in, 93% were arranged on an ad hoc basis. Only 1% of the executives' time was spent in open-ended observational tours. Only 1 out of 368 verbal contacts was unrelated to a specific issue and could therefore be called general planning. Another researcher found that "in *not one single case* did a manager report obtaining important external information from a general conversation or other undirected personal communication."[4]

Is this the planner that the classical view describes? Hardly. The manager is simply responding to the pressures of the job. I found that my chief executives terminated many of their own activities, often leaving meetings before the end, and interrupted their desk work to call in subordinates. One president not only placed his desk so that he could look down a long hallway but also left his door open when he was alone—an invitation for subordinates to come in and interrupt him.

Clearly, these managers wanted to encourage the flow of current information. But more significantly, they seemed to be conditioned by their own work loads. They appreciated the opportunity cost of their own time, and they were continually aware of their ever-present obligations—mail to be answered, callers to attend to, and so on. It seems that a manager is always plagued by the possibilities of what might be done and what must be done.

When managers must plan, they seem to do so implicitly in the context of daily actions, not in some abstract process reserved for two weeks in the organization's mountain retreat. The plans of the chief executives I studied seemed to exist only in their heads—as flexible, but often specific, intentions. The traditional literature notwithstanding, the job of managing does not breed reflective planners; managers respond to stimuli, they are conditioned by their jobs to prefer live to delayed action.

Folklore: The effective manager has no regular duties to perform. Managers are constantly being told to spend more time planning and delegating and less time seeing customers and engaging in negotiations. These are not, after all, the true tasks of the manager. To use the popular analogy, the good manager, like the good conductor, carefully orchestrates everything in advance, then sits back, responding occasionally to an unforeseeable exception. But here again the pleasant abstraction just does not seem to hold up.

Fact: Managerial work involves performing a number of regular duties, including ritual and ceremony, negotiations, and processing of soft information that links the organization with its environment. Consider some evidence from the research:

A study of the work of the presidents of small companies found that they engaged in routine activities because their companies could not afford staff specialists and were so thin on operating personnel that a single absence often required the president to substitute.[5]

One study of field sales managers and another of chief executives suggest that it is a natural part of both jobs to see important customers, assuming the managers wish to keep those customers.[6]

Someone, only half in jest, once described the manager as the person who sees visitors so that other people can get their work done. In my study, I found that certain ceremonial duties—meeting visiting dignitaries, giving out gold watches, presiding at Christmas dinners—were an intrinsic part of the chief executive's job.

Studies of managers' information flow suggest that managers play a key role in securing "soft" external information (much of it available only to them because of their status) and in passing it along to their subordinates.

Folklore: The senior manager needs aggregated information, which a formal management information system best provides. Not too long ago, the words *total information system* were everywhere in the management literature. In keeping with the classical view of the manager as that individual perched on the apex of a regulated, hierarchical system, the literature's manager was to receive all important information from a giant, comprehensive MIS.

But lately, these giant MIS systems are not working—managers are simply not using them. The enthusiasm has waned. A look at how managers actually process information makes it clear why.

Fact: Managers strongly favor verbal media, telephone calls and meetings, over documents. Consider the following:

In two British studies, managers spent an average of 66% and 80% of their time in verbal (oral) communication.[7] In my study of five American chief executives, the figure was 78%.

These five chief executives treated mail processing as a burden to be dispensed with. One came in Saturday morning to process 142 pieces of mail in just over three hours, to "get rid of all the stuff." This same manager looked at the first piece of "hard" mail he had received all week, a standard cost report, and put it aside with the comment, "I never look at this."

Today's gossip may be tomorrow's fact—that's why managers cherish hearsay.

These same five chief executives responded immediately to 2 of the 40 routine reports they received during the five weeks of my study and to 4 items in the 104 periodicals. They skimmed most of these periodicals in seconds, almost ritualistically. In all, these chief executives of good-sized organizations initiated on their

Research on Managerial Work

In seeking to describe managerial work, I conducted my own research and also scanned the literature to integrate the findings of studies from many diverse sources with my own. These studies focused on two different aspects of managerial work. Some were concerned with the characteristics of work—how long managers work, where, at what pace, with what interruptions, with whom they work, and through what media they communicate. Other studies were concerned with the content of work—what activities the managers actually carry out, and why. Thus, after a meeting, one researcher might note that the manager spent 45 minutes with three government officials in their Washington office, while another might record that the manager presented the company's stand on some proposed legislation in order to change a regulation.

A few of the studies of managerial work are widely known, but most have remained buried as single journal articles or isolated books. Among the more important ones I cite are:

• Sune Carlson developed the diary method to study the work characteristics of nine Swedish managing directors. Each kept a detailed log of his activities. Carlson's results are reported in his book *Executive Behaviour*. A number of British researchers, notably Rosemary Stewart, have subsequently used Carlson's method. In *Managers and Their Jobs*, she describes the study of 160 top and middle managers of British companies.

• Leonard Sayles's book *Managerial Behavior* is another important reference. Using a method he refers to as "anthropological," Sayles studied the work content of middle and lower level managers in a large U.S. corporation. Sayles moved freely in the company, collecting whatever information struck him as important.

• Perhaps the best-known source is *Presidential Power*, in which Richard Neustadt analyzes the power and managerial behavior of Presidents Roosevelt, Truman, and Eisenhower. Neustadt used secondary sources—documents and interviews with other parties.

• Robert H. Guest, in *Personnel*, reports on a study of the foreman's working day. Fifty-six U.S. foremen were observed and each of their activities recorded during one eight-hour shift.

• Richard C. Hodgson, Daniel J. Levinson, and Abraham Zaleznik studied a team of three top executives of a U.S. hospital. From that study they wrote *The Executive Role Constellation*. They addressed the way in which work and socioemotional roles were divided among the three managers.

• William F. Whyte, from his study of a street gang during the Depression, wrote *Street Corner Society*. His findings about the gang's workings and leadership, which George C. Homans analyzed in *The Human Group,* suggest interesting similarities of job content between street gang leaders and corporate managers.

My own study involved five American CEOs of middle- to large-sized organizations—a consulting firm, a technology company, a hospital, a consumer goods company, and a school system. Using a method called "structural observation," during one intensive week of observation for each executive, I recorded various aspects of every piece of mail and every verbal contact. In all, I analyzed 890 pieces of incoming and outgoing mail and 368 verbal contacts.

---

own—that is, not in response to something else—a grand total of 25 pieces of mail during the 25 days I observed them.

An analysis of the mail the executives received reveals an interesting picture—only 13% was of specific and immediate use. So now we have another piece in the puzzle: not much of the mail provides live, current information—the action of a competitor, the mood of a government legislator, or the rating of last night's television show. Yet this is the information that drove the managers, interrupting their meetings and rescheduling their workdays.

Consider another interesting finding. Managers seem to cherish "soft" information, especially gossip, hearsay, and speculation. Why? The reason is its timeliness; today's gossip may be tomorrow's fact. The manager who misses the telephone call revealing that the company's biggest customer was seen golfing with a main competitor may read about a dramatic drop in sales in the next quarterly report. But then it's too late.

To assess the value of historical, aggregated, "hard" MIS information, consider two of the managers's prime uses for information—to identify problems and opportunities[8] and to build mental models (e.g., how the organization's budget system works, how customers buy products, how changes in the economy affect the organization). The evidence suggests that the manager identifies decision situations and builds models not with the aggregated abstractions an MIS provides but with specific tidbits of data.

Consider the words of Richard Neustadt, who studied the information-collecting habits of Presidents Roosevelt, Truman, and Eisenhower: "It is not information of a general sort that helps a President see personal stakes; not summaries, not surveys, not the *bland amalgams*. Rather… it is the odds and ends of *tangible detail* that pieced together in his mind illuminate the underside of issues put before him. To help himself he must reach out as widely as he can for every scrap of fact, opinion, gossip, bearing on his interests and relationships as President. He must become his own director of his own central intelligence."[9]

The manager's emphasis on this verbal media raises two important points. First, verbal information is stored in the brains of people. Only when people write this information down can it be stored in the files of the organization—whether in metal cabinets or on magnetic tape—and managers apparently do not write down much of what they hear. Thus the strategic data bank of the organization is not in the memory of its computers but in the minds of its managers.

Second, managers' extensive use of verbal media helps to explain why they are reluctant to delegate tasks. It is not as if they can hand a dossier over to subordinates; they must take the time to "dump memory"—to tell subordinates all about the subject. But this could take so long that managers may find it easier to do the task themselves. Thus they are damned by their own information system to a "dilemma of delegation"—to do too much or to delegate to subordinates with inadequate briefing.

Folklore: Management is, or at least is quickly becoming, a science and a profession. By almost any definition of *science* and *profession*, this statement is false. Brief observation of any manager will quickly lay to rest the notion that managers practice a science. A science involves the enaction of systematic, analytically determined procedures or programs. If we do not even know what procedures managers use, how can we prescribe them by scientific analysis? And how can we call management a profession if we cannot specify what managers are to learn? For after all, a profession involves "knowledge of some department of learning or science" (*Random House Dictionary*).[10]

The Manager's Roles

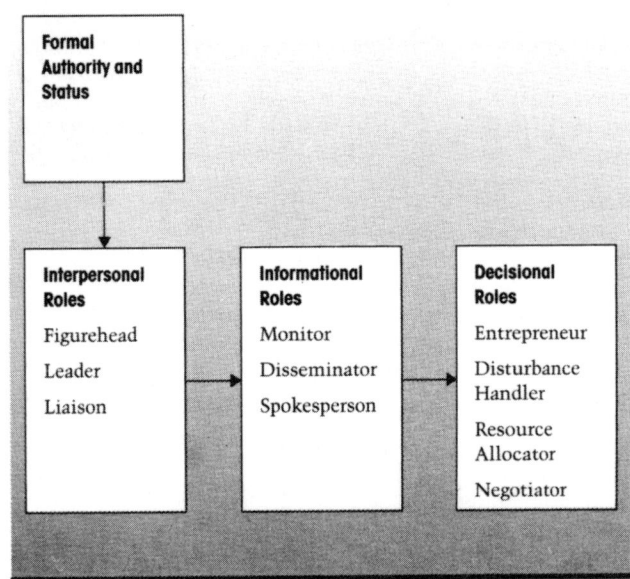

Fact: The managers' programs—to schedule time, process information, make decisions, and so on—remain locked deep inside their brains. Thus, to describe these programs, we rely on words like *judgment* and *intuition*, seldom stopping to realize that they are merely labels for our ignorance.

I was struck during my study by the fact that the executives I was observing—all very competent—are fundamentally indistinguishable from their counterparts of a hundred years ago (or a thousand years ago). The information they need differs, but they seek it in the same way—by word of mouth. Their decisions concern modern technology, but the procedures they use to make those decisions are the same as the procedures used by nineteenth century managers. Even the computer, so important for the specialized work of the organization, has apparently had no influence on the work procedures of general managers. In fact, the manager is in a kind of loop, with increasingly heavy work pressures but no aid forthcoming from management science.

Considering the facts about managerial work, we can see that the manager's job is enormously complicated and difficult. Managers are overburdened with obligations yet cannot easily delegate their tasks. As a result, they are driven to overwork and forced to do many tasks superficially. Brevity, fragmentation, and verbal communication characterize their work. Yet these are the very characteristics of managerial work that have impeded scientific attempts to improve it. As a result, management scientists have concentrated on the specialized functions of the organization, where it is easier to analyze the procedures and quantify the relevant information.[11]

But the pressures of a manager's job are becoming worse. Where before managers needed to respond only to owners and directors, now they find that subordinates with democratic norms continually reduce their freedom to issue unexplained orders, and a growing number of outside influences (consumer groups, government agencies, and so on) demand attention. Managers have had nowhere to turn for help. The first step in providing such help is to find out what the manager's job really is.

Back to a Basic Description of Managerial Work

Earlier, I defined the manager as that person in charge of an organization or subunit. Besides CEOs, this definition would include vice presidents, bishops, foremen, hockey coaches, and prime ministers. All these "managers" are vested with formal authority over an organizational unit. From formal authority comes status, which leads to various interpersonal relations, and from these comes access to information. Information, in turn, enables the manager to make decisions and strategies for the unit.

The manager's job can be described in terms of various "roles," or organized sets of behaviors identified with a position. My description, shown in "The Manager's Roles," comprises ten roles. As we shall see, formal authority gives rise to the three interpersonal roles, which in turn give rise to the three informational roles; these two sets of roles enable the manager to play the four decisional roles.

Interpersonal Roles

Three of the manager's roles arise directly from formal authority and involve basic interpersonal relationships. First is the *figurehead* role. As the head of an organizational unit, every manager must perform some ceremonial duties. The president greets the touring dignitaries. The foreman attends the wedding of a lathe operator. The sales manager takes an important customer to lunch.

The chief executives of my study spent 12% of their contact time on ceremonial duties; 17% of their incoming mail dealt with acknowledgments and requests related to their status. For example, a letter to a company president requested free merchandise for a crippled schoolchild; diplomas that needed to be signed were put on the desk of the school superintendent.

Duties that involve interpersonal roles may sometimes be routine, involving little serious communication and no important decision making. Nevertheless, they are important to the smooth functioning of an organization and cannot be ignored.

Managers are responsible for the work of the people of their unit. Their actions in this regard constitute the *leader* role. Some of these actions involve leadership directly—for example, in most organizations the managers are normally responsible for hiring and training their own staff.

In addition, there is the indirect exercise of the leader role. For example, every manager must motivate and encourage employees, somehow reconciling their individual needs with the goals of the organization. In virtually every contact with the manager, subordinates seeking leadership clues ask: "Does she approve?" "How would she like the report to turn out?" "Is she more interested in market share than high profits?"

The influence of managers is most clearly seen in the leader role. Formal authority vests them with great potential power; leadership determines in large part how much of it they will realize.

The literature of management has always recognized the leader role, particularly those aspects of it related to motivation. In comparison, until recently it has hardly mentioned the *liaison* role, in which the manager makes contacts outside the vertical chain of command. This is remarkable in light of the finding of virtually every study of managerial work that managers spend as much time with peers and other people outside their units as they do with their own subordinates—and, surprisingly, very little time with their own superiors.

In Rosemary Stewart's diary study, the 160 British middle and top managers spent 47% of their time with peers, 41% of their time with people inside their unit, and only 12% of their time with their superiors. For Robert H. Guest's study of U.S. foremen, the figures were 44%, 46%, and 10%. The chief executives of my study averaged 44% of their contact time with people outside their organizations, 48% with subordinates, and 7% with directors and trustees.

The contacts the five CEOs made were with an incredibly wide range of people: subordinates; clients, business associates, and

Article 1. The Manager's Job: Folklore and Fact

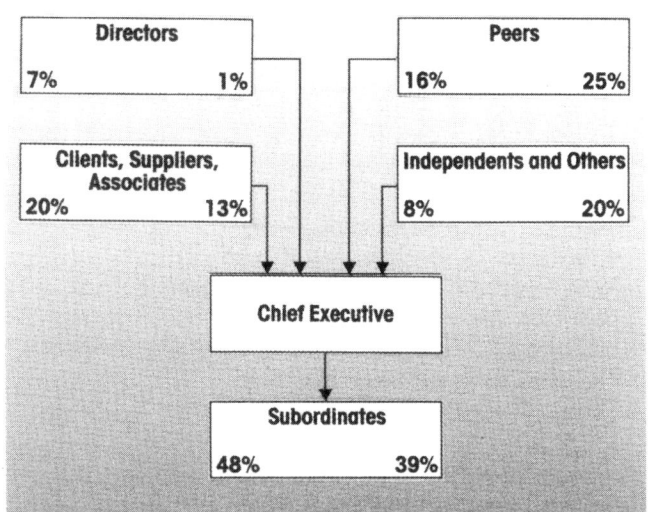

Note: The first figure indicates the proportion of total contact time spent with each group and the second figure, the proportion of mail from each group.

suppliers; and peers—managers of similar organizations, government and trade organization officials, fellow directors on outside boards, and independents with no relevant organizational affiliations. The chief executives' time with and mail from these groups is shown in "The Chief Executive's Contacts." Guest's study of foremen shows, likewise, that their contacts were numerous and wide-ranging, seldom involving fewer than 25 individuals, and often more than 50.

Informational Roles

By virtue of interpersonal contacts, both with subordinates and with a network of contacts, the manager emerges as the nerve center of the organizational unit. The manager may not know everything but typically knows more than subordinates do.

Studies have shown this relationship to hold for all managers, from street gang leaders to U.S. presidents. In *The Human Group*, George C. Homans explains how, because they were at the center of the information flow in their own gangs and were also in close touch with other gang leaders, street gang leaders were better informed than any of their followers.[12] As for presidents, Richard Neustadt observes: "The essence of [Franklin] Roosevelt's technique for information-gathering was competition. 'He would call you in,' one of his aides once told me, 'and he'd ask you to get the story on some complicated business, and you'd come back after a couple of days of hard labor and present the juicy morsel you'd uncovered under a stone somewhere, and *then* you'd find out he knew all about it, along with something else you *didn't* know. Where he got this information from he wouldn't mention, usually, but after he had done this to you once or twice you got damn careful about *your* information.'"[13]

We can see where Roosevelt "got this information" when we consider the relationship between the interpersonal and informational roles. As leader, the manager has formal and easy access to every staff member. In addition, liaison contacts expose the manager to external information to which subordinates often lack access. Many of these contacts are with other managers of equal status, who are themselves nerve centers in their own organiza-

tion. In this way, the manager develops a powerful database of information.

Processing information is a key part of the manager's job. In my study, the CEOs spent 40% of their contact time on activities devoted exclusively to the transmission of information; 70% of their incoming mail was purely informational (as opposed to requests for action). Managers don't leave meetings or hang up the telephone to get back to work. In large part, communication *is* their work. Three roles describe these informational aspects of managerial work.

As *monitor*, the manager is perpetually scanning the environment for information, interrogating liaison contacts and subordinates, and receiving unsolicited information, much of it as a result of the network of personal contacts. Remember that a good part of the information the manager collects in the monitor role arrives in verbal form, often as gossip, hearsay, and speculation.

In the *disseminator* role, the manager passes some privileged information directly to subordinates, who would otherwise have no access to it. When subordinates lack easy contact with one another, the manager may pass information from one to another.

In the *spokesperson* role, the manager sends some information to people outside the unit—a president makes a speech to lobby for an organization cause, or a foreman suggests a product modification to a supplier. In addition, as a spokesperson, every manager must inform and satisfy the influential people who control the organizational unit. For the foreman, this may simply involve keeping the plant manager informed about the flow of work through the shop.

The president of a large corporation, however, may spend a great amount of time dealing with a host of influences. Directors and shareholders must be advised about finances; consumer groups must be assured that the organization is fulfilling its social responsibilities; and government officials must be satisfied that the organization is abiding by the law.

Decisional Roles

Information is not, of course, an end in itself; it is the basic input to decision making. One thing is clear in the study of managerial work: the manager plays the major role in the unit's decision-making system. As its formal authority, only the manager can commit the unit to important new courses of action; and as its nerve center, only the manager has full and current information to make the set of decisions that determines the unit's strategy. Four roles describe the manager as decision maker.

As *entrepreneur*, the manager seeks to improve the unit, to adapt it to changing conditions in the environment. In the monitor role, a president is constantly on the lookout for new ideas. When a good one appears, he initiates a development project that he may supervise himself or delegate to an employee (perhaps with the stipulation that he must approve the final proposal).

The scarcest resource managers have to allocate is their own time.

There are two interesting features about these development projects at the CEO level. First, these projects do not involve single decisions or even unified clusters of decisions. Rather, they emerge as a series of small decisions and actions sequenced over time. Apparently, chief executives prolong each project both to fit

Retrospective Commentary

Henry Mintzberg

Over the years, one reaction has dominated the comments I have received from managers who read "The Manager's Job: Folklore and Fact": "You make me feel so good. I thought all those other managers were planning, organizing, coordinating, and controlling, while I was busy being interrupted, jumping from one issue to another, and trying to keep the lid on the chaos." Yet everything in this article must have been patently obvious to these people. Why such a reaction to reading what they already knew?

Conversely, how to explain the very different reaction of two media people who called to line up interviews after an article based on this one appeared in the *New York Times*. "Are we glad someone finally let managers have it," both said in passing, a comment that still takes me aback. True, they had read only the account in the *Times*, but that no more let managers have it than did this article. Why that reaction?

One explanation grows out of the way I now see this article—as proposing not so much another view of management as another face of it. I like to call it the insightful face, in contrast to the long-dominant professional or cerebral face. One stresses commitment, the other calculation; one sees the world with integrated perspective, the other figures it as the components of a portfolio. The cerebral face operates with the words and numbers of rationality; the insightful face is rooted in the images and feel of a manager's integrity.

Each of these faces implies a different kind of "knowing," and that, I believe, explains many managers' reaction to this article. Rationally, they "knew" what managers did—planned, organized, coordinated, and controlled. But deep down that did not feel quite right. The description in this article may have come closer to what they really "knew." As for those media people, they weren't railing against management as such but against the cerebral form of management, so pervasive, that they saw impersonalizing the world around them.

In practice, management has to be two-faced—there has to be a balance between the cerebral and the insightful. So, for example, I realized originally that managerial communication was largely oral and that the advent of the computer had not changed anything fundamental in the executive suite—a conclusion I continue to hold. (The greatest threat the personal computer poses is that managers will take it seriously and come to believe that they can manage by remaining in their offices and looking at displays of digital characters.) But I also thought that the dilemma of delegating could be dealt with by periodic debriefings—disseminating words. Now, however, I believe that managers need more ways to convey the images and impressions they carry inside of them. This explains the renewed interest in strategic vision, in culture, and in the roles of intuition and insight in management.

The ten roles I used to describe the manager's job also reflect management's cerebral face, in that they decompose the job more than capture the integration. Indeed, my effort to show a sequence among these roles now seems more consistent with the traditional face of management work than an insightful one. Might we not just as well say that people throughout the organization take actions that inform managers who, by making sense of those actions, develop images and visions that inspire people to subsequent efforts?

Perhaps my greatest disappointment about the research reported here is that it did not stimulate new efforts. In a world so concerned with management, much of the popular literature is superficial and the academic research pedestrian. Certainly, many studies have been carried out over the last 15 years, but the vast majority sought to replicate earlier research. In particular, we remain grossly ignorant about the fundamental content of the manager's job and have barely addressed the major issues and dilemmas in its practice.

But superficiality is not only a problem of the literature. It is also an occupational hazard of the manager's job. Originally, I believed this problem could be dealt with; now I see it as inherent in the job. This is because managing insightfully depends on the direct experience and personal knowledge that come from intimate contact. But in organizations grown larger and more diversified, that becomes difficult to achieve. And so managers turn increasingly to the cerebral face, and the delicate balance between the two faces is lost.

Certainly, some organizations manage to sustain their humanity despite their large size—as Tom Peters and Robert Waterman show in their book *In Search of Excellence*. But that book attained its outstanding success precisely because it is about the exceptions, about the organizations so many of us long to be a part of—not the organization in which we actually work.

Fifteen years ago, I stated that "No job is more vital to our society than that of the manager. It is the manager who determines whether our social institutions serve us well or whether they squander our talents and resources." Now, more than ever, we must strip away the folklore of the manager's job and begin to face its difficult facts.

---

it into a busy, disjointed schedule, and so that they can comprehend complex issues gradually.

Second, the chief executives I studied supervised as many as 50 of these projects at the same time. Some projects entailed new products or processes; others involved public relations campaigns, improvement of the cash position, reorganization of a weak department, resolution of a morale problem in a foreign division, integration of computer operations, various acquisitions at different stages of development, and so on.

Chief executives appear to maintain a kind of inventory of the development projects in various stages of development. Like jugglers, they keep a number of projects in the air; periodically, one comes down, is given a new burst of energy, and sent back into orbit. At various intervals, they put new projects on-stream and discard old ones.

While the entrepreneur role describes the manager as the voluntary initiator of change, the *disturbance handler* role depicts the manager involuntarily responding to pressures. Here change is beyond the manager's control. The pressures of a situation are too severe to be ignored—a strike looms, a major customer has gone bankrupt, or a supplier reneges on a contract—so the manager must act.

Leonard R. Sayles, who has carried out appropriate research on the manager's job, likens the manager to a symphony orchestra conductor who must "maintain a melodious performance,"[14] while handling musicians' problems and other external distur-

Article 1. The Manager's Job: Folklore and Fact

Self-Study Questions for Managers

1. Where do I get my information, and how? Can I make greater use of my contacts? Can other people do some of my scanning? In what areas is my knowledge weakest, and how can I get others to provide me with the information I need? Do I have sufficiently powerful mental models of those things I must understand within the organization and in its environment?

2. What information do I disseminate? How important is that information to my subordinates? Do I keep too much information to myself because disseminating it is time consuming or inconvenient? How can I get more information to others so they can make better decisions?

3. Do I tend to act before information is in? Or do I wait so long for all the information that opportunities pass me by?

4. What pace of change am I asking my organization to tolerate? Is this change balanced so that our operations are neither excessively static nor overly disrupted? Have we sufficiently analyzed the impact of this change on the future of our organization?

5. Am I sufficiently well-informed to pass judgment on subordinates' proposals? Can I leave final authorization for more of the proposals with subordinates? Do we have problems of coordination because subordinates already make too many decisions independently?

6. What is my vision for this organization? Are these plans primarily in my own mind in loose form? Should I make them explicit to guide the decisions of others better? Or do I need flexibility to change them at will?

7. How do my subordinates react to my managerial style? Am I sufficiently sensitive to the powerful influence of my actions? Do I fully understand their reactions to my actions? Do I find an appropriate balance between encouragement and pressure? Do I stifle their initiative?

8. What kind of external relationships do I maintain, and how? Do I spend too much of my time maintaining them? Are there certain people whom I should get to know better?

9. Is there any system to my time scheduling, or am I just reacting to the pressures of the moment? Do I find the appropriate mix of activities or concentrate on one particular function or problem just because I find it interesting? Am I more efficient with particular kinds of work, at special times of the day or week? Does my schedule reflect this? Can someone else schedule my time (besides my secretary)?

10. Do I overwork? What effect does my work load have on my efficiency? Should I force myself to take breaks or to reduce the pace of my activity?

11. Am I too superficial in what I do? Can I really shift moods as quickly and frequently as my work requires? Should I decrease the amount of fragmentation and interruption in my work?

12. Do I spend too much time on current, tangible activities? Am I a slave to the action and excitement of my work, so that I am no longer able to concentrate on issues? Do key problems receive the attention they deserve? Should I spend more time reading and probing deeply into certain issues? Could I be more reflective? Should I be?

13. Do I use the different media appropriately? Do I know how to make the most of written communication? Do I rely excessively on face-to-face communication, thereby putting all but a few of my subordinates at an informational disadvantage? Do I schedule enough of my meetings on a regular basis? Do I spend enough time observing activities firsthand, or am I detached from the heart of my organization's activities?

14. How do I blend my personal rights and duties? Do my obligations consume all my time? How can I free myself from obligations to ensure that I am taking this organization where I want it to go? How can I turn my obligations to my advantage?

---

bances. Indeed, every manager must spend a considerable amount of time responding to high-pressure disturbances. No organization can be so well run, so standardized, that it has considered every contingency in the uncertain environment in advance. Disturbances arise not only because poor managers ignore situations until they reach crisis proportions but also because good managers cannot possibly anticipate all the consequences of the actions they take.

The third decisional role is that of *resource allocator*. The manager is responsible for deciding who will get what. Perhaps the most important resource the manager allocates is his or her own time. Access to the manager constitutes exposure to the unit's nerve center and decision maker. The manager is also charged with designing the unit's structure, that pattern of formal relationships that determines how work is to be divided and coordinated.

Also, as resource allocator, the manager authorizes the important decisions of the unit before they are implemented. By retaining this power, the manager can ensure that decisions are interrelated. To fragment this power encourages discontinuous decision making and a disjointed strategy.

There are a number of interesting features about the manager's authorization of others' decisions. First, despite the widespread use of capital budgeting procedures—a means of authorizing various capital expenditures at one time—executives in my study made a great many authorization decisions on an ad hoc basis. Apparently, many projects cannot wait or simply do not have the quantifiable costs and benefits that capital budgeting requires.

Second, I found that the chief executives faced incredibly complex choices. They had to consider the impact of each decision on other decisions and on the organization's strategy. They had to ensure that the decision would be acceptable to those who influence the organization, as well as ensure that resources would not be overextended. They had to understand the various costs and benefits as well as the feasibility of the proposal. They also had to consider questions of timing. All this was necessary for the simple approval of someone else's proposal. At the same time, however, the delay could lose time, while quick approval could be ill-considered and quick rejection might discourage the subordinate who had spent months developing a pet project.

One common solution to approving projects is to pick the person instead of the proposal. That is, the manager authorizes those projects presented by people whose judgment he or she trusts. But the manager cannot always use this simple dodge.

The final decisional role is that of *negotiator*. Managers spend considerable time in negotiations: the president of the football team works out a contract with the holdout superstar; the corporation president leads the company's contingent to negotiate a new strike issue; the foreman argues a grievance problem to its conclusion with the shop steward.

These negotiations are an integral part of the manager's job, for only he or she has the authority to commit organizational resources in "real time" and the nerve-center information that important negotiations require.

The Integrated Job

It should be clear by now that these ten roles are not easily separable. In the terminology of the psychologist, they form a gestalt, an integrated whole. No role can be pulled out of the framework and the job be left intact. For example, a manager without liaison contacts lacks external information. As a result, that manager can neither disseminate the information that employees need nor make decisions that adequately reflect external conditions. (This is a problem for the new person in a managerial position, since he or she has to build up a network of contacts before making effective decisions.)

Here lies a clue to the problems of team management.[15] Two or three people cannot share a single managerial position unless they can act as one entity. This means that they cannot divide up the ten roles unless they can very carefully reintegrate them. The real difficulty lies with the informational roles. Unless there can be full sharing of managerial information—and, as I pointed out earlier, it is primarily verbal—team management breaks down. A single managerial job cannot be arbitrarily split, for example, into internal and external roles, for information from both sources must be brought to bear on the same decisions.

To say that the ten roles form a gestalt is not to say that all managers give equal attention to each role. In fact, I found in my review of the various research studies that sales managers seem to spend relatively more of their time in the interpersonal roles, presumably a reflection of the extrovert nature of the marketing activity. Production managers, on the other hand, give relatively more attention to the decisional roles, presumably a reflection of their concern with efficient work flow. And staff managers spend the most time in the informational roles, since they are experts who manage departments that advise other parts of the organization. Nevertheless, in all cases, the interpersonal, informational, and decisional roles remain inseparable.

Toward More Effective Management

This description of managerial work should prove more important to managers than any prescription they might derive from it. That is to say, *the managers' effectiveness is significantly influenced by their insight into their own work*. Performance depends on how well a manager understands and responds to the pressures and dilemmas of the job. Thus managers who can be introspective about their work are likely to be effective at their jobs. The questions in "Self-Study Questions for Managers" may sound rhetorical; none is meant to be. Even though the questions cannot be answered simply, the manager should address them.

Let us take a look at three specific areas of concern. For the most part, the managerial logjams—the dilemma of delegation, the database centralized in one brain, the problems of working with the management scientist—revolve around the verbal nature of the manager's information. There are great dangers in centralizing the organization's data bank in the minds of its managers. When they leave, they take their memory with them. And when subordinates are out of convenient verbal reach of the manager, they are at an informational disadvantage.

The manager is challenged to find systematic ways to share privileged information. A regular debriefing session with key subordinates, a weekly memory dump on the dictating machine, maintaining a diary for limited circulation, or other similar methods may ease the logjam of work considerably. The time spent disseminating this information will be more than regained when decisions must be made. Of course, some will undoubtedly raise the question of confidentiality. But managers would be well advised to weigh the risks of exposing privileged information against having subordinates who can make effective decisions.

If there is a single theme that runs through this article, it is that the pressures of the job drive the manager to take on too much work, encourage interruption, respond quickly to every stimulus, seek the tangible and avoid the abstract, make decisions in small increments, and do everything abruptly.

Here again, the manager is challenged to deal consciously with the pressures of superficiality by giving serious attention to the issues that require it, by stepping back in order to see a broad picture, and by making use of analytical inputs. Although effective managers have to be adept at responding quickly to numerous and varying problems, the danger in managerial work is that they will respond to every issue equally (and that means abruptly) and that they will never work the tangible bits and pieces of information into a comprehensive picture of their world.

To create this comprehensive picture, managers can supplement their own models with those of specialists. Economists describe the functioning of markets, operations researchers simulate financial flow processes, and behavioral scientists explain the needs and goals of people. The best of these models can be searched out and learned.

In dealing with complex issues, the senior manager has much to gain from a close relationship with the organization's own management scientists. They have something important that the manager lacks—time to probe complex issues. An effective working relationship hinges on the resolution of what a colleague and I have called "the planning dilemma."[16] Managers have the information and the authority; analysts have the time and the technology. A successful working relationship between the two will be effected when the manager learns to share information and the analyst learns to adapt to the manager's needs. For the analyst, adaptation means worrying less about the elegance of the method and more about its speed and flexibility.

Analysts can help the top manager schedule time, feed in analytical information, monitor projects, develop models to aid in making choices, design contingency plans for disturbances that can be anticipated, and conduct "quick and dirty" analyses for those that cannot. But there can be no cooperation if the analysts are out of the mainstream of the manager's information flow.

The manager is challenged to gain control of his or her own time by turning obligations into advantages and by turning those things he or she wishes to do into obligations. The chief executives of my study initiated only 32% of their own contacts (and another 5% by mutual agreement). And yet to a considerable extent they seemed to control their time. There were two key factors that enabled them to do so.

First, managers have to spend so much time discharging obligations that if they were to view them as just that, they would leave no mark on the organization. Unsuccessful managers blame failure on the obligations. Effective managers turn obligations to advantages. A speech is a chance to lobby for a cause; a meeting is a chance to reorganize a weak department; a visit to an important customer is a chance to extract trade information.

Second, the manager frees some time to do the things that he or she—perhaps no one else—thinks important by turning them into obligations. Free time is made, not found. Hoping to leave some time open for contemplation or general planning is tantamount to hoping that the pressures of the job will go away. Managers who want to innovate initiate projects and obligate others to report back to them. Managers who need certain environmental information establish channels that will automatically keep them informed. Managers who have to tour facilities commit themselves publicly.

The Educator's Job

Finally, a word about the training of managers. Our management schools have done an admirable job of training the organization's specialists—management scientists, marketing researchers, accountants, and organizational development specialists. But for the most part, they have not trained managers.[17]

Management schools will begin the serious training of managers when skill training takes a serious place next to cognitive learning. Cognitive learning is detached and informational, like reading a book or listening to a lecture. No doubt much important cognitive material must be assimilated by the manager-to-be. But cognitive learning no more makes a manager than it does a swimmer. The latter will drown the first time she jumps into the water if her coach never takes her out of the lecture hall, gets her wet, and gives her feedback on her performance.

In other words, we are taught a skill through practice plus feedback, whether in a real or a simulated situation. Our management schools need to identify the skills managers use, select students who show potential in these skills, put the students into situations where these skills can be practiced and developed, and then give them systematic feedback on their performance.

My description of managerial work suggests a number of important managerial skills—developing peer relationships, carrying out negotiations, motivating subordinates, resolving conflicts, establishing information networks and subsequently disseminating information, making decisions in conditions of extreme ambiguity, and allocating resources. Above all, the manager needs to be introspective in order to continue to learn on the job.

No job is more vital to our society than that of the manager. The manager determines whether our social institutions will serve us well or whether they will squander our talents and resources. It is time to strip away the folklore about managerial work and study it realistically so that we can begin the difficult task of making significant improvements in its performance.

References

1. All the data from my study can be found in Henry Mintzberg, *The Nature of Managerial Work* (New York: Harper & Row, 1973).
2. Robert H. Guest, "Of Time and the Foreman," *Personnel*, May 1956, p. 478.
3. Rosemary Stewart, *Managers and Their Jobs* (London: Macmillan, 1967); see also Sune Carlson, *Executive Behaviour* (Stockholm: Strombergs, 1951).
4. Francis J. Aguilar, *Scanning the Business Environment* (New York: Macmillan, 1967), p. 102.
5. Unpublished study by Irving Choran, reported in Mintzberg, *The Nature of Managerial Work*.
6. Robert T. Davis, *Performance and Development of Field Sales Managers* (Boston: Division of Research, Harvard Business School, 1957); George H. Copeman, *The Role of the Managing Director* (London: Business Publications, 1963).
7. Stewart, *Managers and Their Jobs*; Tom Burns, "The Directions of Activity and Communication in a Departmental Executive Group," *Human Relations* 7, no. 1 (1954): 73.
8. H. Edward Wrapp, "Good Managers Don't Make Policy Decisions," HBR September–October 1967, p. 91. Wrapp refers to this as spotting opportunities and relationships in the stream of operating problems and decisions; in his article, Wrapp raises a number of excellent points related to this analysis.
9. Richard E. Neustadt, *Presidential Power* (New York: John Wiley, 1960), pp. 153–154; italics added.
10. For a more thorough, though rather different, discussion of this issue, see Kenneth R. Andrews, "Toward Professionalism in Business Management," HBR March–April 1969, p. 49.
11. C. Jackson Grayson, Jr., in "Management Science and Business Practice," HBR July–August 1973, p. 41, explains in similar terms why, as chairman of the Price Commission, he did not use those very techniques that he himself promoted in his earlier career as management scientist.
12. George C. Homans, *The Human Group* (New York: Harcourt, Brace & World, 1950), based on the study by William F. Whyte entitled *Street Corner Society*, rev. ed. (Chicago: University of Chicago Press, 1955).
13. Neustadt, *Presidential Power*, p. 157.
14. Leonard R. Sayles, *Managerial Behavior* (New York: McGraw-Hill, 1964), p. 162.
15. See Richard C. Hodgson, Daniel J. Levinson, and Abraham Zaleznik, *The Executive Role Constellation* (Boston: Division of Research, Harvard Business School, 1965), for a discussion of the sharing of roles.
16. James S. Hekimian and Henry Mintzberg, "The Planning Dilemma," *The Management Review*, May 1968, p. 4.
17. See J. Sterling Livingston, "Myth of the Well-Educated Manager," HBR January–February 1971, p. 79.

Reprinted with permission from *Harvard Business Review*, March/April 1990, pp. 163–176. © 1990 by the President and Fellows of Harvard College. All rights reserved.

Article 2

Why companies fail

CEOs offer every excuse but the right one: their own errors. Here are ten mistakes to avoid.

By Ram Charan and Jerry Useem

HOW MANY MORE MUST FALL? EACH MONTH SEEMS TO BRING the sound of another giant crashing to earth. Enron. WorldCom. Global Crossing. Kmart. Polaroid. Arthur Andersen. Xerox. Qwest. They fall singly. They fall in groups. They fall with the heavy thud of employees laid off, families hurt, shareholders furious. How many? Too many; 257 public companies with $258 billion in assets declared bankruptcy last year, shattering the previous year's record of 176 companies and $95 billion. This year is on pace, with 67 companies going bust during the first quarter. And not just any companies. Big, important, FORTUNE 500 companies that aren't supposed to collapse. If things keep going like this, we may have trouble filling next year's list.

Why do companies fail? Their CEOs offer every excuse in the book: a bad economy, market turbulence, a weak yen, hundred-year floods, perfect storms, competitive subterfuge—forces, that is, very much outside their control. In a few cases, such as the airlines' post–Sept. 11 problems, the excuses even ring true. But a close study of corporate failure suggests that, acts of God aside, most companies founder for one simple reason: managerial error.

We'll get to the errors in a moment. But first let's acknowledge that, yes, failures usually involve factors unique to a company's own industry or culture. As Tolstoy said of families, all happy companies are alike; every unhappy company is unhappy in its own way. Companies even collapse in their own way. Some go out in blinding supernovas (Enron). Others linger like white dwarfs (AT&T). Still others fizzle out over decades (Polaroid). Failure is part of the natural cycle of business. Companies are born, companies die, capitalism moves forward. Creative destruction, they call it.

It was roughly this sentiment that Treasury Secretary Paul O'Neill was trying to convey when he said that Enron's failure was "part of the genius of capitalism." But aside from sounding insensitive, O'Neill got one thing wrong. Capitalism's true genius is to weed out companies that no longer serve a useful purpose. The dot-coms, for instance, were experiments in whether certain businesses were even viable. We found out: They weren't. Yet many recent debacles were of companies that could have lived long, productive lives with more enlightened management—in other words, good companies struck down for bad reasons. By these lights, Arthur Andersen's fall is no more part of the "genius of capitalism" than the terrorism on Sept. 11 was part of the "genius of evolution."

By "failure," we don't necessarily mean bankruptcy. A dramatic fall from grace qualifies too. In the most recent bear market, for instance, 26 of America's 100 largest companies lost at least two-thirds of their market value, including such blue chips as Hewlett-Packard, Charles Schwab, Cisco, AT&T, AOL Time Warner, and Gap. In the 1990 bear market, by contrast, none did, according to money management firm Aronson & Partners.

The sheer speed of these falls has been unnerving. Companies that were healthy just moments ago, it seems, are suddenly at death's door. But this impression may be misleading. Consider, for instance, a certain Houston institution we've heard so much about. There was no one moment when its managers sat down and conspired to commit wrongdoing. Rather, the disaster occurred because of what one analyst calls "an incremental descent into poor judgment." A "success-oriented" culture, mind-numbing complexity, and unrealistic performance goals all mixed until the violation of standards *became* the standard. Nothing looked amiss from the outside until, boom, it was all over.

It sounds a lot like Enron, but the description actually refers to NASA in 1986, the year of the space shuttle *Challenger* explosion. We pull this switch not to conflate the two episodes—one, after all, involved the death of seven astronauts—but to make a point about failures: Even the most dramatic tend to be years in the making. At NASA, engineers noticed damage to the crucial O-rings on previous shuttle flights yet repeatedly convinced themselves the damage was acceptable. Companies fail the way Ernest Hemingway wrote about going broke in *The Sun Also Rises*: gradually, and then suddenly. (For some solutions, see box "Three Quick Fixes.")

What undoes them is the familiar stuff of human folly: denial, hubris, ego, wishful thinking, poor communication, lax oversight, greed, deceit, and other *Behind the Music* plot conventions. It all adds up to a failure to execute. This is not an exhaustive list of corporate sins. But chances are your company is committing one of them right now.

Softened by success

"Those whom the gods would destroy," Euripides wrote nearly 2,500 years ago, "they first make mad." In the modern update, the gods send their victims 40 years of success. Actually, it's a proven fact: A number of studies show that people are less likely to make optimal decisions after prolonged periods of success. NASA, Enron, Lucent, WorldCom—all had reached the mountaintop before they ran into trouble. Someone should have told them that most mountaineering accidents happen on the way down.

Consider the case of Cisco Systems. While by no means a failure, Cisco suffered a remarkable comedown in the spring of 2001—remarkable not only for its swiftness (its shares lost 88% of their value in one year) but also because Cisco, more than any other company, was supposed to be able to see into the future. The basis of this belief was a much vaunted IT system that enabled Cisco managers to track supply and demand in "real time," allowing them to make pinpoint forecasts. The technology, by all accounts, worked great. The forecasts, however, did not. Cisco's managers, it turned out, never bothered to model what would happen if a key assumption—growth—disappeared from the equation. After all, the company had recorded more than 40 straight quarters of growth; why wouldn't the future bring more of the same?

The rosy assumptions, moreover, persisted even when evidence to the contrary started piling up. Customers began going bankrupt. Suppliers warned of a coming dropoff in demand. Competitors stumbled. Even Wall Street wondered if the Internet equipment market was falling apart. "I have never been more optimistic about the future of our industry as a whole or of Cisco," CEO John Chambers declared in December 2000, still projecting 50% annual growth.

What was Chambers thinking? In *The Challenger Launch Decision*, her definitive book on the disaster, Boston College sociologist Diane Vaughan notes that people don't surrender their mental models easily. "They may puzzle over contradictory evidence," she writes, "but usually succeed in pushing it aside—until they come across a piece of evidence too fascinating to ignore, too clear to misperceive, too painful to deny, which makes vivid still other signals they do not want to see, forcing them to alter and surrender the world-view they have so meticulously constructed."

Even when a boss doesn't intend to quash dissent, subtle signals can broadcast the message that bad news is not welcome.

For the perpetually sunny Chambers, that "piece of evidence" did not come until April 2001, when cratering sales forced Cisco to write down $2.5 billion in excess inventory and lay off 8,500 employees. Chambers may have been operating in real time, but he wasn't operating in the real world.

See no evil

With $6.5 billion in cash and a strong competitive position, Cisco will live to fight another day. Polaroid may not be so lucky. Like its fellow old-economy stalwart Xerox, Polaroid was a once-highflying member of the Nifty Fifty group of growth stocks that lost their luster over the years. Eventually the question "What does Polaroid make?" became a latter-day ver-

Ten big mistakes

They are the standard stuff of corporate folly.
Chances are, your company has made at least one.

	Slave to Wall Street	See no evil	Overdosing on risk	Dysfunctional board	Softened by success	Strategy du jour	Acquisition lust	Fearing the boss	Dangerous culture	Death spiral
◆ Enron	●	●	●	●	●			●	●	●
Arthur Andersen			●	●					●	●
◆ Global Crossing	●	●	●	●						
Lucent	●				●	●				
◆ Warnaco	●	●		●					●	
◆ Kmart			●		●		●			
Providian	●		●		●					
◆ Sunbeam	●	●							●	
Tyco	●					●	●			
WorldCom			●			●	●			
Xerox	●	●		●						
AT&T						●	●			
◆ Polaroid			●			●				
Qwest	●		●							

◆ Filed for bankruptcy

FORTUNE TABLE

sion of "Who's buried in Grant's tomb?" Polaroid, that is, made Polaroid cameras—period.

Time had passed the company by, you might say. Not exactly. Think about another company that once seemed doomed to fail: Intel. Back in 1985, competition from Japan was turning Intel's memory chips into cheap commodities, and observers were all but writing the company's obituary. Instead of going the way of Polaroid, though, Intel decided to exit the memory business entirely and become a maker of microprocessors. The key insight occurred when Intel founders Andy Grove and Gordon Moore sat down and asked themselves some tough questions. "If we got kicked out and the board brought in a new CEO," Grove asked Moore, "what do you think he would do?" Get out of memory chips was the answer. From there, they said later, it was just a matter of doing what needed to be done.

Polaroid and Xerox, by contrast, were slow to confront the changing world around them. Executives at both companies repeatedly blamed poor results on short-term factors—currency fluctuations, trouble in Latin America—rather than the real cause: a bad business model. By the time Xerox President (and now CEO) Anne Mulcahy came out and spoke the truth—the company had "an unsustainable business model," she told analysts in 2000—Xerox was flirting with bankruptcy.

Jim Collins, author of the influential management books *Built to Last* and *Good to Great*, has spent years studying what separates great companies from mediocre ones. "The key sign—the litmus test—is whether you begin to explain away the brutal facts rather than to confront the brutal facts head-on," he says. "That's sort of the pivot point." By forcing themselves to think like outsiders, Grove and Moore recognized the brutal facts before it was too late. Polaroid and Xerox didn't.

Fearing the boss more than the competition

Sometimes CEOs don't get the information they need to make informed decisions. The main reason, says Daniel Goleman, a psychologist and author of the book *Primal Leadership*, is that subordinates are afraid to tell them the truth. Even when a boss doesn't intend to quash dissent, subtle signals—a sour expression, a curt response—can broadcast the message that bad news isn't welcome. That's why, according to a study by Goleman and two associates, higher-ranking executives are less likely to have an accurate assessment of their own performance.

Three quick fixes

THE RECENT CORPORATE COLLAPSES HAVE INvolved many breakdowns: in ethics, in trust, in common sense, to name a few. But perhaps the most troubling breakdown is in corporate oversight. Directors, senior executives, and Wall Street analysts all failed miserably by missing—or concealing—danger signals until it was too late. Regulators will no doubt have plenty to say on the issue, but the most zealous reformers should be the companies themselves. They can begin with three changes that, taken together, will provide a better early-warning system against failure:

1 Reengineer the board. Remember reengineering? It was applied to every corner of the corporation at one point or another—except the board. That needs to change. Incompetence is not the problem. Boards can be full of very capable people yet be totally ineffective as a group. The problem is that directors are too nice. Boards seldom convene without the CEO, and raising troubling questions can simply seem rude—which is often the way the CEO wants it. Directors need a forum where they can talk frankly *without* the CEO. Ten minutes at the end of each meeting would be a good start. Better yet, an annual retreat where the board can assess its own performance as well as the CEO's. Collectively, the directors are supposed to serve as a company's peripheral vision. Often at least one director suspects trouble before it becomes a crisis. The trick is getting him or her to say it out loud.

Boards should also appoint the chairperson of the governance committee as lead director. This especially makes sense when the CEO and chairman are the same person, as is the case with most U.S. companies. The lead director would be from the outside, reappointed every two years or so, and authorized to convene a meeting anytime, any place, with or without management.

2 Turn employees into corporate governors. As the Enron debacle has proven, regular employees—not executives, not directors, not shareholders—have the most to lose when a company fails. With their jobs, pensions, and stock-option wealth on the line, it follows that they have a greater incentive than anyone to act as company watchdogs. Yet few companies tap this built-in alarm system. Too often, front-line employees smell something rotten but do not, or cannot, convey the message upward. That's why companies need a mechanism to make it happen.

Whistle-blowing does not count as a mechanism. Whistle-blowing is a last resort—one that's frequently harmful to the whistle blower's health. What's really needed is a survey, carefully designed and administered by an outside agency, that regularly solicits employee feedback on sensitive questions. Do people trust management? Is there any reason to doubt the reported revenue numbers? Are the company's values out of whack? Think of it as a human audit. Send the results directly to the board. And give employees a chance to inspect company finances directly—say, by holding Q&A sessions with the CFO. Corporate governance should ideally include all a company's stakeholders, and employees hold the biggest stake of all.

3 Banish Ebitda. Companies hit the skids for all sorts of reasons, but it's one thing that ultimately kills them: They run out of cash. Yet most managers are too preoccupied with measures like Ebitda (earnings before interest, taxes, debt, and amortization) and return on assets to give cash much notice. Boards don't ask for it. Analysts don't analyze it. Corporate financial statements do typically include a statement of cash flow, but it's a crude snapshot that excludes off-balance-sheet items and doesn't show where the cash comes from. The solution is a detailed, easily readable cash-flow report. Give it to the board. Give it to employees. Break out cash flow by division, letting people track the company's blood flow themselves. Warren Buffett pays close attention to cash flow because, among other reasons, he knows cash is hard to fudge. That's why creative accountants hate it—and why you should learn to love it.

No system survives for long without feedback and controls. So corporate America has a choice: It can implement these controls itself. Or it can wait for regulators and politicians to impose them. Which sounds better to you?

Fear can have its uses, of course; Andy Grove has long espoused the value of competitive paranoia. But in unhealthy situations, employees come to worry more about internal factors—what the boss might say, what management might do—than about threats from the outside world. Certainly this was the case at Enron, where even alarm-ringer Sherron Watkins chose to express her concerns anonymously rather than hazard one of CEO Jeff Skilling's famous tongue-lashings. And she was one of the brave ones.

The same problem hampered Samsung Chairman Lee Kun Hee in 1997 when he decided to take Samsung into the auto business. Knowing the car industry was a crowded field plagued by overcapacity, many of Samsung's top managers silently opposed the $13 billion investment. But Lee was a forceful chairman and a car buff to boot. So when Samsung Motors folded just a year into production, forcing Lee to spend $2 billion of his own money to placate creditors, he expressed surprise: How come nobody had spoken up about their reservations?

ANNUAL EDITIONS

> **During World War II, Churchill set up an office outside the chain of command whose main job was to tell him the unvarnished truth.**

During World War II, Winston Churchill worried that his own larger-than-life personality would deter subordinates from bringing him bad news. So he set up a unit outside his generals' chain of command, the Statistical Office, whose primary job was to feed him the starkest, most unvarnished facts. In a similar vein, Richard Schroth and Larry Elliott, authors of the forthcoming book *How Companies Lie*, suggest designated "counterpointers," whose function is to ask the rudest questions possible. Such mechanisms take information and turn it into information that can't be ignored.

Overdosing on risk

Some companies simply live too close to the edge. Global Crossing, Qwest, 360networks—these telecom flameouts chose paths that were not just risky but wildly imprudent. Their key mistake: loading up on two kinds of risk at once.

The first might be called "execution risk." In their race to band the earth in optical fiber, the telco upstarts ignored some key questions: Namely, would anyone need all of this fiber? Weren't there too many companies doing the same thing? Wouldn't, uh, most of them fail? "People seemed to say, 'Maybe—but it's not going to be us,'" says Darrell Rigby, a Bain & Co. consultant who studies managing during times of turbulence. "Everyone thought they were immune."

> **Ebbers liked to eat. He ate MCI. He ate MFS. Wall Street helped him wash it all down with cheap capital and a soaring stock.**

On top of execution risk was another kind, which we'll call liquidity risk. Global Crossing—run by Gary Winnick, formerly of the junk-bond house Drexel Burnham Lambert—loaded up on $12 billion of high-yield debt. This essentially limited Winnick to a cannonball strategy: one shot, and if you miss, it's bankruptcy.

Bankruptcy it was. Given the utter violence of the telecom shakeout, you might say it was inevitable. But other telcos did manage to escape the carnage. BellSouth, dismissed as hopelessly conservative during the Wild West years, emerged with a pristine balance sheet and a strong competitive position. Its gentlemanly CEO, Duane Ackerman, was guided by a radical idea: "being good stewards of our shareholders' money." What a concept.

Acquisition lust

WorldCom founder Bernard Ebbers liked to eat. He ate MCI. He ate MFS and its UUNet subsidiary. He tried to eat Sprint. Wall Street helped him wash it all down with cheap capital and a buoyant stock price. Pretty soon WorldCom was tipping the scales at $39 billion in revenues. But there was a problem: Ebbers didn't know how to digest the things he ate. A born dealmaker, he seemed to care more about snaring new acquisitions than about making the existing ones—all 75 of them—work together. At least Ebbers was up front about it: "Our goal is not to capture market share or be global," he told a reporter in 1997. "Our goal is to be the No. 1 stock on Wall Street."

The results were frequently chaotic. For a time, sales reps from UUNet competed head-to-head with WorldCom sales teams for corporate telecom contracts. Smaller customers complained they had to call three different customer-service reps for their Internet, long-distance, and local-phone inquiries. If there is such a thing as negative synergy, WorldCom may have discovered it.

Not that acquisitions are always so bad. General Electric combines its acquisitive nature with an impressive ability to break down acquisitions and integrate them into existing operations. But too often CEOs succumb to an undisciplined lust for growth, accumulating assets for the sake of accumulating assets. Why? It's fun. There are lots of press conferences. It's what powerful CEOs do. And like Ebbers, whose WorldCom stock has lost 98% of its value, few wonder if their eyes might be bigger than their stomachs.

Listening to Wall Street more than to employees

No one likes a good growth story better than Wall Street. And in the late 1990s, no one was telling a better one than Lucent CEO Rich McGinn. He knew how to give Wall Street what it wanted—explosive top-line growth—and in return, Wall Street turned McGinn and his team into rock stars. For a bunch of former Bellheads, it was intoxicating stuff.

> **Says an ex-Xerox executive: "I could not present to the board unless things were perfect. Everything had to be prettied up."**

But while McGinn was busy performing for the Street, there were at least two groups he wasn't listening to. The first was Lucent's scientists, who feared the company was missing out on a new optical technology, OC-192, that could transmit voice and data faster. They pleaded in vain for its development, then watched as rival Nortel rolled out OC-192 gear to thunderous success. At the same time McGinn was neglecting Lucent's salespeople, who might have told him that his growth targets were becoming increasingly unrealistic. To meet them, employees were pulling forward sales from future quarters by offering steep discounts and wildly generous financing arrangements, largely to dot-coms. "As we got further and further behind," Chairman Henry Schacht later explained, "we did more and more discounting."

It could only last so long. After Lucent stock had lost more than 80% of its value and he had replaced McGinn as CEO, Schacht sat down with FORTUNE to ponder some hard-earned lessons. "Stock price is a byproduct; stock price isn't a driver," he said. "And every time I've seen any of us lose sight of that, it has always been a painful experience." Top management needs to understand what the folks on Wall Street want—but not necessarily give it to them.

Strategy du jour

When companies run into trouble, the desire for a quick fix can become overwhelming. The frequent result is a dynamic that Collins describes in *Good to Great*: "A&P vacillated, shifting from one strategy to another, always looking for a single stroke to quickly solve its problems. [It] held pep rallies, launched programs, grabbed fads, fired CEOs, hired CEOs and fired them yet again." Lurching from one silver bullet solution to another, the company never gained any traction.

Collins calls it the "doom loop," and it's a killer. Kmart is another victim. In the 1980s and early '90s, Kmart was all about diversification, shifting away from discounting to acquire stakes in chains like Sports Authority, OfficeMax, and Borders bookstores. But in the 1990s a new management team divested those stores and decided to revamp Kmart's supply chain by investing heavily in IT. That lasted for a while, until a new CEO, Chuck Conaway, decided that, actually, Kmart would try to beat Wal-Mart at its own game. This unleashed a disastrous price war that in the end proved to be one mistake too many. "When you look at companies that get themselves into trouble," says Collins, "they're often taking steps of great, lurching bravado rather than quiet, deliberate understanding." Did somebody say AT&T?

A dangerous corporate culture

Arthur Andersen, Enron, and Salomon Brothers were all brought down, or nearly so, by the rogue actions of a tiny few. But the bad apples in these companies grew and flourished in the same kind of environment: a rotten corporate culture. It's impossible to monitor the actions of every employee, no matter how many accounting and compliance controls you put in place. But either implicitly or explicitly, a company's cultural code is supposed to equip front-line employees to make the right decisions without supervision. At Salomon Brothers the culture did just the opposite. The transgressor there was Paul Mozer, a trader who in February of 1991 improperly overbid in auctions of U.S. Treasury bonds. While it was another improper bid on May 22 that finally did him in, the critical event occurred in April, when Salomon Chairman John Gutfreund learned of the February overbid by Mozer and failed to discipline him. Mozer evidently took Gutfreund's lack of action as a green light.

Salomon's culture of swashbuckling bravado encouraged risk taking without accountability. Enron's culture encouraged profit taking without disclosure. Andersen's culture engendered conflicts of interest without safeguards. Rotten cultures produce rotten deeds.

The new-economy death spiral

Alan Greenspan has his own theory on failure. Testifying about Enron in February, he noted, "a firm is inherently fragile if its value-added emanates more from conceptual as distinct from physical assets.... Trust and reputation can vanish overnight. A factory cannot." The speed of some recent crackups would seem to confirm his thesis. The first domino falls when questions are raised, sometimes anonymously. Wrongdoing is suspected. Customers delay new orders. Rating agencies lower their debt ratings. Employees head for the exits. More customers defect. And *voilà*, you have what former Enron CEO Jeff Skilling has called "a classic run on the bank."

Is it possible to halt one? Yes, but only if you stop the spiral from building up speed. Salomon broke the cycle by hiring Warren Buffett as interim CEO —essentially a giant credibility infusion. By waiting several months to step down, on the other hand, Arthur Anderson CEO Joseph Berardino lost whatever chance he had to avoid disaster. Once started, the spiral can bring a company whose main assets are people and ideas to its knees with breathtaking finality.

A dysfunctional board

What was Enron's board thinking? Of all the infamous moments in the company's demise, perhaps the least explicable was the board's decision to waive Enron's code of ethics to accommodate CFO Andrew Fastow's partnerships. "A red flag the size of Alaska," says Nell Minow, founder of the board watchdog group Corporate Library. Even Enron directors belatedly agreed with this assessment. "After having authorized a conflict of interest creating as much risk as this one," the board's special investigation committee wrote in a February report, "the board had an obligation to give careful attention to the transactions that followed. It failed to do this... In short, no one was minding the store."

"The great companies don't make excuses," said Treasury Secretary Paul O'Neill recently. "They do well anyway."

Despite a decade's worth of shareholder activism, Enron's board was not an anomaly. The sorry fact is that most corporate boards remain hopelessly beholden to management. "I was never allowed to present to the board unless things were perfect," says a former senior executive at Xerox, whose board includes Vernon Jordan and former Senator George Mitchell. "You could only go in with good news. Everything was prettied up." At many boards, the CEO oversees meetings, hand-picks directors, and spoon-feeds them information. "Directors know relatively little apart from what management tells them," says John Smale, a former CEO of Procter & Gamble and onetime chairman of General Motors.

Unless, that is, the board demands more. "The CEO is always going to want to turn the board meeting into a pep rally," says Minow. "You've got to say to him 'Look, I'm a busy person. I don't have time for the good news. What I need for you to tell me is the bad news.' It's like what Robert Duvall says in *The Godfather*: 'I have to go to the airport. The Godfather is a man who likes to hear bad news immediately.' That should be emblazoned on every corporate governance policy sheet."

Paul O'Neill may have been wrong about his assessment of Enron, but he was right about something else. "The great companies don't make excuses," he said recently, "including excuses about how they didn't do well because the economy was against them or prices were not good. They do well anyway." It's true. And it's something to think about the next time you hear a CEO railing at the gods.

RAM CHARAN *advises* FORTUNE *500 CEOs and is co-author, with Larry Bossidy, of* Execution: The Discipline of Getting Things Done.

REPORTER ASSOCIATE *Ann Harrington*

Reprinted from the May 27, 2002, issue of *Fortune*, pp. 50-54, 56, 58, 60, 62 by special permission. © 2002 by Time, Inc. All rights reserved.

Article 3

if you think you're HARD enough

In more carefree times, business gurus exalted leaders who admitted to frailty. Not any more. The task of sustaining growth in a sluggish market calls for driven, leather-skinned bosses. Whereas emotional intelligence was the mantra in the touchy-feely '90s, now it's mental toughness. What is that? And who possesses it? **Stefan Stern** reports

Red Auerbach, coach to the all-conquering Boston Celtics basketball team in the 1950s and '60s, knew the difference between life's successes and failures. 'Show me a good loser,' he used to say, 'and I'll show you a loser.' Red's robust attitude might not find favour with some of today's kinder, gentler management theorists. Ever since the publication of Daniel Goleman's book *Emotional Intelligence* in 1995, managers have been encouraged to understand their colleagues' sensitivities, to 'feel their pain', to show a greater awareness of the moods and feelings of those around them.

Goleman's analysis has been developed by others, most notably by Greg Dyke's favourite gurus Rob Goffee and Gareth Jones. In a *Harvard Business Review* article entitled 'Why should anyone be led by you?', Goffee and Jones argued that top managers need to show a degree of vulnerability or frailty to confirm their status as 'regular guys'. 'Leaders should let their weaknesses be known,' they wrote. 'By exposing a measure of vulnerability, they make themselves approachable and show themselves to be human.' Today's leaders have to be 'good situation sensors [able to] collect and interpret soft data'.

However, as Greg Dyke likes to say these days, let's cut the crap. There isn't much room for vulnerability and weakness at the head of businesses and organisations today. A persistently sluggish marketplace, and one that is being joined all the time by new competitors, means that the going is tough. It is time for the tough to get going.

This month, *MT* can exclusively reveal new research on some of life's winners that will cause Dr Goleman and his followers to rethink their theories on touchy-feely management. Professor Graham Jones of the University of Wales has been leading ground-breaking research into what he calls 'mental toughness'—the quality that helps elite performers to prevail while others fall by the wayside.

In extended interviews and discussions with some of this country's most successful sports starts, Jones and his colleagues have identified the characteristics that go to make up the mentally tough competitor. These are the people who keep going and who sustain high levels of performance even under extreme pressure. Over the next few pages, we profile 10 of these leaders, each one of them exemplifying a different characteristic. They make for challenging and at times, perhaps, even rather chilling reading.

Adrian Moorhouse is a director of the management consultancy Lane4, which launched this and further research into elite performers (he also happens to be a former Olympic gold medallist in the 100 metres breaststroke). He says insights into how elite performers function can give Lane4's work with executives a certain edge. 'Coaching people isn't just a case of sitting there saying "we understand", says

Moorhouse. 'It's about identifying what really motivates you.'

'Of course, "toughness" doesn't mean being tough all the time,' he adds. 'The smart bit is knowing when to be tough and when to relax and restore your energies.'

Sceptics will question the use of sports psychology by those who make claims about the skills and attitudes required by people in business. They should think again. Professor Jones is also a partner with Lane4, which has, over the past eight years, been carrying out change management and leadership development programmes with an impressive list of blue-chip clients. The prof and his colleagues have been successful in putting academic theories into practice.

'If you looked at the most successful business leaders,' says Jones, 'their profile would look like the one we have drawn.'

This view is supported by Nigel Walker, once a dashing, try-scoring winger for the Welsh rugby union team and now (armed with an MBA) head of sport for BBC Wales. 'The qualities of mentally tougher performers in sport are inextricably linked to the qualities of leaders in business,' insists Walker. 'These are the people who will run through a brick wall to get what they want.'

Nice guys don't finish first, and for good reason. So wring out that hanky, and get real. Study our 10 main ingredients for true grit and see if you compare favourably to the heavyweights we have lined up. Come and try it, if you think you're hard enough…

> The mentally tough don't let the latest quirk of fate shake them. As Nietzsche said: 'That which does not kill me makes me stronger'

TEN VITAL TOUGH VALUES

self-belief
Being convinced that you possess unique qualities and abilities that will enable you to achieve your goals and make you better than your opponents.

Mental toughness is above all else about self-belief. The face that looks back at you from the mirror: do you believe in it? Does it convince you?

If you do not possess deep self-belief, you are unlikely to convince anyone else that you're worth listening to or worth following. **JACK WELCH** betrayed not the slightest scintilla of doubt as he stormed away for two decades at the head of GE, turning it into one of the world's most successful businesses, a new bellwether for the US economy.

'We will be number one or number two in a business, or we will get out of that business,' Welch famously declared. Funny how he was sometimes prepared to put up with being second-best, if only temporarily. **LORD BROWNE** has succeeded in dazzling both his entire corporation and his industry sector from his base at BP. Although not a showman, his quiet confidence and inner steel stem from a profound self-belief. His leadership has been almost too convincing. Recent downgrades on production targets suggest his managers have not shared the same level of confidence in their ability to deliver.

resilience
Recovering from setbacks as a result of increased determination to succeed.

'We all have setbacks,' commented one of the participants in Graham Jones' research programme, 'but the mentally tough competitor doesn't let them affect him—he uses them.' Or as another one said: 'You have to come back, and stronger.'

This aspect of mental toughness echoes one of Stephen Covey's 'seven habits', that 'between stimulus and response man has the freedom to choose'. In other words, it is not events in themselves that matter, it is how you react to them and cope with them. **ALAN SUGAR** has taken risks, experienced successes and reverses, but has always pressed on to the next challenge, the next launch or target. Where lesser business figures might settle for quiet retirement, Sugar is unstoppable. That is perhaps the essential characteristic of serial entrepreneurs like **SUGAR, STELIOS** and **RICHARD BRANSON**. They do not allow the latest quirk of fate or bad luck to shake them from their purpose. There are even shades here—dangerous thought—of Nietzsche's belief: 'That which does not kill me makes me stronger.' Think about that the next time the chairman is giving you a bollocking.

focus
Remaining fully focused on the task in hand in the face of specific, or personal, distractions.

In the view of one elite performer from the sample group, 'If you want to be the best, you have got to be totally focused on what you are doing'. Another commented: 'There are inevitable distractions and you just have to be able to focus on what you need to focus on.' When **TONY BLAIR** arrives back at the tied cottage that is No 10 Downing Street, and young Leo has a headache, Cherie is preparing for a case and Euan has rung up asking for a top-up on his monthly allowance, does the prime minister have time to feel sorry for himself? Or does he get on with the work in hand, whether it is Saddam Hussein, Jacques Chirac, Gordon Brown or getting himself some supper? Blair's ability to compartmentalise and to focus is one of his greatest leadership skills. Charged with running the country and playing a significant international role, he remains somehow undistracted by family life and pressing domestic concerns. **JOHN BIRT**, meanwhile, could not open a newspaper without seeing himself slagged off by anonymous colleagues during his time at the BBC. He saw through his reforms to the end and, at some personal cost—and arguably at some cost to the Beeb as well—won a renewal of the Charter and an extension of the licence fee, and he created the digital giant that is today's BBC.

drive
Having an insatiable desire and internalised motives to succeed.

Mild-mannered **SIR TERRY LEAHY** can queue up quite unnoticed in one of his Tesco check-out aisles. He passes unremarked through his local high street. It wasn't any outward show that first drew Leahy to Lord MacLaurin's attention as he prepared to find a successor at the end of his long term running the UK's premier retailer. The former marketing director was identified as the crucial talent needed to lead Tesco on to its next stage of development. Leahy's motivation and drive come from within. It is a quality that elite sports stars recognise. 'The motives have to be there for you; you have to really want it, because it's really hard work,' says one. Internalised motives, according to Graham Jones, provide the performer with a frame of reference and meaning when the going gets tough. The desire is so strong that the mentally tough performer 'would do almost anything within the rules to win'. Sainsbury, Safeway and the rest, as well as any farmers dealing with Tesco recently, would confirm this description of Leahy's way of doing business.

control
Regaining psychological control following unexpected, uncontrollable events.

When President **GEORGE W BUSH** went for his morning run on 11 September 2001 he was still that overgrown 'fratboy', goofing around in the Oval Office after a dodgy election result. A few hours later, he was a world leader at one of the most dangerous moments in his nation's history. As Bob Woodward has testified in his recent book, *Bush at War*, daddy's boy seemed to rise to the occasion when facing his greatest test. At a meeting of the key players a few weeks after the al-Qaeda attack, Bush (according to Woodward's friendly account) calmed his colleagues' nerves. 'You know what? We need to be patient,' Bush said. 'We've got a good plan. Look, we're entering a difficult phase. The press will seek to find divisions among us. They will try and force on us a strategy that is not consistent with victory. We've been at this only 19 days. Be steady. Don't let the press panic us. Resist the second-guessing. Be confident but patient… It's all going to work.' Now the control stakes are even higher.

resolve
Pushing back the boundaries of physical and emotional pain, while still maintaining discipline and effort under distress.

Generations of rugby coaches have urged their schoolboy charges to 'get in there where it hurts'. In business as well as sport, sometimes you have to take personal risks with your own safety and go through the pain barrier if you are going to achieve anything big. When **PHILIP GREEN** bought out BHS, the struggling high street chain formerly known as British Home Stores, for £200 million nearly three years ago, he took a massive risk with his personal fortune (£50 million of his own money was invested). BHS was widely regarded as a turkey, and not a particularly appetising one at that. Today, the firm is worth five times as much and Green, the 100% owner, is sitting very pretty. Overcoming the pain of fear or nervousness is the key to success for risk-taking leaders. Only the truly mentally tough can do it. As one of Graham Jones' study group put it, this is all about 'being determined to carry out what you know you've got to do'. Another said: 'It's a question of pushing yourself; it's mind over matter just trying to perform under this distress and go beyond your limits.'

nerves of steel
Accepting that anxiety/pressure is inevitable and knowing that you can cope with it.

How is your investment portfolio looking at the moment? Healthy? Imagine how **WARREN BUFFETT**, the 'sage of Omaha', must have felt in 1999 when teenager scribblers around the world were telling him he'd missed the boat on the dot.coms. This was a one-way bet, a fill-yer-boots chance in a lifetime to get rich quick. Buffett had the last laugh, or course, as investor after investor looked increasingly silly with each wave of dot.bomb disasters. Buffett held his nerve, stuck to what he knew—insurance, power companies, household goods—and is still counting his money.

If the leader is ready for a fight, the team will follow

'I accept that I'm going to get nervous,' said one elite athlete during Graham Jones' research period, 'particularly when the pressure's on. But keeping the lid on it and being in control is crucial.' Mentally tough leaders are not fazed by nerves or fear. They can handle the pressure. They expect it—it goes with the territory of being at the top. It is merely another obstacle to be overcome on the way to success.

independence
Not being adversely affected by others' good or bad performance.

Comparing yourself to others is usually unwise. You'll be filled either with a sense of inferiority or superiority. 'You just have to focus on you and your performance,' said one sports star. Don't look at others and say: 'I can't go that fast' or 'I'm not that brave.' When **LUC VANDEVELDE** inherited the top job at Marks & Spencer a few years ago, he could easily have been intimidated by the performance of other high street businesses. Indeed, for a while he talked up M&S's prospects, promising turnaround within a matter of months. That proved to be a mistake. In time, however, Vandevelde's changes started to take effect, and a spring has returned to the step of the venerable retailer. The lesson is, concentrate on your own results. Don't measure yourself in terms of other people's achievements. That's what the mentally tough leader would do.

competitiveness
Thriving in the pressure of competition.

Mentally tough performers 'are able to raise their game when the occasion demands it, no matter what has happened', according to the Jones research. 'If you are going to achieve anything worthwhile, there is bound to be pressure,' said one participant. 'Mental toughness is being resilient to and using the competition pressure to get the best out of yourself.' **SIR ALEX FERGUSON** creates football teams in his own image. When Manchester United are playing well, they are hard-bitten, fearless and never beaten. When United were one-nil down in the last seconds of the European Cup Final in Barcelona in 1999, the team refused to panic or throw in the towel. Moments later, when even some fans had given up on the game, they were two-one up and crowned as champions of Europe. Few relish competition as much as Fergie. His players certainly know all about his appetite for a fight—as confirmed by the 'hairdryer' moments when Sir Alex lets rip (David Beckham experienced a humdinger last month). If the leader has the stomach for a fight, the team will follow.

chillability
Switching the focus on and off as required.

When *MT*'s own Andrew Davidson first met **GERRY ROBINSON**, then Granada's chief executive, one quiet afternoon in 1995, Robinson calmly served tea and joked how little there was left for him to do. He launched the bloody battle for Forte only a few weeks later. Knowing when to relax, perhaps in preparation for the next big fight, is another key aspect of mental toughness. And if you need a role model for the occasionally laid-back but high-achieving executive, Robinson is your man. Back on the golf course whenever possible, Robinson knows when to stop. Leading a business, he has famously suggested, is all about getting a dozen or so big decisions right a year. The rest of the time, well, why not work on your short game? 'The mentally tough performer succeeds by having control of the on/off switch,' according to one member of Graham Jones' research group. 'There are other important things in my life which deserve my attention... it's important I discipline myself to give them the time.' Lane4's Moorhouse agrees. 'You must be able to leave work behind—take your holidays, enjoy your weekends. Those periods help restore you and make sure you're ready for future challenges.'

Reproduced from *Management Today* magazine, March 2003, pp. 40-46 with the permissions of the copyright owner, Haymarket Business Publications Limited.

Article 4

Spotting Patterns *on the Fly*

A Conversation with Birders David Sibley and Julia Yoshida

To thrive in an information-rich world, executives need to be adept at pattern recognition. They can learn a lot from expert bird-watchers.

RECOGNIZING industry patterns and anticipating change are core competences for today's executives. The ability to grasp complicated phenomena and discern possible trends from seemingly random events can be a source of competitive advantage, allowing managers to capitalize on opportunities before they are apparent to others. At the operational level, technology has laid the foundation for pattern recognition by allowing companies to collect and store huge amounts of data. Wal-Mart, for example, mines the data it collects from supermarket checkouts all over the country to identify patterns in consumer tastes and behavior, knowledge that drives the company's decisions about loyalty programs, cross-selling promotions, and even store layout.

At the strategic level, too, CEOs and their teams routinely make decisions based on the patterns they see in markets and in their competition. While most executives rely on their intuition for spotting and analyzing patterns, a few business thinkers are starting to approach the issue scientifically. In the book *Profit Patterns*, for instance, consultants Adrian Slywotzky and David Morrison theorize that a company's financial performance typically follows one of 30 distinct patterns, determined by its business environment and its strategic direction.

Yet despite the growing realization that recognizing patterns is important for business, companies are far from mastering how to do it, especially at the strategic level, where the data are usually less profuse and much less precise. Pattern recognition is not a new skill, though, at least not to people outside the business world. Since antiquity, naturalists have relied on their ability to spot patterns to make sense of their surroundings. And though it may seem removed from the fast-paced world of business, bird-watching, of all the naturalists' pasttimes, is most like business in terms of the cognitive demands pattern recognition requires. Birders have very little to go on in identifying the birds they see. Most birds, after all, are small, fast-moving creatures, whose survival often depends on their ability to escape detection. Unlike geologists or botanists, who can spend hours studying specimens, most birders have to learn to see as much as they can in a matter of seconds. The best birders, therefore, often rely on a combination of instinct and experience to determine that a particular flash of wings at such and such a place at a certain time is in fact an orange-crowned warbler.

The best birders often rely on a combination of instinct and experience to determine that a particular flash of wings at such and such a place at a certain time is in fact an orange-crowned warbler.

With this in mind, HBR senior editor Diane L. Coutu turned to David Sibley and Julia Yoshida for insight into the nature and challenges of pattern recognition. The author of the birders' bible *The Sibley Guide to Birds,* David Sibley is perhaps the nation's foremost bird-watcher and illustrator. Julia Yoshida, a birder since 1965, is a physician at Lahey Clinic in Burlington, Massachusetts, another occupation that puts a premium on pattern recognition. In a joint interview at Yoshida's home outside Boston, Sibley explained how expert birders draw on a wealth of tacit knowledge built up over the years to make split-second identifications on the basis of incomplete information. Although so fast as to be almost unconscious, the process he describes seems as methodical as one of Yoshida's medical diagnoses. What follows is an edited and abridged transcript of their conversation.

There are more than 700 breeding species in North America, and sightings of more than 900 species have been recorded.

At heart, pattern recognition is the art of finding order in often chaotic masses of data. As you go about identifying birds, just how many species are you dealing with?

Sibley: There are more than 700 breeding species in North America, and sightings of more than 900 species have been recorded. Many of the nonbreeding species that have been recorded on this continent are visitors from Siberia, the Antarctic, South America, or Europe that have made their way across the oceans only once or twice. I've recorded around 730 species myself.

Identifying patterns can be a terrific mental exercise. In birding, each species produces more than a dozen different songs and calls, and individuals' plumage varies widely.

Sibley: Identification is a challenge. Among wood warblers alone, there are about 35 different species appearing regularly in the eastern United States. Each has different juvenile and adult plumage, which also varies by sex and season. So there's a first winter male and female, a first summer male and female, an adult male and female breeding, and an adult male and female non-breeding. Some of these look very different, others quite similar. To add to the complexity, there's variation among individual birds (no two first winter males are identical), and their plumage changes gradually. Their sounds are also quite complex. Each species has two or three different types of songs and probably eight or ten additional call notes that it uses in different situations.

Birders are also using new information from molecular biology and field ornithology.

Can you describe how you begin to identify patterns? In business, pattern recognition still seems to be more of an art than a science.

Sibley: Pattern finding in birding is scientific in the sense that it is very deductive. I'm aware that there are patterns out there, both in the distribution of the birds and in their appearance, and I try to fit my observations to patterns. It's like making hypotheses and then testing them. For instance, if I find a species repeatedly in one location, I'll try to identify what it is about that site that the bird likes and look for other locations with similar characteristics to see if I can find the same species there. Then I'll try to relate that information to patterns that I already know from other species. Similarly, if I'm comparing two species and notice a difference in something like bill shape or feather patterns, I'll try to check that difference on other individuals. I'll ask myself things like, "Can I see this on all these species, all year round?" or "Can I see this at a distance?"

Yoshida: Birders are also using new information from molecular biology and field ornithology. This information expands the repertoire of possible patterns, as well as the necessary explanations for what the birds we are watching are really doing. Nowadays, for example, electronic tracking and blood analyses of migrant birds are producing new information on how birds adapt to changes in habitat and weather. This forces birders to think differently about problems than they used to. As new ways to process data emerge, new patterns are discovered.

One of the goals of pattern recognition is to quickly narrow down your set of possibilities. As birders, is there a particular thing you look for first?

Sibley: The very first questions you consider are "Where am I?" and "What time of year is it?" The answers give you a broad idea of which species are likely to be there. Next you have to look at the type of habitat the bird is in and what it's doing within that habitat. Just with this information and the overall size of the bird, you can narrow down the likely possibilities to a handful of species. One of the examples I use in my *Birding Basics* book is that if you are in Concord, Massachusetts, in July and you see a little yellow bird flitting through the twigs in the trees, moving constantly, it is almost certainly a yellow warbler. All you need to see is a yellow flitting through the twigs of trees. You know what it is because of where you are, what time of year it is, the habitat, and the fact that the bird is moving. But if you see a bright yellow bird sitting on a twig at the top of the tree, not moving for a minute or two at a time, that's not a yellow warbler, it's a goldfinch.

What's the most common mistake a beginner makes in trying to identify a pattern—or, in this case, a bird?

Sibley: Beginners usually latch on to common characteristics; they focus on similarities rather than differences. For example, when I'm at the Hawk Watch at Cape May in New Jersey, people often come to me and say, "I saw a hawk with its wings folded back in a U shape and black wing tips. What would that be?" In fact, all 15 species of hawk that occur at Cape May fold their wings back in a U shape, and all have dark wing tips. What beginners should focus on are the differentiating features; if they really want to identify a hawk in flight, they need to look at the proportion of the wing to the tail; almost everything else is secondary. In general, of course, it is very important to recognize common patterns as completely and clearly as you can. But you can't stop there. Once you've mastered common patterns, the real trick is to educate yourself about where discrepancies are most likely to appear—and to concentrate your attention on those areas.

Medical diagnosis, like birding, involves recognizing different patterns.

How do you spot an unusual pattern?

Sibley: Typically, I've already defined a particular pattern before I go looking for specific features. But then there are many times when I get the sense that something is different, and I take time to explore that difference because it could mean something. I'll be sketching sandpipers, for instance, and after I've sketched a few, I'll think, "This species looks a little bit more slender somehow than that one." Then I'll study the birds more carefully to figure out whether its's longer legs or longer wings or a longer neck that makes it look more slender. And so in the process of my study, different patterns gradually emerge. The more you observe, the more you learn.

In medical diagnosis, pattern recognition is a key skill. Julia, how do birding skills translate into your work as a physician?

Yoshida: Medical diagnosis, like birding, involves recognizing different patterns. The other day, for example, a woman—an ex-smoker—came to see me complaining that she'd had a cold for a month. Since colds normally go away in a couple of weeks, this was clearly not a pattern for a cold. So I asked the patient for more data. It turns out her symptoms persisted despite a course of antibiotics. This made a bacterial infection less likely, but the information could still fit a number of other patterns including a virus, an allergy, or even cancer. Eventually, I found out that things were worse for my patient during the week than on weekends. As it turned out, the cleaners were trying out a new product in the office where my patient worked.

"Once you've mastered common patterns, the real trick is to educate yourself about where discrepancies are most likely to appear—and to concentrate your attention on those areas."

David Sibley

It's fascinating to me how similar the diagnostic process is to birding. In birding, I group information into different patterns. Then I look at the markings, which, like the symptoms of an illness, could indicate various possibilities. For example, a warbler with drab olive coloring could be a Cape May or an orange-crowned warbler or a palm warbler. But if the bird pumps its tail, then I know it's a palm. Of course in medicine, you can do something you can't do in birding: You can conduct a physical diagnostic exam, which for the woman with the cough supported my initial diagnosis of an allergy.

One of the toughest challenges in pattern recognition is knowing when you've looked at enough information to make a reliable judgment. At what point can you be certain that the pattern you've identified is real?

Sibley: Identification is never 100% certain. Even field marks aren't completely dependable, so you have to have an idea of how reliable each mark is or how reliable your judgment of it is, how well you saw it. Say I saw a long bill on a bird, for instance; that's only 70% or 80% reliable as a mark. Or maybe I think I saw a long tail, which is a reliable mark, but I didn't get a good look at it. You put all your information together and say, "OK, there are three 90% characteristics that point this way and a couple of 50% or 70% characteristics that point that way, so I'll go to the 90% side." The identification may or may not be correct, but that's the more likely choice. The more you observe and add bits of evidence, the more certain the identification gets. But you should never kid yourself that you've achieved complete certainty.

Yoshida: The accuracy of a pattern is something that interests me very much as a doctor because in medicine the stakes are so high. In fact, weighing the probability of a particular pattern being right is perhaps the biggest challenge a doctor faces. One way of improving our chances is to implement redundancy in data collection. A doctor will develop not one but several likely diagnoses based on a patient's story. These diagnoses are then ranked, and a physical exam and laboratory tests are conducted to support or discredit each diagnosis. And then, of course, in medicine, we can always review the literature or ask a specialist to consult. The result, ideally, is that we come up with patterns that are really quite reliable and actionable. I would assume that a similar process is possible in deciphering business patterns.

When you're looking at all the data, you're sorting out patterns that may fit your theory. But there must be other patterns you have to ignore. So how do you choose?

Sibley: That's not an easy question to answer. It's inconsistencies that make me stop and think. One time when I was banding birds at Manomet Bird observatory in Massachusetts, I came across one that I thought just didn't fit standard descriptions. Everybody said, "Oh, here's a blackpoll warbler," which is tricky to identify in the fall. But the more I looked at it, the more oddities I saw. After a few minutes, it occurred to me that it might be a hybrid, an unusual cross between a blackpoll warbler and something else. I tried to get other people to take notice of it, saying, "Look at the crown, there's yellow hidden on the crown. And there's a yellow tinge on the rump; these things don't add up." But it was a busy day. People were anxious to move on, so it was banded as a blackpoll warbler and released.

Does randomness have a role to play in birding?

Sibley: Occasionally, individual birds migrate the wrong way and show up as vagrant outside their normal range. When they migrate, most seem to go in a random direction a random distance from the places they were born. But interestingly, even then these vagrant birds tend to show up in places that have a pattern of rare birds turning up. So they're probably not random occurrences but a pattern we haven't worked out yet.

You have the reputation, David, of being able to identify rare birds very quickly. Does intuition play a key role in your identification—or is it something else?

Sibley: There have been times when I've been out birding and have just gotten a strong sense that there might be something unusual around, that I was about to find a rare bird, and sure enough there's a rare bird. The expectation probably comes from deep knowledge—from a sense of the place, the weather conditions, the other species that are around. Last fall, I was in Galveston, Texas, and I was leading a bird walk for 20 or so people in the local Audubon chapter. We went out to the beachfront for an hour to look at birds roosting. And as we were heading out there, I was thinking to myself, "OK, we're going to see all these common Texas gulf coast birds, so what would be something interesting that I can look for? What would be a logical rare bird to find here?" And I thought of the elegant tern. I had been in Florida around the time that one had been sighted there, and so it was on my mind that it would be an exciting bird to find. We went out and parked ourselves next to a flock of about 50 birds resting on the beach. I put up my binoculars, and the second or third bird I looked at was an elegant tern. It was the second sighting ever recorded in Texas, so it was a very rare bird and not at all likely to be there. But I was looking for it. You find rare birds if you're looking for them. I made a conscious decision that an elegant tern was a possibility and then looked for it. You can call this intuition if you like, but then this is intuition based on years of experience.

Recognizing a pattern involves knowing what to look for, what the possibilities are, and then sorting out these patterns when you are actually confronted with the patient.

So sometimes recognizing patterns is a matter of anticipating them?

Yoshida: Yes, and there's a parallel in medicine. I spend a lot of time thinking about it because I teach medical students from Harvard and Tufts. Typically, a student will look at a patient first and then come tell me what he or she thinks. Afterward, we both go in and examine the patient, and then we step out and talk about the patient's condition. Students often tell me that I'm very intuitive because I diagnose with little to go on and before I've seen a patient. But I tell them, "It's really not intuition. When you were telling me the first piece of information, I was thinking this. Then you told me a little bit more, and I was listening to every little detail, refining my preliminary diagnosis." Recognizing a pattern involves knowing what to look for, what the possibilities are, and then sorting out those patterns when you are actually confronted with the patient. I don't think it's a eureka moment at all. It's a methodical process. The more you have in your head, the more you'll see and hear.

"You can't be defensive and cling to the identifications you made in the past because that will only obscure the newer patterns that are turning up as you learn more."

Similarly, in birding, familiarity with features enables a person to identify a bird very quickly, without seeing much of it. The beginner birder typically likes to see everything, but skilled birders don't have to. Just a shadow with a pattern may be enough of a clue for them to make the identification. That works in birding because the stakes are different and one chance may be all you'll get.

Honesty about data is an important quality in people who make decisions based on patterns they recognize. It's said that birders are scrupulously honest about the sightings they record. Is that true?

Sibley: For most people, bird-watching is a personal challenge, so there isn't a lot of incentive to be dishonest. You'd only be cheating yourself. Besides, if you're dishonest, you're going to be discovered and ostracized. Bird-watchers who repeatedly claim that they've seen rare birds when they haven't are quickly found out. There are official committees that rule on these things, and there's also an unofficial cadre of top-notch birders who pass judgment on important sightings—not so much to police the watchers as to be sure that the sightings are good. After all, people reporting false sightings may actually believe that they saw what they needed to see in order to identify a particular bird. Having convinced themselves, they'll dig in their heels. The more they're questioned, the more adamant they become.

The first lesson of birding is that mistakes are an opportunity for learning.

I think some managers will recognize that kind of behavior. Let me ask you, though, who acts as the pattern finder's judge? For instance, who judges you, David?

Sibley: I judge myself. I've had records that I've submitted to committees that have been rejected. I've also misidentified birds. When I was writing the field guide, I pulled out all my old notes from ten or 15 years earlier and found a number of photographs of birds that I could see weren't what I had thought they were. I also discovered a couple of very rare birds in my sketches that I hadn't identified at the time. One bird I'd sketched in California years ago and hadn't recognized I was able to identify as an Arctic loon. At the time I saw it, no one had sighted an Arctic loon in California before. I haven't submitted the record to the California Records committee—I'm not sure how they would respond to a report of a bird identified from a sketch years after it was sighted. But I know now that what I saw was, in fact, an Arctic loon.

If you had to train someone to be a good pattern finder, what would you focus on?

Sibley: A couple of the key things that I would stress would be self-awareness and self-criticism. The lack of ego is also an extremely important trait in a pattern finder because you have to be able to go back and review the decisions you made a year or two ago and admit where you were wrong. Sometimes new experiences just don't fit the patterns you thought you observed before. But you can't be defensive and cling to the identifications you made in the past because that will only obscure the newer patterns that are turning up as you learn more. So in this sense, the first lesson of birding is that mistakes are an opportunity for learning.

"The greatest satisfaction comes from making a discovery that reveals a whole pattern; it's like finding the piece of a jigsaw puzzle that links the two halves together."

Even when you reach my level of experience, you're still learning and seeing new things. These days, I study local patterns of occurrence. I go to places like Cape May or Monterey, California, and I document when, where, and in what numbers specific species turn up. It's a thrill to see a bird that's unusual for that time of year or for that location. The ultimate experience for me is seeing a bird I've never seen before in a place where I never thought it would be—it's even more exciting if a rare sighting happens in a place you go to all the time. Figuring out what the bird is involves trashing all your expectations. You have to recognize it as something different and not try to fit it into your existing patterns.

What attracts people to birding? Is it the adventure of pattern recognition?

Sibley: For some people, it's just an excuse to get outdoors. In many cases, though, people get interested because of some childhood experience. They were out in their yard, they saw a bird that looked odd or that they'd never noticed before, and they went and looked it up in a book or a grown-up helped them find the picture of it in a book. People often tell me that they were just amazed by the idea that these birds have names, that there are specific kinds of birds with specific characteristics, that there's a logic to it all.

For me personally, the greatest satisfaction comes from making a discovery that reveals a whole pattern; it's like finding the piece of a jigsaw puzzle that links the two halves together. I'll be studying some birds and trying to figure out how to tell young from old, and I'll suddenly find a feature that applies across a whole group of species. Thanks to that feature, I can now distinguish between adult and immature birds not only in this one species but also in 20 others. Discoveries of that kind put things into order, and the fact that there are patterns in the world—that it's not just chaos—is very reassuring.

Reprinted with permission from *Harvard Business Review*, November 2002, pp. 45-49. © 2002 by the Harvard School Publishing Corporation. All rights reserved.

Article 5

Restoring Public Confidence in American Business

Murray Weidenbaum

The private enterprise system in the United States is under severe attack, not from people who advocate socialism or another philosophical alternative, but from many citizens appalled by widespread reports of unethical and illegal decisions made by high-level business executives. The initial response has been by government officials—through new legislation from Congress and enhanced enforcement of existing laws by the Securities and Exchange Commission (SEC) and the Department of Justice. Government action is a very good start, but it is not enough.

Many of the governmental reforms have been necessary to address problems in corporate finance, ranging from the accuracy of financial reports to the role of auditors and audit committees. The government actions are valuable to improve the information on corporate performance on which investors rely when making their decisions.

Legislation, however, cannot deal with the fundamental problem: poor judgment and bad decisions by individual business executives. Some of those decisions have had a tragic impact on employees and shareholders who have lost their jobs or their retirement funds as a consequence of business leaders' actions. Macroeconomically, these decisions have had serious, negative effects on the national economy. Business investment has not recovered from its recession lows in part because the disarray in the stock market limits the ability of corporations to raise new investment capital. Sluggish rates of business investment, in turn, prevent a strong recovery in the economy. Restoring public confidence will not rebuild those lost retirement accounts, but greater confidence in business is a key to economic prosperity.

Government action to restore public confidence is a good start, but it is not enough.

Restoring public confidence in the conduct of American business is most fundamentally a challenge for business leadership itself. Until recently, corporate governance, or the way in which company business is conducted, was primarily the province of lawyers and other technical specialists, each of which continue to play an important role. A number of voluntary, private-sector actions in the area of corporate governance could also help restore public confidence in capitalism in the United States. The problems of corporate governance, however, are fundamental, and their solution requires more than a technical response.

The actions of American business leaders—not just shortcomings on the part of technical specialists— have generated the loss of faith on the part of the American people. Only sustained changes in the way that business is conducted—not talk but action—will convince the public that the reforms are real and enduring. Voluntarily yielding some of the powers of what many now call the "imperial presidency," so common in the private sector, is clearly a matter of enlightened self-interest on the part of top business management. The alternative—sooner or later—will be a new round of pervasive government regulation of business, arbitrarily reducing the discretion of management.

Reforms by American Business, for American Business

Corporate governance in the United States is facing an unprecedented variety of pressures to change. Although some of the shortcomings have endured over recent decades, several dramatic bankruptcies, most notably Enron in December 2001, triggered the current wave of concern. More recent reports of companies such as Tyco paying for millions of dollars of personal expenses of CEOs demonstrate that changes in accounting procedures do not suffice. The key issues that have been raised in the national media, as well as in a flurry of congressional investigations, focused too much on auditing firms, financial reporting, audit committees of boards of directors, and similarly important but essentially technical matters. Fundamental reforms in corporate governance surely must deal with financial issues, but they must extend beyond that to the role of the top management.

A typical corporation starts with a board of directors elected by the shareholders. That board, in turn, selects the top management to conduct the day-to-day activities of the enterprise. The board also forms committees to deal with specific matters such as audits, executive compensation, and nomination of board members and officers. A board may consist of "inside" directors (the chief executive officer [CEO] and other management) and "outside" directors, who only serve part-time. The typical board is chaired by the CEO and is comprised primarily of outside directors. Combining the roles of chief executive and board chair generates the potential for, and often ends up with, a very powerful leader who at times can intimidate a dissident board member.

Yet, none of the governmental actions to date address fundamental shortcomings of corporate governance such as the excessive concentration of power in the CEO, nor should they. In an economy organized mainly on the basis of private enterprise, correcting those shortcomings is primarily a task for the private sector itself.

Beyond Legislation

Many companies have been well managed and can produce extremely positive economic as well as financial results. Their senior executives, boards, and outside legal and accounting firms do the effective and honest job that is expected of them. The history of corporate governance in the United States clearly demonstrates the substantial ability of business to reform itself. For example, in 1869 the New York Stock Exchange (NYSE) cracked down on the practice of "watering" stocks (issuing shares in secret). More recently, the NYSE in 1977 required each listed company to establish an audit committee composed of outside directors. In the 1980s, most companies, responding to the critics of the corporate governance then taking place, voluntarily shifted the composition of their boards to a predominance of outside directors.

These and many other voluntary improvements in corporate governance support the notion that not every problem requires a solution based in Washington. Currently, many companies are beginning to treat the issuance of stock options to their executives as a business expense, rather than just burying the information in an obscure footnote to their financial statements. Yet, recent events confirm that serious shortcomings still exist and must be addressed.

Scandalous decisions in giant corporations operating beyond the effective control of their boards of directors appear to have drained public confidence. All business, not just corruptly led ones, could benefit from the types of necessary internal change proposed here. These reforms focus on particular aspects of company management including the CEO's role, the selection processes for various boards and committees, and the specifics of the auditing process. More fundamentally, they aim to meet the challenges that any and every business driven by competition and individual self-interest—those characteristics of American capitalism that at the same time can be credited for its unparalleled success—can expect to face.

How can public interests be protected in an environment dominated by neither sinners nor saints, and how can that protection be provided without inhibiting the efficiency of the private enterprise system that currently generates abundant goods and services, employment, income, wealth, innovation, and progress? Achieving those multiple objectives is a tall order. It surely requires humility in recommending specific courses of action. Unlike the media and congressional coverage of these matters, however, it seems more appropriate to start at the top of the corporate hierarchy rather than in the middle or at the bottom.

RECONSIDERING AND REVISING THE ROLE OF THE CEO

As noted earlier, the CEO, as the corporation's leader, is the focal point of its governing power. He or she sets the organization's tone and runs day-to-day operations. The CEO also controls the resources to support management's ideas. Ninety percent of the time, CEOs chair the board of directors, conducting meetings according to agendas they set.

This procedure makes opposing the recommendations of the chairman/CEO, much less pursuing other approaches, difficult for individual directors. The CEO also often recommends the candidates for the board and frequently contacts potential directors. Board nominating committees that will recommend a new director whom the CEO opposes are most rare. Equally unusual are shareholders who reject the nominations contained in the annual proxy statement submitted for their review and approval.

On the surface, this operation may resemble the structure of an efficient operation. In fact, this model often works quite well. Many dedicated CEOs use this system in an honest attempt to build an effective, profitable organization that produces goods and services that meet the needs of the public and does so in an ethical manner. CEOs can be quick to point out that they may have spent a lifetime with a company while directors, at best, are part-timers and shareholders are often mere transients.

Centralization of power in the CEO, however, has led to a variety of abuses. Skyrocketing CEO compensation is a dramatic symptom of the shortcomings of the status quo in corporate governance. An effective response must go beyond dealing with technical questions such as the accounting treatment of stock options or the adequacy of financial controls on reimbursement of the CEO's personal expenses. The issue boils down to the personal motivations of the CEOs themselves. Expecting subordinates to limit the fiscal appetite of a determined, greedy, and/or ethically insensitive CEO is folly.

Fundamental reforms in corporate governance must extend to top management.

The answer to this basic problem in corporate governance must come from above the CEO—from the board room. The British adopted such a system a long time ago. Many U.S. companies may find it appropriate to adopt the British tradition of appointing an outside director to chair the board and to conduct board meetings. The chairman is usually a very experienced and often prestigious person who is at the stage of life where he is not viewed as a management challenger. Although usually occupied with his own professional matters, the chairman devotes sufficient time and effort to the position so that he or she is not merely a figurehead. For example, Lord Alexander Trotman, retired CEO of Ford Motor Company, now serves as board chairman of Imperial Chemical Industries.

Few U.S. CEOs, of course, can be expected to welcome with enthusiasm such a dilution of their customary authority. The outside chairman, however, is not an unknown phenomenon in the United States. Major investors at times serve as board chairs of new enterprises. During transitional stages, outside directors have been designated chairman, at least for a limited period of time. Moreover, nonprofit organizations—hospitals, museums, and universities—that often have comparable numbers of employees and annual revenue as large corporations have an outside member typically chair the board of trustees.

The views of John G. Smale, retired CEO of Procter & Gamble and former outside chairman of General Motors, are quite instructive. Smale notes that as a CEO/chairman he would not have welcomed a diminution of his authority and that he saw his outside chairmanship at the time as merely a transitional appointment. Reflecting back, he now believes that the board should be chaired by an outside director:

> If the purpose of a board is to represent the shareholders in overseeing management's conduct of the business, such a structure [an outside director serving as chairman] seems considerably more logical than having the board chaired by a manager who is also the subject of such oversight.[1]

Although granting too much authority to the CEO can be dangerous, the constraints that should be placed on the ultimate leader of any business also have limits. An effective enterprise still requires a strong CEO. No committee—and that is the organizational form of any board—can or should try to run a business. Every director should understand that the CEO is the day-to-day leader of the enterprise and provides its public face. That recognition does not, however, require a weak or passive board.

STRENGTHENING THE BOARD OF DIRECTORS

As a longtime corporate director, I can attest from experience that boards of directors often seem asleep at the switch. In the midst of rising public criticism of business, the truly independent members of corporate boards can play a more vital role than ever to assure shareholders and society as a whole that business is being responsibly managed. Most directors take their role very seriously. The lapses from good practice, however, attract public attention and give business in general a bad reputation.

Not every problem requires a solution based in Washington.

When we consider the disgrace that has been heaped upon some Enron directors, it seems clear that exercising independent judgment is not just the prerogative of an outside director. Acting independently of management's interests—overruling a poorly thought-through proposal for expansion, for example—is a basic way of protecting the individual director's integrity as well as that of the enterprise.

In this regard, several director-selection practices should be avoided because they limit the board's independence. Examples include celebrity directors who do not understand the basics of corporate governance; overly committed directors who serve on eight or ten or more boards while holding down a full-time job; personal friends of the CEO; and those directors who simultaneously serve as high-priced consultants or suppliers to the corporation.

Successful board members avoid the extremes of becoming either sycophants or rivals to the management. The board's basic task is oversight—advising and questioning management rather than blindly issuing approvals or independently trying to run the business. No legislation can mandate such wisdom on the part of directors but more public attention to the conduct of boards may encourage a greater dedication to the task.

To improve corporate governance, key board committees must be bolstered. Quite properly, attention has been focused on the audit committee; its watchdog functions should be enhanced. Yet, the role of the relatively recently emerging governance committee (which increasingly replaces the nominating committee) likewise should be developed. Governance committees now regularly review the CEO's and the board's performance. The results of those reviews should be a high-priority item on the full board's agenda. Similarly, if CEO compensation has at times become excessive, that development is an indictment of the compensation committee, which also deserves more notice.

Compensation committees and audit committees of boards of directors would benefit from a greater degree of independence. A compensation committee should consist entirely of truly independent directors, and oftentimes it does. But the selection and pay of outside compensation advisers, whose advice is usually given great weight by the committees, should be determined by the committee and not by the management whose compensation is being decided. This situation is an example of the inability of corporate legal advisers to detect and blow the whistle on what, at least to a layman, appears a blatant conflict of interest: management selecting the individuals who draw up management's compensation plans and then advise the board on those same compensation matters.

WAKING UP THE AUDIT COMMITTEE

Key committees, especially the audit committee, do much of the board of directors' work. A recent analysis revealed the extent to which these financial watchdogs did not bark. In 207 publicly traded companies that filed for bankruptcy in 2001, the audit committee in a dozen cases did not even meet during the year prior to bankruptcy. Another 28 met only once. In a few instances, current or recently departed company executives served on the committee.[2]

The NYSE has rules prohibiting most of these practices. For example, it requires each listed company to establish an audit committee consisting entirely of outside directors. Nevertheless, the effectiveness of audit committees is clearly, to say the least, uneven. Enron's audit committee met all of the formal NYSE and SEC requirements. Yet, it failed to blow the whistle on the outrageous financial practices that were perpetrated on unsuspecting shareholders.

A well-functioning audit committee is truly the conscience of the corporation. Its members review the work of the organization's own internal auditors as well as the activities of the outside accounting firm, which conducts an independent audit of the company's finances. The external audit, when complete, enables the accounting firm to certify that the corporation's financial statements represent its financial position fairly and conform to generally accepted accounting principles. Audit committees have a broad charter to question and investigate the various operations of the company to ensure their financial integrity.

Should the CEO also chair the board of directors? No.

In a world of increasingly sophisticated financial techniques, Enron's audit committee as well as the entire Enron board seems to have violated one of the most elementary rules of management: if you don't understand something, don't approve it. No new legislation is needed for audit committee members to show a greater spirit of inquiring independence. An arm's-length relationship between the audit committee and company management is essential to establish and maintain that independence. As the NYSE proposed, that means no former executives of the company, no consultants to the company, and no employees of companies that sell significant amounts of goods and services to the company should serve on the audit committee.

A reasonable extension of the auditing committee's power is their assumption of the sole authority to hire and set fees for the outside auditing firm. Presently, management tends to make those decisions, subject only to the approval of the committee. Such a seemingly technical and operational shift would help both to bolster the audit committee's authority and strengthen the external auditors' independence.

REFOCUSING THE ROLE OF ACCOUNTING FIRMS

In practice, the accounting firms that conduct the outside audit devote a substantial amount of their resources to ensure integrity of the company's financial reporting and control systems. In recent years, these firms have often devoted much less attention to auditing individual transactions.

The practice of using a firm that conducts a company's outside audit to perform a variety of other services for that company has fallen out of fashion. A great many companies—perhaps the majority—are phasing out the nonaudit functions of their external auditors. In some cases, these ancillary functions were never substantial or are now much smaller than a few years ago. The new corporate reform law quite substantially reduces the array of additional services that an auditor can perform for its client.

Nevertheless, a client trying to eliminate its reliance on its customary auditor to perform other advisory functions faces serious difficulties. For example, the overlap in the knowledge needed to audit a given firm and in the ability to assist in the preparation of its tax returns is considerable. Where should the line be drawn? In any event, the era of nonaudit dominance of auditing firm activity is ending.

Yet, there are other troubling aspects of the role of the accounting firms that remain. For example, an outside auditor that also performs all or a large part of the internal audit function is not unusual. Apparently, this was the case at Enron. Despite talk about Chinese walls separating the two functions, this practice is highly undesirable. Having employees of the same firms conduct the internal audit and then perform the outside review may not be considered a technical conflict of interest. Nevertheless, this practice reduces the effectiveness of the formal checks and balances designed to protect the financial integrity of the enterprise. Here, government can get a jump start on reform; the SEC should revoke its ruling that an outside auditor can perform up to 40 percent of the internal audit.

Fortunately, the history of U.S. corporate governance is based on voluntary reform.

Moreover, too much of today's auditing seems to focus on the computer systems that generate the accounting data, downplaying the traditional review of individual transactions. Both tasks need to be performed. The outlook in this area is now quite positive. In response to the need to bolster the independence of outside auditors, Congress has authorized the establishment, under the auspices of the SEC, of an independent organization to review the practices of the auditors of public companies. It has the power to maintain quality control by disciplining those who fail to maintain adequate accounting systems. That prospect should provide the necessary backbone to accounting firms faced with overly aggressive financial actions by the senior management of their client companies.

HOLDING LAWYERS ACCOUNTABLE

Lawyers have been remarkably successful in ensuring that so much of the liability for current corporate governance problems falls on the accounting profession and so little falls on the members of the bar. To add the proverbial insult to injury, at the same time that attorneys are so actively urging accounting firms to rid themselves of their nonaudit functions, they are campaigning vigorously to expand and strengthen the multidisciplinary practices of their own firms.

Concern for maintaining high levels of legal ethics should extend to the poor advice that some lawyers provided to the corporate decisionmakers who did such a great disservice to investors, employees, and the public generally in the cases of Enron, Worldcom, Tyco, Adelphia, and so forth. The concern extends beyond the notion that what is sauce for the accountant goose should also be administered to the lawyer gander. The point is far more fundamental: many of the highly criticized financial-activities actions by management and auditor alike had been blessed in advance by their house counsel, outside law firm, or both. There is enough criticism to go around, and the onus for bad performance should be shared fairly and more widely, including with Wall Street stock analysts and bond-rating agencies.

Restoring Public Confidence

Corporate governance in the United States is being challenged for good reason. If American business wants to minimize the likelihood of yet another round of burdensome regulation, top management—boards and the most senior corporate officers—must take the lead in cleaning house. Another incentive for such action may be even more basic: to maintain the confidence of the investing public. Fortunately, the history of corporate governance in the United States is one of voluntary change by individual companies in response to developing circumstances. The shift in board-of-director composition from mainly management directors to outside directors is a cogent case in point, as is the rise of independent audit committees.

At its best, the U.S. system of private enterprise delivers an unparalleled combination of rising living standards, attractive employment opportunities, and technological innovation. If uncorrected shortcomings obscured the powerful benefits of the business system, the nation's future would be most adversely affected. Government has responded sufficiently. The onus now is on business leadership.

The hallmark of strong management is the ability to respond to serious problems promptly and proactively; any management can react to the crises that inaction permits to develop. The challenge to American business now is to respond constructively to the severe challenges to corporate governance that it faces. An effective and timely response, more than any government action, will help to maintain investor and public confidence in the private enterprise system.

Notes

1. John G. Smale, "Where Was the Board?" *Across the Board* (May/June 2002): 11–12.

2. Andrew Countryman and Janet Kidd Stewart, "Conflicts in Audit Oversight," *Chicago Tribune*, February 17, 2002, p. 1.

Murray Weidenbaum is the Mallinckrodt Distinguished University Professor at Washington University in St. Louis, where he is also honorary chairman of the Weidenbaum Center on the Economy, Government, and Public Policy.

Case: *Robin Hood*

Robin Hood awoke just as the sun was creeping over the crest of the hill in the very middle of Sherwood Forest. He was not the least rested, for he had not slept well that night. He could not get to sleep because of all the problems he was going to have to face today.

Certainly his campaign against the sheriff was going well, perhaps too well. It had all started out as a personal quarrel between the two of them, but now it was much more than just that. There was a price on his head of 1000 pounds, and there was no doubt that he was causing the sheriff a great deal of trouble, as taxes went uncollected or undelivered to the Crown, and rich men could not sleep soundly at night anywhere near Sherwood.

Things had changed since the early days, however. In those days it was just a small band of men, united in their cause against the sheriff, and for that matter, against Prince John, for the sheriff was simply doing John's bidding. But that was no longer the case. The fame of the Merry Men had grown and with it their numbers. He used to know each man as both a friend and companion, but now he didn't even know all of their names. Little John continued to keep discipline among the men as well as maintaining their skills with the bow, while Will Scarlet kept an eye on the sheriff, as well as any rich prospect who was foolish enough to travel Sherwood. Scarlock took care of the loot as he always had, and Much the Miller's Son continued to keep the men fed.

All this success was leading to problems. Game was, frankly, getting scarce as the number of men in the band increased, and the corresponding demand for food grew. Likely targets for the Merry Men were getting hard to find as more and more wealthy travelers were giving Sherwood a wide berth, as they were reluctant to part with their gold. Finally, the Sheriff and his men were getting better. Robin had always had the advantage of knowing Sherwood better than any man alive, but now there were at least several men who knew it almost as well as he, and some of them wore the colors of Prince John.

All this was leading Robin to reconsider his old ways. Perhaps a simple transit tax through Sherwood might be a part of the answer. But that might destroy his support among the people of the forest, and it had been rejected by the Merry Men, who were proud of their motto "Rob from the rich and give to the poor!" Besides, he needed the support of the poor, as they were his main source of information on the movements of the sheriff.

Killing the sheriff was not the answer. He would just be replaced, and, aside from quenching Robin's personal thirst for revenge, the new sheriff might be even more treacherous. Robin hated his enemy, but he had the advantage of knowing the sheriff's strengths and weaknesses. He would not know a new man's talents.

Prince John, on the other hand, was a vicious tyrant, a good part of which stemmed from his very weakness. The Barons were growing more restless every day, and the people simply hated him. They wanted King Richard back from his jail in Austria. Robin had been discreetly approached by several nobles loyal to Richard to join in the effort to free the King with the promise of a full pardon for him and all his men should they succeed. But Robin knew that if they failed, John would burn Sherwood and the rest of England to the ground to reap his vengeance. Theft and unrest in the provinces were one thing, intrigue at court was another.

Robin knew the days of the Merry Men were numbered. Even as they grew stronger, they grew weaker. Time was on the side of the sheriff, who would draw on all the power of the Crown if he had to, and, if Robin became too much of a threat, would surely do so.

Just then the horn blew for the traditional English breakfast of bread and ale. Robin would have breakfast with the Merry Men and then confer with Will Scarlet, Little John, and Scarlock.

Using the Case of *Robin Hood*

Robin Hood is a perfect example of a manager facing the problems of success. Robin's very success has created his problems.

Questions for Discussion

1. What are some of the problems facing Robin and the Merry Men?
2. What are some of the situations in the environment that will have an impact on whatever Robin decides to do?
3. What are some of the alternatives that Robin is considering for dealing with his problems? Can you identify some additional alternatives?
4. What do you think the reaction of Merry Men will be? The sheriff? The people?
5. What do you think Robin should do?

Exercise: *Managerial Development*

1. Identify the best manager with whom you personally have interacted within the last seven years:

Case: Robin Hood; Exercise: Managerial Development

2. Why did you select that person? I selected him/her because:
   a. s/he:
   b. s/he:
   c. s/he:
4. Of the attributes you listed above, which is the most important for you? A, B, or C?
5. Why do you feel that is the most important attribute of a manager?
6. Identify the best employee with whom you personally have interacted within the past seven years.
7. Why did you select that person? I selected him/her because:
   a. s/he:
   b. s/he:
   c. s/he:
4. Of the attributes you listed above, which is the most important? A, B, or C?
5. Why do you feel that is the most important attribute of an employee?

Using the Exercise for *Managerial Development*

This exercise has been developed to give you the opportunity to establish a role model for managerial and employee behavior. It provides a useful tool for determining your attitude toward what makes a good manager and a good employee.

It might be particularly useful to do the exercise during the first few days of class, discuss it, and then, at the end of the term, redo the exercise to determine if there has been any changes in your perception of the best manager and employee and what they did.

It is recommended that you keep the papers so that they can be used for reference during a class discussion of managerial and employee behavior. The names of the individuals are not important. The ideas, perceptions, and attitudes of those people are what count

Case: Robin Hood; Exercise: Managerial Development, Fred Maidment, McGraw-Hill/Dushkin, 2000.

UNIT 2
Planning

Unit Selections

6. **A New Look at Managerial Decision Making**, Victor H. Vroom
7. **Management Accounting Master: Closing the Gap Between Managerial Accounting and External Reporting**, Soeren Dressler
8. **Michael Porter: What Is Strategy?**, *Thinkers*
9. **Six Priorities That Make a Great Strategic Decision**, Mary Burner Lippitt
10. **The Americanization of Toyota**, *Business Week*
    CASE II. The Fairfax County Social Welfare Agency; Exercise: NASA

Key Points to Consider

- What do you think is the best way to make decisions when other people have to implement them? Do you think some ways are better than others? Explain.

- Many organizations talk about thinking "out of the box," yet few seem able to do so. Why do you think this is? Why is timing critical to the implementation of any plan?

- Many organizations are seeking new ways to implement strategic management in the twenty-first century. What are some of the things that you might consider doing that have not been done in the past?

 **Links: www.dushkin.com/online/**
These sites are annotated in the World Wide Web pages.

American Civil Liberties Union (ACLU)
  http://www.aclu.org/issues/worker/campaign.html
Benchmarking Network
  http://www.well.com/user/benchmar/tbnhome.html
GBN Scenario Planning
  http://www.gbn.com

Managers must plan. Planning must be accomplished before action takes place. The question is, how should managers plan and decide on a course of action?

There are various styles, methods, and techniques that a manager can call upon. As Victor Vroom demonstrates in his classic essay, "A New Look at Managerial Decision Making," the way that the decision is made will be a key factor in the implementation of the plan. People who feel that they have some participation in making important decisions that will affect them are far more likely to support the plan enthusiastically than are people who feel that the decision is a fiat from the upper reaches of the organization chart. Of course, a manager can make some decisions alone or in consultation with a few people. The important part is to select the appropriate planning/decision-making style, so that the action will have the greatest chance for success. The way to accomplish this is to involve the people who will be most directly concerned with the implementation of that decision.

It is basic to the function of a manager that he or she must make decisions. It is not possible for the policy manual to cover every situation that can arise. Managers must be able to evaluate the goals and objectives of the plans for the good of the organization—not an easy task. Because there is always a degree of uncertainty in an important decision, the organization is also obligated to provide the manager with support and resources so that the decisions will succeed. Support includes not only a recognition and knowledge of the firm and its plans, but an understanding of the organization's internal and external environment. These are explored in "Six Priorities That Make a Great Strategic Decision" by Mary Burner Lippitt.

Planning must consider the internal strengths and weaknesses of the organization, including finance, human resources, manufacturing, distribution, and marketing. Capitalizing on strengths while minimizing the impact of weaknesses is vital to successful planning. Strategic decision making also involves an assessment of the environment as well as an understanding of the corporate culture, the importance of which is demonstrated in "The Americanization of Toyota." Organizations must interact with their surroundings and timing is important. Those who manage and plan for organizations must recognize that the only constant is change. Everything is fluid—people, places, and things—and managing the strategic agenda in this changing environment will be a key to success.

Finally, there are many ways to plan and make strategy. The effectiveness of the plans depends on the nature and needs of the business, the styles of the people, and the goals and plans of the firm. The five basic questions in strategic planning are: (1) Where have we been? (2) Where are we now? (3) Where do we want to go? (4) How do we want to get there? (5) How will we know we have arrived? These questions must be answered by each firm's management as they plan for the organization in a changing and uncertain world. It is essential that students of management learn the principles of planning and be able to put them into practice. Opportunities abound and are often found in what might be considered less than traditional areas of planning.

Article 6

A NEW LOOK AT MANAGERIAL DECISION MAKING

Victor H. Vroom

All managers are decision makers. Furthermore, their effectiveness as managers is largely reflected in their track record in making the right decisions. These right decisions in turn largely depend on whether or not the manager has utilized the right person or persons in the right ways in helping him solve the problem.

Our concern in this article is with decision making as a social process. We view the manager's task as determining how the problem is to be solved, not the solution to be adopted. Within that overall framework, we have attempted to answer two broad sets of questions: What decision-making processes should managers use to deal effectively with the problems they encounter in their jobs? What decision-making processes do they use in dealing with these problems and what considerations affect their decisions about how much to share their decision-making power with subordinates?

The reader will recognize the former as a normative or prescriptive question. A rational and analytic answer to it would constitute a normative model of decision making as a social process. The second question is descriptive, since it concerns how managers do, rather than should, behave.

Towards a Normal Model

About four years ago, Philip Yetton, then a graduate student at Carnegie-Mellon University, and I began a major research program in an attempt to answer these normative and descriptive questions.

We began with the normative question: What would be a rational way of deciding on the form and amount of participation in decision making that should be used in different situations? We were tired of debates over the relative merits of Theory X and Theory Y and of the truism that leadership depends upon the situation. We felt that it was time for the behavioral sciences to move beyond such generalities and to attempt to come to grips with the complexities of the phenomena with which they intended to deal.

Our aim was ambitious—to develop a set of ground rules for matching a manager's leadership behavior to the demands of the situation. It was critical that these ground rules be consistent with research evidence concerning the consequences of participation and that the model based on the rules be operational, so that any manager could see it to determine how he should act in any decision-making situation.

Table 1 shows a set of alternative decision processes that we have employed in our research. Each process is represented by a symbol (e.g., AI, CI, GII) that will be used as a convenient method of referring to each process. The first letter in this symbol signifies the basic properties of the process (A stands for autocratic; C for consultative; and G for group). The Roman numerals that follow the first letter constitute variants on that process. Thus, AI represents the first variant on an autocratic process, and AII the second variant.

Conceptual and Empirical Basis of the Model

A model designed to regulate, in some rational way, choices among the decisions processes shown in Table 1 should be based on sound empirical evidence concerning the likely consequences of the styles. The more complete the empirical base of knowledge, the greater the certainty with which we can develop the model and the greater will be its usefulness. To aid in understanding the conceptual basis of the model, it is important to distinguish among three classes of outcomes that bear on the ultimate effectiveness of decisions. These are:

1. The quality or rationality of the decision.
2. The acceptance or commitment on the part of subordinates to execute the decision effectively.
3. The amount of time required to make the decision.

The effects of participation on each of these outcomes or consequences were summed up by the author in *The Handbook of Social Psychology* as follows:

TABLE 1 TYPES OF MANAGEMENT DECISION STYLES

AI You solve the problem or make the decision yourself, using information available to you at that time.

AII You obtain the necessary information from your subordinate(s), then decide on the solution to the problem yourself. You may or may not tell your subordinates what the problem is in getting the information from them. The role played by your subordinates in making the decision is clearly one of providing the necessary information to you, rather than generating or evaluating alternative solutions.

CI You share the problem with relevant subordinates individually, getting their ideas and suggestions without bringing them together as a group. Then you make the decision that may or may not reflect your subordinates' influence.

CII You share the problem with your subordinates as a group, collectively obtaining their ideas and suggestions. Then you make the decision that may or may not reflect your subordinates' influence.

GII You share a problem with your subordinates as a group. Together you generate and evaluate alternatives and attempt to reach agreement (consensus) on a solution. Your role is much like that of chairman. You do not try to influence the group to adopt your solution and you are willing to accept and implement any solution that has the support of the entire group.

(GI is omitted because it applies only to more comprehensive models outside the scope of this article.)
© 1973 by University of Pittsburgh Press

The results suggest that allocating problem solving and decision-making tasks to entire groups requires a greater investment of man hours but produces higher acceptance of decisions and a higher probability that the decision will be executed efficiently. Differences between these two methods in quality of decisions and in elapsed time are inconclusive and probably highly variable.... It would be naive to think that group decision making is always more "effective" than autocratic decision making, or vice versa; the relative effectiveness of these two extreme methods depends both on the weights attached to quality, acceptance and time variables and on differences in amounts of these outcomes resulting from these methods, neither of which is invariant from one situation to another. The critics and proponents of participative management would do well to direct their efforts toward identifying the properties of situations in which different decision-making approaches are effective rather than wholesale condemnation or deification of one approach.

We have gone on from there to identify the properties of the situation or problem that will be the basic elements in the model. These problem attributes are of two types: 1) Those that specify the importance for a particular problem of quality and acceptance, and 2) those that, on the basis of available evidence, have a high probability of moderating the effects of participation on each of these outcomes. Table 2 shows the problem attributes used in the present form of the model. For each attribute a question is provided that might be used by a leader in diagnosing a particular problem prior to choosing his leadership style.

In phrasing the questions, we have held technical language to a minimum. Furthermore, we have phrased the questions in Yes-No form, translating the continuous variables defined above into dichotomous variables. For example, instead of attempting to determine how important the decision quality is to the effectiveness of the decision (attribute A), the leader is asked in the first question to judge whether there is any quality component to the problem. Similarly, the difficult task of specifying exactly how much information the leader possesses that is relevant to the decision (attribute B) is reduced to a simple judgment by the leader concerning whether or not he has sufficient information to make a high quality decision.

We have found that managers can diagnose a situation quickly and accurately by answering this set of seven questions concerning it. But how can such responses generate a prescription concerning the most effective leadership style or decision process? What kind of normative model of participation in decision making can be built from this set of problem attributes?

Figure 1 shows one such model expressed in the form of a decision tree. It is the seventh version of such a model that we have developed over the last three years. The problem attributes, expressed in question form, are arranged along the top of the figure. To use the model for a particular decision-making situation, one starts at the left-hand side and works toward the right asking oneself the question immediately above any box that is encountered. When a terminal node is reached, a number will be found designating the problem type and one of the decision-making processes appearing in Table 1. AI is prescribed for four problem types (1, 2, 4, and 5); AII is prescribed for two problem types (9 and 10); CI is prescribed for only one problem type (8); CII is prescribed for four problem types (7, 11, 13, and 14); and GII is prescribed for three problem types (3, 6, and 12). The relative frequency with which each of the five decision processes would be prescribed for any manager would, of course, depend on the distribution of problem types encountered in his decision making.

Rationale Underlying the Model. The decision processes specified for each problem type are not arbitrary. The model's behavior is governed by a set of principles intended to be consistent with existing evidence concerning the consequences of participation in decision making on organizational effectiveness.

ANNUAL EDITIONS

There are two mechanisms underlying the behavior of the model. The first is a set of seven rules* that serve to protect the quality and the acceptance of the decision by eliminating alternatives that risk one or the other of these decision outcomes. Once the rules have been applied, a feasible set of decision processes is generated. The second mechanism is a principle for choosing among alternatives in the feasible set where more than one exists.

TABLE 2 PROBLEM ATTRIBUTES USED IN THE MODEL

	Problem Attributes	Diagnostic Questions
A.	The importance of the quality of the decision.	Is there a quality requirement such that one solution is likely to be more rational than another?
B.	The extent to which the leader possesses sufficient information/expertise to make a high-quality decision by himself.	Do I have sufficient information to make a high-quality decision?
C.	The extent to which the problem is structured.	Is the problem structured?
D.	The extent to which acceptance or commitment on the part of subordinates is critical to the effective implementation of the decision.	Is acceptance of decision by subordinates critical to effective implementation?
E.	The prior probability that the leader's autocratic decision will receive acceptance by subordinates.	If you were to make the decision by yourself, is it reasonably certain that it would be accepted by your subordinates?
F.	The extent to which subordinates are motivated to attain the organizational goals as represented in the objectives explicit in the statement of the problem.	Do subordinates share the organizational goals to be obtained in solving this problem?
G.	The extent to which subordinates are likely to be in conflict over preferred solutions.	Is conflict among subordinates likely in preferred solutions?

© 1973 by University of Pittsburge Press

Let us examine the rules first, because they do much of the work of the model. As previously indicated, the rules are intended to protect both the quality and acceptance of the decision. In the form of the model shown, there are three rules that protect decision quality and four that protect acceptance.

1. *The Information Rule.* If the quality of the decision is important and if the leader does not possess enough information or expertise to solve the problem by himself, AI is eliminated from the feasible set. (Its use risks a low-quality decision.)

2. *The Goal Congruence rule.* If the quality of the decision is important and if the subordinates do not share the organizational goals to be obtained in solving the problem, GII is eliminated from the feasible set. (Alternatives that eliminate the leader's final control over the decision reached may jeopardize the quality of the decision.)

3. *The Unstructured Problem Rule.* In decisions in which the quality of the decision is important, if the leader lacks the necessary information or expertise to solve the problem by himself, and if the problem is unstructured, i.e., he does not know exactly what information is needed and where it is located, the method used must provide not only for him to collect the information but to do so is an efficient and effective manner. Methods that involve interaction among all subordinates with full knowledge of the problem are likely to be both more efficient and more likely to generate a high-quality solution to the problem. Under these conditions, AI, AII, and CI are eliminated from the feasible set. (AI does not provide for him to collect the necessary information, and AII and CI represent more cumbersome, less effective, and less efficient means of bringing the necessary information to bear on the solution of the problem than methods that do permit those with the necessary information to interact.)

4. *The Acceptance Rule.* If the acceptance of the decision by subordinates is critical to effective implementation, and if it is not certain that an autocratic decision made by the leader would receive that acceptance, AI and AII are eliminated from the feasible set. (Neither provides an opportunity for subordinates to participate in the decision and both risk the necessary acceptance.)

5. *The Conflict Rule.* If the acceptance of the decision is critical, and an autocratic decision is not certain to be accepted, and subordinates are likely to be in conflict or disagreement over the appropriate solution, AI, AII, and CI are eliminated from the feasible set. (The method used in solving the problem should enable those in disagreement to resolve their differences with full knowledge of the problem. Accordingly, under these conditions, AI, AII, and CI, which involve no interaction or only "one-on-one" relationships and therefore provide no opportunity for those in conflict to resolve their differences, are eliminated from the feasible set. Their use runs the risk of leaving some of the subordinates with less than the necessary commitment to the final decision.)

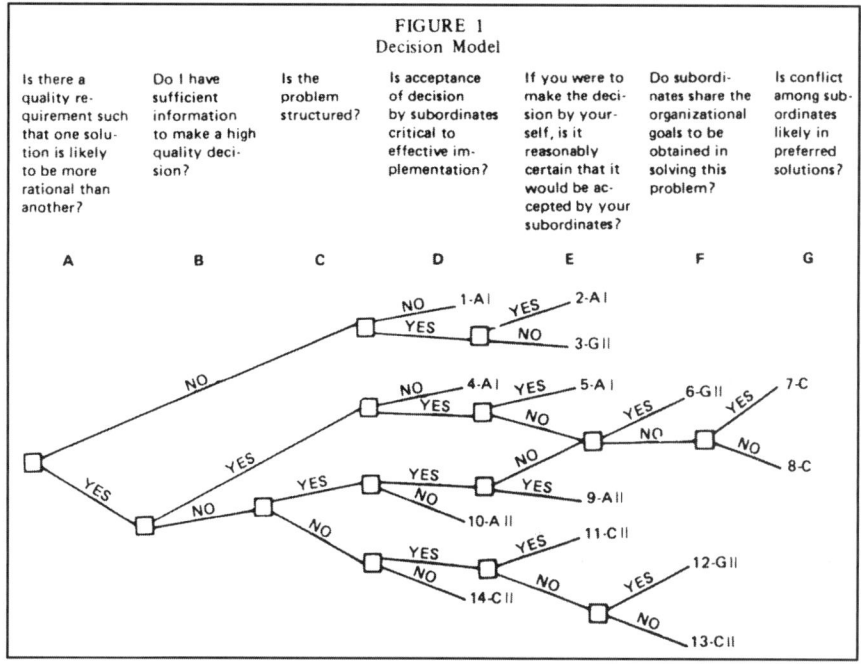

*The rules and figure 1 are reprinted from Leadership and Decision-Making, by Victor H. Vroom and Philip W. Yetton, by permission of the University of Pittsburgh Press. © 1973 by University of Pittsburgh Press

6. *The Fairness Rule.* If the quality of decision is unimportant and if acceptance is critical and not certain to result from an autocratic decision, AI, AII, CI, and CII are eliminated from the feasible set. (The method used should maximize the probability of acceptance as this is the only relevant consideration in determining the effectiveness of the decision. Under these circumstances, AI, AII, CI, and CII, which create less acceptance or commitment than GII, are eliminated from the feasible set. To use them is to run the risk of getting less than the needed acceptance of the decision.)

7. *The Acceptance Priority Rule.* If acceptance is critical, not assured by an autocratic decision, and if subordinates can be trusted, AI, AII, CI, and CII are eliminated from the feasible set. (Methods that provide equal partnership in the decision-making process can provide greater acceptance without risking decision quality. Use of any method other than GII results in an unnecessary risk that the decision will not be fully accepted or receive the necessary commitment on the part of subordinates.)

Once all seven rules have been applied to a given problem we emerge with a feasible set of decision processes. The feasible set for each of the fourteen problem types is shown in Table 3. It can be seen that there are some problem types for which only one method remains in the feasible set, others for which two methods remain feasible, and still others for which five methods remain feasible.

When more than one method remains in the feasible set, there are a number of ways in which one might choose among them. The mechanism we have selected, the principle underlying the choices of the model in Figure 1, utilizes the number of man-hours used in solving the problem as the basis for choice. Given a set of methods with equal likelihood of meeting both quality and acceptance requirements for the decision, it chooses that method that requires the least investment of man-hours. On the basis of the empirical evidence summarized earlier, this is deemed to be the method furthest to the left within the feasible set. For example, since AI, AII, CI, CII, and GII are all feasible as in Problem Types 1 and 2, AI would be the method chosen.

To illustrate application of the model in actual administrative situations, we will analyze four cases with the help of the model. While we attempt to describe these cases as completely as is necessary to permit the reader to make the judgments required by the model, there may remain some room for subjectivity. The reader may wish after reading the case to analyze it himself using the model and then to compare his analysis with that of the author.

CASE I. You are a manufacturing manager in a large electronics plant. The company's management has recently installed new machines and put in a new simplified work system, but to the surprise of everyone, yourself included, the expected increase in productivity was not realized. In fact, production has begun to drop, quality has fallen off, and the number of employee separations has risen.

You do not believe that there is anything wrong with the machines. You have had reports from other companies that are using them and they confirm this opinion. You have also had representatives from the firm that built the machines go over them and they report that they are operating at peak efficiency.

You suspect that some parts of the new work system may be responsible for the change, but this view is not widely shared among your immediate subordinates who are four first-line supervisors, each in charge of a section, and your supply manager. The drop in production has been variously attributed to poor training of the operators, lack of an adequate system of financial incentives, and poor morale. Clearly, this is an issue about which there is considerable depth of feeling within individuals and potential disagreement among your subordinates.

This morning you received a phone call from your division manager. He had just received your production figures for the last six months and was calling to express his concern. He indicated that the problem was yours to solve in any way that you think best, but that he would like to know within a week what steps you plan to take.

You share your division manager's concern with the falling productivity and know that your men are also concerned. The problem is to decide what steps to take to rectify the situation.

Analysis
Questions—
A (Quality?) = Yes
B (Manager's Information?) = No
C (Structured?) = No
D (Acceptance?) = Yes
E (Prior Probability of Acceptance?) = No
F (Goal Congruence?) = Yes
G (Conflict) = Yes
Problem Type—12
Feasible Set—GII
Minimum Man-Hours Solution (from Figure 1)—GII
Rule Violations—
AI violates rules 1, 3, 4, 5, 7
AII violates rules 3, 4, 5, 7
CI violates rules 3, 5, 7
CII violates rule 7

CASE II. You are general foreman in charge of a large gang laying an oil pipeline and have to estimate your expected rate of progress in order to schedule material deliveries to the next field site.

You know the nature of the terrain you will be traveling and have the historical data needed to compute the mean and variance in the rate of speed over that type of terrain. Given these two variables, it is a simple matter to calculate the earliest and latest times at which materials and support facilities will be needed at the next site. It is important that your estimate be reasonably accurate. Underestimates result in idle foremen and workers, and an overestimate results in tying up materials for a period of time before they are to be used.

TABLE 3 PROBLEM TYPES AND THE FEASIBLE SET OF DECISION PROCESSES

Problem Type	Acceptable Methods
1.	AI, AII, CI, CII, GII
2.	AI, AII, CI, CII, GII
3.	GII
4.	AI, AII, CI, CII, GII*
5.	AI, AII, CI, CII, GII*
6.	GII
7.	CII
8.	CI, CII
9.	AII, CI, CII, GII*
10.	AII, CI, CII, GII*
11.	CII, GII*
12.	GII
13.	CII
14.	CII, GII*

*Within the feasible set only when the answer to F is Yes.
© 1973 by University of Pittsurgh Press

Progress has been good and your five foremen and other members of the gang stand to receive substantial bonuses if the project is completed ahead of schedule.

Analysis
Questions—
A (Quality?) = Yes
B (Manager's Information?) = Yes
D (Acceptance?) = No
Problem Type—4
Feasible Set—AI, AII, CI, CII, GII
Minimum Man-Hours Solution (from Figure 1)—AI
Rule Violations—None

CASE III. You are supervising the work of 12 engineers. Their formal training and work experience are very similar, permitting you to use them interchangeably on projects. Yesterday, your manager informed you that a request had been received from an overseas affiliate for four engineers to go abroad on extended loan for a period of six to eight months. For a number of reasons, he argued and you agreed that this request should be met from your group.

All your engineers are capable of handling this assignment and, from the standpoint of present and future projects, there is no particular reason why anyone should be retained over any other. The problem is somewhat complicated by the fact that the overseas assignment is in what is generally regarded as an undesirable location.

Analysis
Questions—
　A (Quality?) = No
　D (Acceptance?) = Yes
　E (Prior Probability of Acceptance?) = No
　G (Conflict?) = Yes
Problem Type—3
Feasible Set—GII
Minimum Man-Hours Solution (from Figure 1)—GII
Rule Violations—
　AI and AII violate rules 4, 5, and 6
　CI violates rules 5 and 6
　CII violates rule 6

CASE IV. You are on the division manager's staff and work on a wide variety of problems of both an administrative and technical nature. You have been given the assignment of developing a standard method to be used in each of the five plants in the division for manually reading equipment registers, recording the readings, and transmitting the scorings to a centralized information system.

Until now there has been a high error rate in the reading and/or transmittal of the data. Some locations have considerably higher error rates than others, and the methods used to record and transmit the data vary among plants. It is probable, therefore, that part of the error variance is a function of specific local conditions rather than anything else, and this will complicate the establishment of any system common to all plants. You have the information error rates but no information on the local practices that generate these errors or on the local conditions that necessitate the different practices.

Everyone would benefit from an improvement in the quality of the data; it is used in a number of important decisions. Your contacts with the plants are through the quality-control supervisors who are responsible for collecting the data. They are a conscientious group committed to doing their jobs well, but are highly sensitive to interference on the part of higher management in their own operations. Any solution that does not receive the active support of the various plant supervisors is unlikely to reduce the error rate significantly.

Analysis
Questions—
　A (Quality?) = Yes
　B (Manager's Information?) = No
　C (Structured?) = No
　D (Acceptance?) = Yes
　E (Prior Probability of Acceptance?) = No
　F (Goal Congruence?) = Yes
Problem Type—12
Feasible Set—GII
Minimum Man-Hours Solution (from Figure 1)—GII
Rule Violations—
　AI violates rules 1, 3, 4, and 7
　AII violates rules 3, 4, and 7
　CI violates rules 3 and 7
　CII violates rule 7

Short Versus Long-Term Models

The model described above seeks to protect the quality of the decision and to expend the least number of man-hours in the process. Because it focuses on conditions surrounding the making and implementation of a particular decision rather than any long-term considerations, we can term it a short-term model.

It seems likely, however, that the leadership methods that may be optimal for short-term results may be different from those that would be optimal over a longer period of time. Consider a leader, for example, who has been uniformly pursuing an autocratic style (AI or AII) and, perhaps as a consequence, has subordinates who might be termed "yes men" (attribute E) but who also cannot be trusted to pursue organizational goals (attribute F), largely because the leader has never bothered to explain them.

It appears likely, however, that the manger who used more participative methods would, in time, change the status of these problem attributes so as to develop ultimately a more effective problem-solving system. A promising approach to the development of a long-term model is one that places less weight on man-hours as the basis for choice of method within the feasible set. Given a long-term orientation, one would be interested in the possibility of a trade-off between man-hours in problem solving and team development, both of which increase with participation. Viewed in these terms, the time-minimizing model places maximum relative weight on man-hours and no weight on development, and hence chooses the style farthest to the left within the feasible set. A model that places less weight on man-hours and more weight on development would, if these assumptions are correct, choose a style further to the right within the feasible set.

We recognize, of course, that the minimum man-hours solution suggested by the model is not always the best solution to every problem. A manager faced, for example with the problem of handling any one of the four cases previously examined might well choose more time-consuming alternatives on the grounds that the greater time invested would be justified in developing his subordinates. Similar considerations exist in other decision-making situations. For this reason we have come to emphasize the feasible set of decision methods in our work with managers. Faced with considerations not included in the model, the manager should consider any alternative within the feasible set, and not opt automatically for the minimum man-hours solution.

As I am writing this, I have in front of me a "black box" that constitutes an electronic version of the normative model discussed on the preceding pages. (The author is indebted to Peter Fuss of Bell Telephone Laboratories for his interest in the model and his skill in developing the "black box.") The box, which is small enough to fit into the palm of one hand, has a set of seven switches, each appropriately labeled with the questions (A through G) used in Figure 1. A manager faced with a concrete problem or decision can "diagnose" that problem by setting each switch in either its "yes" or "no" position. Once the problem has been described, the manager depresses a button that illuminates at least one or as many as five lights, each of which denotes one of the decision processes (AI, AII, etc.). The lights that are illuminated constitute the feasible set of decision processes for the problem as shown in Table III. The lights not illuminated correspond to alternatives that violate one or more of the seven rules previously stated.

In this prototype version of the box, the lights are illuminated in decreasing order of brightness from left to right within the feasible set. The brightest light corresponds to the alternative shown in Figure 1. Thus, if both CII and GII were feasible alternatives, CII would be brighter than GII, since it requires fewer man-hours. However, a manager who was not under any undue time pressure and who wished to invest time in the development of his subordinates might select an alternative corresponding to one of the dimmer lights.

Toward a Descriptive Model of Leader Behavior

So far we have been concerned with the normative questions defined at the outset. But how do managers really behave? What considerations affect their decisions about how much to share their decision-making power with their subordinates? In what respects is their behavior different from or similar to that of the model? These questions are but a few of those that we attempted to answer in a large-scale research program aimed at gaining a greater understanding of the factors that influence managers in their choice of decision processes to fit the demands of the situation. This research program was financially supported by the McKinsey Foundation, General Electric Foundation, Smith Richardson Foundation, and the Office of Naval Research.

Two different research methods have been utilized in studying these factors. The first investigation utilized a method that we have come to term "recalled problems." Over 500 managers from 11 different countries representing a variety of firms were asked to provide a written description of a problem that they had recently had to solve. These varied in length from one paragraph to several pages and covered virtually every facet of managerial decision making. For each case, the manager was asked to indicate which of the decision processes shown in Table I they used to solve the problem. Finally, each manager was asked to answer the questions shown in Table II corresponding to the problem attributes used in the normative model.

The wealth of data, both qualitative and quantitative, served two purposes. Since each manager had diagnosed a situation that he had encountered in terms that are used in the normative model and had indicated the methods that he had used in dealing with it, it is possible to determine what differences, if any, there were between the model's behavior and his own behavior. Second, the written cases provided the basis for the construction of a standard set of cases used in later research to determine the factors that influence managers to share or retain their decision-making power. Each case depicted a manager faced with a problem to solve or decision to make. The cases spanned a wide range of managerial problems including production scheduling, quality control, portfolio management, personnel allocation, and research and development. In each case, a person could readily assume the role of the manager described and could indicate which of the decision processes he would use if he actually were faced with that situation.

In most of our research, a set of thirty cases has been used and the subjects have been several thousand managers who were participants in management development programs in the United States and abroad. Cases were selected systematically. We desired cases that could not only be coded unambiguously in the terms used in the normative model but that would also permit the assessment of the effects of each of the problem attributes used in the model on the person's behavior. The solution was to select cases in accordance with an experimental design so that they varied in terms of the seven attributes used in the model and variation in each attribute was independent of each other attribute. Several such standardized sets of cases have been developed, and over a thousand managers have now been studied using this approach.

To summarize everything we learned in the course of this research is well beyond the scope of this paper, but it is possible to discuss some of the highlights. Since the results obtained from the two research methods—recalled and standardized problems—are consistent, we can present the major results independent of the method used.

Perhaps the most striking finding is the weakening of the widespread view that participativeness is a general trait that individual managers exhibit in different amounts. To be sure, there were differences *among* managers in their general tendencies to utilize participative methods as opposed to autocratic ones. On the standardized problems, these differences accounted for about 10 percent of the total variance in the decision process observed. These differences in behavior between managers, however, were small in comparison with differences *within* managers. On the standardized problems, no manager indicated that he would use the same decision process on all problems or decisions, and most used all five methods under some circumstances.

Some of this variance in behavior within managers can be attributed to widely shared tendencies to respond to some situations by sharing power and others by retaining it. It makes more sense to talk about participative and autocratic situations than it does to talk about participative and autocratic managers. In fact, on the standardized problems, the variance in behavior across problems or cases is about three times as large as the variance across managers!

What are the characteristics of an autocratic as opposed to a participative situation? An answer to this question would constitute a partial descriptive model of this aspect of the decision-making process and has been our goal in much of the research that we have conducted. From our observations of behavior on both recalled problems and on standardized problems, it is clear that the decision-making process has been our goal in much of the research that we have conducted. From our observations of behavior on both recalled problems and on standardized problems, it is clear that the decision-making process employed by a typical manager is influenced by a large number of factors, many of which also show up in the normative model. Following are several conclusions substantiated by the results on both recalled and standardized problems: Managers use decision processes providing less opportunity for participation (1) when they possess all the necessary information than when they lack some of the needed information, (2) when the problem that they face is well-structured rather than unstructured, (3) when their subordinates' acceptance of the decision is not critical for the effective implementation of the decision or when the prior probability of acceptance of an autocratic decision is high, and (4) when the personal goals of their subordinates are *not* congruent with the goals of the organization as manifested in the problem.

So far we have been talking about relatively common or widely shared ways of dealing with organizational problems. Our results strongly suggest that there are ways of "tailoring" one's approach to the situation that distinguish managers from one another. Theoretically, these can be thought of as differences among managers in decision rules that they employ about when to encourage participation. Statistically, they are represented as interactions between situational variables and personal characteristics.

Consider, for example, two managers who have identical distributions of the use of the five decision processes shown in Table I on a set of thirty cases. In a sense, they are equally participative (or autocratic). However, the situations in which they permit or encourage participation in decision making on the part of their subordinates may be very different. One may restrict the participation of his subordinates to decisions without a quality requirement, whereas the other may restrict their participation to problems with a quality requirement. The former would be more inclined to use participative decision processes (like GII) on such decisions as what color the walls should be painted or when the company picnic should be held. The latter would be more likely to encourage participation in decision making on decisions that have a clear and demonstrable impact on the organization's success in achieving its external goals.

Use of the standardized problem set permits the assessment of such differences in decision rules that govern choices among decision-making processes. Since the cases are selected in accordance with an experimental design, they can indicate differences in the behavior of managers attributable not only to the existence of a quality requirement in the problem but also in the effects of acceptance requirements, conflict, information requirements, and the like.

The research using both recalled and standardized problems has also enabled us to examine similarities and differences between the behavior of the normative model and the behavior of a typical manager. Such an analysis reveals, at the very least, what behavioral changes could be expected if managers began using the normative model as the basis for choosing their decision-making processes.

A typical manager says he would (or did) use exactly the same decision process as that shown in Figure 1 in 40 percent of the situations. In two thirds of the situations, his behavior is consistent with the feasible set of methods proposed in the model. In other words, in about one third of the situations his behavior violates at least one of the seven rules underlying the model.

The four rules designed to protect the acceptance or commitment of the decision have substantially higher probabilities of being violated than do the three rules designed to protect the quality or rationality of the decision. One of the acceptance rules, the Fairness Rule (Rule 6) is violated about three quarters of the time that it could have been violated. On the other hand, one of the quality rules, the Information Rule (Rule 1), is violated in only about 3 percent of occasions in which it is applicable. If we assume for the moment that these two sets of rules have equal validity, these findings strongly suggest that the decisions made by typical managers are more likely to prove ineffective due to deficiencies of acceptance by subordinates than due to deficiencies in decision quality.

Another striking difference between the behavior of the model and of the typical manager lies in the fact that the former shows far greater variance with the situation. If a typical manager voluntarily used the model as the basis for choosing his methods of making decisions, he would become both more autocratic and more participative. He would employ autocratic methods more frequently in situations in which his subordinates were unaffected by the decision and participative methods more frequently when his subordinates' cooperation and support were critical and/or their information and expertise were required.

It should be noted that the typical manager to whom we have been referring is merely a statistical average of the several thousand who have been studied over the last three or four years. There is a great deal of variance around that average. As evidenced by their behavior on standardized problems some managers are already behaving in a way that is highly consistent with the model, while others' behavior is clearly at variance with it.

A New Technology for Leadership Development

The investigations that have been summarized here were conducted for research purposes to shed some light on the causes and consequences of participation in decision making. In the course of the research, we came to realize, partly because of the value attached to it by the managers themselves, that the data collection procedures, with appropriate additions and modifications, might also serve as a valuable guide to leadership development. From this realization evolved an important by-product of the research activities—a new approach to leadership development based on the concepts in the normative model and the empirical methods of the descriptive research.

This approach is based on the assumption stated previously that one of the critical skills required of all leaders is the ability to adapt their behavior to the demands of the situation and that one component of this skill involves the ability to select the appropriate decision-making process for each problem or decision he confronts.

Managers can derive value from the model by comparing their past or intended behavior in concrete decisions with that prescribed by the model and by seeing what rules, if any, they violate. Used in this way, the model can provide a mechanism for a manager to analyze both the circumstances that he faces and what decisions are feasible under these circumstances.

While use of the model without training is possible, we believe that the manager can derive the maximum value from a systematic examination of his leadership style, and its similarities to and dissimilarities from the model, as part of a formal leadership development program.

During the past two years we have developed such a program. It is not intended to "train" participants in the use of the model, but rather to encourage them to examine their own leadership style and to ask themselves whether the methods they are using are most effective for their own organization. A critical part of the program involves the use of a set of standardized cases, each depicting a leader faced with an administrative problem to solve. Each participant then specifies the decision-making process that he would use if faced with each situation. His responses are processed by computer, which generates a highly detailed analysis of his leadership style. The responses for all participants in the course are typically processed simultaneously, permitting the economical representation of differences between the person and other participants in the same program.

In its present form, a single computer printout for a person consists of three 15 x 11 pages, each filled with graphs and tables highlighting different features of his behavior. Understanding the results requires a detailed knowledge of the concepts underlying the model, something already developed in one of the previous phases of the training program. The printout is accompanied by a manual that aids in explaining results and provides suggested steps to be followed in extracting full meaning from the printout.

Following are a few of the questions that the printout answers:

1. How autocratic or participative am I in my dealings with subordinates in comparison with other participants in the program?
2. What decision processes do I use more or less frequently than the average?
3. How close does my behavior come to that of the model? How frequently does my behavior agree with the feasible set? What evidence is there that my leadership style reflects the pressure of time as opposed to a concern with the development of my subordinates? How do I compare in these respects with other participants in the class?
4. What rules do I violate most frequently and least frequently? How does this compare with other participants? On what cases did I violate these rules? Does my leadership style reflect more concern with getting decisions that are high in quality or with getting decisions that are accepted?
5. What circumstances cause me to behave in an autocratic fashion; what circumstances cause me to behave participatively? In what respects is the way in which I attempt to vary my behavior with the demands of the situation similar to that of the model?

When a typical manager receives his printout, he immediately goes to work trying to understand what it tells him about himself. After most of the major results have been understood, he goes back to the set of cases to reread those on which he has violated rules. Typically, managers show an interest in discussing and comparing their results with others in the program. Gatherings of four to six people comparing their results and their interpretation of them, often for several hours at a stretch, were such a common feature that they have recently been institutionalized as part of the procedure.

We should emphasize that the method of providing feedback to managers on their leadership style is just one part of the total training experience, but it is an important part. The program is sufficiently new so that, to date, no long-term evaluative studies have been undertaken. The short-term results, however, appear quite promising.

Conclusion

The efforts reported in this article rest on the conviction that social scientists can be of greater value in solving problems of organizational behavior if their prescriptive statements deal with the complexities involved in the phenomena with which they study. The normative model described in this paper is one step in that direction. Some might argue that it is premature for social scientists to be prescriptive. Our knowledge is too limited and the issues too complex to warrant prescriptions for action, even those that are based on a diagnosis of situational demands. However, organizational problems persist, and managers cannot wait for the behavioral sciences to perfect their disciplines before attempting to cope with them. Is it likely that models that encourage them to deal analytically with the forces impinging upon them would produce less rational choices than those that they now make? We think the reverse is more probable—reflecting on the models will result in decisions that are more rational and more effective. The criterion for social utility is not perfection but improvement over present practice.

Victor H. Vroom, Professor, Yale University

From *Readings in Management*, 1986, pp. 132-148. Published by South-Western Publishing Company. Originally from *Organizational Dynamics*, Spring 1972, pp. 66-80. © 1972 by the American Management Association, New York. All rights reserved. Reprinted by permission.

MANAGEMENT ACCOUNTING MASTER: CLOSING THE GAP BETWEEN MANAGERIAL ACCOUNTING AND EXTERNAL REPORTING

Soeren Dressler

Times of significant market adjustments and an uncertain economy spotlight the need for effective decision-support systems. Leadership must have the ability to promptly identify issues and make adjustments based on benchmarks. Financial professionals, however, especially those for multinationals, are challenged to align management accounting with legal reporting requirements. A globally harmonized management accounting master (MAM) can be the answer. It becomes the blueprint for organizational alignment and provides benchmarking for management decision-making. To make it work, the current assortment of business unit structures must be supplemented with local centers comprised of comparable units across divisions and countries. The result is integrated local reporting for management information and control that effectively steers the business from both the local and corporate perspectives, while meeting the various financial reporting requirements.

INTRODUCTION

Especially during a softening economy, finance departments of international corporations are challenged in closing their books—monthly, quarterly, and on a yearly basis. This challenge is basically twofold: on one side, a community of financial analysts thirsts for disclosure of financial figures to guide recommendations for investors and on the other side, management seeks indications of underperforming units and opportunities to streamline its business. The biggest challenge is delivering a set of harmonized and integrated data. Financial professionals and managers, both corporate and of local subsidiaries, are challenged to simplify and harmonize accounting approaches to meet financial reporting requirements and management needs, while balancing diverse, entrepreneurial independence and corporate goals.

In their effort to ensure data transparency for investors, the SEC and the U.S. GAAP have established rigid reporting requirements, relying on standardization and a consistent methodology of profit and loss statements (P&Ls) to derive accurate reporting of corporate business conditions. But even if the investment community is satisfied with the level of detail provided on a corporation and business segment level, the need for information to effectively manage the business is much greater. In particular, international, diversified organizations suffer from inconsistent data provided by their subsidiaries scattered around the globe. Although subsidiaries generally

EXECUTIVE SUMMARY

• *Business leaders, especially those at multinational firms, need effective decision-support systems.*

• *A globally harmonized management accounting master can integrate multiple accounting systems, serving as a "blueprint" for organizational alignments, and providing benchmarks for management decision making.*

• *To make it work, current business units must be reconfigured or supplemented with local centers comprised of comparable units across divisions and countries.*

• *The result is integrated local reporting for management information and control.*

develop and deploy effective internal accounting principles, management reports must be integrated with external reporting, which is based on country-specific legal requirements. The consequence of a global presence is, therefore, a multitude of diverse external reports defined by legal entities. International corporations, however, are not managed according to legal structures but by divisions or product and market segments. The result is financial reporting confusion and inadequate management information.

Local management usually does not understand corporate reporting as its core business.

For a number of reasons, this lack of integration between management reporting and financial reporting often results in reduced impact for deploying corporate objectives and strategies in decentralized units and entities. The primary root of this problem is that management reporting figures have to be derived from financial statements, which are often not detailed enough to identify urgent needs for management intervention.[1] Additionally, local management usually does not understand corporate reporting as its core business, and often resources are not available beyond preparation of consolidated financial statements. The consequences impact both corporate leadership and local management[2]:

- Without appropriately detailed and integrated management information, local managers often make suboptimal decisions.
- Local management is unable to benefit from benchmarking against other local units.
- Corporate leadership cannot optimize its international operations due to missing comparable benchmarking insights.
- Corporate leadership lacks a reliable and accurate overall financial picture.
- Tracking of corporate strategy deployment in decentralized units is quite limited.

This research reviews issues that contribute to financial professionals' challenges in reporting at multinationals, provides a case study example, and suggests and approach based on an MAM and an organizational design of local centers.

This article uses a case study of a construction supply company. We worked with the company for one year, during which time we helped assess their situation and implement numerous changes. The project was guided by the following question: how can corporate reporting be simplified and harmonized to meet financial reporting requirements and management needs, while balancing entrepreneurial independence and corporate goals?

CASE STUDY: CONSTRUCTION SUPPLY COMPANY

The company is a concrete and brick manufacturer based in France that operates across Europe in six countries. It is organized according to two basic principles: each country is an individual operating unit, and the business is organized into four divisions. Overall sales in 2000 were approximately $485 million, with the strongest division contributing nearly $290 million (concrete) and the smallest division $55 million (brick components). The company is headquartered in France, its strongest local market, with Poland and Spain considered emerging markets.

In the last three years, the organizational structure and size of the construction supply company have changed due to massive merger and acquisition activities. The brick business is relatively new to the portfolio and still has to be fully integrated. Overall, the company is well positioned in the market and possesses well-known brands in its industry. As the examples will illustrate, the construction supply company is forced to operate on a global basis, because of transportation costs and access to raw materials. And as a result, harmonizing its management reporting systems has been a significant challenge. This study, reinforced by similar work with other companies during the past three years,[3] is the basis for the local-center accounting model. Details of the construction supply company's business, organization, and reporting provide the examples throughout.[4]

PROBLEMS WITH NONINTEGRATED REPORTING

Consolidated financial statements must be prepared in the United States according to U.S. GAAP. Most international corporations in Europe use the International Accounting Standards (IAS) in order to apply one harmonized standard throughout their entire corporation. Financial reporting normally must meet both legal requirements of each respective country and internationally chosen principles, usually either U.S. GAAP or IAS (for non-U.S. based corporations).[5]

Because management structures rarely are aligned with legal structures, any additional insights that could be gained from consolidated financial statements are quite limited, even if the U.S. GAAP or IAS is applied consistently. The development of international management and cost accounting has not yet succeeded, as external accounting has, in introducing generally accepted principles and guidelines.[6] The lack of convergence is further exacerbated in international corporations by cultural, linguistic, and technological disparities among countries.[7]

Example of Reporting Complications

The France-based construction supplier was challenged by the massive complexity of its reporting structure, which was basically driven by the chosen business unit model and legal entity structure. Because of continuously shrinking margins, especially in the concrete segments, however, cost efficiency needed significant improvement across all countries. Furthermore, as a result of M&A activities, reporting was not fully aligned with corporate principles. The objective was integration for efficiencies and cost savings. Exhibit 1 illustrates why the construction supply company's reporting could not be reconciled with its country-specific consolidated financial statements.

The company experienced numerous business problems that potentially could have been avoided with a better decision-support system. The general manager in Poland, for example, maintained two production units but only one sales organization, which sold products belonging to the brick elements division. His key performance measure was overall revenue growth achieved in Poland; therefore, it was in his interest not to disclose latent underuse in his plants that produced products for the brick division. He kept production at a high level even if these products could not reach the profitability benchmark. If he succeeded in negotiating a transfer price to sell his products to the sales organizations in Austria, Germany, and France as the brick division allowed, he would show an appropriate profitability and continue production levels. The corporate goal, however, is to optimize asset productivity by identifying underutilized production capacities. One essential indicator is profitability; from a corporate perspective, the nonprofitable production of Poland's brick division was not being identified, and value for the corporation further diminished.

ANNUAL EDITIONS

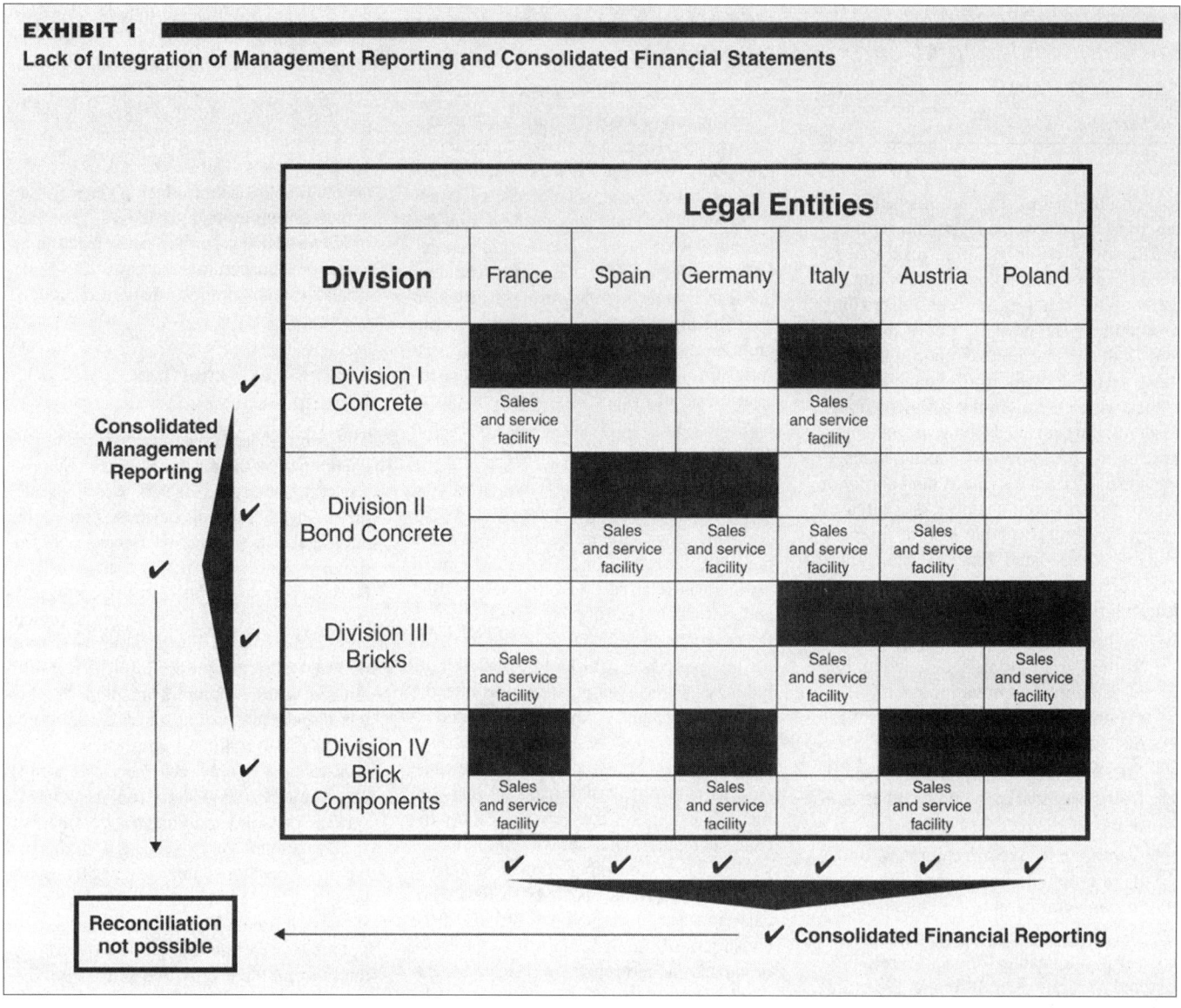

EXHIBIT 1
Lack of Integration of Management Reporting and Consolidated Financial Statements

LOCAL-CENTER ACCOUNTING MODEL

This case example illustrates the usual business problems that can result when normal financial reporting does not produce the information necessary for management's decision-making. Along with the case company's corporate leaders and local managers, a local center accounting model was developed and implemented, based on the MAM—a blueprint for integrating management accounting and external financial reporting.

This local-center accounting model is most effective in corporations with homogeneous business divisions. If the divisions are significantly dissimilar, a refocused accounting model will not result in comparable best practices. If big corporations maintain business units that belong to completely different industry sectors, for example, such as the finance and leasing business automotive companies, it is more appropriate to develop segment-specific MAMs by industry.

If the divisions are significantly dissimilar, a refocused accounting model will not result in comparable best practices.

This approach for integrating financial and managerial accounting for improved business decision-making and simplified reporting has three key elements. Because they are interdependent, the elements are developed concurrently:
1. Management Accounting Master.
2. Center-oriented organizational design.
3. Integrated legal-entity reporting.

MANAGEMENT ACCOUNTING MASTER

The MAM is developed to cope with requirements of both local and corporate management. It is both a conceptual blueprint that guides organizational redesign and a reporting framework that defines key performance indicators and decision rules for alignment across business units, their subunits, and external financial requirements.[8] In particular, it generates information needed to manage the business from a local perspective. An MAM is defined by the following characteristics:

- Harmonized center accounting schemes according to the center function (e.g., manufacturing, sales, and administration).
- Performance indicators of center heads thoroughly linked to their functional roles, responsibilities, and accountabilities.
- Consistent and sustainable transfer pricing rules between cost centers and profit centers based on standard cost mechanism.
- Profit center accounting scheme closely aligned to the country P&Ls.
- Consistent bridging methodologies between profit center accounting and country P&Ls.

Example of Management Accounting Information

The case company example helps explain the purpose of the MAM. The European division head of the bond concrete division, for example, maintains two production facilities that supply its four European sales organizations. Because the plant in Spain is quite remote and is clearly disadvantageous in transportation costs, its use has dropped recently. In addition, Spain has only a small sales organization. Due to more streamlined production and newer machinery and equipment, however, the plant in Spain is more productive than the facility in Germany.

The MAM becomes the blueprint.

Germany's financial statements indicate an overall strong profit position. In fact, its higher profitability is based on an extremely successful sales team and less competitive and price-sensitive market, which compensate for the relative poor productivity of its plant. Even with significant transportation costs, the facility in Spain performs stronger than the one in Germany. Without detailed insights about sales organization effectiveness and plant productivity, however, the division head will not identify these differences or effectively manage assets.

THE BLUEPRINT

As the previous section illustrates, detailed and useful management accounting information is critical for making viable local and corporate business decisions. The division head mentioned above has to make major decisions based on six center reports and four country-specific financial statements. This manager needs clearly defined key performance indicators and decision rules for his center heads and general managers.

The MAM becomes the blueprint for both creating the centers with aligned responsibility for that information, and at the same time, extracting relevant data from financial statements. In all cases where center reports are created, consistent bridging to financial accounts has to be maintained. The added management capability derives from information consistency across centers, not added data.

Example of Management Account Master Benefits

By implementing the MAM, the division head (DH) of bond concrete will receive two reports from the production center that, structure-wise and content-wise, are 100% comparable. The DH will see the same line items, and per line item, will get insights about actual costs and standard cost deviations. In addition, it will be easy for the DH to investigate the root causes for deviations because the major categories, such as bill of material variances or deviations in use, will appear automatically on his or her monthly report. Despite not being an expert in management accounting, the DH will be able to compare cost structures and assess productivity of its plants. In conjunction with the operations head for the country responsible, the DH can work on leveraging efficiency advantages or shifting use for overall value creation.

Furthermore, the MAM will help to separate functional-specific efficiencies. That means, in the situation just described, the relatively poor production efficiency of the Germany-based bond concrete plant was hidden by overperforming sales results. The MAM will reinforce the split of production units and sales units to clearly address improvement potentials. The performance of the sales team will be mirrored primarily in profit-center accounting, whereas plant productivity will be shown in cost center accounting. Because the plant performance is displayed at standard values, the real strength of the German sales team will be visible, and the production team will need to cope with its predefined standard costs. Higher actual costs are the proof of inefficiencies and have to be scrutinized. If necessary, utilization has to be shifted to more productive units such as the one in Spain. Consequently, asset reduction (e.g., line closing) or shut-down of the German operations will have to be considered.

To formulate the MAM, its definitions, rules, and responsibilities must be continually played out against perceived organizational designs and reporting structures. With all of these factors in play and through various modelling exercises, an aligned blueprint will result, leading to the implementation of a center-oriented organizational design across the corporation.

Center-Oriented Organizational Design

An organizational redesign is necessary to create local centers, which supplement and hone the current assortment of business unit structures. Center-oriented organizations are not new, however, their alignment with a harmonized management accounting system is essential. They provide a unique advantage for implementing harmonized structures in a business unit and legal-entity environment without adding a third organizational dimension. The center model is simply used on the level below country entities to provide uniform organizational standards that integrate existent business segments in the respective country. This redesign or refinement forces the development of independent and self-guided organizational centers. Each center head should have the opportunity to optimize his or her center results based on clearly aligned responsibilities.[9] Only when center heads have the ability and opportunity to influence performance and success will they be highly motivated. As well, they will have clear responsibility for major deviations from planned corporate objectives. In any case, a manager should not be able to avoid responsibility by being a great negotiator of internal transfer prices. The management objective is clearly aligned responsibility and control of balance sheet items.

Example of Nonaligned Responsibility

In reality, the opposite of clearly aligned responsibilities is often the case. The construction supply company must often operate relatively small production units, located near its raw-material suppliers and customers. In addition, concrete or brick production is primarily asset intensive, except for the manual concrete reinforcement activities. In the cases of bondless concrete and brick production units, the headcount is on average below 100; for brick production in Austria, it is below 20. To foster the entrepreneurial thinking of its center heads, corporate management decided to assign "virtual" profits to all production units. For the manager of a workforce of 20, this creates quite a challenge. An accurate management accounting system had to be developed that allowed the manager to build in theoretical revenue streams; the manager had to understand the implications of revenue and cost effects on his profitability; and, finally, the manager needed to ensure that appropriate transfer prices had been negotiated. Imagine a production supervisor with an engineering brick processing background. He or she would probably not be able to cope with all of these reporting tasks; more importantly, focus on his core objectives—to process high-quality products at the lowest cost possible and in a timely manner—might be lost.

The MAM can guide necessary redesign across all divisions and countries in the entire corporation.

Local Centers of Responsibility

Local centers are the means to align individual managers' responsibility with their area of highest competence. With this alignment, managers are most able to leverage their creative influence and leadership and, therefore, positively control outcomes. Local centers fall into two basic types according to their primary role in the value chain[10]:

- Profit centers—Have revenue streams and significant costs related directly to the center activities.
- Cost centers—Generate no external revenues but cause significant costs, mostly production costs.

With these basic types of centers, the MAM can guide necessary redesign across all divisions and countries in the entire corporation. The specific design of each center cannot be determined by corporate defaults. Corporate-led redesign guidelines contain only a set of modules and definitions that will drive country-specific center solutions. These guidelines focus on standardization of elements to develop local conformity and therefore overall visibility of information for corporate control. For each center, core activities need to be clarified. And to ensure comparability, it is critically important that equal center types manage equal proportions of the value chain so that insightful cross-country benchmarking analyses can be conducted.

Units below the centers can be structured and organized according to local specifics and the taste of local management. The starting point for tracking the needs of a decentralized management is mapping the decentralized processes and structures. By creating transparency in the basic designs of local units and their interactions, the plausibility of the redesigned organizational structure can be cross checked. Additional reorganization efforts to further harmonize the organizations will be identified.

Exhibit 2 shows the needed redesign of basic center structures for the case company's sales (profit centers) and operations (cost centers). These basic models served as the redesign framework and then were further refined according to country specifics.

Profit Centers

Because of external revenue streams, sales organizations are predestined to be measured according to profits. They are in charge of the margin between revenues and costs of goods sold plus selling costs. Potentially, a relative high profit could be displayed because charges for materials are lower than the effective cost of goods sold. For this reason, profit-center accounting for the major sales organizations in a country is run as part of the P&L-accounting for the respective country. This approach implies that values for overhead such as administration or R&D have to be considered as part of profit center accounting. Because the sales force cannot directly influence overhead costs, however, the values taken should be based on planned figures. The sales organization is only responsible for its "actual" selling costs and will take notice of other "planned" administrative costs that are charged on its profit center account. Exhibit 3 illustrates the basic structure of a profit-center account.

For the profit center organization in France, the case company has developed the following organizational solution. From a sales perspective, only the bricks division requires a regional structure. The current organization according to regions for all divisions, therefore, is not very useful. Instead, the former solution of a countrywide operation sales team for concrete and brick components was reintroduced. Exhibit 4 illustrates the new profit center structure compatible to the basic-center model.

Cost Centers

Cost centers are established for all units without external revenues. Typical cost centers are production, R&D, and administration. Production centers require an effective production control system that monitors productivity, quality, and time. Indicators, such as product cost, the cost effects of different utilization levels, and cost and quality relations are the required bare minimum. For administrative cost centers, it is important to determine the necessary level of quality to be provided. Otherwise, a cost center head might try to stay within budget just by cutting down on certain services.

To apply the basic center model for operation units in France, management agreed on the following center structure, as illustrated in Exhibit 5.

Using the cost center template, the structure could be significantly streamlined. For historical reasons, logistics was previously located in two different parts of the organization. The concrete division maintained logistics resources because of the company's roots in the concrete business. In addition, procurement had its own logistic department that covered issues for the acquired brick component plant. Quality control was also duplicated. The MAM, with its local center model, uncovered these organizational issues, which the agreed on template has solved.

Center Contentions and Balance-Sheet Alignment

The creation of a center-based management accounting approach often brings to light contentions over responsibility for balance sheet items. Through the process of designing and implementing this approach, clear responsibility should be determined, leading to increased corporate value. Commonly, agreement needs to be reached around fixed assets, working capital, and inventories.

As a general rule, cost centers for production should be in charge of fixed assets, in particular, plants, property and equipment. Although cost centers for production have to carry all productive assets, nonpro-

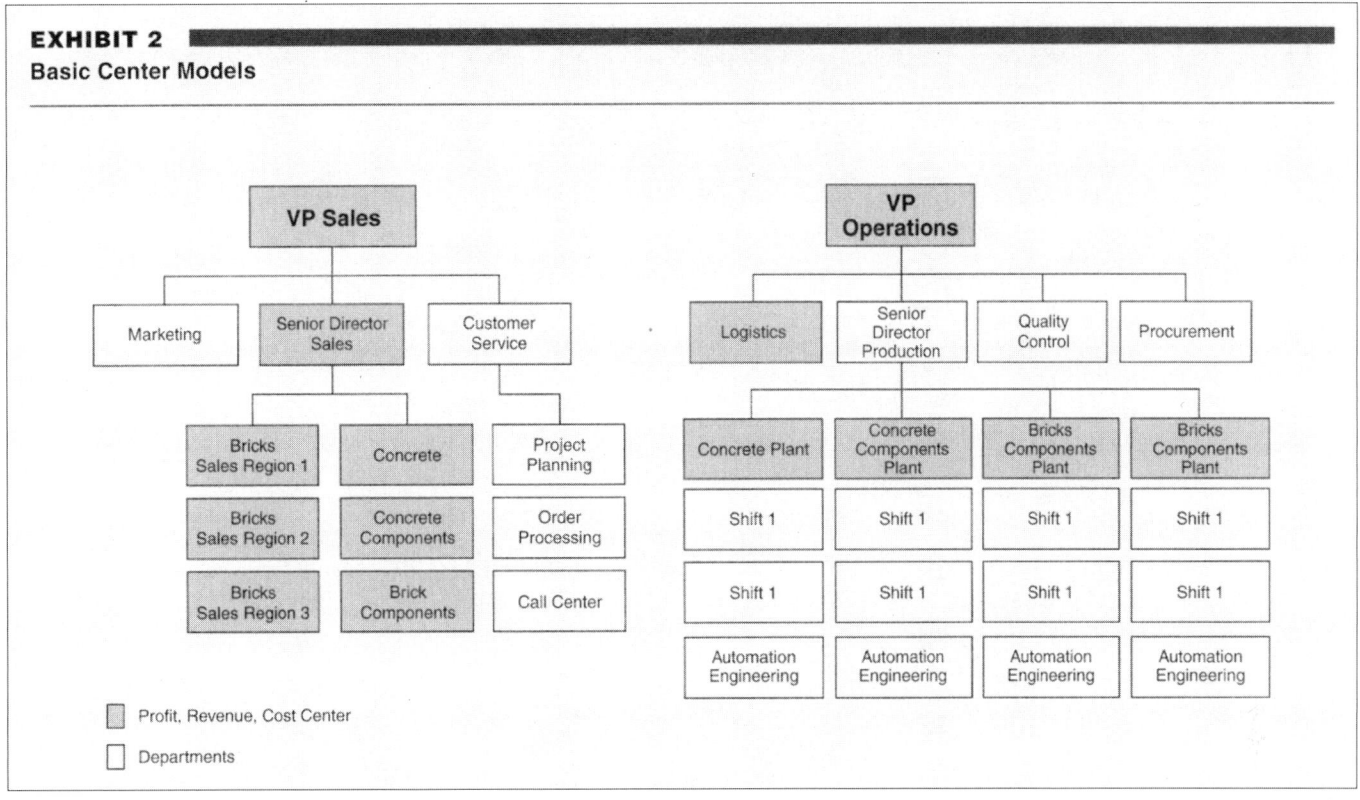

EXHIBIT 2
Basic Center Models

ductive assets, such as nonused real estate or administrative buildings should appear in the cost center account of administrative units.[11]

Often, responsibility for working capital is disputed. Accounts receivable is the easy part; since sales teams normally "own" the customer, they should ensure timely cash inflow. Accounts payable is heavily dependent on supplier relationships. The procurement organization normally negotiates prices and terms and conditions, but actual purchases are made by others. In particular, organizations with a very decentralized sourcing approach face problems in assigning responsibility of accounts payable. Therefore, case-by-case decisions are appropriate for assigning responsibility.

Contentions most often occur around inventories. Plant managers frequently try to improve their profitability on a product basis by ramping up their use—even with significant decreases in demand. When the sales organization is in charge of inventories, plant managers have no problem applying this approach. If the production centers have to carry the inventories, however, they will try to lower inventory levels to a minimum extent. Volatile or even surge customer demand might not be supplied. In both cases, the value of the overall corporation is threatened. As a general rule, the average level of inventory should be agreed upon at the beginning of each planning cycle.[12] Then the production centers will have to optimize their utilization and production costs against this predetermined inventory level, and the sales team will have to cope with unpredicted rises in demand above these levels.

INTEGRATED LEGAL-ENTITY REPORTING

As local centers are implemented, the decision-support system will naturally induce increased demand by the profit center heads for performance indicators. As a result, the potential develops for these self-guided and self-optimizing units to generate a multitude of different reporting formats. Although the MAM is the tool to ensure consistent reporting of comparable business transactions across all centers and countries, it can also drive the development and use of a set of lean, standardized reports that cover most information needs. Close integration of management reporting with legal financial statements is a useful lever to streamline reporting.

Although external reporting according to legal principles has a somewhat different purpose than management reporting, the information can be harmonized as far as format and content. The different purposes will remain: financial statements are primarily prepared to provide investors with a true and fair view about business conditions, management accounting provides insights into the profitability of the business itself and helps identify cost, revenue, and profit drivers. Moreover, the formal harmonization helps center heads, especially those without an accounting background, to correctly understand the financials and derive from them the appropriate business decisions. Any deviations between external reporting figures and management accounting will still be seen and tracked on a country level.

Accurate definitions should be used according to the legal principles.

The following three major steps can be used as a guide for achieving this harmonization:

1. The starting point of the integration is a set of P&L-statement items that should appear in the MAM without any deviation. Normally, these include the revenue items and the major cost items. In the future, the center heads will manage these items. Accurate definitions

ANNUAL EDITIONS

EXHIBIT 3
Illustrative Profit Center Account

Profit Center Account				Sources	Comments
Country: France Sales Unit: Concrete Month: November 2001	Actual ($ MM)	Plan ($ MM)	Δ ($ MM)		
Revenue	29.6	30.3	− 0.7	Financial statements	Actual
— Costs of goods sold	20.1	18.2	+ 1.9	Management Accounting	Standard
— Selling costs	5.2	5.4	− 0.2	Financial statements	Actual
— Administration costs	2.8	2.8	−	Management Accounting	Plan
— General management	1.1	1.1	−	Management Accounting	Plan
— Finance department	0.8	0.8	−	Management Accounting	Plan
— ...	0.9	0.9	−	Management Accounting	Plan
Profit Center total (standard values)	1.5	3.9	2.4		

EXHIBIT 4
Sales Organization — France

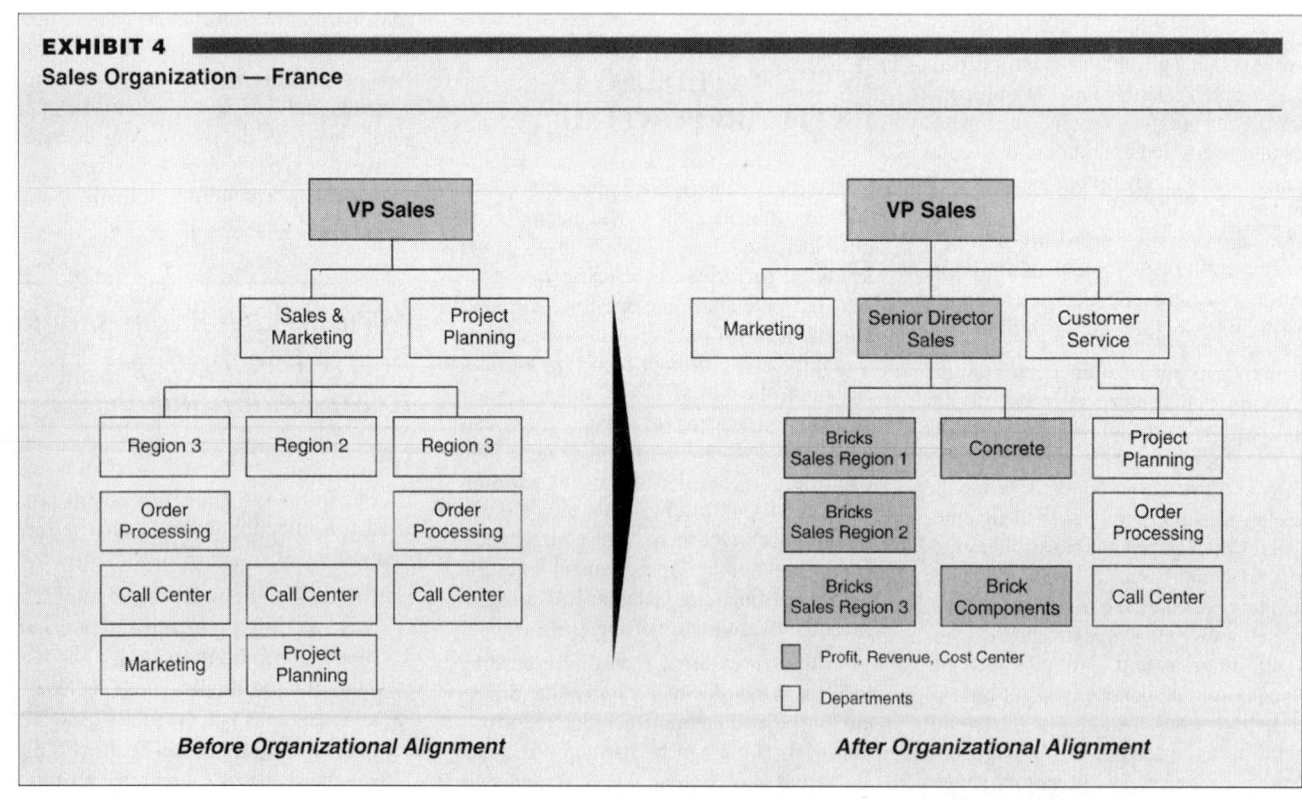

Before Organizational Alignment — After Organizational Alignment

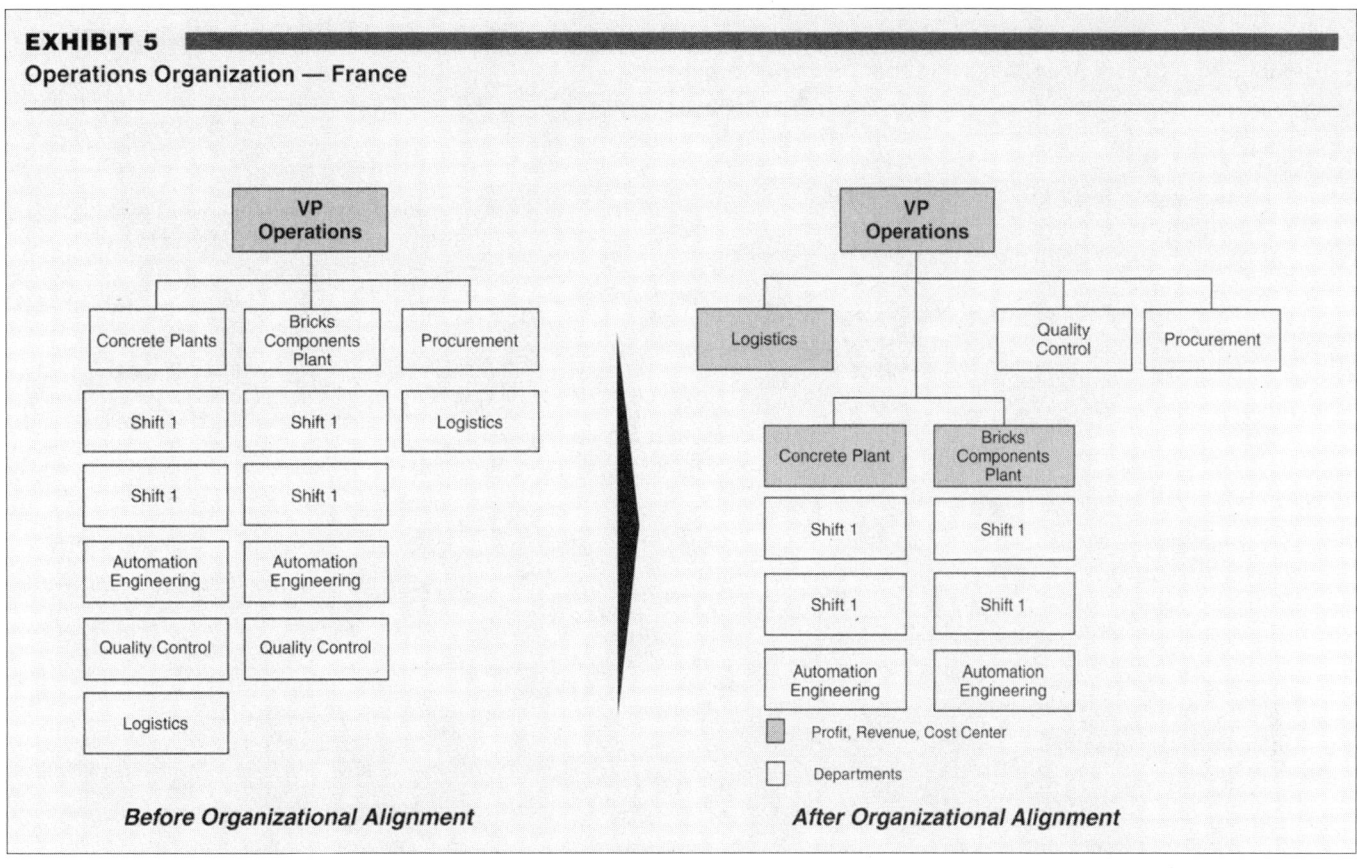

EXHIBIT 5
Operations Organization — France

Before Organizational Alignment → After Organizational Alignment

should be used according to the legal principles.

2. The next step is to identify indicators that are not part of the center heads' responsibility. Examples include non-operating revenues and expenses not under the immediate control of the respective center manager, such as sales of fixed assets.

3. Finally, deviations to the financial statements have to be determined. These deviations must be based on the required level of detail or content. The following examples describe potential content-related deviations:

- Profit centers will value the cost of goods sold in their profit center account based on standard costs.[13] The actual costs for the costs of goods sold will be tracked in the cost center accounts of the supplying cost centers (production). Because the profit center should not be responsible for deviating production cost, it will only be charged with a predetermined standard cost rate per unit taken times the volume of units. The production cost centers will be measured against this standard cost rate. If the actual costs deviate, it will have an immediate impact on the production cost centers' performance evaluation. The cost deviations, however, are not transferred to the profit center; they will be directly tracked in the profit & loss statement of the respective country. This principle ensures comparability and continuity across different centers.

- Internal service charges at actual costs can create a tremendous administrative burden. To simplify the system, accounting can valuate internal service charges with planned figures instead of actual costs.[14] Service and cost receiving centers only have to deal with predetermined planned charges and, therefore, have no deviations in their account caused by service charges. The effective difference between planned service costs and actual service costs will only occur in the center account of the delivering center (e.g., administration or customer support). These centers are in charge of deviations, and as in the other example, they will be tracked directly in the P&L account of the respective country.

The major objective of the integration is to eventually connect all center reports to the single line items of the P&L statement. To create maximum transparency and to keep the financial and accounting systems as streamlined as possible, it is important to use a harmonized approach across the entire corporation on a worldwide level. The system in itself will be greatly efficient, and the foundation is laid for effective benchmarking. Exhibit 6 shows the basic principles of integration.

Example of Bridging Accounting Systems

The essential steps in developing and implementing the MAM at the case company were assessment, concept development, and implementation. Although assessment and concept development required less than four months, the implementation took nearly eight months. Implementation was the most difficult part as well. The local management and division management had to buy into the basic principles and to own the new accounting approach. Implementation of this mindset with managers is not an easy task because they all have concerns about giving up certain local and divisional independence. It is crucial to identify, early in the process, the appropriate performance indicators and to commu-

EXHIBIT 6
Bridging Profit Center Accounting and Profit & Loss Accounting

Profit Center Account		Bridging	Country Profit & Loss Statement (Quarterly Close)	
Country: France **Sales Unit: Division II** **3rd Quarter**	**Values**		**Country: France** **3rd Quarter**	**Values**
Revenue	Actual	Adopt	Revenue	Actual
— Costs of goods sold	Standard	Reconcile	— Costs of goods sold	Actual
— Selling costs	Actual	Adopt	— Selling costs	Actual
— Administration costs	Plan	Replace	— Administration costs	Actual
— ...	Plan	Replace	— ...	Actual
Profit Center total (standard values)			— Non operating revenue and expenses	Actual
			EBIT	Actual

---

nicate and agree on them. The construction supply company has chosen the right path to integrate the MAM in its corporation-wide SAP/R3 configuration, although it was necessary to extend the implementation. If done right, however, the benefits are tremendous. Today, the case company has an integrated center logic in which center reports are created in SAP/R3 CO (controlling) by using primarily data from the modules FI (finance), MM (material management), and SD (sales and delivery). With only minor manual interventions, P&L statements are produced based on the profit center reports for each country and consolidated for the entire corporation on a monthly basis. After conducting intensive training for all managers (including top management), everybody understands the meaning of all information and each report, and all data can easily be reconciled and performance measures can be applied consistently. The concerted initiative to implement the MAM approach has transformed a nightmare into a nearly perfect world of information provision, which has clearly led to an overall increase in productivity and value creation.

SIMPLIFYING FOR THE FUTURE

As businesses continue to globalize and internationally decentralized corporations to proliferate, the need to simplify, harmonize, and standardize corporate control systems becomes more urgent. The MAM and corresponding organizational redesign offer a feasible compromise for balancing local entrepreneurial freedom and strategically important corporation goals.

The concept can easily be implemented, even in small subsidiaries and units abroad. The core element is the MAM, which is used as a blueprint to create centers in all legal entities around the globe and to harmonize their reporting. When integration of management accounting and external financial reporting is managed well, a corporate control system emerges that can cope with the variety of international legal reporting requirements.

Notes

1. P. Sadler, *The Seamless Organization*, 4th Edition (London: Kogan Page, 2001).
2. W. Bay and H-G. Bruns, "Multinational Companies and International Capital Markets," in P. Walton, A. Haller, and B. Raffournier, *International Accounting* (London: Thomson, 1998), pp. 336–355.
3. We have found the problem of nonharmonized management accounting systems in a variety of sizes and industries. Common to all is the need for internationally diversified operations. We worked with an electronic manufacturer of consumer goods, with revenues of $15 billion in 2000, whose need for international production is simply driven by technological

requirements in target markets. In the case of a German automotive supplier of transmission systems and gearbox technology, with $1.6 billion in 2000, the company was forced by its customers to set up production facilities close to assembly plants, leading to unavoidable cost disadvantages.

4. Some structural detail and financial data have been sanitized.

5. T. M. Plank and L. R. Plank, *Accounting Desk Book,* 11th Edition (Upper Saddle River, New Jersey: Prentice Hall, 2000).

6. R. G. Schroeder and C. W. Myrtle, *Accounting Theory* (New York: Wiley, 1998); J. K. Skim and J. G. Siegel, *Modern Cost Management & Analysis,* 2nd Edition (New York: Barron Educational Series, 2000).

7. A. Haller and P. Walton, "Country Differences and Harmonization," in P. Walton, A. Haller and B. Raffournier, *International Accounting* (London: Thomson, 1998), pp. 1–30; S. Klimczuk, "Global Operations and National Roots," *Executive Agenda* (Chicago: AT Kearney, Second Quarter 2001).

8. Additionally, a Balanced Scorecard or Integrated Strategic Measurement Approach should be developed and implemented to fully deploy a value creating decision-culture across the entire organization. A. T. Kearney, Inc., "Making Strategies Pay: A White Paper on Integrated Strategic Measurement" (Chicago: A. T. Kearney, 1999).

9. A. De Waal, *Power of Performance Management: How Leading Companies Create Sustained Value* (New York: Wiley, 2001).

10. J. K. Shank and V. Govindarajan, *Strategic Cost Management* (New York: Wiley, 1993).

11. Schroeder and Myrtle.

12. D. R. Emery and J. D. Finnerty, *Corporate Financial Management* (New Jersey: Prentice Hall, 1997).

13. L. Oliver, *The Cost Management Toolbox* (New York: AMACOM, 1999).

14. Skim and Siegel.

SOEREN DRESSLER, Ph.D., is a principal with A. T. Kearney International Management Consultants and a member of its global strategy and organization practice. He is based in Chicago.

Article 8

Michael Porter: What Is Strategy?

In an age when management gurus are both lauded by the faithful and hounded by the critics, Michael Porter seems to be one of the few who is well-accepted both academically and in the business world. Though he has his critics, Porter has generally been viewed as at the leading edge of strategic thinking since his first major publication, *Competitive Strategy* (1980), which became a corporate bible for many in the early 1980s.

Life and Career

Born in 1947, Porter completed a degree in aeronautical engineering at Princeton and took an economics doctorate at Harvard, joining the faculty there as a tenured professor at the age of 26. He has acted as consultant to companies and to governments and, like many academics, he set up a consulting company—Monitor.

Porter's Thinking

Porter's thinking on strategy has been supported by precision research into industries and companies, and has remained consistent as well as developmental. He has concentrated on different aspects at different times, spinning the threads together with a logic that is irrefutable.

Before *Competitive Strategy*, most strategic thinking focused either on the organisation of a company's internal resources and their adaptation to meet particular circumstances in the marketplace, or on increasing an organisation's competitiveness by lowering prices to increase market share. These approaches, derived from the work of Igor Ansoff, were bundled into systems or processes which provided strategy with its place in the organisation.

In *Competitive Strategy*, Porter managed to reconcile these approaches, providing management with a fresh way of looking at strategy—from the point of view of industry itself rather than just from the point of view of markets, or of organisational capabilities.

Internal Capability for Competitiveness— The Value Chain

Porter describes two different types of business activity—primary and secondary. Primary activities are principally concerned with transforming inputs (raw materials) into outputs (products), and delivery and after-sales support. These usual line management activities include Inbound Logistics (materials handling, warehousing), Operations (turning raw materials into finished products), Outbound Logistics (order processing, and distribution), Marketing and Sales (communication and pricing), and Service (installation and after-sales service).

Secondary activities support the primary and include Procurement (purchasing and supply), Technology Development (know-how, procedures and skills), Human Resource Management (recruitment, promotion, appraisal, reward and development), and Firm Infrastructure (general and quality management, finance, planning).

To be able to survive competition and supply what customers want to buy, the firm has to ensure that all these value-chain activities link together and fit, as a weakness in any one of them will impact on the chain as a whole and affect competitiveness.

The Five Forces

Porter argued that in order to examine its competitive capability in the marketplace, an organisation must choose between three generic strategies: cost leadership—becoming the lowest-cost producer in the market; differentiation—offering something different, extra or special; and focus—achieving dominance in a niche market. The question is to choose the right one at the right time. These generic strategies are driven by five competitive forces which the organisation has to take into account:

- the power of customers to affect pricing and reduce margins
- the power of suppliers to influence the organisation's pricing
- the threat of similar products to limit market freedom and reduce prices and thus profits
- the level of existing competition which impacts on investment in marketing and research and thus erode profits

- the threat of new market entrants to intensify competition and further impact on pricing and profitability.

In recent years, Porter has revisited his earlier work and emphasises the acceleration of market change that means companies now have to compete not just on a choice of strategic front, but on all fronts at once. Porter has also said that a company that tries to position itself in relation to the five competitive forces misunderstands his approach, since positioning is not enough. What companies have to do is ask how the five forces can help to re-write industry rules in the organisation's favour.

Diversification

Instead of going it alone, an organisation can spread risk and attain growth by diversification and acquisition. While the blue-chip consulting companies such as Boston Consulting Group (Market growth/market share matrix) and McKinsey (7-S framework) have developed analytical models for discovering which companies will rise and fall, Porter prefers three critical tests for success:

1. The attractiveness test. Industries chosen for diversification must be structurally attractive. An attractive industry will yield a high return on investment but entry barriers will be high, customers and suppliers will have only moderate bargaining power and there will be only a few substitute products. An unattractive industry will be swamped by a range of alternative products, high rivalry and high fixed costs.
2. The cost-of-entry test. If the cost of entry is so high that it prejudices the potential return on investment, profitability is eroded before the game has started.
3. The better-off test. How will the acquisition provide advantage to either the acquirer or the acquired? One must offer significant advantage to the other.

Porter devised seven steps to tackle these questions:

1. As competition takes place at the business unit level, identify the interrelationships among the existing business units.
2. Identify the core business which is to be the foundation of the strategy. Core businesses are those in attractive industries and where competitive advantage can be sustained.
3. Create horizontal organisational mechanisms to facilitate interrelationships among core businesses.
4. Pursue diversification opportunities that allow shared activities and pass all three critical tests.
5. Pursue diversification through transfer of skills if opportunities for sharing activities are limited or exhausted.
6. Pursue a strategy of restructuring if this fits the skills of management or if no good opportunities exist for forging corporate partnerships.
7. Pay dividends so that shareholders can become portfolio managers.

National Competitiveness

Why do some companies achieve consistent capability in innovation, seeking an ever more sophisticated source of competitive advantage? For Porter the answer lies in four attributes which affect industries: These attributes are: Factor Conditions (the nations skills and infrastructure to enable a competitive position), Demand Conditions (the nature of home-market demand), Related and Supporting Industries (presence or absence of supplier/feeder industries), and Firm Strategy, Structure and Rivalry (the national conditions under which companies are created, grow, organise and manage).

These are the chief determinants which create the environment in which firms flourish and compete. The points on the diamond constitute a self-reinforcing system, where the effect of one point often depends on the state of the others and any weaknesses at one point will impact adversely on an industry's capability to compete.

The New Strategic Wave

Somewhere between 1980 and 1990 strategic planning came unstuck. Old theories no longer worked as customers became more demanding and changeable, and markets and technologies rose and fell ever more rapidly. Even industries that were once distinct with definable products and services now converged and became blurred. A new wave of more subversive strategic thinking—with Gary Hamel and Strategy as Revolution, and Mintzberg with The Fall and Rise of Strategic Planning—emerged to replace the old rule-book. Porter's main contribution to date—What is strategy?—argues that strategic planning lost its way because managers failed to distinguish between strategic and operational effectiveness and confused the two. The old strategic model—which still held up in the 1980s—was based on productivity, increasing market share and lowering costs. Hence total quality management, benchmarking, outsourcing and re-engineering were all at the forefront of change in the 1980s as the key drivers of operational improvements. But continuing incremental improvements to the way things are done tend, over time, to bring different players up to the same level, not differentiate them. To achieve differentiation means that:

- Strategy rests on unique activities based on customers' needs, customers' accessibility or the variety of a company's products or services.
- The company's activities must fit and link together. In terms of the value chain, one link is prone to imitation but with a chain, imitation is very difficult.
- Making trade-offs: excelling at some things means making a conscious choice not to do others—a question of being a 'master of one trade' to stand out from the crowd as opposed to being a 'jack of all trades' and lost in the crowd. Trade-offs purposefully limit what a company offers. The essence of strategy lies in what not to do.

The Internet

In 2001 Porter addressed the assertion that the Internet renders strategy obsolete. He admits that the Internet is in its infancy, but observes that lack of strategy and reliance on Internet technologies to gain market penetration is already proving not to be a sound approach. In a Harvard Business Review article in March 2001 Porter says:

> 'In our quest to see how the Internet is different, we have failed to see how the Internet is the same' (pp 63–78)

Porter argues that many Internet companies are competing through unsustainable, artificial means, usually propped up by short-term capital investment. He also argues that while the excitement of the Internet appeared to throw up new rules of competition, the first wave of excitement is now clearly over, and the old rules and strategic principles appear to be re-establishing themselves. He gives examples such as:

1. The right goal—healthy long-term return on investment.
2. Value—a company must offer a set of benefits which set it apart from the competition.
3. A company's value chain has to do things differently or do different things from rivals to reflect, produce and deliver that value.
4. Trade-offs—make conscious deliberate sacrifices in some areas in order to excel, or even be unique, in others.
5. All the different components in the value chain must fit together, reinforcing each other to create uniqueness and value: it is this which makes a core competence—something that is difficult to imitate.
6. Continuity—not only from a customer perspective but also in order to build and develop skills that bring competitive edge.

Porter foresees that, as most businesses embrace the Internet, it will become nullified as a source of advantage, while traditional strengths such as uniqueness, design and service relationships will reemerge. For Porter the next phase of Internet evolution will be more holistic, with a shift from e-business to business, from e-learning to learning, within which the Internet will be a communications medium and not necessarily a source of advantage.

In Perspective

It is a mark of Porter's achievement that much of his work on Competitive Strategy, researched in the 1970s, still has high value and relevance in the late 1990s, and still shapes mainstream thinking on competition and strategy.

Although now much quoted, the following was intended to be as much a compliment as the Economist would muster: "His work is academic to a fault... Mr. Porter is about as likely to produce a blockbuster full of anecdotes and booserish catchphrases as he is to deliver a lecture dressed in bra and stockings." (Professor Porter Ph.D., Economist, 8 October 1994, p 97)

While his work is academically rigorous, his ability to abstract his thinking into digestible chunks for the business world has given him wide appeal to both the academic and business worlds. It is now standard practice for organisations to think and talk Value Chains, and the Five Forces have entered the curriculum and every management programme. Porter's later thinking on strategy rides the new wave of revolutionary strategic thinking led by Hamel and links consistently with his earlier work. One suspects that there is not only more to come from Michael Porter, but also that it will be wholly consistent with what he has said in the past.

Key works by Porter

Books

Competitive strategy: techniques for analyzing industries and competitors New York: Free Press, 1980

Competitive advantage: creating and sustaining superior performance London: Collier Macmillan, 1985

Competitive advantage of nations London: Macmillan, 1990

Cases in competitive strategy London: Collier Macmillan, 1983

Competition in global industries (ed) Boston, Mass.: Harvard Business School Press, 1986

Journal Articles

From competitive advantage to corporate strategy Harvard Business Review, May/June 1987, vol. 65 no 3, pp 43–59

The competitive advantage of nations Harvard Business Review, Mar/Apr 1990, vol. 68 no 2, pp 73–93

What is strategy? Harvard Business Review, Nov/Dec 1996, vol. 74 no 6, pp 61–78

Corporate strategy: the state of strategic thinking Economist, 23 May 1998, pp 21–22, 27–28. Revised Apr 2002

From *Thinkers*, April 2002. © 2002 by Harvard Business School Publishing.

SIX PRIORITIES THAT MAKE A GREAT STRATEGIC DECISION

Good strategies don't arise spontaneously, they come from attention to a spectrum of important priorities.

Mary Burner Lippitt

When telecom companies were the darlings of Wall Street, Iridium seemed to have everything going for it. The company was committed to a far-sighted vision for a satellite phone system; had identified and targeted a potentially profitable niche—consumers not served by cellular communications; and was part of a worldwide consortium that included heavy-hitters Motorola and Sprint. In pursuit of its vision, Iridium spent $5 billion to launch a first-to-market product and another $150 million in advertising. Iridium faced, and conquered, the daunting technical challenge of putting 66 satellites into space and creating a worldwide telecommunication system.

Iridium had the jump on its competitors when it opened for business in 1998 offering a global communication network for international voice, data, and fax communication. It filed for bankruptcy a year later.

How did such a promising venture fall? Hindsight makes it clear that Iridium overlooked external realities. At a time when the cell market saw hardware prices falling, wireless standards coalescing, and new features being added, Iridium pursued its own course. Its hardware was expensive and bulky, and, worse, it couldn't be used indoors. A competitor, Globalstar, was 18 months behind Iridium, but operated with a business plan that targeted the international businessperson and local service in developing areas. It also offered less expensive and lighter equipment along with "get-acquainted" pricing as low as $.50 per minute in the U. S. versus a $2 to $7 per minute charge from Iridium.

Could Iridium's leaders have foreseen these problems? The answer is yes—if their thinking had been broad, deep, and comprehensive, rather than pre-cooked or disconnected from reality. Iridium focused all of its resources on just one priority—becoming the technical leader. It ignored five other important priorities that would have provided a more balanced, and realistic, perspective.

Critical Thinking Framework

A critical and comprehensive analysis must go beyond traditional SWOT analysis. What we see as opportunities, threats, strengths, and weaknesses depends on our perceptions, and perception clouds reality more often than revealing it. Strategic thinking must also go beyond belief in a one-stop strategic fix. Putting all strategic eggs in a basket named quality, Six Sigma®, customer relationship management, niche selection, first to market, or innovation can lead to disaster.

The single strategy solution leads us astray if it assumes stability in our era of turbulence just as surely as if it assumes everything will change. Using one lens to view strategic options magnifies potential benefits, overlooks limiting variables, and confirms preexisting inclinations. Taking into account a wide array of factors during decision making may appear to muddy the analytic process, but it also increases the likelihood of success.

Information doubles on the World Wide Web every 2.8 years. Clearly, therefore, it is not the availability of information that is the issue, it is our ability to grasp it and use it wisely. Leaders must not only drill into the details when red flags start to surface, but also confront conventional practices and ascertain opportunities more quickly than ever before. Escalating speed and complexity cannot be handled with linear thinking. It requires continuous reassessment through an objective and exhaustive inquiry.

Strategic leaders must concentrate on asking questions that tap multiple perspectives in order to avert the single lens trap as well as develop strategic thinking throughout their organization. Six priorities or desired outcomes can be used to generate balanced decisions, manage risk, and build a communication plan. The six priorities are:

1. Keeping products/services up-to-date and/or being state-of-the art.
2. Gaining and maintaining market share and/or serving customers.
3. Minimizing confusion by building an infrastructure and systems to establish and sustain high performance.
4. Improving processes and procedures for efficiency, quality, and return.
5. Developing committed and competent workforce and/or building a supportive environment and identity.
6. Positioning for the long-term by identifying trends, assumptions, and issues that offer opportunities or potential threats.

These priorities represent the pressing business issues leaders must address if they hope to sleep through the night. Leaders who understand and continuously adjust priorities to reflect workforce and business realities develop more solid strategies. Priorities are objective and dynamic, reflecting information, alternatives, and consequences as events shift or erupt. Knowing the priorities enhances flexibility, commitment, focus, and success.

Being able to interpret trends, judge events, predict opportunities, and persuade an organization is not a matter of charisma or conviction. It relies on an accurate assessment of reality derived from an inclusive and extensive examination of six priorities.

Product Leadership

Intel strives for faster chips and new products because it recognizes the transient benefits of technology. The current recession has not sidetracked Intel's research and development spending, which grew from $2.7 billion in 1998 to $4 billion in 2002. The reliance on this proven strategy drew both praise and concern from Wall Street. The research and development investment positions Intel effectively for the recovery, but it also could hurt the company's financial performance in a prolonged recession. The added lens complicates strategy, but strategy cannot be an easy call. Leaders face a tough act to create a sound direction.

Iridium, too, focused on technical leadership, but with considerably less success. It is possible that its leaders failed to ask the right questions about this priority. Those questions include:

1. What are the options, new alternatives, and synergies?
2. If there were no constraints, what could we do?
3. How can we take our existing procedures/methods to a new level?
4. What has never been tried before?
5. What have we given up on in the past that might be viable now?

This analysis can extend product range. The zipper was limited to securing bales of grain, until it was expanded to clothing. Likewise, Novocaine was developed as a nonaddictive anesthesia for treating battlefield wounds, until practical applications in dentistry eclipsed the original purpose. In addition to these extensions, breakthrough products from the Walkman to the personal digital assistant have surfaced using these questions.

Problems associated with alluring, groundbreaking products can derail efforts, consume funds, and waste time.

But a new idea is not necessarily a good idea. Problems associated with alluring, groundbreaking products can derail efforts, consume funds, and waste time. Genetically modified foods have tremendous appeal for producers and distributors. But from another perspective, the substantial hurdle of customer acceptance looms large. A one-pound Iridium phone had customer problems as well as competitive forces working against it. A promising idea cannot equate with a successful strategy.

Customer Focus

The second threshold of analysis centers on the customer, market share, and meeting customer expectations.

Understanding current customers reveals cross-selling opportunities, identifies potential customers, and pinpoints the level of customer loyalty.

Questions to test the feasibility of an original game plan include:

1. What is our competitive advantage?
2. How can we grow our existing key customers?
3. Who is the competition?
4. What new customers can be targeted?
5. What is the expected market share?

Understanding current customers reveals cross-selling opportunities, identifies potential customers, and pinpoints the level of customer loyalty. The experiences of Target and Home Depot demonstrate that strong benefits stem from understanding your customer and meeting their needs. Firms such as Harley-Davidson benefit from following customers after the sale; Harley's customer rallies enhance customer retention as well as sell clothing and ancillary products.

But you can get so close to the customer that you can miss opportunities. SmithKline and Glaxo focused on relieving customers' pain when they developed Tagament and Zantac. Ulcer and heartburn patients flocked to the new products, which blocked the production of stomach acid. But customer desire for relief and strong market share overshadowed an even more critical need—preventing ulcers that stimulated acid secretion in the first place. Johnson & Johnson pursued this avenue, and the success of its purple pill, Prilosec, has been astounding. J & J recently reformulated the medication to address the erosion in the esophagus. The firm has advertised Nexium heavily in the hope that it would attract new patients as patent protection on Prilosec expires.

Infrastructure Development

Knowing what customer wants is not enough. The organization has to deliver the goods. The third priority area explores aspects from an internal systems viewpoint.

The third priority questions include:

1. What are the risks?
2. What is the best distribution channel?
3. Are there potential partners or allies?
4. Are our current systems capable of sustained excellence?
5. How should the structure/governance change to deliver results?

This structural analysis frequently results in a quest for mergers, acquisitions, or alliances. The promise of reduced overhead, increased system efficiencies, and cross-selling within the firm produces larger and larger firms.

With demographic trends warning of a dire shortage of talent in a decade, the ability to be an employer of choice and retain talent is vital.

However, goals of increasing business breadth, rolling-up local firms into national firms, or building market cap are not, by themselves, successful strategies. ITT could not maintain its size and was dismantled. The expected synergies evaporated in the AOL Time Warner merger, while culture clashes and flagging stock price distracted management. Magellan Health Services' acquisition spree to become the nation's largest provider of mental health services burdened the firm with so much debt that it was delisted from the New York Stock Exchange.

Efficiency, Quality, and Return

Being first to market, commanding strong customer loyalty, and having a solid infrastructure, without also being profitable makes little sense. The fourth priority digs into the details to discover whether an option can build a sustainable business.

Questions addressing the issues of quality and efficiency include:

1. Is the option financially viable in the short and long term?
2. What economies of scale exist?
3. What level of quality can be attained?
4. What data and measures can be used to monitor progress?
5. How can technology increase efficiencies?

In our competitive and complex environment, excellence in one area can be a recipe for disaster. For example, although other firms benchmark their systems, cycle time, or resource utilization efforts against Amazon.com's vaunted systems, these alone cannot guarantee success. And while Motorola developed legendary Six Sigma skills, it lost market share in hand-held phones to Nokia.

A Workforce Advantage

Getting it right means mastering multiple priorities, the easily quantifiable facets as well as the quality aspects of the workforce and the work environment. In the information age, the workers' discretionary effort creates the high-performing workplace. Even though individual behavior cannot be effectively monitored constantly, performance can be measured.

To discover the scope of this fifth priority, the questions include:

1. Do we currently have the talent needed? Can we develop it internally?
2. Are we an employer of choice? Can we retain key talent?
3. What is consistent with our culture, operations, values, and practices?
4. What level of commitment is needed? Can we gain support in the requisite time frame?
5. What are the applicable lessons we have learned about our culture and workforce?

This may sound soft or just nice to have, but evidence is clear, a workforce advantage is a must have. In an industry noted for slim margins and decidedly hostile labor-management relations, Southwest Air has maintained both a profit and strong worker support for 26 years. While the former CEO's practice of dressing as

Elvis Presley at employee meetings or hiding in a baggage compartment can be duplicated, the high-performing environment and fast plane turnaround times cannot be. In fact, the competitive advantage that is the hardest to replicate is internal culture.

The power of culture was evident in the highly charged debate prior to Hewlett-Packard's merger with Compaq. Concerned that their culture, the HP Way, would be sacrificed, several stakeholders vigorously fought the merger. This priority may seem bound to the past, but it also positions the firm for the future.

Only a priority framework produces an in-depth understanding and avoids the traps inherent in the narrow view.

Slogans, promises, or parties cannot manufacture a high performance culture. Only a sound strategic choice—supported by action—can. Although most technological advances can be easily adopted, culture and talent are difficult to replicate. With demographic trends warning of a dire shortage of talent in a decade, the ability to be an employer of choice and retain talent is vital.

Tracking the External Environment

Leaders must understand trends and competitive opportunities if they are to ensure that their firms are effectively positioned for the long term. Evaporating trends strand grand plans and drain resources. Even when the crystal ball can be deciphered, reading the impact and implications requires both art and science.

Questions that can uncover the sixth priority include:

1. What assumptions are no longer valid?
2. What are the nontraditional threats from regulators, technology, or competitors?
3. Are our short- and long-term goals aligned?
4. What are the opportunities or trends on the horizon?
5. How can we capture emerging trends?

Unanticipated circumstances and consequences both erode and erupt. Linux, the open source operating system, has taken market share from Microsoft in Spain. The locally coordinated effort has spurred other "open source" efforts. Whether this is an isolated incident or emerging trend requires study, but the benefit of reevaluating assumptions and operating practices is solid, even in established industries.

A Spanish retailer, Zara, challenged standard retail operating practices by designing new merchandise and restocking every two weeks instead of following the traditional 12-week cycle. Its manufacturing costs are about 15% higher than other firms' because it relies on higher cost factories in developed countries to respond quickly to fashion trends. However, Zara's strong brand reputation translates into reduced marketing costs and profit margins 43% higher than at the Gap.

Putting Priorities to Work

Successful strategy neither emerges magically nor is it contingent on bet-the-ranch hunches. Solid corporate blue-prints emerge from probing and balancing six priorities. Judgment plays a part, but it must follow the identification, quantification, and evaluation of information. Starting with a strong premise means that facts conform to expectations and assumptions go untested.

Iridium Satellite LLC purchased Iridium's assets for $25 million and repositioned the business. Rejecting the predecessor firm's reliance on the commercial sector, the new Iridium negotiated a long-term contract with the U. S. Department of Defense and cut costs. This strategy appears viable, since it reflects reality rather than promise.

When there are so many variables to consider, only a priority framework produces an in-depth understanding and avoids the traps inherent in the narrow view. It has the added benefits of promoting the development of feasible plans, milestones, and checkpoints; providing a map to develop critical thinking skills in others; and drawing attention to the benefits that must be communicated to gain support for a strategic decision. Getting it right is not easy, but it gets easier when a systematic examination precedes the strategic decision.

Dr. Mary Burner Lippitt is a trainer, consultant, researcher, and speaker in the areas of leadership/executive development and the optimization of strategic and tactical thinking within the organization. She is the author of The Leadership Spectrum: 6 Priorities That Get Results. *Her inventory,* Leadership Spectrum Profile® (Davies-Black, 2002), *was cited among the top 10 training tools by* Human Resource Executive *magazine. She can be reached at mlippitt@enterprisemgt.com*

AUTOS

THE AMERICANIZATION OF TOYOTA

Its U.S. success is a lifeline, as other important markets languish

Since moving to the U.S. 15 years ago, Nicaragua-born Roberto Castillo has had a series of jobs at car dealerships—first Ford, then Pontiac, and eventually Hyundai. But two years ago, he landed the job he really wanted: selling Toyotas. "Toyotas are easier to sell than any other car," he says. "Everyone knows the reputation," he says. "So you never have to sell [people] on the benefits." Nowadays, Castillo works at Longo Toyota in the Los Angeles suburb of El Monte. Last year he piled up commissions worth more than $80,000. As he says: "You can make good money with Toyota."

Tell that to Tetsuo Kawano. He runs a Toyota dealership in a beachfront suburb of Yokohama, Japan. Recently Kawano held a promotion featuring FM deejay Haruhisa Kurihara. The event drew about 75 young Japanese with bleached hair, baggy pants, and goatees. The idea was to move a few Toyota Vitz subcompacts. The crowd enjoyed the music and free doughnuts, but there wasn't much interest in the product. "I'm here because I like the deejay," said Kidokoro Katsumi, 21. And the cars? "I just bought a Honda." Says a rueful Kawano: "We're selling into a shrinking market."

Booming in the U.S., but running out of gas in Japan? That was never Toyota Motor Corp.'s global strategy. Ten years ago the auto maker had a multipronged attack plan: grow steadily at home, make modest gains in the U.S., make money in Europe, and take over Southeast Asia. Well, things have changed. Japan has become the incredible shrinking market. The European conquest, though still possible, is a dream deferred. And Southeast Asia has stalled out. That leaves the U.S., the one market where sales remain robust. Toyota's American strategy, in short, has become Toyota's lifeline.

The importance of the U.S. raises questions about what kind of company Toyota will become. How far will the Japanese leadership let the Americanization of Toyota go? How will the importance of the North American market affect Toyota's international thrust? And most important, with future profits so dependent on the U.S., how easy will it be for Toyota to drive its current 10% share of the U.S. market to 15%—or even 20%?

Toyota, the world's third-largest auto maker—2001 sales are expected to hit $108 billion and operating profits $4.2 billion—will struggle with these and other questions over the next few years. Still, despite trepidation about the company's increasingly American tilt back at headquarters in Toyota City, about 100 km east of Nagoya, the way forward seems clear. Says Toyota Chief Executive Fujio Cho: "We must Americanize."

The process is already well under way. Consider the following facts, including some statistics that scare the wits out of Toyota's rivals in Detroit:

- Last year, Toyota sold more vehicles in the U.S. (1.74 million) than in Japan (1.71 million). Analysts figure that almost

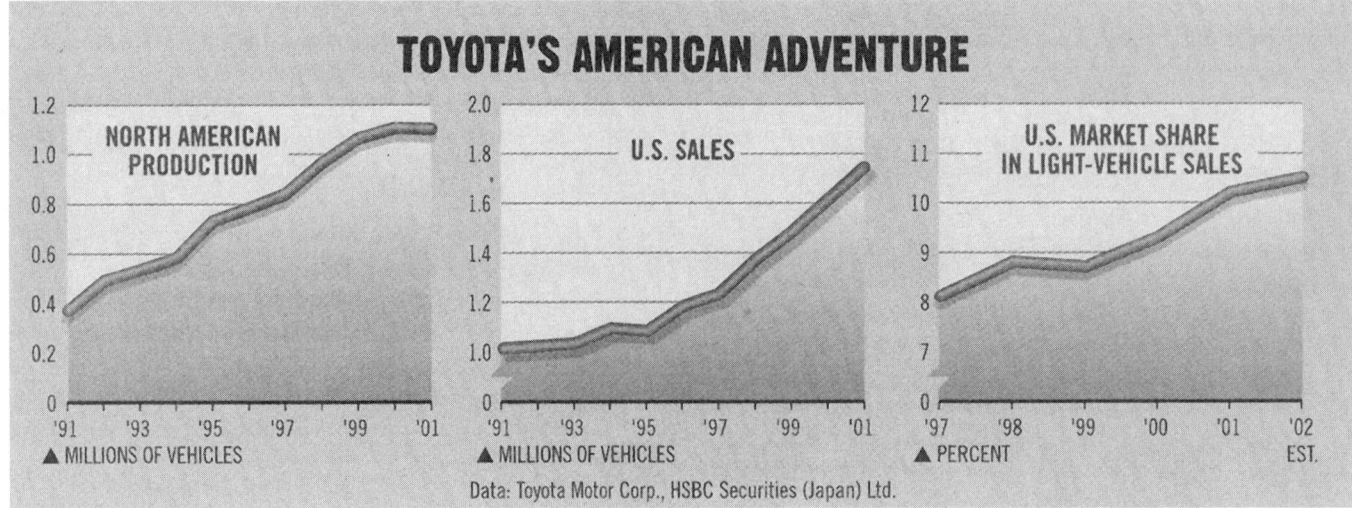

Data: Toyota Motor Corp., HSBC Securities (Japan) Ltd.

CHART BY ALBERTO MENA/BW

two-thirds of the company's operating profit comes from the U.S.
• Toyota's U.S. factories and dealerships currently employ 123,000 Americans—that's more than Coca-Cola, Microsoft, and Oracle combined.
• Toyota's top U.S. execs are, increasingly, local hires. The recently appointed manager of the key Georgetown (Ky.) plant, which makes the Camry, is Ford Motor Co. veteran Gary Convis. "Thirty years ago, we were more dependent on Japan," says James Press, chief operating officer of Toyota Motor Sales USA Inc. in Torrance, Calif. Now, Press says, "there's not much Japanese influence on a day-to-day basis."
• Toyota's big hits in the U.S.—the Camry sedan, Tundra pickup, and Sequoia sport-utility vehicle—were all designed with the American consumer in mind with significant input from U.S. design teams. Now, Toyota is launching a third brand: Scion, aimed at America's youth.
• With its 10% U.S. market share, Toyota is within striking distance of DaimlerChrylser's 14.5%. Some auto executives think it's only a matter of time before Toyota steals DaimlerChrysler's place in the Big Three.

It's easy to see why Toyota has become so focused on the U.S. While the company has never forfeited its dominant position in Japan, its market share is slipping steadily, while profit margins per vehicle are now an estimated 5%, vs. 13% in the U.S. In recessionary Japan, Toyota failed to shift production quickly enough into minivans and cheaper subcompacts. Its rivals, by contrast, have adapted to changing demand, putting unaccustomed pressure on Toyota. "The Japanese market has gotten much more competitive, with Nissan back on track and Honda on a roll," says Chris Richter, an analyst at HSBC Securities Inc. in Tokyo. And Toyota's move into Europe has been slower than expected.

Toyota's top brass won't discuss market-share goals—The last thing the company wants to do is ruffle feathers in Washington by publicly targeting DaimlerChrysler. However, "The American market is our top priority, bar none," says Cho, who in February became one of a few Japanese executives to be in-

ducted into the U.S. Automotive Hall of Fame. "We'll do whatever it takes to succeed there." The company is already planning to ramp up production capacity in the U.S. to more than 1.45 million units by 2005, from 1.25 million now. In the next two to three years, Toyota hopes to be selling a total of 2 million vehicles a year, including imports, in the American market.

Of course, deep inside the company, ambivalence lingers about the growing clout of the U.S. division. Toyota traditionalists are reluctant to stray from the Toyota Way, a philosophy set forth by the company's legendary founder, Kiichiro Toyoda, a zealot for consensus-style decision-making, merciless costcutting, and fanatical devotion to quality and customer satisfaction. So, to ensure that Toyota doesn't lose the essence of what makes it great, the company in February opened the Toyota Institute, an internal, MBA-style program near Toyota City whose faculty will comprise Toyota execs and visiting professors from the University of Pennsylvania's Wharton School.

Fact is, Toyota and its U.S. subsidiaries don't always see eye to eye, especially when it comes to making design choices for the American market. Sometimes the conflicts are over small issues; one Toyota official in Japan, for example, says interior color schemes are a constant source of friction. At other times, there are clashes over crucial product-strategy decisions. "They have to be dragged kicking and screaming into bigger products," says Jim Olson, a senior vice-president at Toyota Motor North America Inc. in New York City.

In the late 1990s, Japanese product planners resisted their U.S. colleagues' idea that the company should produce a V8 pickup truck for the American market. To change their minds, U.S. executives took their Japanese counterparts to a Dallas Cowboys football game—with a pit stop in the Texas Stadium parking lot. There, the Japanese saw row upon row of full-size pickups. Finally, it dawned on them that Americans see the pickup as more than a commercial vehicle, considering it primary transportation. Result: the red-hot Tundra, which sells for about $25,000.

Now, it's harder than ever for executives in Japan to second-guess their American colleagues. "Once we started building

Article 10. THE AMERICANIZATION OF TOYOTA

products [in the U.S.]," says Donald V. Esmond, senior vice-president of the Torrance sales arm, "then the chief engineers started listening a lot closer in terms of what products we need in the market." The proof that American marketers know their business is in the numbers. March sales of the $20,000 Camry, a sedan revamped for the U.S., surged 24.1% over the same month last year. Sales of the Highlander SUV jumped 28.4%.

However successfully Toyota blends the essence of the Toyota Way with a dash of American salesmanship, increasing market share in the U.S. from now on will be a bigger challenge. "Toyota [has] very complete product coverage," says George Peterson, president of AutoPacific Group Inc., a market-research company in Tustin, Calif. "There are very few holes in its lineup." More ominously, Toyota could face in the U.S. the same problem it does in Japan: smaller rivals taking daring design steps that attract new customers. Already, Nissan Motor Co.'s redesigned Altima and Infiniti G35, with their head-turning styling, are luring Americans from the Camry and Lexus line. And South Korea's Hyundai is moving upscale with such cars as the XG350, a family sedan that is thousands of dollars cheaper than the Camry.

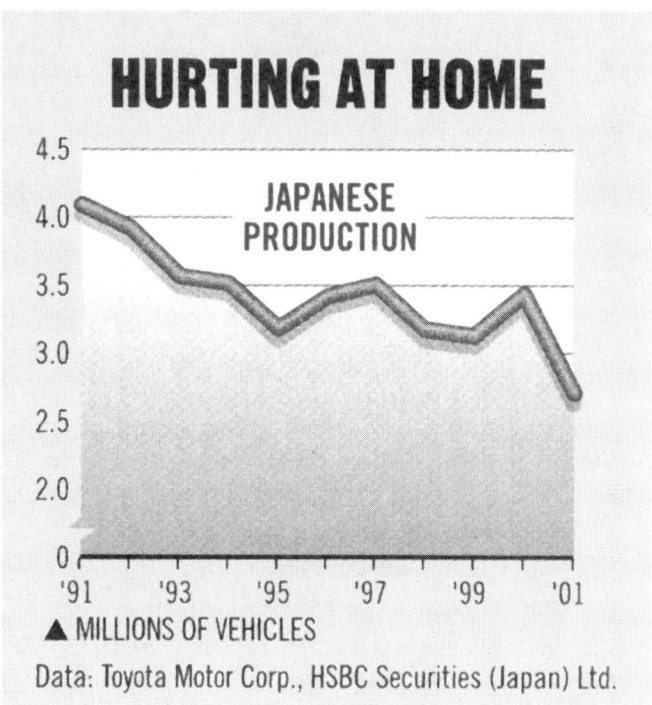

CHART BY ALBERTO MENA/BW

The average age of Toyota drivers in the U.S. is 45—the highest for any Japanese carmaker

Still, given Toyota's U.S. momentum, even stiffer competition from Honda and Nissan won't have a dramatic impact in the short term. Indeed, to increase market share, all Toyota needs to do is crank up U.S. production. Right now there is more demand for such models as the Lexus RX 300 and Highlander SUV than Toyota can fill. "They could get a full share point just by bringing Highlander production to the U.S.," says a well-placed analyst. The company already plans to make the RX 300 in Canada. As a result, Toyota should have no trouble "dialing up their U.S. sales through the remainder of the decade," says one analyst.

But Toyota does have an Achilles' heel: its aging customer base. The average age of a Toyota buyer in the U.S. is 45, the highest among Japanese carmakers. Press, the U.S. chief operating officer, says that Toyota has already halted the aging process by revamping the Celica coupe and MR2 Spyder roadster. Yet neither sold well last year. Nor did the Echo, the first Toyota subcompact aimed at Generation Y and younger. A moderate hit in Japan, it is a flop with young drivers in the U.S., who prefer the Ford Focus or any Volkswagen.

It's too early to tell, but the new $15,000 Matrix subcompact could be the winner Toyota is hoping for. The company's strongest prospect to close the generation gap, however, will be Scion, the new brand to be launched in California next summer. The first Scion models will be the bbX, a modified version of the bB—or black box—a particularly blocky looking van that is now being sold in Japan, as well as a car that is rumored to be derived from the Japanese-market Ist (pronounced "east"). In 2004, the Scion brand will go national in the U.S. and roll out models designed specifically for the American market. One prospect is the ccX, a sporty coupe with additional cargo space and not one, but two sunroofs to provide an open-air feeling.

Will Scion work? Many analysts say that Toyota should have launched its youth-oriented line as part of the Toyota marque—and in doing so bring some verve to the whole brand. However, AutoPacific Group analyst James N. Hall believes that Scion has "no downside." With luck, he says, the brand will bring a new breed of buyers into Toyota showrooms. If it doesn't, he adds, the core Toyota franchise won't suffer. Besides, while the bbX may look bizarre to older buyers, some analysts are convinced that young Americans will like Scion products.

Toyota Chairman Hiroshi Okuda jokingly said last year that his company should move its headquarters to the U.S. That's unlikely. Still, this most Japanese of Japanese auto makers knows its U.S. strategy is crucial to its future. The company that Kiichiro Toyoda founded still has its roots in Japan, but Toyota's destiny is all-American.

By Chester Dawson in Toyota City, with Larry Armstrong in Los Angeles and Joann Muller and Kathleen Kerwin in Detroit

---

Reprinted from the April 15, 2002 issue of *Business Week*, pp. 52-54 by special permission. © 2002 by the McGraw-Hill Companies, Inc.

Case: *The Fairfax County Social Welfare Agency*

The Fairfax County Social Welfare Agency was created in 1965 to administer services under six federally funded social service grants:
- The Senior Citizens' Developmental Grant (SCD).
- The Delinquent Juvenile Act Grant (DJA).
- The Abused Children's Support Grant (ACS).
- The Job Development and Vocational Training Grant JDVT).
- The Food Stamp Program (Food).
- The Psychological Counseling and Family Therapy Fund (Counseling).

The agency's organizational structure evolved as new grants were received and as new programs were created. Staff members—generally the individuals who had written the original grants—were assigned to coordinate the activities required to implement the programs. All program directors reported to the agency's executive director, Wendy Eckstein, and had a strong commitment to the success and growth of their respective programs. The organizational structure was relatively simple, with a comprehensive administrative department handling client records, financial records, and personnel matters. (See below.)

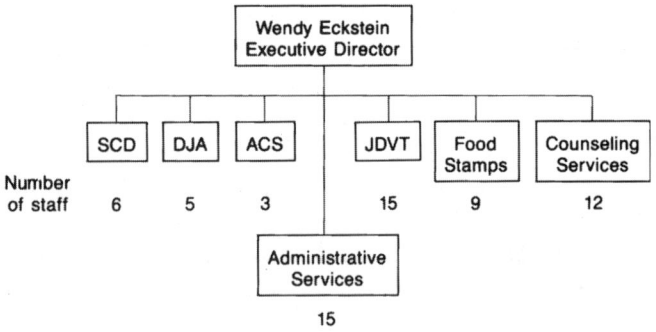

The sense of program "ownership" was intense. Program directors jealously guarded their resources and only reluctantly allowed their subordinates to assist on other projects. Consequently, there was a great deal of conflict among program directors and their subordinates.

The executive director of the agency was concerned about increasing client complaints regarding poor service and inattention. Investigating the matter, Eckstein discovered that:

1. Staff members tended to "protect" their clients and not refer them to other programs, even if another program could provide better services.
2. There was a total absence of integration and cooperation among program directors.
3. Programs exhibited a great deal of duplication and redundancy; program directors acquired administrative support for their individual programs.

Eckstein concluded that the present client or program-based structure no longer met the agency's needs. A major reorganization of this county social welfare agency is being considered.

Discussion Questions

1. What structural attributes of the agency could be causing the client complaints?
2. What actions could Eckstein take without actually changing the organization's structure?
3. Redesign the structure of the agency to improve cooperation and increase efficiency. How would you implement your newly designed structure?

Using the Case on *The Fairfax County Social Welfare Agency*

This case provides an outstanding opportunity to use Vroom's model of decision-making. Included with this discussion is some material developed by the Center for Creative Leadership, which takes Vroom's model and creates a schematic for decision purposes.

It is suggested that the instructor make a copy of the material for each of you or, perhaps, make an overhead for use in the classroom as you try to decide which decision-making approach would be best.

Questions for Discussion

1. How do you think Ms. Eckstein should proceed with making her decision?
2. What parts of the agency are going to be affected by the decision?
3. What are some of the likely outcomes from various decision-making approaches that Eckstein could use?

Case: The Fairfax County Social Welfare Agency; Exercise: NASA

Exercise: *NASA Exercise*

As you approach the moon for a rendezvous with the mother ship, the lateral dissimilar malfunctions, forcing your ship and crew to land some 17 craters, or 145 Earth miles, from the mother ship. The touchdown results in a great deal of damage to the ship but, luckily, none to the crew. Survival is dependent upon reaching the mother ship. The most critical items must be chosen for the trip.

Instructions: Below are the only 15 items left intact after the landing. Rank the items in order of importance they hold to you and your crew in reaching the rendezvous point. Place 1 by the most important item, 2 by the next most important, and so on, through all fifteen items. You should complete this section in 10 minutes.

Your Decision	Articles	Group Decisions
_____	Box of matches	_____
_____	Food concentrate	_____
_____	50 feet of nylon rope	_____
_____	Parachute silk	_____
_____	Portable heating unit	_____
_____	Two .45 caliber pistols	_____
_____	One case of dehydrated Pet milk	_____
_____	Two 100-pound tanks of oxygen	_____
_____	Stellar map of the moon's constellation	_____
_____	Self-inflating life raft	_____
_____	Magnetic compass	_____
_____	Five gallons of water	_____
_____	Signal flares	_____
_____	First-aid kit containing injection needles	_____
_____	Solar-powered FM receiver/transmitter	_____

Because you have survived as a group, the most appropriate decision-making method is group consensus. Each member of the group has to agree upon the rank order. Because the consequence of a wrong decision is so severe—death—you want to be as logical as you can and avoid arguments. In addition, you want to be sure to agree with that ranking that somewhat meets your solution. Be sure not to employ any voting, averaging, or trading techniques that might stifle and embitter one of your companions on this survival journal. *(See answers below.)*

Scoring

1. Subtract the group score on each item from your individual score on each item. Write down the difference. For example, you put down an item as 3 on your list, and the group ended up ranking it 6. There is a net difference of 3.

2. Add all the net differences together to get your par score.

3. Collect all the scores in the group, add them, then divide by the number of people in the group. Your net difference-score _____ Average Individual score _____

4. Now take the NASA-computed rankings and compare the group's ranking with it, computing the net difference between the group's ranking and the correct ranking. Net Difference Score—Group and Correct _____

What do these differences mean?

Answers:

15—Box of matches; 4—Food concentrate; 6—50 feet of nylon rope; 8—Parachute silk; 13—Portable heating unit; 11—Two .45 caliber pistols; 12—One case dehydrated Pet milk; 1—Two 100 lb. tanks of oxygen; 3—Stellar map of the moon's constellation; 9—Rubber life raft; 14—Magnetic compass; 2—Five gallons of water; 10—Signal flares; 7—First-Aid kit containing injection needles; 5—Solar-powered FM receiver-transmitter.

Case: The Fairfax County Social Welfare Agency; Exercise: NASA Exercise, Fred Maidment, McGraw-Hill/Dushkin, 2000.

UNIT 3
Organizing

Unit Selections

11. **Classifying the Elements of Work**, Frank B. Gilbreth and Lillian M. Gilbreth
12. **Beyond Empowerment: Building a Company of Citizens**, Brook Manville and Josiah Ober
13. **Creating a Learning Organization**, Neal McChristy
14. **The Change-Capable Organization**, Patricia A. McLagan
    CASE III. Resistance to Change; Exercise: Organizing

Key Points to Consider

- Some of the early work that was done by management theorists was in classifying and analyzing jobs. Do you think that this type of analysis style still applies? Explain.

- As different groups enter the labor force, they are going to have different demands than the more traditional sources of labor. What impact do you think this is going to have on organizations? How do you think employees from the more traditional sources of labor are going to react?

- Do you think that organizations are going to have to trust their employees more than they did in the past? Why or why not?

 **Links: www.dushkin.com/online/**
These sites are annotated in the World Wide Web pages.

From Foosball to Flextime: Dotcommers Are Growing Up
http://www.fastcompany.com/articles/2000/12/act_childcare.html

Sympatico: Careers
http://www.ntl.sympatico.ca/Contents/Careers/

U.S. Department of Labor (DOL)
http://www.dol.gov

Work and Organizational Psychology, Stockholm University
http://www.psychology.su.se/units/ao/ao.html

After the managers of an organization have planned a course of action, they must organize the firm to accomplish the goals. Many early writers in management were concerned with organization. Frederick W. Taylor was one of the first to apply scientific principles to organizing work. He was followed by Frank and Lillian Gilbreth, pioneers in the field of time and motion studies. Their work contributed to the development of the assembly line and other modern production techniques and is shown in the classic essay "Classifying the Elements of Work."

The questions that constantly confront managers today are how best to organize the firm, given the internal and external environment, and how to approach the problem, not only from the company's perspective, but also from the perspective of the economy as a whole. Are large organizations better than small ones? Each has advantages and disadvantages. Which is better able to compete in the global environment against organizations from different countries with different expectations and rules? Add to these uncertainties the fact that society is evolving, so that new types of organizations will be needed in the future as well as new forms of commerce.

There are several ways that a company can grow. One is to merge with or acquire other firms. The second is to expand the current business internally by building on already established business units. A third is to utilize the new technology that is available as we start the twenty-first century. A recent trend in U.S. industry has been to grow via the merger and acquisition route, but growing internally or through the use of new technology can often be more rewarding.

Technology is forcing organizations to change the way that they do business and how people do their jobs. People are not machines; they are looking for fulfilling and enjoyable work. Managers, therefore, must design jobs to be interesting and rewarding. The days of assembly-line workers doing the same task over and over are numbered. Such positions are being replaced by jobs that vary in the types of tasks the worker performs each day. Technology is also changing the content for jobs that have traditionally required lower-level skills and less effort.

Today, firms must be designed to meet the increasingly competitive environment of a global economy. Organizations must learn to do more with fewer resources and fewer people; management overlap and deadwood can no longer be tolerated. Organizations, therefore, try to be lean and mean, but is that necessarily the best way to go? As firms cut back, are they crippling the future of the organization by looking only at the short term? The opposite side of this coin is that the middle manager who is able to survive and prosper in this environment will be a better leader, having been tempered in a much hotter furnace than his or her predecessors.

As seen in "The Change-Capable Organization," to remain competitive in a rapidly changing environment, organizations

must evolve to meet the rapidly developing global economy with which they will have to interact. "Creating a Learning Organization" will be a top priority for all organizations as new challenges appear for them to overcome. Managers will have to trust their employees more and share information with them. Organizations will have to advance "Beyond Empowerment: Building a Company of Citizens," if they are to succeed. In the future organizations will have the world as their market and their competitor. They must be able to foresee changes in their environment and to react quickly to turn those changes to their advantage. Organizations will need strength and flexibility to meet change or they will suffer the fate of the dinosaurs, which failed to adapt to new environments.

Classifying the Elements of Work

Frank B. Gilbreth and Lillian M. Gilbreth

This paper presents a complete method of visualizing a classification of all the subdivisions and the true motion-study elements of The One Best Way to Do Work.

NEED FOR SUCH A CLASSIFICATION

Such a classification is vitally necessary in order that fundamental super-standards shall be made by the scientific method of selecting and measuring the best units, for synthesis into methods of least waste.

This classification furnishes the basis of a definite mnemonic classification for filing all motion-study and time-study data for the work of the industrial engineer, the machine designer, and the behavior psychologist—that their various pieces of information, usually obtained through entirely different channels and methods of attack, may be automatically brought together, to the same filing folders, under the same filing subdivisions.

So far as we are able to learn, there are no other classifications or bases for filing that accomplish this purpose, and we have found that such a classification is absolutely necessary for our work of finding The One Best Way to Do Work, standardizing the trades, and making and enforcing standing orders for best management.

It is hoped that teachers of industrial engineering in our colleges will learn that *one* demonstration of building up The One Best Way to Do Work from the ultimate elements, in any kind of activity, will do more to teach a student the principles of motion study and most efficient methods of management than dozens of lessons dealing with generalities.

The coming generation should be taught a definite filing system for data of scientific management, laid out under a complete classification of all work; should be taught the method of selecting the right units to measure and the methods of measuring these units; and should be furnished with the devices for making the cost of measuring cheap, and with a method for synthesizing the resulting information. This would result in a general progress in world efficiency and an increase in quality of living that would mark an epoch in the history of industry and civilization.

USE OF FUNDAMENTAL ELEMENTS

The literature of scientific management abounds with examples of units of work improperly called "elements," which are in no sense elements. A classification for finding The One Best Way to Do Work must deal with *true elements*, not merely with subdivisions that are arbitrarily called "elements."

There has recently appeared a well-written biography of a great engineer[1] in which subdivisions of operations, requiring in many instances more than 30 seconds to perform, have been erroneously described as "elements." That error will again mislead many people. These so-called elements should be taken for what they really are, namely subdivisions and not elements, and not confused with true elements, or fundamental units which cannot be further subdivided.

SCOPE OF THE CLASSIFICATION

This classification for finding The One Best Way to Do Work is applicable to all kinds of work. It was used by one of the authors while serving as ranking officer in the field under the training committee of the General Staff, standardizing the methods of The Best Way to Do Work for teaching the five million men and officers in the World War. It has also been used in analyzing the work of the surgeon, nurse, hospital management, large department stores, selling a great many kinds of manufacturing, accounting, office work in general, and many other kinds of work.

TRUE ELEMENTS OF WORK

The classification of all work of any and all organizations for the purpose of finding The One Best Way to Do Work may be visualized as follows:

Article 11. Classifying the Elements of Work

I. A complete organization, which consists of
II. Processes, such as
   (a) Financing
   (b) Advertising
   (c) Marketing
   (d) Distributing
   (e) Selling
   (f) Accounting
   (g) Purchasing
   (h) Manufacturing
   (i) Planning
   (j) Teaching
   (k) Charting
   (l) Maintaining
   (m) Filing
   These processes consist of
III. Operations, which consist of
IV. Cycles of motions, which consist of
V. Subdivisions, or events, or therbligs[2] of a cycle of motions which consist of
   (a) Search
   (b) Find
   (c) Select
   (d) Grasp
   (e) Transport loaded
   (f) Position
   (g) Assemble
   (h) Use
   (i) Disassemble
   (j) Inspect
   (k) Pre-position for next operation
   (l) Release load
   (m) Transport empty
   (n) Rest for overcoming fatigue
   (o) Other periods of unavoidable delay
   (p) Avoidable delay
   (q) Plan
VI. Variables of motions
   (a) Variables of the worker
    1. Anatomy
    2. Brawn
    3. Contentment
    4. Creed
    5. Earning power
    6. Experience
    7. Fatigue
    8. Habits
    9. Health
    10. Mode of living
    11. Nutrition
    12. Size
    13. Skill
    14. Temperament
    15. Training
   (b) Variables of the surroundings, equipment, and tools
    1. Appliances
    2. Clothes
    3. Colors
    4. Entertainment, music, reading, etc.
    5. Heating, cooling, ventilating
    6. Lighting
    7. Quality of material
    8. Reward and punishment
    9. Size of unit moved
    10. Special fatigue-eliminating devices
    11. Surroundings
    12. Tools
    13. Union rules
    14. Temperament
   (c) Variables of the motion
    1. Acceleration
    2. Automaticity
    3. Combination with other motions and sequences
    4. Cost
    5. Direction
    6. Effectiveness
    7. Foot-pounds of work accomplished
    8. Inertia and momentum overcome
    9. Length
    10. Necessity
    11. Path
    12. "Play for position"
    13. Speed

Under I, a complete organization, are included all kinds of organizations, including financial, industrial, commercial, professional, educational, and social.

Under II, processes, it should be noted that processes are divided in the same way from a motion-study analyst's standpoint, regardless in which department or in which function they are found.

Under III, operations, the operations include mechanical as well as physiological, and mental as well as manual. The reasons for these inclusions are:

1. From the motion-study standpoint there are not always clear dividing lines between the *operations of devices* and the *mental and manual operations of the human being*, for they are often mutually interchangeable, sometimes in part and sometimes as a whole.[3]

2. Records of many and probably all mental operations can now be obtained by the chronocyclegraph and micromotion photographic methods, and each year such photographic records can more and more be deciphered and used to practical advantage. Enough can already be read and used to serve our present needs. Careful examination of all our old micromotion and chronocyclegraph films taken under conditions of actual practice show that they are literally full of examples of such records of mental processes.

Under IV, cycles of motions are arbitrary subdivisions of operations. They have distinct and natural boundaries of beginning and ending. Usually and preferably there are certain sequences of therbligs that are especially suitable for standardization and transference to other kinds of work, and serve every purpose of finding The One Best Way to Do Work.

Under V, therbligs, we would emphasize that we do not place "motions" as the next subdivision under "cycle of motions" because "motions" have neither distinct and definite boundaries nor beginnings and endings. For example: It is difficult to determine correctly how many "motions" are required to take a fountain pen from the pocket and prepare to write with it. It will be found difficult to agree on just how many "motions" are made and as to where are located the boundaries of the "motions" of so simple a cycle as this, or of any other similarly common cycle of motions.

However, the 17 subdivisions, or events, or therbligs, as they are variously called, seem to be all that are necessary from which to synthesize all of the *cycles of motions* of all the *operations* of all the *processes* of all the *organizations* of every kind whatever. The science of motion study consists, therefore, of finding The One Best Sequence of therbligs for each kind of work and the science of management consists of deriving, installing, and enforcing the conditions that will permit the work to be done repeatedly in The One Best Way. It is conceivable that sometime in the future an eighteenth and possibly more therbligs will be found, and we seem near to their discovery at the present time. The discovery of additional therbligs pertaining to the phenomena of skill and automaticity seems inevitable.[4]

Under VI, variables of motions, provision is made for filing all information regarding any kind of motion made by either hand, device, or machine. It provides for all information regarding the structures in which work is performed. It provides for filing all data regarding human behavior—supernormal, normal, and subnormal. It supplies the basis of filing all data of the educator, psychologist, psychiatrist, and the expert in personnel, placement, and promotion problems.

This classification can be carried on and subdivided indefinitely. It furnishes an efficient and quickly usable plan for synthesizing the components of The One Best Way to Do Work in such shape that they can be cumulatively improved.

However, our present information regarding the 17 therbligs is sufficient to revolutionize all kinds of work, and if the industries of the various nations would eliminate the obviously unnecessary therbligs and standardize the kinds, sequences, and combinations of the remaining efficient therbligs, the resulting savings each year would be sufficient to pay the outstanding debts of most nations.

HISTORY OF THIS CLASSIFICATION

For many years we have used these therbligs as divisions for dissecting cycles of motions of a great many different kinds of work, but it was not until we began to use photography in motion study in 1892 that we made our greatest progress. It was not until 1912, when we used our first micromotion processes intensively, that we were able to make such great advances as projecting the motions of experts faster and slower, as well as at the speed of experts' demonstration. We were then also able to project and examine therbligs backwards, or in the reversed directions. This enabled us to get a new fund of information that resulted in many suggestions from seeing, measuring, and comparing the therbligs performed in the reversed sequence and opposite directions. This was used to great advantage in finding the methods of least waste and especially in the process of taking machines apart and putting them together again in front of a motion picture camera, and then running the film backwards, showing the films of assembling as dissembling and vice versa.

EXAMPLES OF PROFITABLE USE

Running films of superexperts backwards, to see what we could get for automatically suggesting inventions, or as "thought detonators" when seeing the operation done thus, presented peculiarities and combinations of therbligs never seen before. This was, of course, supplemented by examining one picture, or frame, at a time which, with motion study experts, will always be the most efficient method for getting facts from the films. Great progress was made, for example, in *pre-positioning for next operation* (therblig k) parts and tools so that *grasp* (therblig d) was performed with quite the same motions and actions and performed within a time equal to that of *release load* (therblig l).

As an example of the importance of recognizing the therblig as the fundamental element, the result of that particular study in 1912 was that our organization enabled a client to have his machine assemblers put together 66 machines per day with less fatigue than they had previously accumulated while assembling 18 machines per day. Because this method was synthesized from fundamentally correct units, the same methods are still in use today in this same factory.[5]

This increase in output should not be considered as an exceptional case. On the contrary, it is quite typical. In fact we have a great many illustrations that we could give where the savings were much greater. For example: One large motion-study laboratory, as a result of this method of attack, synthesized and demonstrated new methods which averaged an output of five times as much product per man. This method used in assembling carburetors enabled messenger boys to do the work in one-tenth the time required by skilled mechanics.[6] It has been used on work of assembling pumps with still greater results.[7]

THERBLIG SEQUENCES

It was early recognized that certain similar operations have similar sequences of therbligs. For example: The operations of feeding pieces into a drill press or into a punch press, time tickets into a time stamp, and paper into a printing press, have practically the same sequence of therbligs. A typical sequence of therbligs for one complete cycle of handling one piece on a drill press is *search, find, select, grasp, transport loaded, position, assemble, use, disassemble, inspect, transport loaded, pre-position for next operation, release load* and *transport empty*. This cycle of motions can and should be done with the following therbligs: *grasp, transport loaded, position, assemble, use, release load* and *transport empty*, which are half the number of therbligs of the usual method.

While the former is the usual sequence of therbligs on a drill press, it is by no means the best one. There is The One Best Sequence of therbligs on each machine and each kind of work, and it should always be found, standardized, taught, and maintained.

Table 1	
PAIRED THERBLIG USUALLY PERFORMED BEFORE USE	PAIRED THERBLIG USUALLY PERFORMED AFTER USE
d. Grasp... Use	.... *l*. Release load
e. Transport loaded.................................. Use	.... *m*. Transport empty
f. Position... Use	.... *k*. Pre-position for next operation
g. Assemble... Use	.... *i*. Disassemble
q. Plan... Use	.... *j*. Inspect

Table 2 Unpaired Therbligs	
ORDER NO. 4	ORDER NO. 5
a. Search..Use	*n*. Rest for overcoming fatigue
b. Find..Use	*o*. Other forms of unavoidable delay
c. Select...Use	*p*. Avoidable delay

ANOTHER WORK CLASSIFICATION

Now let us look at another method of subdividing and classifying all work. There is another and better known type of division and classification for visualizing all activity which was early recognized. The importance of considering this simple classification can be seen in the unfairness and trouble that have been caused by giving the same piece rate for large lots as for small. This classification divides all work, both large and small, into three parts, as follows:

1. Get ready
2. Do it, or make it.
3. Clean up.

Now, applying this division to one piece on the drill press, we have:

1. *Get ready*, or pick up the piece and put it under the drill. This consists of all therbligs that come before *use* (therblig *h*).
2. *Drill it* (do it or make it). This consists of only one therblig, namely *use* (therblig *h*).
3. *Clean up*, or take the piece out from under the drill and inspect it and lay it down. This consists of all therbligs that come after *use* (therblig *h*).

THE IMPORTANCE OF USE

It should be recognized that the therblig *use* is the difficult one to learn in mastering a trade. It is the most productive and, therefore, the most important therblig of all.

All other therbligs of all kinds of work are desirable and necessary only so far as they facilitate, prepare for, or assist in increasing *use*. Any therbligs that do not foster *use* should be under suspicion as being unnecessary. Use is the highest paid therblig, because it usually requires the most skill. The more of the therbligs of "get ready" and "clean up" that are performed by less skilled and consequently lower priced workers the better for all workers, for they all will be employed a larger portion of the day at the highest priced work at which they are each individually capable. This is true not only in the consideration of the therbligs

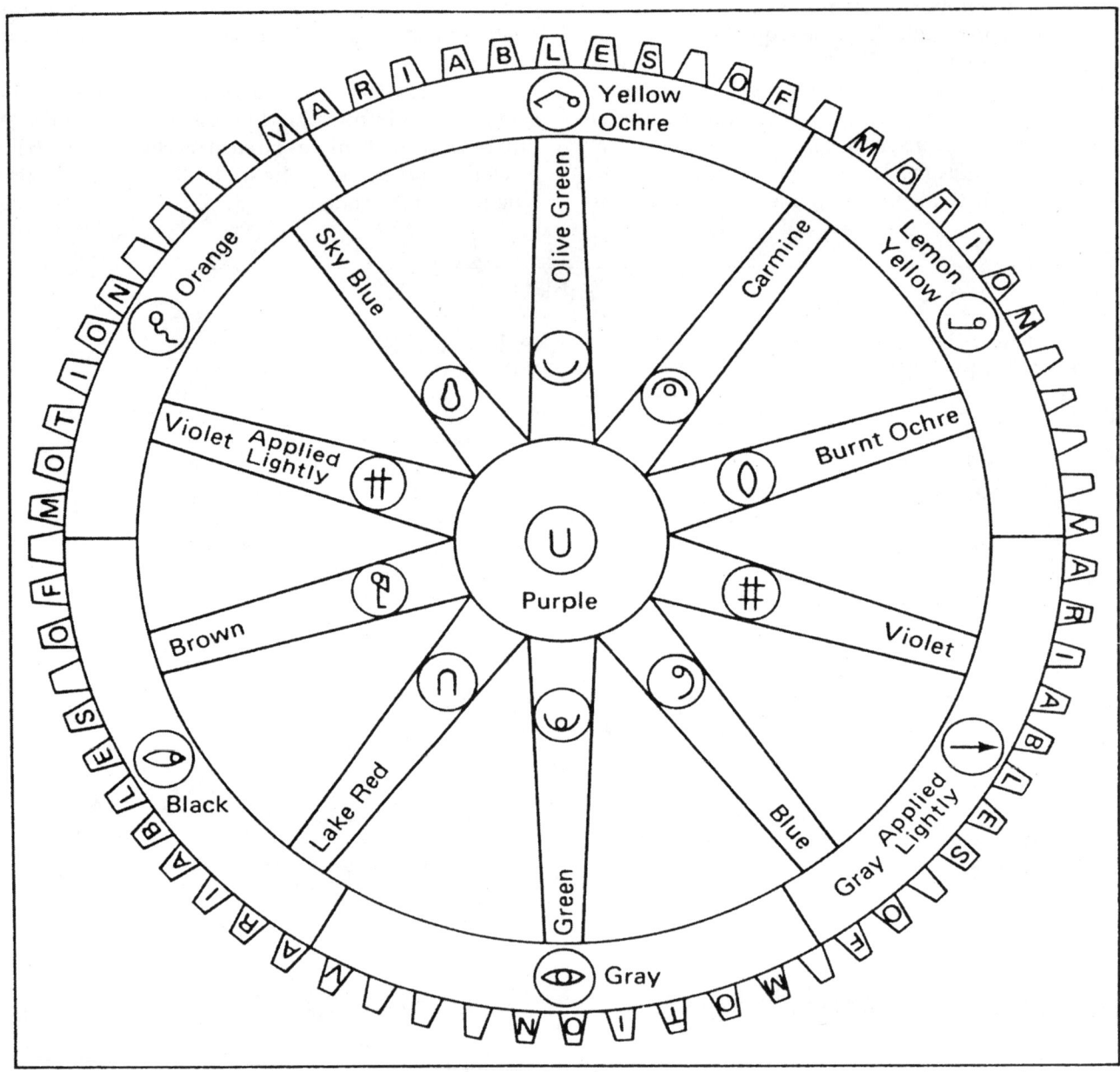

Figure 1. The Wheel of Motion

but also in the trades in general. For example: The bricklayer, the plumber, the steamfitter, the office executive, and many others, each have their specially assigned helpers, but they still habitually do much pay-reducing work for which in the long run they suffer a loss due to less personal activity. It will help to analyze and classify all work if it is recognized that the hod carrier bears the same relation to the bricklayer, and the secretary to the executive, as do the therbligs that compose "get ready" bear to the therblig *use*; and the laborer's work of "clean up" after the work of the bricklayer, is quite the same as the therbligs that compose "clean up" after therblig *use*.

Further investigations of a typical sequence of therbligs, such as on the drill press or other examples cited, from the standpoint of the classification of the therbligs show that *grasp* (therblig d) of "get ready" is used before *use* (therblig h) and that *release load* (therblig l) done after *use* may be quite the same except that it is performed in motions that are the reverse of those of *grasp*.

PAIRED THERBLIGS

There are a number of such paired therbligs which are almost always separated by the therblig *use*.

For example:

It was the absence of a therblig on the other side of *use* to pair with *inspect*, together with the fact that *plan* is actually found in the photographic records regardless of how much planning may be done prior to the beginning of an operation, that caused us to add to the list of therbligs,

Article 11. Classifying the Elements of Work

plan (therblig *q*). The therblig *plan* may occur in any place in the sequence of therbligs, but we have put it last in the list before cited because it was added last, and also to distinguish it from the "planning" that should be done before any "performing" of the operation is begun.

There are two more kinds of divisions, or orders, making a total of five orders of therbligs, namely one consisting of *search*, *find* and *select* (therbligs *a*, *b*, and *c*) which usually come before *use*, and *rest for overcoming fatigue*, *other forms of unavoidable delay* and *avoidable delay* (therbligs *n*, *o*, and *p*) which usually come after *use*. Thus we have two orders of unpaired therbligs separated by *use*, as follows:

In analyzing an operation of any kind a simultaneous motion cycle chart is prepared. The therbligs of motion are applied to this chart in studying it for present methods and determining the altered sequence which should be adopted to establish The One Best Way to Do Work. This brought up the problem of graphic presentation of the therbligs for ready identification.

To make these 17 therbligs more real, tangible, and easier to visualize and remember, different colors are used to distinguish them on the simultaneous motion cycle chart.[8] One member of our organization, Paul M. Vanderhorst, who conceived the idea of adding *plan* to our list of therbligs, also suggested the idea of showing the 17 therbligs in the design of a wheel, and we have adopted a "Wheel of Motion" not altogether unlike the "Wheel of Life" of Hindus, for explaining therblig study to the employees of our

		STANDARD SYMBOLS, COLORS AND PENCILS FOR SIMO-CHARTS (Simultaneous Motion Cycle Charts)		
Symbol	Name of Symbol	Symbol Color	Name of Color	Name and Number of Pencil or Crayon
⌒o	Search		Black	Dixon's Best Black #331
⊚	Find		Gray	Dixon's Best Gray #352½
→	Select		Light Gray	Dixon's Best Gray #352½ Applied Lightly
∩	Grasp		Lake Red	Dixon's Best Lake Red #321½
\o/	Transport Loaded		Green	Dixon's Best Green #354
9	Position		Blue	Dixon's Best Blue #350
#	Assemble		Violet	Dixon's Best Violet #323
U	Use		Purple	Dixon's Best Purple #323½
‡	Dis-assemble		Light Violet	Dixon's Best Violet #323 Applied Lightly
○	Inspect		Burnt Ochre	Dixon's Best Burnt Ochre #335½
ᵷ	Pre-position for Next Operation		Sky Blue	Dixon's Best Sky Blue #320
⌒o	Release Load		Carmine Red	Dixon's Best Carmine Red #321
∪	Transport Empty		Olive Green	Dixon's Best Olive Green #325
ℓ	Rest for Overcoming Fatigue		Orange	Ruben's "Crayola" Orange
⌒o	Unavoidable Delay		Yellow Ochre	Dixon's Best Yellow Ochre #324½
∟o	Avoidable Delay		Lemon Yellow	Dixon's Best Lemon Yellow #353½
℘	Plan		Brown	Dixon's Best Brown #343

Figure 2. Symbols, Colors, and Pencils for Simo-Charts. In practice, column 3 is solid colors, not crosshatching.

clients. Each part of the wheel representing a therblig has its own individual color, and each of the colors has a special meaning and is also mnemonic. See Figs. 1 and 2.

It should be noted that *use* is the hub of the wheel. *Use* is the most important therblig. The more *use*, the more production.

The therbligs that have like characteristics, although they may represent reversed action, are shown as paired spokes on opposite sides of the wheel.

The rim of the wheel consists of two different kinds, or orders, of three parts each, and the cogs on the rim are shaped like the letter V and are to remind the motion-study student that the variables affect all of the therbligs and must be all carefully considered in order to obtain The One Best Way to Do Work. There are at least a hundred variables that are important on nearly all kinds of work and our complete list contains several thousand variables. It is extremely important to recognize that information relating to the variables is applicable to all kinds of work. The application of this information is simply a matter of degree required in the particular study in hand.

The same colors are always used on the same therbligs wherever they are represented or shown. This permits instant visualization of all the therbligs of any one kind. These colors are specially important in connection with quickly visualizing, grouping, comparing, and interpreting the behavior and happenings on simultaneous motion cycle charts. The use of the standard colors enables the micromotion study engineer to acquire a proper sense of the proper time for each therblig, even before a new study is made. This is particularly important when studying an operator for his first time, as it will show whether or not he is fully cooperating.

In fact, too much stress can hardly be laid on the importance of showing each and every therblig and all possible happenings on the simultaneous motion cycle chart in finding The One Best Way to Do Work. We know of no other method in finding The One Best Way to Do Work. It answers all purposes satisfactorily.

After sufficient experience and study, preferably in a motion-study laboratory, the interrelations, peculiarities, and suitabilities of the therbligs on several simultaneous motion cycle charts of different kinds of work will be recognized by an engineer trained in motion study. When he has the proper training he is invariably able to improve and completely revolutionize any work on which the micromotion study method of attack has not already been used.

RELATION OF THERBLIG STUDY TO STOPWATCH TIME STUDY

The symbols here shown furnish a sort of shorthand which makes for greater speed in making notes regarding best sequences of therbligs and motion study in general, and for remembering the therbligs easily. The results of careful study of the peculiarities of the therbligs individually and in combination with those that immediately precede and immediately follow, as well as those that are executed simultaneously by other anatomical members, will remove for all time any idea that scientific motion study of the behavior of the workers can be accomplished with any such obsolete device as a stopwatch, or that time study and motion study are the same thing or even similar.

The literature of scientific management is full of examples where time study and motion study are confused. This confusion abounds even in books that are considered classics. It should be recognized that "Time study is the art of finding how long it takes to do work." This was Taylor's original definition, and it is still good. Time study is the great invention of Dr. Taylor. Taylor never did any motion study[9] of any kind whatever.[10]

The definition of motion study is: "Motion study is the science of finding The One Best Way to Do Work." Of course micromotion study gives records in indisputable permanent form of the motions and behavior of the demonstrator of the methods and of the individual errorless times of each therblig of each cycle of motions and of the overall times of the operator.

TRANSFERABLE DATA

Intensive study of the resulting therbligs furnishes information that is interchangeable in all kinds of work for finding The One Best Way to Do Work. It is this feature of the great value of the interchangeability of the indisputable detailed data that makes it most desirable to select as demonstrator of a method that person only who is *the best demonstrator obtainable* of the best methods extant or the best known, and in a motion-study laboratory[11] equipped for the purpose, and under controlled conditions.

It is obvious that records of the methods of recognized champions are most desirable. It must be recognized, however, that champions are usually champions because others are so inefficient. The synthesis of the best components of the methods of two or more champions will make a method better than that of the method of the champion of champions and better than the method of *the one best demonstrator obtainable*.

Data regarding the therbligs of a champion or a superexpert in any one kind of work are usable on a great many different kinds of work, for the times and skill on each therblig are transferable. It is also desirable, but not absolutely necessary, that *the best demonstrator obtainable*, of the best method extant, shall have sufficient experience to perform the cycles of motions and the complete operation in the shortest time for that operation. However, it is often difficult to obtain anyone who can demonstrate the combination of the *best method known* and also the *best speed of performance*. Oftentimes the expert of motion study can demonstrate the sequence of therbligs which constitute The One Best Way to Do Work, yet, because of his lack of practice and speed, is not able at first to equal the times nor the relativity of simultaneity of therbligs performed by different anatomical members of those with a much poorer method, but with much greater natural dexterity who have had so much practice that they have arrived at a state of motion automaticity.

The usual standards obtained by rule-of-thumb methods will always be temporary and transitory.

It is here that the method of recording lateness of therbligs previously cited is of importance. Here again the detailed records of the therbligs are of great value for the correct times of individual therbligs and the proper relativity of simultaneity can be obtained even from inferior sequences where great dexterity and automaticity have been recorded under the wrong method. When the best sequence is known, the correct time for task management for performing The One Best Way to Do Work *can be prophesied before anyone can demonstrate it.* The importance of prophesying the time for accomplishing The One Best Way to Do Work before it can be demonstrated will be appreciated when it is realized that there is not a single case on record where The One Best Way to Do Work has been derived by the wasteful fumbling methods of evolution.

RELATION OF THIS CLASSIFICATION TO FATIGUE STUDY

Much has been written in generalities regarding unnecessary fatigue. Because of the dreadful working conditions in nearly all factories, some improvements can almost always be made by anyone with good intentions and authority together with sufficient continuity of purpose. However, such improvements are only part of what could be done and often lapse after the passing of the regime of the untrained enthusiast who is merely interested in the elimination of unnecessary fatigue. The One Best Way to Do Work is that sequence of therbligs which permits the work to be done in least time, with least fatigue, and entails having the periods of *unavoidable delay* (therblig *o*) and *avoidable delay* (therblig *p*) utilized for *rest for overcoming fatigue* (therblig *n*).

The data relating to therbligs that cause or eliminate unnecessary fatigue can be filed in orderly fashion for future use under the classification shown herein.

Unnecessary fatigue should be recognized as the badge of ignorance of the therbligs and consequently of motion study. To eliminate unnecessary fatigue, there must be complete recognition that the therbligs are the fundamental elements of The One Best Way to Do Work, and are units for the application of the laws of motion study and fatigue study.

RELATION TO STANDARDIZATION

Much has been written also of standardization, and The One Best Way to make standards is to proceed from the standpoint that the best standard is the one that best complies with the laws of motion study. It is quite impossible to standardize a method for quickest achievement of the state of automaticity without recognition and standardization of the individual therbligs involved and their combinations and sequences.

Automaticity of the wrong method, so prevalent in highly repetitive vocations like those of the textile trades, is the shame and disgrace of industry today. However, it will be quite useless for executives and managers to talk standardizations of the correct sequences of the therbligs for The One Best Way to Do Work until they know from personal experience the possibilities of micromotion study and set the example in their own duties. For this purpose the simplest device is the executive's cross-sectioned desk which serves as a permanent reminder, and if used properly will furnish a permanent proof. It permits doing all manual work with almost exactly the same motions every time. It soon becomes strikingly evident how much faster work can be accomplished when the motions are made over the same locations each and every time. The next step is the search for The One Best Way to Do Work.

… the evils of deadening monotony do not exist where there is sufficient knowledge of the therblings …

Because of the rule-of-thumb methods used in the past for obtaining standards, almost anyone can make improvements in the present state of standardization encountered in all organizations. The usual standards obtained by rule-of-thumb methods will always be temporary and transitory. If standards are based upon the permanent records of indisputable knowledge of the ultimate components of the cycles obtained by the micromotion methods, they will be in shape for cumulative improvement without any additional study. Comparatively few organizations have given proper attention to the possibilities of standardization built upon indisputable measured elements, and but few standards have been made with due regard to the extra outputs in the savings of time and fatigue that result if the standards are made to conform with the laws of automaticity, which is the greatest free asset of the working man, whatever his occupation.

RELATION TO THE LEARNING PROCESS

For greatest speed with least effort and fatigue in learning, The One Best Sequence of therbligs should be used whenever possible from the very beginning of the learning period so that automaticity may be achieved in the shortest possible learning period and with least habit interference. The study of the 17 therbligs of this classification furnishes a means to shorten the period required to learn any kind of art, trade, profession, or other activity. Hence, there will be more time available to learn more jobs and thus gain promotion, and, by reason of more knowledge of the theory combined with the practice, prolong one's earning periods by teaching others, when one is too old to do a young man's total quantity of output.

Finally, the evils of deadening monotony do not exist where there is sufficient knowledge of the therbligs and the variables affecting them. As two cycles of motions can never be made exactly alike, the quest of perfection of methods is much more interesting and absorbing than the desire to know which part of the whole structure is the piece which is being worked upon, although the latter is supposed to be the millennium by the academic enemies of standardization.

Knowledge of measuring, selecting, and studying of therbligs makes all work fascinating, for while the best method known and performed under given conditions may be called for practical purposes "The One Best Way to Do Work," a still better method with new tools and conditions is ever possible. There is no instance or example that cannot be improved with greater knowledge of the therbligs pertaining to that work. There are so many possible combinations of therbligs that the skilled worker with the knowledge of therbligs performing any work ordinarily considered monotonous has the opportunity to improve the temporary One Best Way to Do Work almost without limit.

It is not the fault of the skilled worker, if he has not been taught to visualize the therbligs, that he has not been given sufficient incentives to enlist and hold all of his zeal continuously, has not been taught the science that underlies his work, has not been induced to search for the scheme of perfection, has not been taught a filing method for his knowledge that he may have systematized improvement from his additional experience, and has not desired to teach the apprentices and other learners the best way that he knew.

The results derived under the method of attack that this classification embodies have been successful in every kind of work in which it has been used.

It is hoped that this description of this filing classification will be of service to those who are interested in efficiency, in making waste elimination attractive, and in finding and enforcing the managerial conditions which will permit The One Best Way to Do Work.

NOTES AND REFERENCES

1. See *Frederick W. Taylor* by E B. Copley.
2. This word was coined for the purpose of having a short word which will save the motions necessary to write such long descriptions as "The 17 categories into which the motion-study elementary subdivisions of a cycle of motions fall."
3. In 1910 and the years following, we collected and specially devised in our own laboratory, many devices for supplying, mechanically, the therbligs of cycles of motions that the crippled soldiers could not perform, due to their injuries. Such collections should be made by all museums and colleges that intend to teach motion study.
4. See Society of Industrial Engineers Bulletin, November 1923, pp. 6-7. "A Fourth Dimension for Recording Skill," by Frank B. Gilbreth and L. M. Gilbreth. The lateness in starting or finishing of a therblig performed by any one anatomical member as compared with the time of beginning or finishing of a therblig performed by another anatomical member is a most important unit for measuring skill and automaticity.
5. See *Management Engineering*, February 1923, p. 87. "Ten Years of Scientific Management," by John G. Aldrich, M. E., and also his discussion of paper 1378 on page 1131, vol. 34, 1912, American Society of Mechanical Engineers Transactions.
6. See Proceedings of the Institution of Automobile Engineers (English), "The Fundamentals of Cost Reduction," by H. Kerr Thomas, Member of the Council.
7. See Society of Industrial Engineers Transactions, vol. 2, 1920, "The One Best Way to Do Work," by Frank B. Gilbreth and L. M. Gilbreth.
8. See "Applied Motion Study" by Frank B. Gilbreth and L. M. Gilbreth, p. 138.
9. See Bulletin of The Taylor Society, June 1921.
10. This can easily be proved by reading Taylor's own writings, and it is also a matter of record in our own office. This fact is entirely missed, perhaps unintentionally, by Taylor's biographer, Copley.
11. Laboratory motion study has been criticized as being done under conditions of the shop. The conditions of the shop should be changed until they duplicate the most desirable conditions of the laboratory.

Frank Bunker Gilbreth graduated from the English high school in Boston in 1885, passed the entrance examinations at M.I.T., but decided to work for a firm of consulting engineers and to complete his technical training at night. In 1911, he established Gilbreth, Inc., an engineering consulting firm, which advanced the specialty of Motion Study. His achievements in scientific engineering were recognized by the University of Maine, which conferred on him an LL.D. degree in 1920. Gilbreth died in 1925.

Lillian Moller Gilbreth married Frank Gilbreth in 1904. Her education included a Bachelor of Letters and a Master of Letters from the University of California and a Ph.D. from Brown University (1915). She traveled widely as a lecturer on technology and human relations problems, served as president of Gilbreth, Inc., and received numerous awards and medals. Lillian Gilbreth died in 1972.

Article 12

Beyond Empowerment:
Building a Company of Citizens

We're in a knowledge economy, but our managerial and governance systems are stuck in the industrial era. It's time for a whole new model.

by Brook Manville
and Josiah Ober

WE LIVE TODAY IN A KNOWLEDGE ECONOMY. The core assets of the modern business enterprise lie not in buildings, machinery, and real estate, but in the intelligence, understanding, skills, and experience of employees. Harnessing the capabilities and commitment of knowledge workers is, it might be argued, the central managerial challenge of our time. Unfortunately, it is a challenge that has not yet been met. Corporate ownership structures, governance systems, and incentive programs—despite the enlightened rhetoric of business leaders—are still firmly planted in the industrial age. We grant ownership rights only to the providers of financial capital, not to the providers of intellectual capital. We govern through small management teams at the top of hierarchies. We motivate people through Pavlovian carrot-and-stick incentives.

It's true that business organizations have become less bureaucratic in recent years and that authority has been pushed down through the ranks. People at lower levels—unit managers, factory workers, customer service representatives—have greater autonomy today than they did a generation ago. But such "empowerment," as it's commonly called, is limited. Workers are able to make decisions about their immediate jobs or to participate in somewhat broader decisions about their own units, but they still have little or no voice in decisions about the direction of the overall company. They remain essentially disenfranchised. It should be no surprise, therefore, that many knowledge workers feel estranged from their organizations—their outlook distrustful, their attitude cynical, their loyalty tenuous.

At the heart of the problem is a lack of adequate models. Although we know how command-and-control management works in an industrial company, we have no working template for a truly democratic system of management—one suited to the knowledge worker's need for and expectation of self-determination and self-government. But if a usable model for a democratic organization does not yet exist in the business world, history offers a compelling, if unexpected, prototype. Some 2,500 years ago, the city-state of ancient Athens rose to unprecedented political and economic power by giving its citizens a direct voice and an active role in civic governance. Although not without its flaws, the city's uniquely participative system of democracy helped unleash the creativity of the Athenian people and channel it in ways that produced the greatest good for the society as a whole. The system succeeded in bringing individual initiative and common cause into harmony. And that is precisely the synthesis that today's companies need to achieve if they're to realize the full power of their people and thrive in the knowledge economy.

An Ancient Model

It is the year 480 BC. Dawn is breaking over the small Greek island of Salamis, just off the coast of Athens. Thousands of Athenian citizens huddle on slender, wooden galleys, clutching weapons and oars. Facing them are hundreds of powerful, hulking warships, the majestic fighting navy of the Persian Empire. That force is poised to complete the Persian takeover of the Greek mainland and its prize jewel, the flourishing city of Athens. Across the narrow strait, on a commanding hill, sits the Great King of Persia himself, eager to witness the culmination of years of preparation. He expects that victory will come easily. After all, the Athenians are a ragtag bunch. They do not even have a king of their own to dispense orders.

Yet by the time dusk falls, the Persian king's grandiose plans are in ruins. The Athenians have successfully carried out a bold and innovative battle plan, using the agility of their lighter ships, together with their deep knowledge of local geography and weather, to outmaneuver and ultimately defeat their far more powerful foe. Spurred by a deep sense of civic duty, the Athenians have fought together with especial valor, and their superior ingenuity, motivation, and commitment carry the day. Against all odds, a small community of 30,000 citizens defeats a colossal, monarchic military machine.

In the years following their great victory at Salamis, the Athenians were quick to exploit their advantage, steadily expanding their influence across the Aegean Sea. Skillfully combining diplomacy and military might, and resiliently rebounding from setbacks, they built the first great Greek empire. They not only kept the Persians at bay, but swept pirates from the sea, making the Aegean a safer place to trade. Commerce boomed, and many individuals prospered. Private and public wealth soared, as the city-state collected the modern-day equivalent of billions of dollars in taxes and tributes from a rapidly expanding group of subject states.

At the same time, Athens spawned a cultural florescence the likes of which the world had never seen. The atmosphere of the democratic city was open, experimental, and entrepreneurial. Philosophers, artists, scientists, and poets from across the Mediterranean world flocked to Athens's academies, workshops, and public squares. Not only was the great Parthenon built, but many other masterpieces of architecture and sculpture were created too. Moral philosophy came into being, the craft of history writing emerged, and drama became a great art form. Scientists developed new theories about everything from the atomic structure of matter to the relationship of the earth to heavenly bodies.

Underpinning all the achievements was a system of governance based on personal freedom, collective action, and an open, democratic culture. Athens was at heart a community of citizens—a "politeia," to use the Greek word—and each of those citizens had both the right and the obligation to play an active role in the society's governance. (Although the Athenian conception of democracy marked a historic leap forward in civic and political thinking, it is important to note that it did not extend to the enfranchisement of women or immigrants, much less the freeing of chattel slaves.) Our emaciated modern conception of democracy makes it difficult to understand the richness of the original Athenian concept. What we call "citizenship" today—an essentially passive legal status involving only minimal civic obligations and relying on a distant and entrenched governing elite—is but a shadow of the Athenian politeia.

The Architecture of Citizenship

What made the democracy of ancient Athens so successful, and why does it stand as a good model for businesses today? First, the system was not imposed on the Athenian people, but rather it grew organically from their own needs, beliefs, and actions—it was as much a spirit of governance as a set of rules or laws. Any managerial structure that is to have true meaning to knowledge workers must also emerge naturally from their own aspirations and initiatives. And second, the system was holistic—it was successful because it informed all aspects of the society, just as a productive corporate culture must inform all aspects of an organization and its management. The Athenian democracy encompassed *participatory structures* for making decisions, resolving disputes, and managing activities; a set of *communal values* that defined people's relationships with one another; and an array of *practices of engagement* that ensured the broad participation of the entire citizenry. By looking more carefully at this architecture of citizenship, we gain hints of what the business organization of the future might look like.

Participatory Structures. The Athenian system of governance had what might be called a radically flat organization—much flatter than even the leanest of corporate structures today. A set of clearly defined and universally understood processes and institutions—including councils, courts, assemblies, and executive offices—served to minimize hierarchy, inhibit the development of a ruling class, and engage citizens in governance and jurisprudence. In addition to taking part in local policy making, every adult male Athenian had the opportunity to attend the great citizen assembly, which met almost weekly to debate and vote on matters of importance, from financing the construction of a new road to fighting a war. The assembly was steered by a council of 500 citizens whose membership rotated annually. The councilors took turns setting the assembly's agenda and presiding over its deliberations.

To ensure that the decisions of the populace would be executed swiftly and well, the Athenian governance structure also included teams of "executives"—generals, administrators, managers—who were selected by election or lottery. Turnover in executive positions was systematic: At some point in their lives, most of Athens's 30,000 citizens had the opportunity to participate as a leader. Individual performance was carefully monitored, and outgoing executives were rewarded or punished accordingly—but only by their peers, the body of citizens themselves. The administration of justice was similarly open and participatory. Citizen arbitrators settled most conflicts, but when arbitration failed or the crime was particularly serious, juries representing the entire citizenry made the judgments and set the penalties.

Transparent procedural rules governed judicial and policy-making processes, keeping them simple, fair, and flexible. But the processes also allowed, even encouraged, passion and emotion. Many decisions made by the citizens were literally matters of life and death; no one was ejected from meetings for speaking loudly or heatedly—as long as the rights of others were respected. Expertise in technical matters was deeply valued, but the concept of professionalism played little part in the system. Amateur engagement was seen as preferable to professional management because it encouraged the constant sharing of fresh viewpoints and knowledge. It was expected that people with expertise in a particular area would come forward whenever their skills were needed, without becoming part of any standing bureaucracy. Laws and policies were stated in plain language; professional prosecutors and lawyers were unknown. Time limits on debate in courts and assemblies allowed each citizen to have his voice heard and prevented any bloc from dominating the proceedings. And voting on policy was open and mostly "by consensus," though secret ballots were employed for judicial decisions to ensure fairness.

> People with expertise came forward whenever their skills were needed, without becoming part of any standing bureaucracy.

In combination, these democratic structures ensured that no obstacles or barriers would arise to separate the Athenians from their government. More important, they reflected the people's deep trust in their own ability to chart the course of their state. Think how different such a notion is from the beliefs that underlie corporate management structures today. In most companies, major decisions continue to be made by small, insular elites behind the closed doors of executive offices and conference rooms. Tightly scripted planning, budgeting, and approval processes deter rather than encourage free thinking and honest debate. The entire shape of the modern company reflects a fundamental distrust of its members—a distrust that, as recent American business scandals have shown, can all too easily give rise to a malignant arrogance.

Communal Values. Establishing democratic structures is not enough, of course. People do not walk miles to attend meetings, forsake precious time to play temporary executive roles, or risk their lives in wars merely for the sake of "structures." For ancient Athenians, as for knowledge workers today, motivation came from a higher purpose—from a sense of shared ownership in their community's destiny. A distinctive set of values made the personal communal and the communal personal. In most companies today, by contrast, there is a tension between the employee's individual will and the will of the organization. Management is forever arbitrating the bounds between personal freedom and the corporate interest. In Athens, there was no such tension. The interest of the citizen was indistinguishable from the interest of the government.

The society placed the highest possible value on individuality, diligently protecting each person's right to self-determination, equality of opportunity, and security. Every citizen was free to— and encouraged to—express himself publicly, debate and dissent, and participate actively in all decisions that would materially affect him. But he was also free to pursue his private interests; he was not expected to engage constantly in public matters, but to contribute only when his skills and perspectives were needed. All citizens were given an equal chance to fulfill their personal potential while making their greatest possible contributions to the society. Finally, each citizen was secure, protected from the physical coercion and verbal abuse that would have made it impossible to enjoy either freedom or equality. As members of a community devoted to the common good, citizens were expected to band together not only to guarantee their collective security from external threats, but to guarantee the security of each individual from vicious behavior on the part of any aberrant internal member or group. The public welfare depended on the protection of each of the community's members.

A second set of Athenian values, balancing those that focused on individuality, centered on community, on the belief that the people *are* the state. So deeply held was this concept that it was embedded in the language: "Athens" was only the name of a place; the name of the community was "the Athenians." The physical manifestations of the city paled in importance to its people. The historian Thucydides memorably quotes an Athenian general's address to the citizenry on the eve of a great battle: "Not ships, not walls, but men make our city." How many knowledge workers today, hearing a similar pronouncement from their company's top management, would believe it? How many would automatically embrace the company's interest as their own?

Critical to the day-to-day integration of individual and community was a third set of values having to do with moral reciprocity. The sense of moral reciprocity provided the all-important link between "What's in it for me?" and "What's in it for us?" Its essence was the shared belief that engagement in the life of the community was educational in the broadest sense: It gave each individual the chance to become better, to grow wiser, and to fully develop his talents. As a citizen, you owed the community your best effort; the community, in return, owed you every opportunity to fulfill your potential. By providing unfettered opportunity to each of its members, the society understood that it would arrive at the best solutions to problems facing everyone.

On the surface, moral reciprocity may seem like an ancient version of what in business has come to be called "the employability contract": An employer promises to further the employee's professional development (and thus career prospects) in return for the employee's commitment to perform at the highest possible level throughout his or her tenure. There are, however, two significant differences between the modern concept of employability and the Athenian concept of moral reciprocity. First, employability does not foster long-term loyalty—indeed, it envisions each worker's likely departure. Employability is a short-term bargain that assumes a conflict between the interest of the community and that of its individual members. Athenian citizens, by contrast, could not ordinarily be "fired" from their organization, nor were they likely to leave it for any but the direst of reasons. Whether modern global business can (or should) ever return to a goal of long-term employment remains to be seen. But the contract between the individual and community will be richer and more productive for both if it has a meaningful chance of durability.

The second difference between employability contracts and moral reciprocity is less obvious but perhaps more important. Whereas moral reciprocity is integrally tied to a broader dependency between the individual and the community, employability is simply a quid pro quo understanding about working and learning on the job. Without the chance to meaningfully participate in steering one's own destiny, without the opportunity to gain the sincere respect of one's peers, without an honest stake in making the community more successful through one's own work and ideas, employability can quickly decay into generic training programs or bogus choices among short lists of uninspiring assignments. Narrowly construed employability contracts will motivate knowledge workers only so far.

How many knowledge workers today would automatically **embrace the company's interest as their own?**

Practices of Engagement. The structure and values of Athenian democracy outlined above provided the framework for citizenship. Ultimately, however, citizenship must be expressed in action—in day-to-day practices—or it will quickly degenerate into bureaucracy, routines, and self-interest. An organization's practices define its culture, how work gets done. To the Athenians, though, the practices of democracy were not just about "doing citizenship" but also about "learning citizenship." They continually refined their understanding of the workings of democracy through their actions and interactions in public squares, in leadership roles, and in jury trials.

The practices that animated the Athenian system can be broken out into subgroups, though it is essential to think about them in their totality—and as embedded in the structures and values to which they gave life.

Practices of access ensured that every citizen had free and equal opportunity to participate in self-governance. Athenians volunteered in both making and executing decisions, sharing their knowledge by participating in forums and initiatives at both the local and statewide level. The rotation of roles was crucial to the dynamism of governance, enabling all citizens to have opportunities to lead, to assume executive positions, and in general to take turns at ruling and being ruled.

Practices of process were essential in ensuring that deliberations, decision making, and execution were carried out in ways that were consistent, fair, and timely. Citizens sought consensus, making decisions and judgments based on trust among well-intentioned individuals (the polar opposite of today's partisan politics). All governmental and judicial processes were transparent, ensuring that every decision was based on information freely offered and supported by clearly expressed reasons. The populace also believed in making decisions swiftly; citizens maintained a sense of urgency in bringing debates to a conclusion. Finally, it was expected that all would support and, as necessary, assist in executing decisions, regardless of one's point of view prior to the final vote.

Practices of consequence ensured that citizens did not come to see process as an end in itself (a sure recipe for bureaucracy), but rather maintained a focus on achieving practical and concrete results. Fundamental to the society's emphasis on outcomes was the concept of merit; the people strove to ensure that every decision was based on the best argument, never on the position, privilege, or prejudice of those deciding. Another cherished concept was accountability—accepting personal responsibility for respecting the values of the citizen culture in all decision-making and executive settings, supporting those values in one's own conduct, and accepting peers' judgments about one's performance. Finally, the Athenians considered it an obligation to challenge the process—to seek to reverse misguided policies, appeal bad decisions, and call attention to, and act upon, misbehavior that threatened the community or any of its members.

Each of these three sets of practices was governed by an overarching group of *jurisdiction practices,* which ensured that every decision was made in the right place, by the right people, and at the right time. The community believed that decisions should be made by those with the greatest knowledge of the issues and the greatest stake in the consequences. This meant that technical decisions tended to be left to experts; decisions about battle strategy, for example, were reserved for generals. Decisions of great consequence, from levying taxes to declaring war, demanded full-scale debate by the society as a whole. Other, more mundane decisions—scheduling festivals or resolving disputes between neighbors, for example—were made locally. So precious was the possession of citizenship for Athenians that the entire citizen body had the jurisdiction to consider any proposal to confer citizenship upon a foreigner.

The culture of citizenship created by the Athenians—with its interplay of structures, values, and practices—encouraged every person to zealously pursue individual excellence and at the same time created, through shared processes of self-governance, an emotional commitment to efforts for the common good. This kind of "both/and" thinking has recently been promoted by Jim Collins and other management thinkers. It seeks to break the conflict between self-interest and corporate interest. Pericles, the Athenian statesman, expressed the essence of this attitude. Every citizen, he said, was "the rightful lord and owner of his own person," exhibiting "an exceptional grace and versatility." And, he went on, thanks to their politeia and their entire way of life, the citizens were collectively able to be a great and powerful community.

Indeed, this "school is the rest of Greece," as Pericles called his city, was the envy of and an object of fear to its enemies. One of Athens's rivals spoke in awe of how the motivation of its citizens yielded outstanding performance: "They regard their bodies as expendable for their city's sake, and each man cultivates his own intelligence, for doing something notable for the common cause… Of the Athenians alone it may be said, they begin to possess something almost as soon as they desire it, so quickly are they able to act upon something once they have made a decision…and when they are successful, they regard that success as nothing compared to what they will do next."

Looking Ahead

The Athenian model of organizational democracy is just that—a model. It does not provide a simple set of prescriptions for modern managers. It does, however, offer a window into how sizable groups of people can successfully govern themselves with dignity and trust and without resorting to a stifling bureaucracy. Most important, it shows the need to combine structures, values, and practices in a coherent, self-sustaining system.

Article 12. Beyond Empowerment: Building a Company of Citizens

Simply creating forums or processes for group decision making will not be enough—half-hearted measures will only amplify employee cynicism. Building and sustaining a company of citizens requires a genuine change in organizational and managerial culture.

Most of today's workers are familiar with the basic values and structures of democracy, and most have experience with some forms of communal action at work, whether it's serving on self-managed teams, reaching decisions through consensus building, or sharing leadership responsibilities. The idea of moving toward a more democratic structure should not, therefore, be a foreign one. Still, what we're talking about is a radical change in the corporate mind-set, and complications abound. Consider a few of the most obvious: Technological advances, demographic shifts, and the increasing globalization of markets have dispersed workforces, undermined traditional assumptions about job security and employee loyalty, and created far more open markets for labor. The very definition of an "employee" has grown fuzzy, as companies rely increasingly on freelancers, contractors, and temporary workers.

One of the first hurdles a company will need to clear is simply to define what constitutes a "citizen." What are the benefits, rights, and responsibilities that go along with formal citizenship in an organization? Should limited citizenship be available, with lesser rights and responsibilities? Should contractors and partners be given some form of citizenship? How should different levels of citizenship be managed? How should ownership rights and other rewards be distributed? These are hard questions, and every company will need to answer them in its own way, taking account of its size, circumstances, and goals.

One thing, however, is certain: The practice of citizenship cannot be imposed from above. It must grow out of the actions and beliefs of the citizens themselves. The transition to a more democratic business organization will thus take time, requiring many experiments and many successes and failures. While an organization's managers will necessarily play key roles in establishing basic goals and values—as a series of great leaders did for Athens—they must also have the courage to take their turn in being led, as the self-confidence of the citizenry grows. It is a process that must never cease: The experience of democracy must continually refine the practice of democracy.

Pericles told his fellow Athenians that "future ages will wonder at us, even as the present age wonders at us now." Over two thousand years later, his bold prediction rings true. But our attention to Athens should not be limited to wonder. It should encompass emulation as well.

Brook Manville *is the chief learning officer of Saba Software, a provider of software and services for human capital development and management based in Redwood Shores, California.* **Josiah Ober** *is the David Magie Professor of Classics and the acting director of the University Center for Human Values at Princeton University in New Jersey. They are the authors of* A Company of Citizens: What the World's First Democracy Teaches Leaders About Creating Great Organizations, *forthcoming from Harvard Business School Press.*

Reprinted with permission from *Harvard Business Review*, January 2003, pp. 48-53. © 2003 by the Harvard School Publishing Corporation. All rights reserved.

CREATING A learning organization

Creating a learning environment in the workplace is not only vital to keeping employees up to date on rapidly changing technology, but can also help to bring revenue to the company.

by Neal McChristy

JOE MILLER OWNS AN office supply store in a midsize town in the Midwest with a restaurant next door and a drugstore across the street. Joe is manager over a copier salesman, two clerks who handle requests for office supplies, and two technicians who work on the machines. When a customer comes in, Joe notices that he goes directly to Betty, one of his clerks, and starts asking her questions. In fact, at other times, Joe has noticed that when Georgette, his other clerk, is there alone, this customer will ask about when Betty will return so he can talk to her.

Joe notices that Betty listens with care to the customer and shows him two types of paper, he picks one and buys a box. This day, Joe asks the customer to come into his office saying, since he's a long-time customer, he'd like to ask him a few questions about customer service. The customer complies, and Joe asks him why he seems to prefer having Betty wait on him rather than Georgette, the newest employee of the two.

"She tells me everything I need about every product," the customer said. "I've asked her about paper, toner, pens—everything. She knows the latest about each product in the store—soup to nuts." Joe nodded.

"She just saved me money, too, by showing me a new type of paper that's processed chlorine free. Our company wants to try that to help the environment. She also knew where to find the partially recycled paper, and that's also something we're going towards. "She's the best salesman you have, Joe. She knows her stuff."

After the customer left, Joe brought Georgette into his office. "I'm going to see what I can do to help you learn about some of the supplies in this business. You're a good employee, but I think a little training will help you and the store even more."

It's likely that Georgette, in this fictional account, has already learned a lot in her years with the company by watching Betty and asking her questions, then doing it herself. This type of learning is one of the most effective learning tools available in the workplace.

Should Joe add a new employee, Georgette would likely find the new employee would bring new ideas and knowledge, maybe even challenging her own. And if Joe would face a complete shift in the office supplies or equipment he carries, his training process would need to be accelerated to accommodate a rapid, substantial change in how he does business. It's all part of learning in the workplace, and visible managers like Joe need knowledge to stay ahead of the competition.

In spite of the crucial role of training in an industry changing as much as office equipment, service, and supplies, an owner looking at cost reduction often considers training expendable, especially in these times of recession. But providing a learning environment adds real dollars to the company. "I believe if your people are learning something every day, most of it will translate into better service for clients and that translates into revenue growth real quickly," says Warren Whitlock, president of Landmark Printer Service, Rialto, California.

Learning is critical

Learning is "absolutely vital" in the process of having loyal employees who will stay with a company, according to Ronelle Ingram, director of technical service for FKM Copier Products, Irvine. Calif. So how do you keep employees as motivated at work on Monday morning as Friday afternoon? Or, put another way, "Are they as motivated about work as what they do on Saturday?" asks Tim Conlon, Rochester, N.Y., chief learning officer for Xerox Corp.

Regardless of whether you are a multinational corporation or a small startup, educating and training employees remain a key element of your business' health and future.

"Nothing kills a learning plan quicker than some boring lecturer droning on about things people already know," says Paul Schwartz, president of CopierCareers.com, Minneapolis, Minn., which specializes in working with technicians and employers for copier-industry placement. "Dry, factual, elementary material delivered by uninspired instructors can put your brightest stars in a coma. Spice it up and it will sink in," he advises.

Various studies done in workplaces have shown that:

- learning new skills are crucial to keep employees on the job—not for helping them go somewhere else. Employees will gauge a large amount of job satisfaction on the training opportunities in a job. "There's a tremendous employee value associated with learning," says Conlon.
- employees learn more easily by interacting with each other than in classroom-type teaching. Schwartz suggests employees read, study, and report on materials that are proven winners, such as gurus in the training world, before undertaking training. "This exercise 'limbers up' the employees' minds, preparing them to receive the training you are paying for, thus making it eventually more effective," Schwartz says.
- people learn by doing much more readily than through traditional training. "Instructor-based training—one of our traditional training methods—is not one of the best training modes," says Conlon.

Schwartz states that a learning plan must be tailored to the students. And, he says, ask which employees have "a fire in their belly to do the best by you, your customers, and their fellow employees. Those are the people who will benefit from the training you provide." You can't exactly discriminate against those who can't, or won't, learn and grow, but you don't have to throw good resources out the window, either.

"The bottom line is there are buffalo and there are steers," Schwarz says. "Buffalo roam the prairie, play in the snow, they have spirit and verve, and they thunder. Steers stand around munching and complaining."

Creating a future

Sometimes outcomes-based learning needs to be configured a different way in order to make it seem more attainable. Conlon uses the example of the person wanting to diet whose focus is on his or her weight. To turn this around, he says, the person could think about building a healthier lifestyle. Weight then becomes just one of the outcomes instead of the main drive for the diet. He calls this "creating a future instead of solving a problem."

Rapidly rising technology always creates a challenge that needs an immediate training solution. A majority of the office equipment and supplies training of late was first on the transition to digital sales and service and then the convergence of printers and copiers. "As many businesses look to transit from products to service to solutions," Conlon says, "this is where knowledge comes into play."

In the process of teaching people, Katherine Richard, regional director for the Kansas Small Business Development Center at Pittsburg State University, Pittsburg, Kan., says those training need to be aware that people have different traits and ways of learning; some learn by seeing, some by hearing, and some by doing. "Hands-on learning is really critical to making *what is learned* an everyday part of our mode of operation," she says.

It's a truism that if someone needs something bad enough to survive in the workplace, they'll do it. "Real learning occurs," Conlon states, "at the point of need in the work you do."

Schwartz says any educational endeavor should be field-tested and proven before being applied internally. "One must get employees to collaborate, endorse, and embrace," he says, "and there must be real-time evaluation of effectiveness while the teaching happens, plus long-term measurement of tangible results."

Some employers have resisted training because they're afraid their trained employees will then seek work elsewhere. But FKM's Ingram says they've retained most of their employees who have gained new certifications. FKM service technicians who succeed at acquiring Microsoft Certified Systems Engineer (MCSE) or A+ certification status receive not only recognition and their name on the wall, but also bonuses and raises. FKM requires a signed one-year noncompete agreement, Ingram says, and "it works out well for everybody." And she says the accomplishment and recognition from their peers has been a powerful positive force for those who complete it. Of the 23 technicians who have taken A+ certification, only one has left, Ingram says.

Employees who internalize effective practices in the workplace will lead the business to productivity and profit and gain personal satisfaction, Schwartz says. "They have to make it something that lives in their guts 24/7," he says. "Passion isn't conjured: it's electrified by a mystical combination of the individual's predisposition to excellence and the organization's genius in nurturing, inspiring, and challenging individuals to higher levels of performance."

Lessons from larger companies

For larger companies, one of the ideas floating around is that teams meet the needs of people in the organization. Ron Armstrong, Hardy, Va., of R.V. Armstrong and Associates, says the top executive must make the commitment to such an organizational structure. Learning provided by the organization helps the team members perform and achieve at the level sought by management, according to Armstrong, and there's an accompanying return on the training investment by increasing productivity, quality, and customer satisfaction.

"Execs have more time for making strategic decisions," Armstrong states, "managers make better decisions regarding their functional responsibilities, and supervisors don't carry the burden of accountability for large groups of people (teams carry the responsibility, authority, and accountability for their performance) —they become the resource persons and the coaches; staff employees' expertise is needed; *and* clerical, production, and service employees develop a sense of self-worth, ownership, and satisfaction in their work."

Peter Senge, author of *The Fifth Discipline: The Art and Practice of the Learning Organization*, was suggested as a resource by both Whitlock and Conlon.

Senge advocates a learning structure that differs from what he calls the current assembly-line model of schools and emphasizes an organic-like learning process that creates, acquires, and transfers knowledge, changing with the acquisition of new knowledge.

Conlon says Xerox has done work with Senge's model as well as the Center for Creative Leadership (CCL) model. (The CCL overview Web page states, "... we believe leadership development is the cornerstone of organizational effectiveness").

Much of the Xerox training has departed from classroom training toward e-learning, Conlon says, which gives everyone at Xerox access to training and feedback. In addition, mentors and chat rooms enhance the ability for employees to interact.

But Xerox's e-learning matrix doesn't have to be just for larger companies. An innovative manager or owner with a computer and access to the Internet has access to resources that can be used for learning, Conlon adds. "E-learning is available in a lot of different avenues out there."

Mom and pop need to stay current

Many of the old-timers who have owned stores in the copier and printer industry for 10–30 years are street savvy and don't necessarily have college training, Ingram says, and may not be as convinced of the value of teaching and training. "They've learned through the school of hard knocks," she says. But all that's changing as others join the office equipment area. Says Ingram, "The new generation is willing to learn, take the lead, and ask questions."

In the technical area such as Ingram's, the training is from within and uses a template. This is because of the task-oriented nature of office equipment service, she says. With competition for the customer as close as the nearest computer, Richard says there's a real need for mom-and-pop stores to stay current on what's going on in their industry and how to compete with it. A lot of this is customer service, she says—staying abreast of current technology and what products the customer wants. She adds, "And if you don't have it, they'll go somewhere else."

Training opportunities are readily available through classes offered by junior colleges or vo-tech schools and from places such as small-business development centers throughout the United States, Richard says. The centers can offer in-store seminars on improving customer service.

Learning and training doesn't have to be formal. "Brown bag" lunches and sharing ideas among employees, making sure everyone participates in some way, are easily done. And such get-togethers foster not only education, but also interaction, which it seems is a vital conduit to learning.

Whatever the setting, think of training that has inspired and motivated in order to keep the attention of your audience and then do likewise, say experts on training.

"Learning plans should be full of real-life stories, emotional word pictures, and compelling and inspiring examples of what real people accomplished when they applied time-tested principles and practices," Schwartz says.

Neal McChristy is a freelance writer from Pittsburg, Kan. He may be contacted by e-mail at freelance9@kscable.com.

The Change-Capable Organization

Part 3 of this series focuses on transforming your organization so that it embraces change as an ongoing way of life. Parts 1 and 2 appear in the November and December 2002 issues of T+D.

By Patricia A. McLagan

Change is a relatively recent management topic everywhere in the world. While it has always been an issue, it's now one of *the* issues. The number of books and articles on change management has increased more than 100 times since the 1960s. In addition, the costs of change failures are rising as organizations try (and fail) or make costly and repeated mistakes to implement complex and organization-wide initiatives such as reengineering, diversity awareness, globalization, quality and productivity programs, as well as complex alliances, mergers, and acquisitions. Many surveys put change management at the top of the list of executive concerns.

One way to deal with change is to notice when major changes are happening and to implement each change using methods such as those described in part 2 of this series. (**"Success With Change," November** *T+D*) A managing change approach is especially important when an organization isn't fundamentally designed for success with change—and most organizations aren't. A managing change approach is needed when, in order to implement change, you must override and supplement the normal processes of the business. But managing changes as they occur isn't enough these days. With the number and complexity of changes increasing, it's time to rethink how we design organizations. It's time to admit that change is a way of life and not an appendage to "business as usual." It's time to take a new view of how your organization works and must work every day so that it isn't constantly trying to override the usual organizational processes. That requires a structural and mental redesign of the organization—a transformational approach.

Transformation

The world's research is beginning to provide insights about the qualities of organizations that have an inbuilt capacity for change. Specifically, these organizations

- link present and future
- make learning a way of life
- actively support and encourage day-to-day improvements and changes
- ensure diverse teams
- encourage mavericks
- shelter breakthroughs
- integrate technology
- build and deepen trust.

How to implement those practices is just becoming clear. Creating a change-friendly organization is a new and still emerging pursuit. There are many experiments and some promising results, but there are as yet no robust models. We live in a time of transition, in which our concept of *organization* is being challenged and changed. One thing we can say with certainty is that what we mean by *organization* will be vastly different in the future. We can also say that the following practices are proving to create what Daryl Conner calls a "nimble" organization.

Link the present and the future. Research suggests that change occurs more fluidly when people bring the future into current work. That means that instead of—or in addition to—seeing work as an extension of the past, we need to think about the world, markets, competitors, and opportunities that may exist months and years hence, and factor them into today's decisions.

There are several ways to do that. Several studies suggest that when teams consist of some people who are present-oriented and others who are future-oriented, the teams perform better over time. One study of 108 executives in technology-based startups assessed whether each executive was more present- or future-oriented. Then they looked at communication among the executives. The findings were that significantly better performance occurred when a team contained both present- and future-oriented executives and when there was a lot of communication among the exec team.

Another way to link the present and future is to conduct low-cost experiments with new ideas in the current markets. One study of changes in eight computer companies in the United States, Europe, and Asia made this discovery: Successful projects often incorporate emerging ideas into present products, rather than just developing entirely new products.

For example, Swatch added communications capability to its watches, creating a pager watch, representing a futuristic yet anchored approach to innovation. The company has one eye on what it does well and one eye on the possibilities beyond current capabilities—with the intent to bring them together in the present. Part of the lesson from those and other studies is to be continually looking for new ideas that build on core competencies.

Make learning a way of life. Knowledge is becoming an increasingly more important source of competitive advantage. That includes knowledge about markets and the outside world, about what works and what to avoid doing, and about where to find expertise and information. Organizations that find, spread, and manage knowledge well can respond and innovate faster. They have less waste from people failing in the same way over and over. Recent research tells us that change-friendly organizations excel in knowledge movement and management. Another way to say that is they excel in learning.

Several important themes related to accelerating learning are emerging. One, it's important to expose frontline people to new ideas. Many—perhaps most—innovations and performance improvements happen in the course of daily work. Such improvements and innovations spread when frontline people talk to each other and to suppliers. But people at the top of the organization focused on the big picture often don't support worker communication with suppliers and across work groups. Worse, they may even discourage such contacts. One interesting study examined 73 technical innovations in a 38,000-person firm with 13 different locations. Only seven of the 73 innovations spread between units. The innovations that did spread did so primarily through direct contact between employees and suppliers. The conclusion: Make it easy for workers to talk with and learn from each other and from suppliers, or else develop more formal ways to keep frontline people aware of what's going on related to their work. Some ways to do that are field trips to suppliers and involving frontline people in purchasing decisions.

On a more formal level, accumulating evidence indicates that designing organizations to manage knowledge more systematically and effectively has high payoffs. One study of 158 global companies in North America, Europe, and Asia discovered such benefits as productivity improvements, faster speed to market, increased market share, improved sales volume, and cost reductions and avoidance.

Another study examined 24 companies to discover the keys to using knowledge in an organization successfully. Success occurred in these conditions:

- a knowledge-friendly culture
- a reward system for sharing knowledge
- multiple channels for knowledge transfer, especially encouragement of personal contact across work groups.

All of those are embedded conditions that go beyond any specific change project or program.

It's all about creating and supporting a learning and information-sharing orientation. A study of 268 Australian organizations found that customer retention, new product success, sales growth, and return-on-investment are significantly better in companies with a learning orientation. That is, such companies are better at creating, acquiring, and spreading knowledge and helping people bring that knowledge into action. That study also indicates that a learning orientation has a more positive impact on overall performance than just a market orientation, which focuses on needs that customers say they have. Market orientation is good for adaptive change but seems to prevent radical change: Customers usually want refinements but don't request products when they don't yet feel a need. Learning orientation appears to go beyond that, supporting the kind of creativity that anticipates and even creates new customer demands.

The behaviors of top management have a significant effect on an organization's learning. If the top team actively supports learning, learning orientation goes up significantly. If the team is risk-averse, learning orientation goes down.

Support and encourage day-to-day improvements and changes. Most management interest focuses on the big and planned changes driven by formal strategies or specific challenges. Though some change occurs within a framework of strategic priorities, most change happens almost imperceptibly on local and team levels. One typical study of changes in four industries (biochemical, animal feed, steel, electronics) found that 77 percent of changes at the work-group level were reactions to a specific, current problem or to a suggestion from someone outside of the team; 68 percent of those changes occurred in the course of day-to-day work. Those changes focused on work processes not directly related to work tasks, product and service changes, or changes in how group members work together.

The point is that change is occurring all of the time in organizations. Great organizations encourage—or at least don't inhibit—ongoing change at the individual, team, and inter-team levels. This topic deserves more study, but research-based insights do support that conclusion.

A massive review of the world's organization change literature concludes that in organizations constantly improving, change is "a way of life for the entire organization, not a one-time program." Collins reached the same conclusion after identifying the 11 companies (out of 1435) that achieved breakthrough performance that continued to exceed industry standards. In those few organizations, "relentless commitment" to excellence, rather than a grand program, was part of the success secret. A study of eight computer companies on three continents used the same word, *relentless,* saying that optimal innovation occurred when there was a "relentless pace of change," in which continuous innovation was punctuated by periodic formal innovation planning sessions.

It's clear that the most change-friendly organizations are developing and encouraging skills for ad hoc and emergent change actions—not only for formal and planned change.

Ensure diverse teams. Diversity is an antidote to business as usual. It seems to help stir the pot. And diversity at senior-management levels is especially important to having a nimble organization. When top management teams are diverse in time orientation (combing present and past); tenure; and experience, strategic change is more likely. A global, 14-year study of 67 semiconductor firms found that the most strategic change occurred when the top executive and his or her team had relatively short but different lengths of time on the job. Another comprehensive study based on a six-year review of the two largest companies in each of 16 industries found that more diverse top management teams implemented more complex changes, though the tendency was not to sustain them. The challenge is keeping all diversity headed in the same direction.

Diversity isn't only important at the top. Research has long shown that diversity within any team, though it increases the potential for conflict and sometimes makes it difficult to sustain new directions, leads to more innovative solutions.

Encourage mavericks. Mavericks frequently are essential champions of the new directions that create an organization's future. Mavericks take the risks and do the early experimentation that an organization won't easily fund. By definition, mavericks are not part of the mainstream. They stand for radical change, not evolutionary change. Their ideas and approaches aren't standard and, therefore, cause a lot of resistance and reaction. Evidence is growing that to have transformational capacity, an organization must encourage and be a home for mavericks.

Research is helping to clarify the qualities of disturbers of the status quo. In one study, executives in each of 24 companies of various sizes in the United States, the United Kingdom, and Canada describe the qualities of people who had led small but effective changes in their organizations. The executives said those change leaders were energetic, independent but committed to the organization, questioning of the system, impatient and not put off by resistance, and willing to go beyond the requirements of their jobs to make a difference. These mavericks usually didn't get formal support until they'd proven their ideas. They were driven by the needs of the organization, not by rewards or promotion.

Another report describes 300 people who had led successful customer-focus transformations. They had these qualities: enthusiasm and energy, knowledge of customer needs, communicativeness, and the ability to not only understand customer needs, but also to interpret them creatively.

A large international study of 4405 respondents from 43 companies in 68 countries sums up the maverick profile: "These change champions have the same profile as entrepreneurs."

Sadly, many mavericks who are inside organizations don't find ongoing support there, especially when their ideas challenge the status quo radically. They usually leave and start new businesses. An extensive global review of innovations in several industries found that although every breakthrough innovation in the computer industry from 1973 to 1995 was born in an established organization, none were developed and commercialized in those organizations. A quote from the findings: "Some changes that will make an organization viable are radical changes. When these present themselves, most leaders go where the customers, budget processes, and promotions systems drive them—to incremental and safe decisions." Under those conditions, mavericks leave.

Research is beginning to tell us that it is possible for mavericks to live and prosper in organizations. Creating an environment that doesn't evict them appears to be important to ongoing organizational transformation.

Shelter breakthroughs. When breakthroughs occur in an existing organization, they meet enormous resistance. The resistance forces are so powerful and integrated (the whole organization is often set up for the old ways) that the best course of action may be to create a new organization to

The World's Research

Here's a sampling of the studies and literature on which this article is based.

- *Good to Great: Why Some Companies Make the Leap… and Others Don't,* by Jim Collins (Harper, 2001)
- "Navigating the Competitive Landscape: The Drivers and Consequences of Competitive Aggressiveness," *Academy of Management Journal* (August 2001)
- *The Innovator's Dilemma,* by C. Christensen (Harper Business, 2000)
- "The Development of Product and Process Improvement in Work Groups," *Group and Organization Management* (September 2000)
- "Developing a Market-Oriented Learning Organization," *Australian Journal of Management* (September 2000)
- "Beyond Knowledge Management: New Ways to Work and Learn," *The Conference Board* (March 2000)
- *Research in Organizational Change and Development, vol. 12: An Annual Series Featuring Advances in Theory, Methodology, and Research,* Editors Passmore and Woodman (JAI Press, 1999)
- "Change and Complementarities in the New Competitive Landscape: A European Panel Study, 1992–1996." *Organization Science* (September/October 1999)
- "What's a Good Reason to Change? Motivated Reasoning and Social Accounts in Promoting Organizational Change," *Journal of Applied Psychology* (August 1999)
- *Leading at the Edge of Chaos: How to Create the Nimble Organization,* by D. Conner (John Wiley & Sons, 1998)
- *Enhancing Organizational Performance,* Editors Druckman, Singer, and Van Cott (National Academy Press, 1997)
- "The Corporate Entrepreneur: Leading Organizational Transformation," *Long-Range Planning* (June 1997)
- "Igniting Organizational Change From Below: The Power of Personal initiative," *Organizational Dynamics* (May 1997)
- "The Art of Continuous Change: Linking Complexity Theory and Time-Paced Evolution in Relentlessly Shifting Organizations," *Administrative Science Quarterly* (March 1997)
- "Strategic Change: The Influence of Managerial Characteristics and Organizational Growth," *Academy of Management Journal* (February 1997)
- "Temporal Dimensions of Opportunistic Change in Technology-Based Ventures," *Entrepreneurship Theory and Practice* (Winter 1997)
- "Success Stories in the Strategic Use of Telecommunications: Companies That Made It Work," *Telecommunication* (September 1996)
- "Are Champions Different From Non-Champions?" *Journal of Business Venturing* (September 1994)
- "The Diffusion of Innovation Within Multi-Unit Firms," *International Journal of Operations and Production Management* (October 5, 1990)

shelter and grow the change. Change-friendly organizations have institutionalized ways to provide such shelters.

Christensen's intense and thorough study of breakthrough innovations in the computer, retail, printer, and mechanical excavator industries makes this lesson clear: Successful changes are more frequent in organizations that routinely create small, independent units, in which breakthroughs have their own budgets, suppliers, markets, and cultures. These independent units also receive more resources for learning and trial-and-error. They tend to have different attitudes to the market, often leading the market rather than following its stated needs.

Companies known for their high rates of innovation and large proportion of new-to-old products have long had a policy of sheltering breakthrough ideas. 3M is a good example. It has a formal process for moving new ideas into a protected organization with a separate budget and where those ideas can grow.

Integrate technology. Technology isn't just nice to have; it's critical for creating transformational capacity. However, technology must be a means to an end, not an end in itself. The largest global and ongoing study of changes occurring in organizations throughout the world drew a surprising conclusion: Of all factors reviewed, only IT had a significant and positive relationship to performance. But that was true only when it was integrated with other changes related to creating a more network-like and less top-down organization. Another comprehensive study of companies that achieved and sustained breakthrough performance in their industries concludes that those companies don't use technology as a change driver. But they aren't technology-shy. They use technology to help implement their strategies and enhance their core competencies.

Build and deepen trust. Trust as a theme emerges throughout the change research. People are more likely to support changes when the general atmosphere in and around their organization is trusting and when formal leaders have personal credibility. One study found that nurses were more likely to believe a change was legitimate when they trusted management. If trust was low, they were more likely to resist and look for reasons what managers wanted wasn't right.

Trust is also key theme from a 1999 review of change research to discover barriers to change success. When the researchers asked what affected people's commitment to change, they found that the credibility and honesty of the change agent were critical. They also found that those trust-related qualities were built over time, making them bigger than any single change program or initiative. That partly explains why opinion leaders make such good change agents: They're people others trust.

Trust is a fragile condition in organizations, as in all relationships. A comprehensive report notes: "Many current change practices (such as downsizing) erode trust, making future change initiatives harder to implement." Because trust takes time to build, it must be developed on a day-to-day basis so that it becomes a ready foundation supporting ad hoc and planned changes as they arise.

What all this means

Change isn't just something to manage when strategies shift or crises occur. It's an ongoing challenge and condition in organizational life. Yet, most organizations are designed to support stability. We plan, organize, and control. We operate according to rigid organizational charts and old-style decision and innovation processes. Though we need some of that, most organizations overemphasize control, rules, decision and communication lines, and precedence. Increasingly, success depends on fluidity, openness, learning, and a pervasive capacity to make evolutionary and even radical changes.

In order to open up to change as a natural and ongoing aspect of our organizations, we have to adopt some new ways of thinking about life as well as organizations. Many actions managers and others take indicate that we think organizations are rational systems that we can plan and control from the top and break into functional units for ease of control. The model for that thinking comes from 17th-century science and mechanics, in which the machine is a key metaphor for an organization and a key challenge is how to make things work routinely and consistently. In that world order, change is something to be managed and minimized. The emphasis is on stopping undesirable changes, overcoming resistance, and ensuring that rationally developed strategies will be implemented with limited failure and error.

Now things are different. The mechanical, top-down view of organizations doesn't work well in our global and networked economy and world, except for simple and predictable problems. Research confirms that principles from life sciences are a better framework for thinking about organizations. Life sciences examine how living systems perform and change. Here are a few characteristics from biology and the life sciences that reflect and shed light on many of the research-based findings mentioned in this article.

- As an organism's environment becomes more complex and unpredictable, the organism must develop adaptive and transformative capabilities. The evolution of the brain is a prime example.

- The organism's own capabilities interact with the environment to produce a unique path of evolution. No change can happen that doesn't build on existing capacity.

- When stress and tension build to a breaking point, surprising and unpredictable new actions and directions often occur in nature (for example, feet on fish) that may lead to dramatically improved capabilities. Organisms must have an ability to create their own breakthroughs—and so must organizations. In organizations, people who don't feel they have to preserve the status quo often initiate breakthroughs. Sadly, many organizations aren't designed to embrace breakthroughs and mavericks, so those creativities leave and grow somewhere else.

- In complex, unpredictable environments, all parts of the organism are mobilized for action. That is, parts of any organism operate with a great deal of local authority and responsibility. In the human body, it's not just up to the brain (top management) to decide what to do. Without consulting the thinking part of the brain, the body reacts instantly to stress, temperature changes, air-quality changes, viruses, and so forth. That capacity to respond at all levels becomes more important as more forces challenge and stress the organism. In other words, thinking and acting have to be delegated to the body (people) for adaptive action. That means change is everybody's business and everyone needs the skills and mindset to play an active role.

Next month in the final article in this series, we'll look more closely at the idea that change is everybody's business. We'll stress that in change, there are and can be no bystanders. Leaders can't make changes alone. People throughout the organization are powerful even when they don't act or when they resist.

Editor's note: You can order Parts 1 and 2 of this article at *store.astd.org*

Patricia A. McLagan *is chairman of McLagan International and the author or co-author of many books and articles on management, change, and organization effectiveness, including the newly released* Change Is Everybody's Business. *She's also publisher of a series of research-to-practice reports,* theRITEstuff Reports, *and is co-host of an Internet radio show,* The Changing World of Work; *www.thechangingworldofwork.com.*

This article was based, in part, on her research reported in "Success With Change: Lessons From the World's Research." The full report is available for purchase at www.mclaganinternational.com.

Case: *Resistance to Change*

What This Incident Is About: Employees face the threat of the unknown when consultants arrive to study their performance. The incident involves the process of successful change: gaining acceptance, coordination, use of consultants, attitudes, and morale.

As office manager of the Duncan Paper Products Corporation, Robert Hale was responsible for the work of approximately 45 employees, of whom 26 were classified as either stenographers or file clerks. Acting under instructions from the company president, he agreed to allow a team of outside consultants to enter his realm of responsibility and make time and systems-analysis studies in an effort to improve the efficiency and output of his staff.

The consultants began by studying job descriptions, making observations, and recording each detail of the work of the stenographers and file clerks. After three days, they indicated to Hale and his employees that they were prepared to begin more detailed studies, observations, and interviews on the following day.

The next morning, five employees participating in the study were absent. On the following day, 10 employees were absent. Concerned, Hale investigated the cause of the absenteeism by telephoning several absentees. Each employee related approximately the same story. Each was nervous, tense, and tired after being viewed as a "guinea pig" for several days. One stenographer told Hale that her physician had advised her to ask for a leave of absence if working conditions were not improved.

Shortly after the telephone calls, the chief of the systems-analysis team explained to Hale that, if there were as many absences on the next day, his team would have to drop the study and proceed to another department. He said that a valid analysis would be impossible to conduct with 10 employees absent. Realizing that he would be held responsible for the failure of the systems analysis, Hale began to create and evaluate alternative actions that would provide the conditions necessary for the study. He was also concerned about implementing the procedural changes that he knew would be mandated after the study was completed. Hale was astute enough to realize that policies declared and orders issued are not always followed by instant compliance, even in the military, and that this wasn't a military situation.

Using the Case on *Resistance to Change*

This case is a classic example of how people will react to situations that are imposed upon them as opposed to situations in which they themselves have been active in producing. These employees are responding in this manner because they fear for their jobs and their well-being. They have no input into the decisions leading to the study, and they are refusing to cooperate with the company by simply not showing up for work. This passive/aggressive behavior is typical in this type of situation, although mass absenteeism is a very strong form of protest, just short of mass resignation.

Questions for Discussion

1. How do you think the company could have handled the situation so as to get greater cooperation?
2. What are some of the alternatives that Robert Hale could implement to get greater cooperation from the employees?
3. What do you think Robert Hale and the company should do?

Exercise: *Organizing*

The purpose of this exercise is to increase your awareness of the importance of structure in organization. In addition, the exercise focuses on the importance of management in organizing a venture.

The Problem

Select one of the following situations to organize. Then read the background material before answering the questions.

- The registration process at your university or college
- A new hamburger fast-food franchise
- A Jet-ski rental in an ocean resort area

Do steps 1–7, below, as homework. In preparing your answers, use your own experience or think up logical answers to the questions.

Background

Organization is a way of gaining some power against an unreliable environment. The environment provides the organization with input, which includes raw materials, human resources, and financial resources. There is a service or product to produce that involves technology. The output is to be sold to a client, a group that must be nurtured. The complexities of the environment and the technology determine the complexity of the organization.

Planning Your Organization

1. In a few sentences, write the mission or purpose of your organization.

Case: Resistance to Change; Exercise: Organizing

2. From the mission statement you should be able to write down specific things that must be done in order to accomplish the mission.
3. From the list of specifics that must be accomplished, an organizational chart can be devised. Each position on the chart will perform a specific task or is responsible for a specific outcome.
4. Add duties to each job position on your organizational chart. This will form a job description.
5. How would you ensure that the people you placed in these positions work together?
6. What degree of skill and abilities is required at each position and level in order to hire the right person for each position?
7. Make a list of the decisions that would have to be made while you planned and built the organization. Make a second list of those decisions you would have to make just after your organization began operating.

In Class

1. Form into groups of up to three members that organized the same project and share your answers to the questions.
2. Come to agreement on the way to organize, utilizing everyone's responses.
3. Present your group's approach to the class.

Case: Resistance to Change; Exercise: Organizing, Fred Maidment, McGraw-Hill/Dushkin, 2000.

UNIT 4
Directing

Unit Selections

15. **The Abilene Paradox: The Management of Agreement**, Jerry B. Harvey
16. **The Myth of Charismatic Leaders**, Joseph A. Raelin
17. **Effective Performance Counseling,** Leadership for the Front Lines
18. **The Myth of Synergy**, James Surowiecki
19. **When You Disagree With the Boss's Order, Do You Tell Your Staff?**, Carol Hymowitz
    CASE IV. Cub Scout Pack 81; Exercise: Listening

Key Points to Consider

- Why do you think people have trouble managing agreement? Are they just trying to get along? Explain.
- To be effective, a leader has to be able to achieve results and be accountable for those results. Do you see that happening in today's world? Defend your answer.
- How much incentive is there for cooperation between supervisors in different departments in your organization? Do people cooperate, or are they concerned with "turf"? Discuss.

 **Links: www.dushkin.com/online/**
These sites are annotated in the World Wide Web pages.

ADR (Alternative Dispute Resolution): General
http://www.opm.gov/er/adrguide/

Equity Compensation, Employee Ownership & Stock Options
http://www.fed.org

Office.com: The Intranet for Small Business
http://www.individual.com

Managers spend most of their time directing the organization. They have learned, however, that just telling people what to do is not good enough. To achieve the maximum possible results, people must first clearly understand the firm's goals, and then management must find a way to motivate them. Miscommunication and assumptions can often lead to poor choices and highly ineffective courses of action, as seen in the classic article by Jerry Harvey, "The Abilene Paradox: The Management of Agreement."

People enter business situations with a history of experiences, attitudes, and beliefs, and effectively communicating with them can be difficult. Open communication must be based upon trust. If there is fear, confusion, or lack of understanding, then communication will not be as effective as it could be. Managers must be able to communicate both in writing and orally. Effective communication involves the ability to design a letter, memo, or conversation so that both the sender and the receiver have a clear understanding of what was said and what is now expected of both parties. This frequently involves telling the receiver not only the message, but how the message was generated, because an employee's understanding of the reasons for an instruction can be the key to effective motivation. In today's environment, the problem is not a lack of ways to communicate but, rather, selecting the important information. This can even be applied in situations where the subordinate does not agree with the instructions of his or her superior as seen in "When You Disagree With the Boss's Order, Do You Tell Your Staff?"

Of all the various components of management, leadership is probably the most discussed, analyzed, and misunderstood. Indeed, some would argue that leadership and management are two separate and distinct activities. Leadership may be overdiscussed, but it is not well understood. Leaders come in all shapes and sizes and styles, but they need to be developed and they need to demonstrate leadership. There have been good leaders and evil leaders, saints and brutes, but they all share certain characteristics. One is the ability to communicate an idea to their

followers and have them accept it as their own. This results in motivation of the followers. The second characteristic is genuine caring, enthusiasm, and dedication to the dream. A manager who is successful in communicating with, motivating, and leading people will experience enhanced performance and productivity. The Japanese have led other nations in this area with the application of many techniques, such as quality circles. However, not all forms of worker participation have resulted in enhanced productivity.

There are those who would say that there is a leadership crisis facing industry as not enough qualified people are available for these kinds of positions. But, there are also those who would disagree with that assertion and say that not all types of leaders are right for all types of situations as seen, for instance, in "The Myth of Charismatic Leaders."

Effective managers are people who are able to direct an organization successfully. They know how to communicate, motivate, and lead, achieving enhanced productivity and performance that will accomplish the goals and mission of the organization in a fluid environment. These attributes are further discussed in "Effective Performance Counseling."

Article 15

The Abilene Paradox: The Management of Agreement

Jerry B. Harvey

JERRY B. HARVEY *is professor of management science at the George Washington University in Washington, D.C. He is a graduate of the University of Texas in Austin, where he earned an undergraduate degree in business administration and a Ph.D. in social psychology. A member of the International Consultant's Foundation, a Diplomate of the American Board of Professional Psychology, and a member of the O.D. Network, he has served as a consultant to a wide variety of industrial, governmental, religious, and voluntary organizations. He has written a number of articles in the fields of organizational behavior and education and currently is involved in the exploration of moral, ethical, and spiritual issues of work. In the pursuit of that interest, his book,* The Abilene Paradox and Other Meditations on Management, *was published by Lexington Books in 1988.*

The July afternoon in Coleman, Texas (population 5,607) was particularly hot—104 degrees as measured by the Walgreen's Rexall Ex-Lax temperature gauge. In addition, the wind was blowing fine-gained West Texas topsoil through the house. But the afternoon was still tolerable—even potentially enjoyable. There was a fan going on the back porch; there was cold lemonade; and finally, there was entertainment. Dominoes. Perfect for the conditions. The game required little more physical exertion than an occasional mumbled comment, "Shuffle 'em," and an unhurried movement of the arm to place the spots in the appropriate perspective on the table. All in all, it had the makings of an agreeable Sunday afternoon in Coleman—this is, it was until my father-in-law suddenly said, "Let's get in the car and go to Abilene and have dinner at the cafeteria."

I thought, "What, go to Abilene? Fifty-three miles? In this dust storm and heat? And in an unairconditioned 1958 Buick?"

But my wife chimed in with, "Sounds like a great idea. I'd like to go. How about you, Jerry?" Since my own preferences were obviously out of step with the rest I replied, "Sounds good to me," and added, "I just hope your mother wants to go."

"Of course I want to go," said my mother-in-law. "I haven't been to Abilene in a long time."

So into the car and off to Abilene we went. My predictions were fulfilled. The heat was brutal. We were coated with a fine layer of dust that was cemented with perspiration by the time we arrived. The food at the cafeteria provided first-rate testimonial material for antacid commercials.

Some four hours and 106 miles later we returned to Coleman, hot and exhausted. We sat in front of the fan for a long time in silence. Then, both to be sociable and to break the silence, I said, "It was a great trip, wasn't it?"

No one spoke. Finally my mother-in-law said, with some irritation, "Well, to tell the truth, I really didn't enjoy it much and would rather have stayed here. I just went along because the three of you were so enthusiastic about going. I wouldn't have gone if you all hadn't pressured me into it."

I couldn't believe it. "What do you mean 'you all'?" I said. "Don't put me in the 'you all' group. I was delighted to be doing what we were doing. I didn't want to go. I only went to satisfy the rest of you. You're the culprits."

My wife looked shocked. "Don't call me a culprit. You and Daddy and Mama were the ones who wanted to go. I just went along to be sociable and to keep you happy. I would have had to be crazy to want to go out in heat like that."

Her father entered the conversation abruptly. "Hell!" he said.

He proceeded to expand on what was already absolutely clear. "Listen, I never wanted to go to Abilene. I just thought you might be bored. You visit so seldom I wanted to be sure you enjoyed it. I would have preferred to play another game of dominoes and eat the leftovers in the icebox."

After the outburst of recrimination we all sat back in silence. Here we were, four reasonably sensible people who, of our own volition, had just taken a 106-mile trip across a godforsaken desert in a furnace-like temperature through a cloud-like dust storm to eat unpalatable food at a hole-in-the-wall cafeteria in Abilene, when none of us had really wanted to go. In fact, to be more accurate, we'd done just the opposite of what we wanted to do. The whole situation simply didn't make sense.

At least it didn't make sense at the time. But since that day in Coleman, I have observed, consulted with, and been a part of more than one organization that has been caught in the same situation. As a result, they have either taken a side-trip, or, occasionally, a terminal journey to Abilene, when Dallas or Houston or Tokyo was where they really wanted to go. And for most of those organizations, the negative consequences of such trips, measured in terms of both human misery and economic loss, have been much greater than for our little Abilene group.

This article is concerned with that paradox—the Abilene Paradox. Stated simply, it is as follows: Organizations frequently take actions in contradiction to what they really want to do and therefore defeat the very purposes they are trying to achieve. It also deals with a major corollary of the paradox, which is that *the inability to manage agreement is a major source of organization dysfunction*. Last, the article is designed to help members of organizations cope more effectively with the paradox's pernicious influence.

As a means of accomplishing the above, I shall: (1) describe the symptoms exhibited by organizations caught in the paradox; (2) describe, in summarized case-study examples, how they occur in a variety of organizations; (3) discuss the underlying causal dynamics; (4) indicate some of the implications of accepting this model for describing organizational behavior; (5) make recommendations for coping with the paradox; and, in conclusion, (6) relate the paradox to a broader existential issue.

SYMPTOMS OF THE PARADOX

The inability to manage agreement, not the inability to manage conflict, is the essential symptom that defines organizations caught in the web of the Abilene Paradox. That inability to manage agreement effectively is expressed by six specific subsymptoms, all of which were present in our family Abilene group.

1. Organization members agree privately, as individuals, as to the nature of the situation or problem facing the organization. For example, members of the Abilene group agreed that they were enjoying themselves sitting in front of the fan, sipping lemonade, and playing dominoes.

2. Organization members agree privately, as individuals, as to the steps that would be required to cope with the situation or problem they face. For members of the Abilene group "more of the same" was a solution that would have adequately satisfied their individual and collective desires.

3. Organization members fail to accurately communicate their desires and/or beliefs to one another. In fact, they do just the opposite and thereby lead one another into misperceiving the collective reality. Each member of the Abilene group, for example, communicated inaccurate data to other members of the organization. The data, in effect, said, "Yeah, it's a great idea. Let's go to Abilene," when in reality members of the organization individually and collectively preferred to stay in Coleman.

4. With such invalid and inaccurate information, organization members make collective decisions that lead them to take actions contrary to what they want to do, and thereby arrive at results that are counterproductive to the organization's intent and purposes. Thus, the Abilene group went to Abilene when it preferred to do something else.

5. As a result of taking actions that are counterproductive, organization members experience frustration, anger, irritation, and dissatisfaction with their organization. Consequently, they form subgroups with trusted acquaintances and blame other subgroups for the organization's dilemma. Frequently, they also blame authority figures and one another. Such phenomena were illustrated in the Abilene group by the "culprit" argument that occurred when we had returned to the comfort of the fan.

6. Finally, if organization members do not deal with the generic issue—the inability to manage agreement—the cycle repeats itself with greater intensity. The Abilene group, for a variety of reasons, the most important of which was that it became conscious of the process, did not reach that point.

To repeat, the Abilene Paradox reflects a failure to manage agreement. In fact, it is my contention that the inability to cope with (manage) agreement, rather than the inability to cope with (manage) conflict, is the single most pressing issue of modern organizations.

OTHER TRIPS TO ABILENE

The Abilene Paradox is no respecter of individuals, organizations, or institutions. Following are descriptions of two other trips to Abilene that illustrate both the pervasiveness of the paradox and its underlying dynamics.

> *Case No. 1: The Boardroom.* The Ozyx Corporation is a relatively small industrial company that has embarked on a trip to Abilene. The president of Ozyx has hired a consultant to help discover the reasons for the poor profit picture of the company in general and the low morale and productivity of the R&D division in particular. During the process of investigation, the consultant be-

comes interested in a research project in which the company has invested a sizable proportion of its R&D budget.

When asked about the project by the consultant in the privacy of their offices, the president, the vice-president for research, and the research manager each describes it as an idea that looked great on paper but will ultimately fail because of the unavailability of the technology required to make it work. Each of them also acknowledges that continued support of the project will create cash flow problems that will jeopardize the very existence of the total organization.

Furthermore, each individual indicates he has not told the others about his reservations. When asked why, the president says he can't reveal his "true" feelings because abandoning the project, which has been widely publicized, would make the company look bad in the press and, in addition, would probably cause his vice-president's ulcer to kick up or perhaps even cause him to quit, "because he has staked his professional reputation on the project's success."

Similarly, the vice-president for research says he can't let the president or the research manager know of his reservations because the president is so committed to it that "I would probably get fired for insubordination if I questioned the project."

Finally, the research manager says he can't let the president or vice-president know of his doubts about the project because of their extreme commitment to the project's success.

All indicate that, in meetings with one another, they try to maintain an optimistic facade so the others won't worry unduly about the project. The research director, in particular, admits to writing ambiguous progress reports so the president and the vice-president can "interpret them to suit themselves." In fact, he says he tends to slant them to the "positive" side, "given how committed the brass are."

The scent of the Abilene trail wafts from a paneled conference room where the project research budget is being considered for the following fiscal year. In the meeting itself, praises are heaped on the questionable project and a unanimous decision is made to continue it for yet another year. Symbolically, the organization has boarded a bus to Abilene.

In fact, although the real issue of agreement was confronted approximately eight months after the bus departed, it was nearly too late. The organization failed to meet a payroll and underwent a two-year period of personnel cutbacks, retrenchments, and austerity. Morale suffered, the most competent technical personnel resigned, and the organization's prestige in the industry declined.

Case No. 2: The Watergate. Apart from the grave question of who did what, Watergate presents America with the profound puzzle of why. What is it that led such a wide assortment of men, many of them high public officials, possibly including the President himself, either to instigate or to go along with and later try to hide a pattern of behavior that by now appears not only reprehensible, but stupid? (*The Washington Star* and *Daily News*, editorial, May 27, 1973.)

One possible answer to the editorial writer's question can be found by probing into the dynamics of the Abilene Paradox. I shall let the reader reach his own conclusions, though, on the basis of the following excerpts from testimony before the Senate investigating committee on "The Watergate Affair."

In one exchange, Senator Howard Baker asked Herbert Porter, then a member of the White House staff, why he (Porter) found himself "in charge of or deeply involved in a dirty tricks operation of the campaign." In response, Porter indicated that he had had qualms about what he was doing, but that he "... was not one to stand up in a meeting and say that this should be stopped.... I kind of drifted along."

And when asked by Baker why he had "drifted along," Porter replied, "In all honesty, because of the fear of the group pressure that would ensue, of not being a team player," and "... I felt a deep sense of loyalty to him [the President] or was appealed to on that basis." (*The Washington Post,* June 8, 1973, p. 20.)

Jeb Magruder gave a similar response to a question posed by committee counsel Dash. Specifically, when asked about his, Mr. Dean's, and Mr. Mitchell's reactions to Mr. Liddy's proposal, which included bugging the Watergate, Mr. Magruder replied, "I think all three of us were appalled. The scope and size of the project were something that at least in my mind were not envisioned. I do not think it was in Mr. Mitchell's mind or Mr. Dean's, although I can't comment on their states of mind at that time."

Mr. Mitchell, in an understated way, which was his way of dealing with difficult problems like this, indicated that this was not an "acceptable project." (*The Washington Post,* June 15, 1973, p. A14.)

Later in his testimony Mr. Magruder said, " .... I think I can honestly say that no one was particularly overwhelmed with the project. But I think we felt that this information could be useful, and Mr. Mitchell agreed to approve the project, and I then notified the parties of Mr. Mitchell's approval." (*The Washington Post,* June 15, 1973, p. A14.)

Although I obviously was not privy to the private conversations of the principal characters, the data seem to reflect the essential elements of the Abilene Paradox. First, they indicate agreement. Evidently, Mitchell, Porter, Dean, and Magruder agreed that the plan was inappropriate. ("I think I can honestly say that no one was particularly overwhelmed with the project.") Second, the data indicate that the principal figures then proceeded to implement the plan in contradiction to their shared agreement. Third, the data surrounding the case clearly indicate that the plan multiplied the organization's problems rather than solved them. And finally, the organization broke into subgroups with the various principals, such as the President, Mitchell, Porter, Dean, and Magruder, blaming one another for the dilemma in which they found themselves, and internecine warfare ensued.

In summary, it is possible that because of the inability of White House staff members to cope with the fact that they agreed, the organization took a trip to Abilene.

ANALYZING THE PARADOX

The Abilene Paradox can be stated succinctly as follows: Organizations frequently take actions in contradiction to the data they have for dealing with problems and, as a result, compound their problems rather than solve them. Like all paradoxes, the Abilene Paradox deals with absurdity. On the surface, it makes little sense for organizations, whether they are couples or companies, bureaucracies or governments, to take actions that are diametrically opposed to the data they possess for solving crucial organizational problems. Such actions are particularly absurd since they tend to compound the very problems they are designed to solve and thereby defeat the purposes the organization is trying to achieve. However, as Robert Rapaport and others have so cogently expressed it, paradoxes are generally paradoxes only because they are based on a logic or rationale different from what we understand or expect.

Discovering that different logic not only destroys the paradoxical quality but also offers alternative ways for coping with similar situations. Therefore, part of the dilemma facing an Abilene-bound organization may be the lack of a map—a theory or model—that provides rationality to the paradox. The purpose of the following discussion is to provide such a map.

The map will be developed by examining the underlying psychological themes of the profit-making organization and the bureaucracy and it will include the following landmarks: (1) Action Anxiety; (2) Negative Fantasies; (3) Real Risk; (4) Separation Anxiety; and (5) the Psychological Reversal of Risk and Certainty. I hope that the discussion of such landmarks will provide harried organization travelers with a new map that will assist them in arriving at where they really want to go and, in addition, will help them in assessing the risks that are an inevitable part of the journey.

ACTION ANXIETY

Action anxiety provides the first landmark for locating roadways that bypass Abilene. The concept of action anxiety says that the reasons organization members take actions in contradiction to their understanding of the organization's problems lies in the intense anxiety that is created as they think about acting in accordance with what they believe needs to be done. As a result, they opt to endure the professional and economic degradation of pursuing an unworkable research project or the consequences of participating in an illegal activity rather than act in a manner congruent with their beliefs. It is not that organization members do not know what needs to be done—they do know. For example, the various principals in the research organization cited *knew* they were working on a research project that had no real possibility of succeeding. And the central figures of the Watergate episode apparently *knew* that, for a variety of reasons, the plan to bug the Watergate did not make sense.

Such action anxiety experienced by the various protagonists may not make sense, but the dilemma is not a new one. In fact, it is very similar to the anxiety experienced by Hamlet, who expressed it most eloquently in the opening lines of his famous soliloquy:

> To be or not to be; that is the question:
> Whether 'tis nobler in the mind to suffer
> The slings and arrows of outrageous fortune
> Or to take arms against a sea of troubles
> And by opposing, end them?...
> (*Hamlet*, Act III, Scene II)

It is easy to translate Hamlet's anxious lament into that of the research manager of our R&D organization as he contemplates his report to the meeting of the budget committee. It might go something like this:

> To maintain my sense of integrity and self-worth or compromise it, that is the question. Whether 'tis nobler in the mind to suffer the ignominy that comes from managing a nonsensical research project, or the fear and anxiety that come from making a report the president and V.P. may not like to hear.

So, the anguish, procrastination, and counterproductive behavior of the research manager or members of the White House staff are not much different from those of Hamlet; all might ask with equal justification Hamlet's subsequent searching question of what it is that

> makes us rather bear those ills we have than
> fly to others we know not of.
> (*Hamlet*, Act III, Scene II)

In short, like the various Abilene protagonists, we are faced with a deeper question: Why does action anxiety occur?

Negative Fantasies

Part of the answer to that question may be found in the negative fantasies organization members have about acting in congruence with what they believe should be done. Hamlet experienced such fantasies.

Specifically, Hamlet's fantasies of the alternatives to the current evils were more evils, and he didn't entertain the possibility that any action he might take could lead to an improvement in the situation. Hamlet's was not an unusual case, though. In fact, the "Hamlet syndrome" clearly occurred in both organizations previously described. All of the organization protagonists had negative fantasies about what would happen if they acted in accordance with what they believed needed to be done.

The various managers in the R&D organization foresaw loss of face, prestige, position, and even health as the outcome of confronting the issues about which they believed, incorrectly, that they disagreed. Similarly, members of the White House staff feared being made scapegoats, branded as disloyal, or ostracized as non-team players if they acted in accordance with their understanding of reality.

To sum up, action anxiety is supported by the negative fantasies that organization members have about what will happen as a consequence of their acting in accordance with their understanding of what is sensible. The negative fantasies, in turn, serve an important function for the persons who have them. Specifically, they provide the individual with an excuse that releases him psychologically, both in his own eyes and frequently in the eyes of others, from the responsibility of having to act to solve organization problems.

It is not sufficient, though, to stop with the explanation of negative fantasies as the basis for the inability of organizations to cope with agreement. We must look deeper and ask still other questions: What is the source of the negative fantasies? Why do they occur?

Real Risk

Risk is a reality of life, a condition of existence. John Kennedy articulated it in another way when he said at a news conference, "Life is unfair." By that I believe he meant we do not know, nor can we predict or control with certainty, either the events that impinge upon us or the outcomes of actions we undertake in response to those events.

Consequently, in the business environment, the research manager might find that confronting the president and the vice-president with the fact that the project was a "turkey" might result in his being fired. And Mr. Porter's saying that an illegal plan of surveillance should not be carried out could have caused his ostracism as a non-team player. There are too many cases when confrontation of this sort has resulted in such consequences. The real question, though, is not, Are such fantasized consequences possible? but, Are such fantasized consequences likely?

Thus real risk is an existential condition, and all actions do have consequences that, to paraphrase Hamlet, may be worse than the evils of the present. As a result of their unwillingness to accept existential risk as one of life's givens, however, people may opt to take their organizations to Abilene rather than run the risk, no matter how small, of ending up somewhere worse.

Again, though, one must ask, What is the real risk that underlies the decision to opt for Abilene? What is at the core of the paradox?

Fear of Separation

One is tempted to say that the core of the paradox lies in the individual's fear of the unknown. Actually, we do not fear what is unknown, but we are afraid of things we do know about. What do we know about that frightens us into such apparently inexplicable organizational behavior?

Separation, alienation, and loneliness are things we do know about—and fear. Both research and experience indicate that ostracism is one of the most powerful punishments that can be devised. Solitary confinement does not draw its coercive strength from physical deprivation. The evidence is overwhelming that we have a fundamental need to be connected, engaged, and related and a reciprocal need not to be separated or alone. Everyone of us, though, has experienced aloneness. From the time the umbilical cord was cut, we have experienced the real anguish of separation—broken friendships, divorces, deaths, and exclusions. C. P. Snow vividly described the tragic interplay between loneliness and connection:

> Each of us is alone; sometimes we escape from our solitariness, through love and affection or perhaps creative moments, but these triumphs of life are pools of light we make for ourselves while the edge of the road is black. Each of us dies alone.

That fear of taking risks that may result in our separation from others is at the core of the paradox. It finds expression in ways of which we may be unaware, and it is ultimately the cause of the self-defeating, collective deception that leads to self-destructive decisions within organizations.

Concretely, such fear of separation leads research committees to fund projects that none of its members want and, perhaps, White House staff members to engage in illegal activities that they don't really support.

THE PSYCHOLOGICAL REVERSAL OF RISK AND CERTAINTY

One piece of the map is still missing. It relates to the peculiar reversal that occurs in our thought processes as we try to cope with the Abilene Paradox. For example, we frequently fail to take action in an organizational setting because we fear that the actions we take may result in our separation from others, or, in the language of Mr. Porter, we are afraid of being tabbed as "disloyal" or are afraid of being ostracized as "non-team players." But therein lies a paradox within a paradox, because our very unwillingness to take such risks virtually ensures the separation and aloneness we so fear. In effect, we reverse "real existential risk" and "fantasied risk" and by doing so transform what is a probability statement into what, for all practical purposes, becomes a certainty.

Take the R&D organization described earlier. When the project fails, some people will get fired, demoted, or sentenced to the purgatory of a make-work job in an out-of-the-way office. For those who remain, the atmosphere of blame, distrust, suspicion, and backbiting that accompanies such failure will serve only to further alienate and separate those who remain.

The Watergate situation is similar. The principals evidently feared being ostracized as disloyal non-team players. When the illegality of the act surfaced, however, it was nearly inevitable that blaming, self-protective actions, and scapegoating would result in the very emotional separation from both the President and one another that the principals feared. Thus, by reversing real and fantasied risk, they had taken effective action to ensure the outcome they least desired.

One final question remains: Why do we make this peculiar reversal? I support the general thesis of Alvin Toffler and Philip Slater, who contend that our cultural emphasis on technology, competition, individualism, temporariness, and mobility has resulted in a population that has frequently experienced the terror of loneliness and seldom the satisfaction of engagement. Consequently, though we have learned of the reality of separation, we have not had the opportunity to learn the reciprocal skills of connection, with the result that, like the ancient dinosaurs, we are breeding organizations with self-destructive decision-making proclivities.

A POSSIBLE ABILENE BYPASS

Existential risk is inherent in living, so it is impossible to provide a map that meets the no-risk criterion, but it may be possible to describe the route in terms that make the landmarks understandable and that will clarify the risks involved. In order to do that, however, some commonly used terms such as victim, victimizer, collusion, responsibility, conflict, conformity, courage, confrontation, reality, and knowledge have to be redefined. In addition, we need to explore the relevance of the redefined concepts for bypassing or getting out of Abilene.

- *Victim and victimizer.* Blaming and fault-finding behavior is one of the basic symptoms of organizations that have found their way to Abilene, and the target of blame generally doesn't include the one who criticizes. Stated in different terms, executives begin to assign one another to roles of victims and victimizers. Ironic as it may seem, however, this assignment of roles is both irrelevant and dysfunctional, because once a business or a government fails to manage its agreement and arrives in Abilene, all its members are victims. Thus, arguments and accusations that identify victims and victimizers at best become symptoms of the paradox, and, at worst, drain energy from the problem-solving efforts required to redirect the organization along the route it really wants to take.

- *Collusion.* A basic implication of the Abilene Paradox is that human problems of organization are reciprocal in nature. As Robert Tannenbaum has pointed out, you can't have an autocratic boss unless subordinates are willing to collude with his autocracy, and you can't have obsequious subordinates unless the boss is willing to collude with their obsequiousness.

Thus, in plain terms, each person in a self-defeating, Abilene-bound organization *colludes* with others, including peers, superiors, and subordinates, sometimes consciously and sometimes subconsciously, to create the dilemma in which the organization finds itself. To adopt a cliche of modern organization, "It takes a real team effort to go to Abilene." In that sense each person, in his own collusive manner, shares responsibility for the trip, so searching for a locus of blame outside oneself serves no useful purpose for either the organization or the individual. It neither helps the organization handle its dilemma of unrecognized agreement nor does it provide psychological relief for the individual, because focusing on conflict when agreement is the issue is devoid of reality. In fact, it does just the opposite, for it causes the organization to focus on managing conflict when it should be focusing on managing agreement.

- *Responsibility for problem-solving action.* A second question is, Who is responsible for getting us out of this place? To that question is frequently appended a third one, generally rhetorical in nature, with "should" overtones, such as, Isn't it the boss (or the ranking government official) who is responsible for doing something about the situation?

The answer to that question is no.

The key to understanding the functionality of the no answer is the knowledge that, when the dynamics of the paradox are in operation, the authority figure—and others—are in unknowing agreement with one another concerning the organization's problems and the steps necessary to solve them. Consequently, the power to destroy the paradox's pernicious influence comes from confronting and speaking to the underlying reality of the situation, and not from one's hierarchical position within the organization. Therefore, any organization member who chooses to risk confronting that reality possesses the necessary leverage to release the organization from the paradox's grip.

In one situation, it may be a research director's saying, "I don't think this project can succeed." In another, it may be Jeb Magruder's response to this question of Senator Baker:

> If you were concerned because the action was known to you to be illegal, because you thought it improper or unethical, you thought the prospects for success were very meager, and you doubted the reliability of Mr. Liddy, what on earth would it have taken to decide against the plan?

Magruder's reply was brief and to the point:

> Not very much, sir. I am sure that if I had fought vigorously against it, I think any of us could have had the plan cancelled. (*Time*, June 25, 1973, p. 12.)

• *Reality, knowledge, confrontation.* Accepting the paradox as a model describing certain kinds of organizational dilemmas also requires rethinking the nature of reality and knowledge, as they are generally described in organizations. In brief, the underlying dynamics of the paradox clearly indicate that organization members generally know more about issues confronting the organization than they don't know. The various principals attending the research budget meeting, for example, knew the research project was doomed to failure. And Jeb Magruder spoke as a true Abilener when he said, "We knew it was illegal, probably, inappropriate." (*The Washington Post*, June 15, 1973, p. A16.)

Given this concept of reality and its relationship to knowledge, confrontation becomes the process of facing issues squarely, openly, and directly in an effort to discover whether the nature of the underlying collective reality is agreement or conflict. Accepting such a definition of confrontation has an important implication for change agents interested in making organizations more effective. That is, organization change and effectiveness may be facilitated as much by confronting the organization with what it knows and agrees upon as by confronting it with what it doesn't know or disagrees about.

Real Conflict and Phony Conflict

Conflict is a part of any organization. Couples, R&D divisions, and White House staffs all engage in it. However, analysis of the Abilene paradox opens up the possibility of two kinds of conflict—real and phony. On the surface, they look alike. But, like headaches, they have different causes and therefore require different treatment.

Real conflict occurs when people have real differences ("My reading of the research printouts says that we can make the project profitable." "I come to the opposite conclusion.") ("I suggest we 'bug' the Watergate." "I'm not in favor of it.")

Phony conflict, on the other hand, occurs when people agree on the actions they want to take, and then do the opposite. The resulting anger, frustration, and blaming behavior generally termed "conflict" are not based on real differences. Rather, they stem from the protective reactions that occur when a decision that no one believed in or was committed to in the first place goes sour. In fact, as a paradox within a paradox, such conflict is symptomatic of agreement!

Group Tyranny and Conformity

Understanding the dynamics of the Abilene Paradox also requires a "reorientation" in thinking about concepts such as "group tyranny"—the loss of the individual's distinctiveness in a group, and the impact of conformity pressures on individual behavior in organizations. Group tyranny and its result, individual conformity, generally refer to the coercive effect of group pressures on individual behavior. Sometimes referred to as Groupthink, it has been damned as the cause for everything from the lack of creativity in organizations ("A camel is a horse designed by a committee") to antisocial behavior in juveniles ("My Johnny is a good boy. He was just pressured into shoplifting by the kids he runs around with").

However, analysis of the dynamics underlying the Abilene Paradox opens up the possibility that individuals frequently perceive and feel as if they are experiencing the coercive organization conformity pressures when, in actuality, they are responding to the dynamics of mismanaged agreement. Conceptualizing, experiencing, and responding to such experiences as reflecting the tyrannical pressures of a group again serves as an important psychological use for the individual: As was previously said, it releases him from the responsibility of taking action and thus becomes a defense against action. Thus, much behavior within an organization that heretofore has been conceptualized as reflecting the tyranny of conformity pressures is really an expression of collective anxiety and therefore must be reconceptualized as a defense against acting.

A well-known example of such faulty conceptualization comes to mind. It involves the heroic sheriff in the classic Western movies who stands alone in the jailhouse door and singlehandedly protects a suspected (and usually innocent) horse thief or murderer from the irrational, tyrannical forces of group behavior—that is, an armed lynch mob. Generally, as a part of the ritual, he threatens to blow off the head of anyone who takes a step toward the door. Few ever take the challenge, and the reason is not the sheriff's six-shooter. What good would one pistol be against an armed mob of several hundred people who *really* want to hang somebody? Thus, the gun in fact serves as a face-saving measure for people who don't wish to participate in a hanging anyway. ("We had to back off. The sheriff threatened to blow our heads off.")

The situation is one involving agreement management, for a careful investigator canvassing the crowd under conditions in which the anonymity of the interviewees' responses could be guaranteed would probably find: (1) that few of the individuals in the crowd really wanted to take part in the hanging; (2) that each person's participation came about because he perceived, falsely, that others wanted to do so; and (3) that each person was afraid that others in the crowd would ostracize or in some other way punish him if he did not go along.

DIAGNOSING THE PARADOX

Most individuals like quick solutions, "clean" solutions, "no risk" solutions to organization problems. Furthermore, they tend to prefer solutions based on mechanics and technology, rather than on attitudes of "being." Unfortunately, the underlying reality of the paradox makes it impossible to provide either no-risk solutions or action technologies divorced from existential attitudes and realities. I do, however, have two sets of suggestions for dealing with these situations. One set of suggestions relates to diagnosing the situation, the other to confronting it.

When faced with the possibility that the paradox is operating, one must first make a diagnosis of the situation, and the key to diagnosis is an answer to the question, Is the organization involved in a conflict-management or an agreement-management situation? As an organization member, I have found it relatively easy to make a preliminary diagnosis as to whether an organization is on the way to Abilene or is involved in legitimate, substantive conflict by responding to the Diagnostic Survey shown in the accompanying figure. If the answer to the first question is "not characteristic," the organization is probably not in Abilene or conflict. If the answer is "characteristic," the organization has a problem of either real or phony conflict, and the answers to the succeeding questions help to determine which it is.

In brief, for reasons that should be apparent from the theory discussed here, the more times "characteristic" is checked, the more likely the organization is on its way to Abilene. In practical terms, a process for managing agreement is called for. And finally, if the answer to the first question falls into the "characteristic" category and most of the other answers fall into the category "not characteristic," one may be relatively sure the organization is in a real conflict situation and some sort of conflict management intervention is in order.

COPING WITH THE PARADOX

Assuming a preliminary diagnosis leads one to believe he and/or his organization is on the way to Abilene, the individual may choose to actively confront the situation to determine directly whether the underlying reality is one of agreement or conflict. Although there are, perhaps, a number of ways to do it, I have found one way in particular to be effective—confrontation in a group setting. The basic approach involves gathering organization members who are key figures in the problem and its solution into a group setting. Working within the context of a group is important because the dynamics of the Abilene Paradox involve collusion among group members; therefore, to try to solve the dilemma by working with individuals and small subgroups would involve further collusion with the dynamics leading up to the paradox.

The first step in the meeting is for the individual who "calls" it (that is, the confronter) to own up to his position first and be open to the feedback he gets. The owning up process lets the others know that he is concerned lest the organization may be making a decision contrary to the desires of any of its members. A statement like this demonstrates the beginning of such an approach:

> I want to talk with you about the research project. Although I have previously said things to the contrary, I frankly don't think it will work, and I am very anxious about it. I suspect others may feel the same, but I don't know. Anyway, I am concerned that I may end up misleading you and that we may end up misleading one another, and if we aren't careful, we may continue to work on a problem that none of us wants and that might even bankrupt us. That's why I need to know where the rest of you stand. I would appreciate any of your thoughts about the project. Do you think it can succeed?

What kinds of results can one expect if he decides to undertake the process of confrontation? I have found that the results can be divided into *two* categories, at the technical level and at the level of existential experience. Of the two, I have found that for the person who undertakes to initiate the process of confrontation, the existential experience takes precedence in his ultimate evaluation of the outcome of the action he takes.

• *The technical level.* If one is correct in diagnosing the presence of the paradox, I have found the solution to the technical problem may be almost absurdly quick and simple, nearly on the order of this:

"Do you mean that you and I and the rest of us have been dragging along with a research project that none of

ORGANIZATION DIAGNOSTIC SURVEY

Instructions: For each of the following statements please indicate whether it is or is not characteristic of your organization.

1. There is conflict in the organization.
2. Organization members feel frustrated, impotent, and unhappy when trying to deal with it. Many are looking for ways to escape. They may avoid meetings at which the conflict is discussed, they may be looking for other jobs, or they may spend as much time away from the office as possible by taking unneeded trips or vacation or sick leave.
3. Organization members place much of the blame for the dilemma on the boss or other groups. In "back room" conversations among friends the boss is termed incompetent, ineffective, "out of touch," or a candidate for early retirement. To his face, nothing is said, or at best, only oblique references are made concerning his role in the organization's problems. If the boss isn't blamed, some other group, division, or unit is seen as the cause of the trouble: "We would do fine if it were not for the damn fools in Division X."
4. Small subgroups of trusted friends and associates meet informally over coffee, lunch, and so on to discuss organizational problems. There is a lot of agreement among the members of these subgroups as to the cause of the troubles and the solutions that would be effective in solving them. Such conversations are frequently punctuated with statements beginning with, "We should do…"
5. In meetings where those same people meet with members from other subgroups to discuss the problem they "soften their positions," state them in ambiguous language, or even reverse them to suit the apparent positions taken by others.
6. After such meetings, members complain to trusted associates that they really didn't say what they wanted to say, but also provide a list of convincing reasons why the comments, suggestions, and reactions they wanted to make would have been impossible. Trusted associates commiserate and say the same was true for them.
7. Attempts to solve the problem do not seem to work. In fact, such attempts seem to add to the problem or make it worse.
8. Outside the organization individuals seem to get along better, be happier, and operate more effectively than they do within it.

us has thought would work? It's crazy. I can't believe we would do it, but we did. Let's figure out how we can cancel it and get to doing something productive." In fact, the simplicity and quickness of the solution frequently don't seem possible to most of us, since we have been trained to believe that the solution to conflict requires a long, arduous process of debilitating problem solving.

Also, since existential risk is always present, it is possible that one's diagnosis is incorrect, and the process of confrontation lifts to the level of public examination real, substantive conflict, which may result in heated debate about technology, personalities, and/or administrative approaches. There is evidence that such debates, properly managed, can be the basis for creativity in organizational problem solving. There is also the possibility, however, that such debates cannot be managed, and substantiating the concept of existential risk, the person who initiates the risk may get fired or ostracized. But that again leads to the necessity of evaluating the results of such confrontation at the existential level.

• *Existential results.* Evaluating the outcome of confrontation from an existential framework is quite different from evaluating it from a set of technical criteria. How do I reach this conclusion? Simply from interviewing a variety of people who have chosen to confront the paradox and listening to their responses. In short, for them, psychological success and failure apparently are divorced from what is traditionally accepted in organizations as criteria for success and failure.

For instance, some examples of success are described when people are asked, "What happened when you confronted the issue?" They may answer this way:

> I was told we had enough boat rockers in the organization, and I got fired. It hurt at first, but in retrospect it was the greatest day of my life. I've got another job and I'm delighted. I'm a free man.

Another description of success might be this:

> I said I don't think the research project can succeed and the others looked shocked and quickly agreed. The upshot of the whole deal is that I got a promotion and am now known as a "rising star." It was the high point of my career.

Similarly, those who fail to confront the paradox describe failure in terms divorced from technical results. For example, one may report:

> I didn't say anything and we rocked along until the whole thing exploded and Joe got fired. There is still a lot of tension in the organization, and we are still in trouble, but I got a good performance review last time. I still feel lousy about the whole thing, though.

From a different viewpoint, an individual may describe his sense of failure in these words:

> I knew I should have said something and I didn't. When the project failed, I was a convenient whipping boy. I got demoted; I still have a job, but my future here is definitely limited. In a way I deserve what I got, but it doesn't make it any easier to accept because of that.

Most important, the act of confrontation apparently provides intrinsic psychological satisfaction, regardless of the technological outcomes for those who attempt it. The real meaning of that existential experience, and its relevance to a wide variety of organizations, may lie, therefore, not in the scientific analysis of decision making but in the plight of Sisyphus. That is something the reader will have to decide for himself.

THE ABILENE PARADOX AND THE MYTH OF SISYPHUS

In essence, this paper proposes that there is an underlying organizational reality that includes both agreement and disagreement, cooperation and conflict. However, the decision to confront the possibility of organization agreement is all too difficult and rare, and its opposite, the decision to accept the evils of the present, is all to common. Yet those two decisions may reflect the essence of both our human potential and our human imperfectability. Consequently, the choice to confront reality in the family, the church, the business, or the bureaucracy, though made only occasionally, may reflect those "peak experiences" that provide meaning to the valleys.

In many ways, they may reflect the experience of Sisyphus. As you may remember, Sisyphus was condemned by Pluto to a perpetuity of pushing a large stone to the top of a mountain, only to see it return to its original position when he released it. As Camus suggested in his revision of the myth, Sisyphus's task was absurd and totally devoid of meaning. For most of us, though, the lives we lead pushing papers or hubcaps are no less absurd, and in many ways we probably spend about as much time pushing rocks in our organizations as did Sisyphus.

Camus also points out, though, that on occasion as Sisyphus released his rock and watched it return to its resting place at the bottom of the hill, he was able to recognize the absurdity of his lot and, for brief periods of time, transcend it.

So it may be with confronting the Abilene Paradox. Confronting the absurd paradox of agreement may provide, through activity, what Sisyphus gained from his passive but conscious acceptance of his fate. Thus, through the process of active confrontation with reality, we may take respite from pushing our rocks on their endless journeys and, for brief moments, experience what C. P. Snow termed "the triumphs of life we make for ourselves" within those absurdities we call organizations.

SELECTED BIBLIOGRAPHY

Chris Argyris in *Intervention Theory and Method: A Behavioral Science View* (Addison-Wesley, 1970) gives an excellent description of the process of "owning up" and being "open," both of which are major skills required if one is to assist his organization in avoiding or leaving Abilene.

Albert Camus in *The Myth of Sisyphus and Other Essays* (Vintage Books, Random House, 1955) provides an existential viewpoint for coping with absurdity, of which the Abilene Paradox is a clear example.

Jerry B. Harvey and R. Albertson in "Neurotic Organizations: Symptoms, Causes and Treatment," Parts I and II, *Personnel Journal* (September and October 1971) provide a detailed example of a third-party intervention into an organization caught in a variety of agreement-management dilemmas.

Irving Janis in *Victims of Groupthink* (Houghton-Mifflin Co., 1972) offers an alternative viewpoint for understanding and dealing with many of the dilemmas described in "The Abilene Paradox." Specifically, many of the events that Janis describes as examples of conformity pressures (that is, group tyranny) I would conceptualize as mismanaged agreement.

In his *The Pursuit of Loneliness* (Beacon Press, 1970), Philip Slater contributes an in-depth description of the impact of the role of alienation, separation, and loneliness (a major contribution to the Abilene Paradox) in our culture.

Richard Walton in *Interpersonal Peacemaking: Confrontation and Third Party Consultation* (Addison-Wesley, 1969) describes a variety of approaches for dealing with conflict when it is real, rather than phony.

Article 16

The Myth of Charismatic Leaders

It can be foolish, futile, and even dangerous to follow leaders just because they're charismatic. Be careful of hero worship, and step forward.

By Joseph A. Raelin

Perhaps no subject has captivated the American business audience more than leadership. Within the practice of leadership, charisma is thought to be the quality that, though often considered metaphysical, represents the hallmark of inspirational leadership.

If leadership has something to do with inspiring a cadre of followers to do things in their own interest but also for the greater good, then we certainly need individuals who have a special talent to recruit others to work together towards a common cause.

Often, such individuals have heroic qualities because they're thought to persist in spite of the odds against them. They're also thought to possess particular heroic characteristics, such as courage and persistence, to face and prevail against those who would resist their noble efforts.

Many social critics have begun to challenge that heroic view of leadership. Should leadership rest upon the shoulders of one individual? We're beginning to see that many of the tasks that we need to perform in order to achieve our missions cannot be accomplished awaiting orders from just one person. All of us need to act and take a leadership role within our own domains.

Is it possible, then, that leadership may be as much a collective as an individual property? Do we need a savior to steer us out of trouble, or can we rely upon each other to find our way in the world?

If leadership is something other than being in charge of others—if it belongs not to the hero (without whom the followers will surely founder) but to the collective urged to face their own problems, then there may be a need to revise the ancient, obdurate concept of charisma.

The sway of charisma

Charisma comes from the Greek word meaning "gift," suggesting that leaders have special gifts to distribute. Their gifts aren't necessarily physical; they're more likely to be social. In fact, it's commonly thought that the pleasing personality of a charismatic person is his or her greatest gift. So, by definition, charismatics sway people and shape the future by their sheer presence and personality.

Charismatic leaders are thought to differ from mere mortal leaders by their ability to formulate and articulate an inspirational vision, as well as by actions that foster the impression that they *are* extraordinary people. Some observers go as far as to suggest that divine qualities exist in charismatic leaders—following Max Weber, who in *Economy and Society* asserted that these people are "set apart from ordinary [people] and treated as endowed with supernatural, superhuman, or at least exceptional powers and qualities... [that] are not accessible to the ordinary person but are regarded as divine or as exemplary."

Unfortunately, even if we were to decide on what are the ingredients of a charismatic personality, I doubt we would ever find that charismatics are persuasive in all environments and for all times. The post-war demise of Winston Churchill is a sufficient case. Except for exceptional circumstances when a community is in dire straits and genuinely asks for the direction of an outspoken member, there are severe problems in allowing a given individual—particularly a charismatic—to control a community.

As soon as one attempts to identify the particular characteristics that make up a charismatic personality, one begins to exclude a host of candidates for leadership. Here's how perennial CEO Lawrence Bossidy, formerly of Allied-Signal and Honeywell, unwittingly characterizes leaders in his chapter, "Reality-Based Leadership: Changes in the Workplace," in *The Book of Leadership Wisdom* (John Wiley & Sons, 1998):

> *You all know the maxim, "Leaders are born, not made." That's only half true. Some people are, indeed, born leaders, and you can spot them a mile away. The trouble is, there simply aren't enough of them to go around So, we need to find individuals with innate intelligence, an eagerness to learn, and a desire to work with others, and give them the tools and encouragement they need to become effective leaders, too. They may never run the company, but they can make enormous contributions to the success of your organization.*

Bossidy's comments show that he identified in advance the also-rans because of a notion of what it takes to be a leader.

Using the Freudian term *narcissist*, Michael Maccoby and Roy Lubit point out in separate articles (Maccoby: "Narcissistic Leaders," *Harvard Business Review*; Lubit: "The Long-Term Organizational Impact of Destructively Narcissistic Managers," *Academy of Management Executive*) that though charismatics can charm the masses with their rhetoric and can draw the big picture, they tend to be grandiose and distrustful. Narcissists tend to keep themselves emotionally distant from others and generally don't tolerate dissent. They're also poor listeners, show little empathy, can be brutally exploitative, seldom mentor, and aren't restrained by conscience. Their excessive promotion of self and lack of concern for others can become utterly destructive to their organizations because they're prone to make reckless business decisions, divert people's energies away from their real work, and ultimately drive away the community's most talented people.

In what strikes me as a stark contrast to democratic practice, followers working under narcissists are advised to find out what their bosses think before presenting their own views. That way, they can keep any dissent to a minimum. People are advised to generally let the narcissistic boss take credit for the followers' ideas and contributions.

In addition to claiming to have a unique vision and compelling language, a charismatic leader might also attempt to acquire the symbolic accouterments of the role of savior. Depending on the society in question, this might be represented by a certain look or stature, by particular vestments or possessions, or by a relationship or lineage to prior historical figures. It was reported that during the Taliban control of Afghanistan, the spiritual leader, Mullah Mohammad Omar, rose to power by acquiring the very cloak of the Prophet Mohammed, which had been folded and padlocked in a series of chests in a crypt in the royal mausoleum at Kandahar. Myth had it that the padlocks to the crypt could be opened only when touched by a true *amir-ul-momineen*, a king of the Muslims. After the collapse of the Taliban regime, the people of Afghanistan came to know of Omar's brutality and how he duped them into obedience through the Taliban's rigid interpretations of the Koran. In the words of a young Kandahari: "We trusted men we thought were holy and educated in the Koran, and because many of us did not know Arabic, we could not study the Koran carefully ourselves. When we saw Omar in the cloak, all of Afghanistan hoped that… the rains would begin. But, in truth, we did not know what he was saying. We only followed." (*Boston Globe*)

The charisma-followership connection

Charisma is increasingly being seen as a condition interconnected with followership. The qualities of charisma need to be appreciated by followers or by a following community. Often, a charismatic emerges within the community as it faces some level of psychic distress. Distress occurs when people are unable to understand the direction in which the surrounding environment might be changing, what the potential impact of those changes on the organization might be, and whether particular responses by management might or might not be successful. Further, people might perceive that any erroneous decision on the part of management could risk the survival of the organization. In that instance, people may look to a leader for psychological comfort in order to reduce their stress and anxiety. Such leaders might be able to turn the uncertainty of their followers into a vision of opportunity and success.

Yet, it's precisely at that point followers are particularly susceptible to charismatic salvation. They find themselves in a dependent state and look to their leaders to satisfy their needs. Charismatics are all too willing to comply by offering them hope, and usually, paternal direction. That's in contrast to leaders who might choose to work with their followers to face and manage their conflicts.

Some observers have suggested that in the presence of charismatics, followers can experience inspiration, empowerment, and even awe. Those states are created by specific acts undertaken by leaders—behaviors such as dramatizing a mission, assuring followers of their competency, projecting self-assurance, and enhancing their own image. Other accounts of charismatic leaders unabashedly assert that leaders need to engage in impression management, in image building, and in manipulation of meaning in order to bind "subordinates" closely to them and to their vision. It's no wonder, then, that charismatic leaders are granted enormous license to direct an organization—be that in a direction of pro- or anti-social practices.

There's always a chance that followers might learn to manage their affairs on their own, by which time they may no longer need the charismatic. Followers might even feel ashamed for having debased themselves. When that happens, they might develop resentment against the charismatic, especially if they discover that he or she has an underlying weakness—referred to as "feet of clay." That phenomenon is well captured in a story recounted by one of my former students:

> *I will tell a story about meeting a celebrity. This person was a very popular singer in a 1980s band. From age 12 to 18, I was obsessed with this individual. My friends weren't all that impressed with him, and I was made fun of quite a bit, but that didn't dissuade me. Well, the 1980s came and went, and I moved on. But just last year, I found out that a co-worker's husband is my teenage heartthrob's first cousin, and she gave me tickets to a concert with the band, on a comeback tour. I was thrilled; all of the excitement came back. I was, after all, on my way to meet the subject of my awe. I'm sure by now you realize where this is going. Meeting this person was a big disappointment. I went backstage and shook his hand and talked a bit. He was arrogant and conceited, and his behavior made me feel stupid for wanting to meet him. My awe was destroyed by the close encounter.*

Most charismatic leaders are capable of capitalizing on awe, offering their followers a set of idealized goals. The more idealized those goals are, the more likely it is the leaders will be credited with extraordinary vision. An idealized vision further serves to highlight the uniqueness of the charismatic leader, making him or her even more admirable and worthy of identification and imitation. Jay Conger, Rabindra Kanungo, and Sanjay T. Menon say in their article "Charismatic Leadership and Follower Effects" (*Journal of Organizational Behavior*) that it's "this idealized quality of the charismatic leader's goals—supported by appealing rhetoric—that distinguishes him or her from other leaders."

We might note that charismatics need not be narcissistic, egocentric, or hard-driving. More critical is that they're seen as saviors who, through their superb vision, can appeal to the masses and save the day. Indeed, Jim Collins, in his book *Good to Great*, depicts his "level-5 leaders" as humble and shy and as people committed to diverting credit to others. Yet, they're at the same time recognized as having individually turned companies around or having led them in a strategic direction that, though unpopular, resulted in success.

For example, in an article in the *Harvard Business Review*, Collins refers to Alan Wurtzel as a leader "responsible for turning Circuit City from a ramshackle company on the edge of bankruptcy into one of America's most successful electronics retailers." Collins cites Charles R. "Cork" Walgreen II as the iron-willed leader who transformed dowdy Walgreens by proclaiming to his executive staff, "OK, now I am going to draw the line in the sand. We are going to be out of the restaurant business completely in five years." Can you imagine the silence in the room? "Cork" may have had a quiet demeanor, but he was resolute. His followers knew that the leader, their charismatic leader, had spoken. Yet, did he truly act alone?

The contagion of charisma

Views that disentangle leadership from individual action don't coincide with the charismatic mindset because they don't credit control as emanating from a single individual. People don't require salvation from the top; salvation is produced by their own mutual hard work and compassion towards each other. One folds into one's own community. Although we may temporarily focus attention on a speaker, we simultaneously seek connections to ourselves and to others.

James Meindl, author of "On Leadership: An Alternative to the Conventional Wisdom" (*Research in Organizational Behavior*) and a professor of organization and human resources at the State University of New York at Buffalo, goes as far as to suggest that charisma is no more than a romantic notion that people conjure to uplift their spirits. Most of us tend to overemphasize a leader's prowess. As followers interact, they begin to define a social reality of leadership representing special mythical qualities endowed only by very special people. Although those qualities may not, in fact, exist, they're often ascribed to a leader by either an implicit or carefully conceived orchestration by particular members of the follower community. Called "carriers," those members essentially spread the news of the charismatic leader's mythical qualities throughout society. In that way, charisma becomes a contagion. What is spread, though, isn't necessarily real but rather reactions that represent no more than pre-existing shared profiles of what leaders are supposed to be like. And we know what the profile tends to be: the hero who can save us! Meindl suggests that followers are predisposed to look for a cause and a leader for whom they can become true believers.

I see charisma as not necessarily a set of personality or emotional characteristics that define the attributes of leadership. Charisma is more of a social process, often implicitly set up between follower and leader to keep the leader in power. Charismatics rely on that process to sustain their charismatic effect. They enjoy enhancing the romantic images of themselves.

But it's important to deconstruct the romantic view of leadership embedded in the idea of charisma, because its effect can deprive a community of its own power and utility and, left unexamined, can lead to demagogic behavior and deleterious effects on groups not affiliated with the leader. Moreover, the romantic view can lead to carrier abuse among followers, who can exalt a leader's image either without his or her knowledge or after the leader steps aside. In extreme cases, a leader's death may spur martyrdom, a hyper-romantic construct that can be used for practically any purpose. The ultimate end of charismatic practices of that ilk is disempowerment. People no longer control their own destiny, having handed it over to their saviors.

Back down to Earth

We need a leadership that subsists without charismatics, or heroes. It won't be easy. Though we advocate the value of participative leadership and other forms of organizational democratic practice, the drive to have a spiritual leader whom we can love and who can save us sneaks back into our consciousness just as we prepare to assert our own worth and independence. Part of the reason for that is that our culture still seems to value, even revere, individualism while preaching teamwork. Whatever the walk of life—be it a corporate setting, a professional sports team, or an opera—we tend to focus on the star performer, even when he or she may depend entirely on the team or group to achieve prominence.

Another possible explanation for hero worship is a fear of the future, in spite of our era's advances in science and technology. The tragic events of 9/11 heighten our fear. Under that cloud of uncertainty, many people look to heroes, or surrogate parent figures, who can bring us comfort and assurance, who can inspire us and explain the future.

Hero worship is outdated in our age. Indeed, it might have become outdated ever since the common man or woman was thought to be able to go out into the world and make decisions on his or her own. Relying on a single charismatic leader to part the seas for us works as long as the leader can successfully diagnose the environment and make correct decisions. But what happens when this same leader errs? What happens when his or her followers realize that they have the maturity to make their own decisions? What happens when the environment becomes so complex that no single individual could possibly discern all of its elements? What happens when a leader dies and no one is available to take his or her place?

We must graduate from our reliance on charismatics because, sooner or later, they will need us as collaborators in leadership. We no longer need dependent subordinates who are waiting to act on command. We want our colleagues to act on their own initiative, not as loose cannons but as a well-oiled community of members who trust and need their independence and interdependence. Naturally, these initiators will check back with their groups as appropriate. But if we insist that they wait for the proverbial go-ahead, they may lose their chance to act by the time permission is received.

We can no longer afford to be mechanistic in our view of the world. We can't rely on a coterie to await orders from the top, from detached bosses who have sole possession of problem fixes even across the remote corners of the organization. We need organizations that empower anyone who is capable and willing to assume leadership in the moment in his or her relationships with peers, team members, customers, suppliers, and other organizational partners.

Alas, we are in it together. The essence of leadership is collaboration and mutuality.

Joseph A. Raelin *is the Knowles Chair at Northeastern University in Boston, heading up the Center for the Study of Practice-Oriented Education; j.raelin@neu.edu. He's the author of* Creating Leaderful Organizations: How to Bring Out Leadership in Everyone *(Berrett-Koehler, February 2003).*

From *Training & Development*, March 2003, pp. 47-54. © 2003 by ASTD, Inc. Reprinted by permission.

Article 17

Effective Performance Counseling

Supervisor Cam Arnold turned the page of his monthly planner. *It's that time of the year again*, he thought. *Performance evaluations—not my favorite thing. I wish I felt more comfortable with the whole process. I wish I felt that I was doing something positive for my people. There has to be a better way…*

All supervisors and managers need to assess employees periodically in order to explain to them just how they're doing and what action is required for progress. Whether you do this at specified times under a formal evaluation system or on a continuing basis under a less formal system, you'll be more effective if you concentrate on…

The Things That Count

The key to fair appraisal and effective counseling is carefully choosing the factors that you take into consideration when evaluating employees. Some supervisors make the mistake of considering too many factors. For example, when the HR director in one workplace asked a group of supervisors what specific characteristics should be considered on a new evaluation form, she ended up with a total of 73 factors!

The key to fair appraisal and effective counseling is carefully choosing the factors that you take into consideration.

The HR director pointed out that even if there were enough time to rate employees on that many factors, the result would include a lot of unnecessary details. She suggested keeping on the list only those characteristics that could actually be observed in a worker's performance and were obviously important for effective work. The group distilled the list to six: dependability, quality, quantity, attitude, knowledge, and skills.

Remember Your Fellow Supervisors

When you evaluate your people, remember these two factors. Either of them could adversely affect an appraisal.

1. **Avoid being influenced by occurrences that are not typical** of employees or their work. Consider one factor at a time, and don't let your reaction to any one incident affect your ratings. Consider an employee's actions over the *entire* review period, not just his or her most recent ones.

2. **Always think of your fellow supervisors when you do your evaluating.** Nothing can upset morale more quickly than ratings that are either too liberal or too rigid in comparison with those of other departments.

Performance Counseling Success

Because a counseling interview is not part of the day-to-day work pattern, it takes on great importance in the minds of employees. You may be affected, too. Because you are in an unusual position, you may act and speak in a stilted manner, quite different from your normal conversational tone.

Paying attention to what employees are saying, in addition to listening to the words, is a must for effective counseling.

Here are some guidelines to help you make the chore of conducting counseling interviews easier for both you and your employees:

- **Keep the interview balanced.** A successful counseling interview remains faithful to the appraisal. Let's suppose you're talking to an employee who is rated above average in everything but job skills. He's competent enough in the work he does, but he has no interest in increasing his skills or learning different jobs.

The great temptation is to spend a minute or so commending him for his above-average rating in five categories and half an hour lecturing about the one where he's only average. While it isn't necessary to divide time equally between praise and criticism, overemphasis on the critical side produces resentment rather than the extra effort you are trying to bring forth.

- **Don't expect too much.** You can't expect to remake employees in one short counseling session. It's much more practical to set modest, attainable objectives. Asking employees to improve their performance in several areas simultaneously will only discourage them. Short-term goals that can be maintained after they've been achieved are more realistic.

- **Pay attention and listen.** Paying attention to what employees are saying, in addition to listening to the words, is a must for effective counseling. Unfortunately, it's not an easy thing to do. For one thing, while the other person is talking, you may be thinking about your own views on the subject; consequently, you'll respond to your own thoughts rather than to the thoughts being expressed.

Another reason listening is difficult is that you may have already decided what the other person is going to say. After all, you probably know the person well and have heard him or her talk about a lot of things. The result is that you hear only what you expect to hear.

The obvious result of not listening is that you don't understand what the employee is trying to tell you. You'll never be able to guide workers toward improving their performance or attitudes if you don't know what might motivate them to do it.

When workers know that they're being evaluated fairly and are being given an attainable target to shoot for, they'll change their performance to try to meet that standard.

From *Leadership for the Front Lines,* February 15, 2002, pp. 3-4. © 2002 by Aspen Publishers, Inc.

THE Myth OF Synergy

IT'S A SLIPPERY CONCEPT, SYNERGY. FEW REALLY UNDERSTAND IT. YET THE WORD IS THROWN AROUND TO JUSTIFY ALL BIG MERGERS TODAY. TOO BAD IT'S A BASELESS IDEA.

BY JAMES SUROWIECKI

Eight months ago, when Carly Fiorina unveiled Hewlett-Packard's proposed multi-billion-dollar acquisition of Compaq, she offered a dizzying array of reasons the deal made sense. The new company, she indicated, would be able to satisfy customers' demands for "solutions capability on a truly global basis." It would have product leadership "from top to bottom, from low end to high end." It would be able to compete in services and storage. Fiorina saved her most important point for last. The new company would flourish, she said, because it would enjoy—you guessed it—"synergies that are compelling."

Synergy: It is the business buzzword that will not die. For almost 40 years now, CEOs have been justifying high-priced acquisitions by trumpeting the benefits of synergy, and even though after 40 years those benefits remain remarkably elusive, the faith in synergy has not dimmed. In the 1960s, for instance, conglomerates such as LTV—which ran businesses in electronics, aerospace, steel, sporting goods, meatpacking, and pharmaceuticals—argued that by acquiring lots of different companies and then running them all out of one headquarters, they would be able to save on overhead and wring out inefficiencies. They weren't able to. In the late '70s and early '80s, synergy was called on to justify a host of mergers in banking and financial services. Customers, companies argued, wanted a financial supermarket that offered one-stop shopping. Checking, lending, insurance, real estate, stocks: They could all fit under the same umbrella. Sears took the idea to its logical extreme, trying to combine all those financial services with its traditional department-store business. Sears would be, the argument went, the everything store. Instead, customers shied from the idea of the financial supermarket—which has since returned at places like E*Trade and Citigroup—and Sears ended up treading water for more than a decade.

Today, synergy is used most often to justify media mergers. Synergy provided the impetus for Tina Brown's failed *Talk* magazine venture, which was co-owned by Miramax and Hearst. It was the reason behind the Viacom-CBS merger, and it helped explain the AOL–Time Warner deal too. Media moguls like nothing better than to envision all of their different properties cross-fertilizing each other: CNN.com, an AOL–Time Warner company, pushing Time Inc. magazines to its users, for example, or Simon & Schuster, a Viacom property, publishing books about MTV, also a Viacom property. Still, as the HP–Compaq deal (pending at press time) suggests, the media moguls don't have a monopoly on the idea. Just the other day I came across a press release from the Zamboni Company touting its "long history of synergy with the NHL."

MOST FIRMS JUMP IN AT THE DEEP END WITHOUT A LIFE JACKET.

So what, really, is synergy? In the crudest sense, a merger creates synergy if it allows you to add one and one and get three. In economic terms, the profits that the new company earns post-merger have to be bigger than the cumulative profits the two merged companies made pre-deal. For HP's acquisition of Compaq to make sense, the new HP will have to be better—more efficient, more profitable, more productive—on its own than HP and Compaq were apart.

Given how often CEOs promise billions of dollars in savings from synergy, you'd think that wouldn't be too hard to achieve. But in fact it's almost impossible. Synergy is, for the most part, a myth. The vast majority of companies that merge in order to reap the benefits of synergy fail. According to a study by Mark Sirower of the Boston Consulting Group, about two thirds of all acquisitions actually destroy value for the acquiring company. Another study found that three quarters of all acquisitions fail to live up to their financial and strategic objectives. Part of this, to be sure, is simply because companies hurry deals and don't do enough homework before shelling out their money. When NationsBank bought BankAmerica in 1998, for instance, NationsBank reportedly spent only a few days on due diligence. Indeed, Sirower says that 8 out of 10 companies that make deals do "little pre-acquisition planning." They just jump in at the deep end without a life jacket on.

The more serious problem, though, is that companies—and, for that matter, analysts and the press—have a misguided idea of what synergy means. My favorite example of this is the cable executive who, after the AOL–Time Warner deal, was reported to have said, "MovieFone is now part of AOL. So you can call MovieFone and book your seat for the latest Warner release." This is exactly the kind of cross-promotion and cross-selling that companies like AOL Time Warner call synergy. But it isn't synergistic at all.

Why not? Well, just slapping two companies together doesn't give you synergy. You only get it when putting two companies together allows them to make goods or sell services more efficiently—or to sell more of them—than they were able to before. In the case of MovieFone and Warner Bros., even before the AOL–Time Warner merger, you could call MovieFone and buy tickets to a Warner Bros. movie. MovieFone would take its cut, Warner Bros. would get your business, and everyone would be happy. The merger changed nothing about that. All the revenue and all the profits from your transaction may now go to one company instead of two, but the total revenue and the total profit are exactly the same. The synergy here is an illusion.

Similarly, take the case of *The Rugrats Movie*. Nickelodeon owned the TV show it was based on. Paramount produced the film. Viacom owned both. A classic case of synergy, right? Not really. If Paramount had been owned by a different company, Viacom could still have sold the rights to *Rugrats* to Paramount and made a certain amount of money, and Paramount would have made the movie and made a certain amount of money, and together the two companies would have made as much as Viacom did. Nor is Paramount, as some might think, going to work especially hard to market a movie just because Viacom owns it. Paramount wants every movie it releases to succeed, and putting special emphasis on one film over others would hurt the studio, not help it.

A similar dynamic helps explain why most high-profile mergers, including Daimler-Chrysler, Vivendi–Seagram–Canal Plus, even Disney–Capital Cities/ABC, don't create any real value. In all these cases, tremendous synergies were promised, but when you look at the numbers, the mergers seem to have accomplished very little. That doesn't mean the new companies are bad companies. It just means they are not good enough to justify all the money that was spent on the deals.

Think of it this way. When you buy a company, you generally pay a premium to its current stock price. Now, the stock price reflects all the profits investors think that company will produce in the foreseeable future. So if you're going to pay more than the going rate, you have to be able to increase those profits beyond investors' expectations. If you're Viacom, you can't just have CBS grow as fast as investors thought it was going to grow. You need it to grow faster (much faster, in fact, since you spent more than $39 billion to buy CBS).

That is a very hard thing to do. This is a ferociously competitive economy. There are not too many CEOs out there who aren't keeping costs down or trying to sell their products and services in as many ways as possible. That makes it difficult to buy a company and add value. Again, take Viacom and CBS. It's hard to believe that Mel Karmazin ran CBS worse when he was by himself than he does now that he has to deal with Sumner Redstone. And if you accept that, then it's hard to see what value Viacom has added to CBS. Viacom plus CBS is certainly one plus one. But it adds up to two, not three. Of course, if cross-selling and cross-promotion were really corporate panaceas, then the merger would have been a match made in heaven. But they're not.

Synergy isn't always an illusion. Companies in similar businesses can save money by combining operations when they merge, though the savings can easily be overestimated. There are cases where customers really do prefer one-stop shopping, and if a company is able to offer a full product line, then it has profit opportunities that otherwise wouldn't have existed. And, occasionally, companies have been better off doing things in-house instead of outsourcing them. One of the greatest examples of synergy in business history—though it's not usually called that—was General Motors' acquisition of Fisher Body in 1926. Fisher made the bodies for GM cars, but when GM's needs increased, management decided it made the most sense to acquire Fisher, thereby getting the best results for the lowest possible cost. By acquiring Fisher, GM was able to make its assembly lines run the way it wanted them to, enhancing productivity and saving all the time and energy that had been wasted on bargaining.

The truth, though, is that what made sense in 1926 makes less sense today. In fact, even as companies like AOL Time Warner and HP are arguing that mergers are the only way to real efficiency, other companies have demonstrated that well-organized networks and alliances allow you to reap the benefits of partnership without any of the hassle or expense of buying another company. Dell Computer, for instance, works very closely with its suppliers, who are integral to Dell's just-in-time system (Dell builds computers to order, so it keeps almost no inventory on hand, counting on its suppliers to deliver parts as soon as it needs them). But Dell does not own its suppliers and would probably be worse off if it did. And Microsoft makes operating systems for every PC maker on the planet. But it's never felt any need to buy a PC company.

Even so, most CEOs still prefer acquisitions despite their terrible track record, which raises the obvious question: Why does the dream of synergy remain so alluring? In part, it is synergy's very ephemerality that makes it attractive. As Thomas Wilson of PricewaterhouseCoopers put it, synergies are "easy to understand… but hard to forecast accurately." It's precisely because estimates of the value of real synergies are hard to calculate, though, that it's easy to make them excessively optimistic. Or as Warren Buffett famously said, "While deals often fail in practice, they never fail in projections."

There also appears to be something deeper at work, too, which researchers Mathew Hayward and Donald Hambrick call "CEO hubris." In their 1997 study Hayward and Hambrick researched 106 major acquisitions and found that companies that were run by high-profile, overly self-confident CEOs paid the heftiest premiums when they made acquisitions. Having read their own press clippings, these CEOs believed that they could see value where the market couldn't and that they could create synergies that no one else could. But they couldn't. On average, those companies lost money for their shareholders in the end. Anticipating imaginary synergies, they spent more than they should have and set up expectations they could not fulfill. And if CEO hubris is the disease, then the perpetual quest for synergy is its most important symptom.

From *MBS Jungle*, May 2002, pp. 58–61. © 2002 by Jungle Media Group, `mbajungle.com`.

Article 19

IN THE LEAD

When You Disagree With the Boss's Order, Do You Tell Your Staff?

By Carol Hymowitz

LAST WEEK I wrote about how managers who are excluded from decision making that affects their work can try to get included and make their views known to senior executives. But what should they do when their bosses insist that they implement decisions the managers disagree with?

Should they present a united front with senior executives and stay tight-lipped in front of subordinates in an effort to rally their staff's support? Or should they make their views known to those who report to them, while acknowledging that they have to go along with their boss's decision?

Traditionally managers have been expected to follow the former course. They have been told that they should serve as mouthpieces for their bosses and avoid voicing any dissent about a corporate decision they have been asked to implement. And they have been warned that following that approach may stir discontent and opposition among subordinates.

But a new breed of executives, many of whom have weathered mergers and other upheavals that have required them to carry out difficult directives, believe frankness is the best policy.

"No manager is ever going to agree with every decision senior management makes," says Douglas Emond, senior vice president and chief technology officer of Eastern Bank, Lynn, Mass. And employees can usually discern when their bosses disagree with their bosses, and they will respect managers more if the managers acknowledge their opinions while still motivating their staffs to implement the decision, Mr. Emond believes.

"The key is to know why senior management wants you to do what it asks, to understand its thought process, and to be able to convey that to subordinates," he adds.

MR. Emond has held management posts in the U.S. and overseas at a half dozen financial service and other companies. With each move, he has taken on new challenges and learned to trust his own thinking, he says. "As a manager, you're not paid to agree with everything your bosses decide, but to perform tasks."

Four years ago he was chief operating officer and chief technology officer at BankBoston when Fleet Financial acquired it. While many BankBoston senior executives quickly headed for the door, he stayed on and became a member of the merger integration team. His responsibility was to integrate eight businesses at the two companies, helping to decide strategy and a new management team while also cutting staff.

When he disagreed with a decision about which senior executive would oversee one particular business and what the business's future strategy would be, Mr. Emond decided that he wasn't going to hide his views. "I told them I was given orders, and this is the way it's going to go," he says. His frankness, he believes, "better prepared people to handle what was coming" and also won him the trust and support of his management staff, which was involved in the tough task of cutting about 50% of the staff.

Mr. Emond ties his willingness to be frank with employees to a leadership lesson he learned from his father, also a banker. When his father learned that a hard-working subordinate had lied on his job application about graduating from college, "instead of firing him, he took the employee aside and asked him, 'what is it going to take for you to get that degree,'" Mr. Emond says. "My father believed in doing the right thing, and he taught me that being a leader means being true to yourself and to your people."

LAURIE SPOON, vice president of corporate communications and investor relations at software-maker Selectica Inc. in San Jose, Calif., says that when she is handed a decision she doesn't agree with, she always asks the company's chief executive and chief financial officer, "what's the reason for this? Sometimes they tell me something I didn't know, so I can explain the issues behind the decision to my staff," she says.

She also asks her bosses for help when they ask her to implement a tough task. Recently, when she and her staff were asked to put together the company's annual report in 10 days, she told the CEO and chief financial officer that they would have to be available to help her plan content. "We sat together in a room and wrote the open letter to stakeholders, whereas if we had more time we would have gone back and forth with drafts," she says.

Meanwhile, a designer on her staff suggested that adding a pocket to the back of the report for business cards would allow it to be used by the company's sales team, serving two purposes. "I encourage my staff to make adjustments to decisions they're handed, in order to make them better," she says.

From the *Wall Street Journal*, Eastern Division, April 16, 2002, p. 61 by Carol Hymowitz. © 2002 by Dow Jones & Co. Inc. Reproduced with permission.

Case: *Cub Scout Pack 81*

Things certainly have changed over the past six years for Cub Scout Pack 81. Six years ago, the pack was on the verge of disbanding. There were barely enough boys for an effective den, and they had been losing membership for as long as anyone could remember. The cub master was trying to pass his job onto any parent foolish enough to take the helm of a sinking ship, and the volunteer fire department that sponsored the pack was openly considering dropping it.

But that was six years ago. Today the pack has one of the largest memberships of any in the Lancaster/Lebanon Council. It has started its own Boy Scout troop, into which the Webelos can graduate, and it has received a presidential citation for its antidrug program. The pack consistently wins competitions with other packs in the Council, and the fire department is very happy about its sponsorship. Membership in the pack is now around 60 cubs at all levels, and they have a new cub master.

"Parents want their boys to be in a successful program," says Cub Master Mike Murphy. "Look, I can't do everything. We depend on the parents and the boys to get things done. Everybody understands that we want to have a successful program, and that means that we all have to participate to achieve that success. I can't do it all, but if we can unleash the energy these boys have, there isn't anything in the Cub Scout Program we can't do!"

It was not always like that. "About five years ago we placed fourth for our booth in the Scout Expo at the mall," says Mike. "Everybody was surprised! Who was Pack 81? We were all elated! It was one of the best things to happen to this pack in years. Now, if we don't win at least something, we're disappointed. Our kids expect to win, and so do their parents."

Fourth place at the Scout Expo eventually led to several first places. Success leads to success, and the community around pack 81 knows it.

"Last year, we made our annual presentation to the boys and their parents at the elementary school. We were with several other packs, each one trying to drum up interest in their program. When everyone was finished, the boys and their parents went over to the table of the pack that most interested them. We must have had well over half of the people at our table. I was embarrassed! They were standing six or seven deep in front of our table, and there was virtually nobody in front of the others."

Using the Case on *Cub Scout Pack 81*

This case shows what can happen to any organization when the people in the organization are motivated and have goals. Success builds upon success, and pack 81 is now successful. The role of the leader is to ensure the success of the organization by creating an environment in which the participants (the Cubs and their families) can continue to be winners.

Questions for Discussion

1. What do you think was the major change in pack 81's situation?
2. How does the cub master "spread the wealth"? That is, the credit and the work associated with operating the pack?
3. How do you think the success of pack 81 has affected the other Cub Scout packs in the area? Why?
4. If you were a potential Cub Scout, or a parent of a potential Cub Scout, why would you be interested in pack 81?
5. Part of leadership has been defined as getting others to accept your goals as their own. Do you think that Cub Master Mike Murphy has been successful in doing that? Why or why not?

Exercise: *Listening*

Procedure

The instructor should:

1. Instruct the students to write down the numbers 1 through 10 on a sheet of paper.
2. Advise the student that the questions will be read to them twice, and their task is to record an answer to each question on the sheet of paper.
3. Emphasize to the students that they will not be allowed to ask for any clarification. Likewise, they may not discuss the question or answer with any other student.
4. Read each of the following questions (twice) aloud to the class.

Questions

1. Does England have a fourth of July?
2. Why can't a man living in Winston-Salem, North Carolina, be buried west of the Mississippi River?

Case: Cub Scout Pack 81; Exercise: Listening

3. If you had only one match and entered a room in which there was a kerosene lamp, an oil burner, and a woodburning stove, which would you light first?
4. Some months have 30 days, some have 31; how many have 28?
5. If a doctor gave you three pills and told you to take one every half hour, how long would they last?
6. I have in my hand three U.S. coins totalling 55 cents in value. One is not a nickel. What are the coins?
7. Is it legal in Louisiana for a man to marry his widow's sister?
8. How many two-cent stamps are there in a dozen?
9. How many animals of each species did Moses take aboard the Ark with him?
10. An archaeologist claimed to have discovered some gold coins dated 46 B.C. Do you believe that she did? Why, or why not?

Alternate Question A: An aircraft flying south crashes so that the wreckage is half in the United States and half in Mexico. In which country would you bury the survivors?

Alternate Question B: How many birthdates does the average woman have?

Alternate Question C: A farmer had seventeen sheep. All but nine died. How many did he have left?

Alternate Question D: How far can a dog run into the woods?

Questions for Discussion

1. Think about the barriers to effective communication. Which, if any, of these barriers affected the communication process in this exercise (perceptual differences, language and meaning, noise, etc.)?
2. How did the medium of communication affect the communication process? Do you think you could have done better if the questions had been presented in written form rather than vocal form?
3. What effect did the time constraint have on your interpretation of the message?

Answers:

1. Yes, it follows July 3rd; 2. The man is not dead so he cannot be buried; 3. Light the match first; 4. All months have 28 days; 5. One hour. Take one immediately, followed by a second a half-hour later, and the third one hour after the first; 6. Two quarters and a nickel (the question says one is not a nickel); 7. No, the man is dead; 8. Twelve; 9. None—Noah was aboard the Ark, not Moses; 10. No, since at the time the coin was made, there was no way for someone to know it was 46 years before Christ was born; Alternate Question A: You don't bury survivors; Alternate Question B: One birthdate; Alternate Question C: Nine; Alternate Question D: Half way (because then it is on the way out).

Case: Cub Scout Pack 81; Exercise: Listening, Fred Maidment, McGraw-Hill/Dushkin, 2000.

UNIT 5
Controlling

Unit Selections
20. **An Uneasy Look at Performance Appraisal**, Douglas McGregor
21. **The Cost of Failure**, Edward S. Robins
22. **How Safe Is Your Job? The Threat of Workplace Violence**, Laurence Miller
23. **Mail Preparation Total Quality Management**, Richard W. Pavely
    CASE V. Evaluation of Organizational Effectiveness; Exercise: Win as Much As You Can!

Key Points to Consider
- Control in any organization takes a variety of forms. Which one do you think is the most important for a profit-making organization? A not-for-profit organization?
- What impact do you think technology will have on the way that organizations control their operations in the future?
- How should organizations respond to violence in the workplace? What can be done to prevent it? What can be done once it has happened?

 **Links: www.dushkin.com/online/**
These sites are annotated in the World Wide Web pages.

Bill Lindsay's Home Page
http://www.nku.edu/~lindsay/

Computer and Network Security
http://www.vtcif.telstra.com.au/info/security.html

Internal Auditing World Wide Web
http://www.bitwise.net/iawww/

Office of Financial Management
http://www.doi.gov/

The Potential Downside of the National Information Infrastructure
http://www.annenberg.nwu.edu/pubs/downside/

Total Quality Leadership (TQL) vs. Management by Results
http://deming.eng.clemson.edu/pub/den/files/tql.txt

Workplace Violence
http://www.osha-slc.gov/SLTC/workplaceviolence/

Managers must plan, organize, and direct the organization, but how do they know if they are doing a good job? Controlling is the function of management that evaluates their efforts. Is the plan a good one? Is the firm adequately organized to implement the plan effectively? Is the plan being implemented so as to maximize the desired results? What changes need to be made in the plan, or the organization, or the implementation, or any combination thereof to help the firm better achieve its goals?

It is necessary to evaluate the firm's results against some sort of criteria. For most firms, those criteria are often financial, defined in terms of profits. However, it is necessary to define and understand control and to actively engage in procedures that will lead to effective management, as Douglas McGregor wrote in the classic article, "An Uneasy Look at Performance Appraisal."

Profitability is not the only measure of effectiveness. In fact, the entire not-for-profit sector of the economy refuses to use profitability as a measure of success. Measures come in other forms for not-for-profits as exemplified by the unqualified success of the March of Dimes in winning the battle against the deadly, crippling disease of polio. The March of Dimes was a success by any standard, but profitability would not be an appropriate criterion for it or other similar ventures. The key is whether the organization has achieved its goals, which may or may not include profitability.

When managers talk about control in the modern corporate sense, they really are talking about two different levels of control. The first is the traditional approach to controlling the firm's operation. This control is centered around the flow of information to determine what is going on in the organization as a whole. New technologies are making this easier. As for the second level of control, in this era of hostile takeovers, mergers, and acquisitions, managers are seeking to maintain control of their firms and not lose them to someone else in some new financial arrangement.

Management is discovering that decisions concerning the firm can no longer be made solely on the basis of a good financial return. Decision-makers must consider what is socially and politically acceptable to the stockholders. The decision of many firms to leave South Africa to protest apartheid was just one manifestation of the new awareness of nonfinancial goals and objectives. With the new government in place in South Africa, many firms have decided to return.

But financial control is important and "The Cost of Failure" is high. It is obviously a chief concern of all firms, especially small ones, because it is usually the area where they run into trouble. Financial control is the basis of all the other types of control in the organization, because the people who own it have the final say about what the firm does. Such control makes it possible for management to protect itself from corporate raiders as well as enabling managers to direct the organization successfully.

Security has also taken on new importance. With the advent of the computer and the World Wide Web, most information that was once the sole possession of the organization may now become public knowledge. "How Safe Is Your Job?" is a question of greater concern than it was in the past as firms need to know what they can do to prevent workplace violence. But traditional concerns of employee theft must also be addressed.

Production control is probably the area where the Japanese have made the biggest strides in recent years. U.S. and European firms have imported many of the ideas and techniques used in Japan over the past 20 years, including Total Quality Management (TQM), which is now being applied to many areas including "Mail Preparation" by the U.S. Postal Service. The Japanese themselves have set up their own plants in the United States, demonstrating that their techniques are transferable. Many changes have taken place in the area of production, including the introduction of computers and robots. Developments do not just involve machines; they include standards, policies, and, most especially, people. As organizations strive to become more effective and efficient, it will become necessary to redesign the processes that a company uses.

The control of cost vs. quality and customer service is now the hottest area in the business world. Supply chain management is bringing all the pieces together, from raw material to the final customer in the most efficient and economical manner, and customer service grows even more important as an aspect of every organization's efforts.

Article 20

Are managers more responsive to human values than personnel people? If so, we had better join them in taking...

An Uneasy Look at Performance Appraisal

By Douglas McGregor

Performance appraisal within management ranks has become standard practice in many companies during the past twenty years, and is currently being adopted by many others, often as an important feature of management development programs. The more the method is used, the more uneasy I grow over the unstated assumptions which lie behind it. Moreover, with some searching, I find that a number of people both in education and in industry share my misgivings. This article, therefore, has two purposes:

- To examine the conventional performance appraisal plan which requires the manager to pass judgment on the personal worth of subordinates.
- To describe an alternative which places on the subordinate the primary responsibility for establishing performance goals and appraising progress toward them.

Current Programs

Formal performance appraisal plans are designed to meet three needs, one for the organization and two for the individual:

1. They provide systematic judgments to back up salary increases, promotions, transfers, and sometimes demotions or terminations.
2. They are a means of telling a subordinate how he is doing, and suggesting needed changes in his behavior, attitudes, skills, or job knowledge; they let him know "where he stands" with the boss.
3. They also are being increasingly used as a basis for the coaching and counseling of the individual by the superior.

Problem of Resistance

Personnel administrators are aware that appraisal programs tend to run into resistance from the managers who are expected to administer them. Even managers who admit the necessity of such programs frequently balk at the process—especially the interview part. As a result, some companies do not communicate appraisal results to the individual, despite the general conviction that the subordinate has a right to know his superior's opinion so he can correct his weaknesses.

The boss's resistance is usually attributed to the following causes:

- A normal dislike of criticizing a subordinate (and perhaps having to argue about it).
- Lack of skill needed to handle the interviews.
- Dislike of a new procedure with its accompanying changes in ways of operating.
- Mistrust of the validity of the appraisal instrument.

To meet this problem, formal controls—scheduling, reminders, and so on—are often instituted. It is common experience that without them fewer than half the appraisal interviews are actually held. But even controls do not necessarily work. Thus:

> In one company with a well-planned and carefully administered appraisal program, an opinion poll included two questions regarding appraisals. More than 90% of those answering the questionnaire approved the idea of appraisals. They wanted to know how they stood. Some 40% went on to say that they had never had the experience of being told—yet the files showed that over four-fifths of them had signed a form testify-

ing that they had been through an appraisal interview, some of them several times!

The respondents had no reason to lie, nor was there the slightest supposition that their superiors had committed forgery. The probable explanation is that the superiors, being basically resistant to the plan, had conducted the interviews in such a perfunctory manner that many subordinates did not recognize what was going on.

Training programs designed to teach the skills of appraising and interviewing do help, but they seldom eliminate managerial resistance entirely. The difficulties connected with "negative appraisals" remain a source of genuine concern. There is always some discomfort involved in telling a subordinate he is not doing well. The individual who is "coasting" during the few years prior to retirement after servicing his company competently for many years presents a special dilemma to the boss who is preparing to interview him.

Nor does a shift to a form of group appraisal solve the problem. Though the group method tends to have greater validity and, properly administered, can equalize varying standards of judgment, it does not ease the difficulty inherent in the interview. In fact, the superior's discomfort is often intensified when he must base his interview on the results of a *group* discussion of the subordinate's worth. Even if the final judgments have been his, he is not free to discuss the things said by others which may have influenced him.

The Underlying Cause

What should we think about a method—however valuable for meeting organizational needs—which produces such results in a wide range of companies with a variety of appraisal plans? The problem is one that cannot be dismissed lightly.

Perhaps this intuitive managerial reaction to conventional performance appraisal plans shows a deep but unrecognized wisdom. In my view, it does not reflect anything so simple as resistance to change, or dislike for personnel technique, or lack of skill, or mistrust for rating scales. Rather, managers seem to be expressing very real misgivings, which they find difficult to put into words. This could be the underlying cause:

> The conventional approach, unless handled with consummate skill and delicacy, constitutes something dangerously close to a violation of the integrity of the personality. Managers are uncomfortable when they are put in the position of "playing God." The respect we hold for the inherent value of the individual leaves us distressed when we must take responsibility for judging the personal worth of a fellow man. Yet the conventional approach to performance appraisal forces us, not only to make such judgments and to see them acted upon, but also to communicate them to those we have judged. Small wonder we resist!

The modern emphasis upon the manager as a leader who strives to *help* his subordinates achieve both their own and the company's objectives is hardly consistent with the judicial role demanded by most appraisal plans. If the manager must put on his judicial hat occasionally, he does it reluctantly and with understandable qualms. Under such conditions it is unlikely that the subordinate will be any happier with the results than will the boss. It will not be surprising, either, if he fails to recognize that he has been told where he stands.

Of course, managers cannot escape making judgments about subordinates. Without such evaluations, salary and promotion policies cannot be administered sensibly. But are subordinates like products on an assembly line, to be accepted or rejected as a result of an inspection process? The inspection process may be made more objective or more accurate through research on the appraisal instrument, through training of the "inspectors," or through introducing group appraisal; the subordinate may be "reworked" by coaching or counseling before the final decision to accept or reject him; but as far as the assumptions of the conventional appraisal process are concerned, we still have what is practically identical with a program for product inspection.

On this interpretation, then, resistance to conventional appraisal programs is eminently sound. It reflect an unwillingness to treat human beings like physical objects. The needs of the organization are obviously important, but when they come into conflict with our convictions about the worth and the dignity of the human personality, one or the other must give.

Indeed, by the fact of their resistance managers are saying that the organization must yield in the face of this fundamental human value. And they are thus being more sensitive than are personnel administrators and social scientists whose business it is to be concerned with the human problems of industry!

A New Approach

If this analysis is correct, the task before us is clear. We must find a new plan—not a compromise to hide the dilemma, but a bold move to resolve the issue.

A number of writers are beginning to approach the whole subject of management from the point of view of basic social values. Peter Drucker's concept of "management by objectives"[1] offers an unusually promising framework within which we can seek a solution. Several companies, notably General Mills, Incorporated, and General Electric Company, have been exploring different methods of appraisal which rest upon assumptions consistent with Drucker's philosophy.

Responsibility on Subordinate

This approach calls on the subordinate to establish short-term performance goals for *himself*. The superior enters the process actively only *after* the subordinate has (a) done a good deal of thinking about his job, (b) made a careful assessment of his own strengths and weaknesses, and (c) formulated some specific plans to accomplish his goals. The superior's role is to help the man relate his self-appraisal, his "targets," and his plans for the ensuing period to the realities of the organization.

The first step in this process is to arrive at a clear statement of the major features of the job. Rather than a formal job description, this is a document drawn up *by the subordinate* after studying the company-approved statement. It defines the broad areas of his responsibility as they actually work out in practice. The boss and employee discuss the draft jointly and modify it as may be necessary until both of them agree that it is adequate.

Working from this statement of responsibilities, the subordinate then establishes his goals on "targets" for a period of, say, six months. These targets are *specific* actions which the man proposes to take, i.e., setting up regular staff meetings to improve communication, reorganizing the office, completing or undertaking a certain study. Thus, they are explicitly stated and accompanied by a detailed account of the actions he proposes to take to reach them. This document is, in turn, discussed with the superior and modified until both are satisfied with it.

At the conclusion of the six-month period, the subordinate makes *his own* appraisal of what he has accomplished relative to the targets he had set earlier. He substantiates it with factual data wherever possible. The "interview" is an examination by superior and subordinate together of the subordinate's self-appraisal, and it culminates in a resetting of targets for the next six months.

Of course, the superior has veto power at each step of this process; in an organizational hierarchy anything else would be unacceptable. However, in practice he rarely needs to exercise it. Most subordinates tend to underestimate both their potentialities and their achievements. Moreover, subordinates normally have an understandable wish to satisfy their boss, and are quite willing to adjust their targets or appraisals if the superior feels they are unrealistic. Actually, a much more common problem is to resist the subordinates' tendency to want the boss to tell them what to write down.

Analysis vs. Appraisal

This approach to performance appraisal differs profoundly from the conventional one, for it shifts the emphasis from *appraisal* to *analysis*. This implies a more positive approach. No longer is the subordinate being examined by the superior so that his weaknesses may be determined; rather, he is examining himself, in order to define not only his weaknesses but also his strengths and potentials. The importance of this shift of emphasis should not be underestimated. It is basic to each of the specific differences which distinguish this approach from the conventional one.

The first of these differences arises from the subordinate's new role in the process. He becomes an active agent, not a passive "object." He is no longer a pawn in a chess game called management development.

Effective development of managers does not include coercing them (no matter how benevolently) into acceptance of the goals of the enterprise, nor does it mean manipulating their behavior to suit organizational needs. Rather, it calls for creating a relationship within which a man can take responsibility for developing his own potentialities, plan for himself, and learn from putting his plans into action. In the process he can gain a genuine sense of satisfaction, for he is utilizing his own capabilities to achieve simultaneously both his objectives and those of the organization. Unless this is the nature of the relationship, "development" becomes a euphemism.

Who Knows Best?

One of the main differences of this approach is that it rests on the assumption that the individual knows—or can learn—more than anyone else about his own capabilities, needs, strengths and weaknesses, and goals. In the end, only he can determine what is best for his development. The conventional approach, on the other hand, makes the assumption that the superior can know enough about the subordinate to decide what is best for him.

No available methods can provide the superior with the knowledge he needs to make such decisions. Ratings, aptitude and personality tests, and the superior's necessarily limited knowledge of the man's performance yield at best an imperfect picture. Even the most extensive psychological counseling (assuming the superior possess the competence for it) would not solve the problem because the product of counseling is self-insight on the part of the *counselee*.

(Psychological tests are not being condemned by this statement. On the contrary, they have genuine value in competent hands. Their use by professionals as part of the process of screening applicants for employment does not raise the same questions as their use to "diagnose" the personal worth of accepted members of a management team. Even in the latter instance the problem we are discussing would not arise if test results and interpretations were given *to the individual himself*, to be shared with superiors at his discretion.)

The proper role for the superior, then, is the one that falls naturally to him under the suggested plan: helping the subordinate relate his career planning to the needs and realities of the organization. In the discussions the boss can use his knowledge of the organization to help the subordinate establish targets and methods for achieving them which will (a) lead to increased knowledge and skill, (b) contribute to organizational objectives, and (c) test the subordinate's appraisal of himself.

This is help which the subordinate wants. He knows well that the rewards and satisfactions he seeks from his career as a manager depend on his contribution to organizational objectives. He is also aware that the superior knows more completely than he what is required for success in this organization and *under this boss*. The superior, then, is the person who can help him test the soundness of his goals and his plans for achieving them. Quite clearly the knowledge and active participation of *both* superior and subordinate are necessary components of this approach.

If the superior accepts this role, he need not become a judge of the subordinate's personal worth. He is not telling, deciding, criticizing, or praising—not "playing God." He finds himself listening, using his own knowledge of the organization as a basis for advising, guiding, encouraging his subordinates to develop their own potentialities. Incidentally, this often leads the superior to important insights about himself and his impact on others.

Looking to the Future

Another significant difference is that the emphasis is on the future rather than the past. The purpose of the plan is to establish realistic targets and to seek the most effective ways of reaching them. Appraisal thus becomes a means to a *constructive* end. The 60-year-old "coaster" can be encouraged to set performance goals for himself and to make a fair appraisal of his progress toward them. Even the subordinate who has failed can be helped to consider what moves will be best for himself. The superior rarely finds himself facing the uncomfortable prospect of denying a subordinate's personal worth. A transfer or even a demotion can be worked out without the connotation of a "sentence by the judge."

Performance vs. Personality

Finally, the accent is on *performance*, on actions relative to goals. There is less tendency for the personality of the subordinate to become an issue. The superior, instead of finding himself in the position of a psychologist or a therapist, can become a coach helping the subordinate to reach his own decisions on the specific steps that will enable him to reach his targets. Such counseling as may be required demands no deep analysis of the personal motivations or basic adjustment of the subordinate. To illustrate:

Consider a subordinate who is hostile, short-tempered, uncooperative, insecure. The superior need not make any psychological diagnosis. The "target setting" approach naturally directs the subordinate's attention to ways and means of obtaining better interdepartmental collaboration, reducing complaints, winning the confidence of the men under him. Rather than facing the troublesome prospect of forcing his own psychological diagnosis on the subordinate, the superior can, for example, help the individual plan ways of getting "feedback" concerning his impact on his associates and subordinates as a basis for self-appraisal and self-improvement.

There is little chance that a man who is involved in a process like this will be in the dark about where he stands, or that he will forget he is the principal participant in his own development and responsible for it.

A New Attitude

As a consequence of these differences we may expect the growth of a different attitude toward appraisal on the part of superior and subordinate alike.

The superior will gain real satisfaction as he learns to help his subordinates integrate their personal goals with the needs of the organization so that both are served. Once the subordinate has worked out a mutually satisfactory plan of action, the superior can delegate to him the responsibility for putting it into effect. He will see himself in a consistent managerial role rather than being forced to adopt the basically incompatible role of either the judge or the psychologist.

Unless there is a basic personal antagonism between the two men (in which case the relationship should be terminated), the superior can conduct these interviews so that both are actively involved in seeking the right basis for constructive action. The organization, the boss, and the subordinate all stand to gain. Under such circumstances the opportunities for learning and for genuine development of both parties are maximal.

The particular mechanics are of secondary importance. The needs of the organization in the administration of salary and promotion policies can easily be met within the framework of the analysis process. The machinery of the program can be adjusted to the situation. No universal list of rating categories is required. The complications of subjective or prejudiced judgment, of varying standards, of attempts to quantify qualitative data, all can be minimized. In fact, *no* formal machinery is required.

Problems of Judgment

I have deliberately slighted the many problems of judgment involved in administering promotions and salaries. These are by no means minor, and this approach will not automatically solve them. However, I believe that if we are prepared to recognize the fundamental problem inherent in the conventional approach, ways can be found to temper our present administrative methods.

And if this approach is accepted, the traditional ingenuity of management will lead to the invention of a variety of methods for its implementation. The mechanics of some conventional plans can be adjusted to be consistent with this point of view. Obviously, a program utilizing ratings of the personal characteristics of subordinates would not be suitable, but one which emphasizes *behavior* might be.

Of course, managerial skill is required. No method will eliminate that. This method can fail as readily as any other in the clumsy hands of insensitive or indifferent or power-seeking managers. But even the limited experience of a few companies with this approach indicates that managerial *resistance* is substantially reduced. As a consequence, it is easier to gain the collaboration of managers in developing the necessary skills.

Cost in Time

There is one unavoidable cost: the manager must spend considerably more time in implementing a program of this kind. It is not unusual to take a couple of days to work through the initial establishment of responsibilities and goals with each individual. And a periodic appraisal may require several hours rather than the typical 20 minutes.

Reaction to this cost will undoubtedly vary. The management that considers the development of its human resources to be the primary means of achieving the economic objectives of the organization will not be disturbed. It will regard the necessary guidance and coaching as among the most important functions of every superior.

Conclusion

I have sought to show that the conventional approach to performance appraisal stands condemned as a personnel method. It places the manager in the untenable position of judging the personal worth of his subordinates, and of acting on these judgments. No manager possesses, nor could he acquire, the skill necessary to carry out this responsibility effectively. Few would even be willing to accept it if they were fully aware of the implications involved.

It is this unrecognized aspect of conventional appraisal programs which produces the widespread uneasiness and even open resistance of management to appraisals and especially to the appraisal interview.

A sounder approach, which places the major responsibility on the subordinate for establishing performance goals and appraising progress toward them, avoids the major weaknesses of the old plan and benefits the organization by stimulating the development of the subordinate. It is true that more managerial skill and the investment of a considerable amount of time are required, but the greater motivation and the more effective development of subordinates can justify these added costs.

Note

1. See Peter Drucker, *The Practice of Management* (New York, Harper & Brothers, 1954).

Reprinted with permission from *Harvard Business Review*, May/June 1957, pp. 89-94. © 1957 by the President of Harvard College. All rights reserved.

The Cost of FAILURE

Carefully formulating analytics and business practices can be the best way to avoid financial catastrophe

EDWARD S. ROBINS

Catastrophic financial failure is rarely on the agenda of most organizations, and most managers expect to have plenty of warning before hitting the ropes. That's a dangerous assumption. With the advent of business-critical, enterprisewide IT systems, it might only take one key person to put an organization at risk for failure.

Threats can arise from inside or outside the organization and originate largely from two sources: misleading or poor reporting of an organization's accounting and financial risk exposure, and poor technological safeguards that enable malfeasant or maverick employees to operate beyond corporate control.

Business procedures alone can't guard against such behavior. Furthermore, standard accounting practices are no saviors in detecting oncoming disasters. However, you can mitigate catastrophic failure by incorporating management and risk analytic capabilities during corporate IT system upgrades. For example, you could establish different accounting standards or practices that meet high-, medium-, and low-risk scenarios, which would make managers savvier about the risks of specific decisions and corporate policies.

IT'S NOTHING NEW

Managers are accustomed to thinking of failure as a process of slow degradation over time—a whittling away of revenue in a bad economy, or from carrying outdated products that aren't selling. Reality suggests otherwise: Business cycles turn faster than businesses can adapt to them, and the recent spate of spectacular corporate bankruptcies due to management misconduct has put managers, investors, governments, and stock exchanges on edge. To name a few cases: Great Britain's Barings Bank was brought down by Nick Leesen, a single maverick trader; the Enron Corp. meltdown was enabled by corporate executive malfeasance apparently in collusion with Arthur Andersen; and Peregrine Systems Inc. is now suing Arthur Andersen for alleged misleading accounting. (Criminal behavior isn't the only means for catastrophic failure; unexpected bank foreclosures kill many small- and medium-sized businesses as well.)

Even with these well-publicized cases, business failure due to criminal behavior is a subject most people prefer to sweep under the rug. It might be high on the talk agenda, but often there's little in the way of action.

Operating within legal accounting regimens, however, is no guarantee of avoiding catastrophic collapse. For example, in the 1980s, savings-and-loan institutions were legally allowed excessively low equity holdings, as well as accounting practices that misrepresented their solvency. (Sound familiar?)

With many corporations and organizations rethinking their accounting and business practices, conservatism is

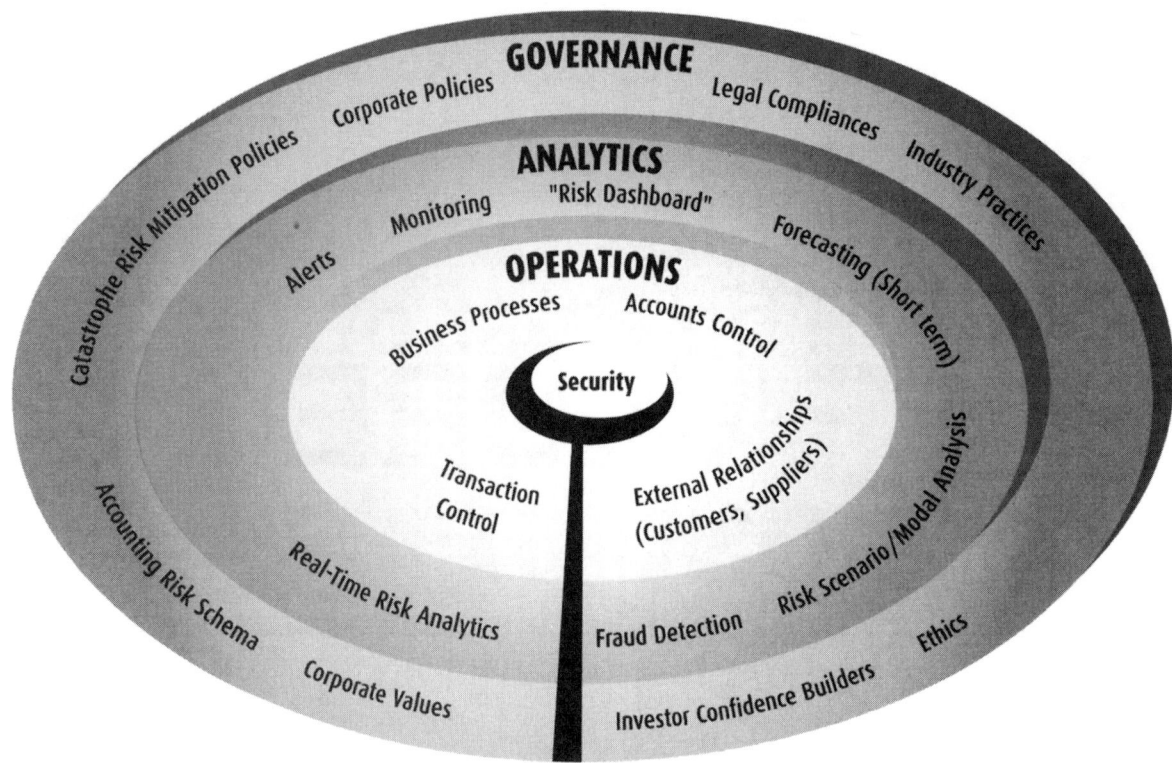

FIGURE 1 *Rules hierarchy showing top-level rule classes with catastrophe–avoidance components. Rule configurations are dependent on specific applications.*

back. But even if the CFO and auditors sign on the bottom line, that doesn't mean the company is healthy—"What if" questions aren't supported in static financial statements. Thus, the CEO and the board are left to explain unexpected failures to their investors.

Few people realize that the Sarbanes-Oxley Act calls for a move from rules-based to principles-based accounting practices. The impact of this shift is still unknown, as the new Auditors' Oversight Board, established under the act, is still developing rules. Thus far, the focus has been on auditor, corporate executive, and board responsibilities. Eventually, the need to achieve "reasonable" accounting quality control and board or audit committee "compliance" may require commoditized, technologically possible risk assessment, forecasting, and fraud and malfeasant behavior detection, which may well have business implications beyond the scope of this article.

Part of the solution may lie in the architecture of IT systems. To cope with the unpredictable, architectures must be adaptive. In other words, if something just hurt you or a similar organization, the ability to clean house quickly is a big advantage. To do that, your business "organism" has to be agile, able to learn, and able to transform knowledge into codified behavior—or what is commonly called governance. If it's willing to think in these terms, your company can protect its integrity as effectively as it protects data. (See Figure 1.)

Governance rules are implemented in many IT enterprise products and custom-coded schema, although more often implicitly than explicitly, and rarely systematically or as a primary concern. Two other classes of rules—operational rules that enable daily business processes, and analytic rules that provide metric feedback, forecasting, and watchdog functions—complete the solution. Dividing the problem this way enables management to ensure implementations are flexible and adaptable. When selecting ERP and business intelligence (BI) systems, however, few managers consider these capabilities. Rather, they get boxed in by vendor perspectives, cost pressures, and functional concerns.

THE GROUND RULES

Let's outline the ground rules for preventing financial disasters. The goal is to reduce the likelihood of being caught unprepared and to mitigate the impact of unexpected events. The side effects should be flexibility for change, better corporate management, and more honest, transparent business processes that maintain personal initiative and individuality.

Separate rules from business processes. The first step is to identify and expose rules that enable your business to function and divide them up appropriately. For example, buyers can be prevented from making unauthorized purchases by a simple governance rule. Conversely, more complex rules can give flexibility to buyers while maintaining a limit on discretionary purchasing.

According to the Association of Certified Fraud Examiners, business organizations lose about 6 percent of their revenues to all forms of fraud and abuse. The cost is estimated at more than $400 billion in the U.S. annually.

All rules should evolve as business needs change, but governance must always be present. Rules are maintained in a database, allowing authorized managers or analysts to change them as part of the natural course of managing processes. Rules-engine technologies that support this approach are available and can be integrated with existing ERP, BI, and other systems.

Another critical governance concept is risk management. For example, HR is rarely capable of estimating the business risk of option plans and executive compensation. Option plans may need to be taken into the realm of the what-if so that potential risks can be weighed against the demands of the current hiring environment. To do so, fairly sophisticated decision-support tools may be required.

Educate managers and investors about risk. Many boards are selecting CEOs with CFO backgrounds. Unfortunately, this approach may guarantee that risk estimates are put in financial terms, which will miss the point if not viewed through different accounting lenses with uncertainty added to the mix. Analytic systems for managing uncertainty exist, but they are complex and counterintuitive. Modal schemas, such as conservative, moderate, and risky accounting scenarios, should be considered to help users make sense of their results.

Protect against fraud. Fraud isn't just a problem of external suppliers and customers knowingly cheating. It can also be an internal matter, involving personnel who misrepresent results because of job pressures or who are illegally lining their pockets.

The types of fraud along the money trail are extensive and vary by industry. False accounting, for example, can be detectable through Benford's Law, which can indicate if a sequence of numbers has been artificially created. Abnormal purchasing or selling patterns, illegitimate intrusions (allowed or otherwise) that modify accounting records, subtle misuse of corporate property, establishing questionable financial vehicles or customer accounts, and even money-laundering activities can be uncovered by fraud-detection systems. These systems are as diverse as the types of fraud and are only now achieving reasonable levels of sophistication, ranging from simple scoring techniques to industry-specific behavioral analytics algorithms. Many vendors, for example, focus on telephone fraud.

CASE STUDY: GOOD NEWS AND BAD NEWS

NEWLY ON THE job as R&D manager at a small discrete manufacturing company, I soon found that the system of procurement for each bill of materials had been left to the engineers. Consequently, the sourcing of some materials represented a significant risk, particularly as supplies of one critical component, for which there was at the time only one supplier, would be delayed by several months.

Neither the engineer responsible nor the former manager had identified this procurement risk. In addition, the engineers were more preoccupied with current technical problems and gave little thought to raising the sourcing issue with management.

The potential impact on cash flow, customer confidence, and manufacturing costs represented a critical risk to the company's financial integrity. Without an internal risk-analytic system in place—at least, one affordable for a small company—it was impossible to ensure this situation would not recur, so my focus shifted toward production policing and away from new product development.

Although an engineering solution was eventually found, its weaknesses highlight the need for a rules at three different levels:

- Analytics: A "warning flag" would indicate when the critical part hadn't been ordered in time, despite the fact it was known in advance that delivery could take several weeks. Furthermore, downstream financial impact couldn't be assessed, even though preventing delivery delays to a major customer were critical to the company's survival.
- Operations: The business process of servicing a discrete order was more informal than structured, so chief stakeholders and decision-makers remained out-of-the-loop.
- Governance: Management remained unaware of supply risk.

In this case, establishing rules of engagement among chief stakeholders, higher level decision-makers, and line engineers would probably have avoided unnecessary and costly work. In addition, a rules engine may have identified the risk adequately enough to enable risk-reducing actions to be taken—perhaps entirely avoiding problems at the product design stage.

Use watchdog and proactive systems. Senior managers don't want to waste precious time chasing poltergeists; they need alarms to sound early. Unfortunately, although base technology is available, no generic product can help protect against fraudulent activities at the operational level for various reasons (such as the existence of differing accounting practices across business units, industries, and national boundaries). In the early 1990s, for example, both Sybase and Bausch & Lomb discovered business practices that seriously overstated sales figures and affected their corporate integrities. Sudden changes in sales patterns should have set alarm bells ringing, but they didn't. There were no watchdogs on duty.

Modern BI tools can serve as crude watchdogs, but more sophisticated third-party products are appearing. Examples include Mantas Inc.'s Behavior Detection Platform, which proactively detects suspicious patterns or events in the financial services industry; NetMap Analytics' Link Analysis technology, which finds links among unrelated events for the insurance and retail sectors; Neural Technologies' Minotaur, which provides neural networks to detect money laundering and other fraudulent activities in the utilities, financial, and telecom industries; and ViPS Inc.'s STARS and IBM DecisionEdge, which target healthcare fraud.

Align people and IT. You should engage in at least some rules separation, a process in which business rules are made explicit and automated. Essentially, the modeling must move from IT coders, legacy code, and database modelers to the value chain stakeholders involved in governance, operations, analytic, and auditing functions. If it doesn't, implementing anything suggested in this article is likely to be a costly nightmare.

Rules implementations are not all-or-nothing exercises because systems can be structured incrementally. As a start, perform a risks audit—a separation of rules based on their priority and ability to provide governance in the context of planned IT upgrades.

In some cases, you may need internal or external consulting analysts to separate the rules and identify the kinds of rules needed. Such analysts are essential to help manage and develop systems. Most BI and ERP companies provide rules analyst services. However, most of them are prepackaged solutions that won't give you the control and flexibility you need. Third party rules-engine middleware vendors—Fair, Isaac & Co. and Corticon among others—are good alternatives worth investigating.

Manage the cultural impact. More tightly governed systems may entail changes in corporate culture and likely place a higher demand on honesty. Managers may need to be more forgiving of human error and judgment, at least initially. In the high stakes area of drug discovery, for example, reducing drug discovery costs is causing a cultural tsunami: Systems coming online to capture and share the knowledge of individual scientists and doctors (two groups that jealously guard their personal knowledge capital) enable management and peers to judge their individual competency and efficacy, which also threatens the bargaining position of these high-value individuals. If undesirable behaviors are uncovered, sensitive remedial action will need to be taken.

BENEFITS AND DRAWBACKS

Besides overall improvements in flexibility, efficiency, and change management, rules systems containing catastrophe-avoiding procedures can be built to help managers better appreciate the risks in making decisions. Having a risk dashboard, for example, will enable better strategic thinking. It will make more demands on the senior management to understand risk and equally challenge the designers of such systems.

The planning should include considerations to inculcate more honesty in the workforce. Studies in this area suggest that corporate cultures with high ethics and honesty are more successful companies. A company that doesn't hold to such standards inevitably breeds a culture of theft and can collapse. Furthermore, investors should know that catastrophic risk management is being performed; a CEO looking to enhance value and confidence may find it a valuable tool for his or her kit bag.

The downside is the risk of discovering unpleasant surprises at an awkward moment. In addition, the presence of a cybernetic Big Brother isn't conducive to a pleasant work environment, although such a presence is increasingly common. Staff buy-in through involvement in development is often critical.

Interface design must hide complexity to help overcome estrangement and enable users to feel accommodated as changed processes are implemented. If these needs aren't satisfied, management may find itself with unhappy employees and customers. Good project managers, programmers, and interface designers will be needed for the grinding work of getting it done.

BOTTOM LINE

Catastrophic failure is an underestimated mode of corporate failure, and today, more sophistication should be demanded of management and their tools. Investors should also be aware that management has potential disaster in check.

IT can help, but it'll never be the complete solution; standard accounting practices are also no guarantee against even short-term risk of catastrophic failure. Rather, more sophistication is needed on the part of vendors, managers, and investors in understanding this complex problem. In effect, the risk of catastrophic failure can and should be factored in as part of general business practice.

RESOURCES

Bergeron, Bryan and R. Kurzweil. *The Eternal E-Customer*, McGraw-Hill, 2000.

Beroggi, Giampiero. *Decision Modeling in Policy Management: An Introduction to Analytic Concepts*, Kluwer Academic Publishers, 1999.

Starbuck, William H. and P. Narayan Pant. "Trying to Help S&Ls: How Organizations With Good Intentions Jointly Enacted Disaster," in *Organizational Decision Making*, Zur Shapira (Ed.), Cambridge University Press, 1997.

Von Halle, Barbara. *Business Rules Applied*, Wiley, 2001.

Business Rules Community: www.brcommunity.com

Securities industry Association's *Preliminary Guidance for Deterring Money Laundering Activity:* www.sia.com/moneyLaundering/pdf/AMLguidance.pdf

For more information about the role of analytics in fraud detection, see Girish Keshav Palshikar's "The Hidden Truth" (May 28, 2002). Read it online at www.intelligententerprise.com/020528/509feat3_1.shtml.

EDWARD S. ROBINS, Ph.D. [esro@attbi.com] is general manager of Esrotech, a technology-based consulting company, and on the faculty of the College of Arts and Science at Northeastern University in Boston. He has more than 20 years of experience in discrete product development and manufacturing, software development, decision support and analytics, and systems architecture.

From *Intelligent Enterprise*, March 1, 2003, pp. 35-39. © 2003 by CPM Media LLC.

How Safe Is *Your* Job?

The Threat of WORKPLACE VIOLENCE

"Changes in the American workplace have created fertile ground for breeding discontent and potential violence."

BY LAURENCE MILLER

"A DISGRUNTLED [pick one: postal worker, law client, insurance claimant, store customer, hospital patient, factory worker] stormed into a place of business yesterday, killing six people before turning the gun on himself. Film at 11." You've heard this one before. Often, the lead story is followed by interviews with coworkers or associates whose comments almost invariably follow one of two main themes:

"He was always a little strange, you know, quiet. Kept to himself a lot, didn't get along with too many people, but came in, did his job, and never caused any real trouble. Certainly, nobody figured him for the violent type. Man, we didn't see this one coming." Or: "Damnit, I knew it was just a matter of time till something like this happened. This guy was bad news, a ticking bomb, and we all knew it. But there were no precautions or any real kind of discipline at all. We tried to tell management, but they just got annoyed, said there was nothing they could do, and told us not to stir up trouble. When he finally snapped, we were sitting ducks."

Most traumas I deal with in my clinical and forensic psychology practice strike suddenly and without warning or control. In those cases, the emphasis is on treating the victims, survivors, and their families after the fact. However, in virtually no other high-risk area is education, training, planning, and prevention so vital as in the case of workplace violence. In many cases, you *can* see this one coming and you *can* do something about it.

The National Institute of Occupational Safety and Health reports that homicide is the second-leading cause of death in the workplace. Murder is the number-one workplace killer of women and the third-leading cause of death for men, after motor vehicle accidents and machine-related fatalities. The majority of workplace homicides are committed by firearms. For every actual killing, there are anywhere from 10 to 100 sublethal acts of violence committed at work.

According to Michael Mantell and Steve Albrecht in *Ticking Bombs: Defusing Violence in the Workplace*, the cost of workplace violence for American businesses runs more than $4,000,000,000 annually, including lost work time, employee medical benefits, and legal expenses. Additional costs of workplace violence include replacing lost employees and retraining new ones, decreased productivity, higher insurance premiums, raised security costs, bad publicity, lost business, and expensive litigation.

While demographics suggest that the majority of workplace violence is committed by strangers—robbers, disaffected clients and/or customers, etc.—the news media tend to focus attention on acts of lethal aggression committed by coworkers. That is because there is an almost visceral fear we all have of someone we see and talk with every day—someone *we thought we knew*—suddenly turning into a demon of destruction.

Joseph Kinney, executive director of the National Safe Workplace Institute, warns in *Violence at Work: How to Make Your Company Safer for Employees and Customers* that current and future generations of workers will continue to have less emotional maturity, greater feelings of unearned entitlement, poorer social skills, little experience in nonviolent conflict resolution, less respect for older generations, a lower attention span, poorer self-discipline, and higher rates of violence. The newly emerging young workforce is ill-equipped for the world of work, work culture, and work ethic. High turnover encouraged by low wages and poor management reinforces the impression that everyday work is for "chumps," and further denigrates loyalty and authority.

Kinney points out that, for the past 20 years, people have been bombarded by the egocentric message that all personal problems are caused by "society." Individuals are not responsible for their actions, and all blame is externalized. At the same time, there has been a breakdown in traditionally stabilizing institutions such as family, home, church, school, and community. Some workplace violence perpetrators have been quite up front in stating that they want to "strike back" and hurt as many people as they can, no matter who those people are, because of the supposed wrongs committed against them.

In practice, I've found that reported workplace threats actually vary widely in terms of their explicitness. A few threats are direct and unambiguous ("I'm gonna blow that SOB away"), while a far-greater number are nonspecific, falling into a gray zone ("You'll be sorry" or "He deserves whatever's coming to him") that makes it difficult for managers to take action against. Some threats may occur in the form of commiseration with violent news events ("Too bad about all those people, but I know how that restaurant shooter felt").

Indeed, glamorized violence is a staple of the entertainment media, and they have naturally taken an enormous interest in workplace violence, though they often misinterpret and misrepresent those events and the reasons behind them. The common conclusion of this sound-bite journalism is that the lethal perpetrator is either a "nut case" or else engaged in a crusade of "righteous" retribution against an unfair or even darkly conspiratorial employer. This may lead marginally disturbed viewers to "justify" their own future acts of violence.

Changes in the American workplace have created fertile ground for breeding discontent and potential violence. Levels of stress accumulate in many work settings as survivors of downsized corporations are made to take on extra work and fill multiple jobs. For the terminated, anger and hopelessness mount at the inability to replace lost jobs, compounded by the accompanying financial and family stresses. The sense of long-term common corporate purpose that once may have existed between managers and the rank and file has largely disappeared. The changed culture of resentment and entitlement in the workplace says that "This company *owes* me something, and if they don't give it to me, I'm gonna take it the hard way."

Managers and supervisors are increasingly unable or unwilling to use effective discipline or promote fair and effective management practices. Like dysfunctional families, dysfunctional workplaces share common characteristics, such as chronic labor-management disputes, frequent grievances filed by employees, excessive numbers of stress disability claims, persistent pilfering and/or tampering, understaffing and overwork, and a rigidly authoritarian and/or inconsistent management style.

According to forensic psychiatrist Robert Simon in *Bad Men Do What Good Men Dream*, satisfying work affords more than just an income. For most people, it provides stability, direction, security, a sense of achievement, self-worth, camaraderie, and a feeling of belonging. Most workers would regard losing a job as a traumatic event, but one they eventually come to resolve by picking up the pieces, going forward, and searching for new opportunities. However, for a small minority of vulnerable personalities, job loss—especially if perceived as "unfair"—is a devastating blow to the psyche, a mortal narcissistic wound. If the situation is further compounded by financial difficulties, health problems, family friction, and lack of personal support, the person may feel bereft of options.

For such individuals, job stress or job loss can trigger overwhelming rage. Blame is externalized, and vengeance brews as the worker begins to think, "Who do they think they are? I'll show them they can't do this to me and get away with ruining my life." For some, the intolerability of the job loss leads to hopelessness and suicidal intentions with a retaliatory sting: "If they wanna screw me, I can screw them back—big time. Why should other people go on living their happy lives, having what they want, when I can't? I may be going out, but I'm not going out alone." The idea percolates in the perpetrator's mind that, after he's gone, his Ramboesque exploits will be reported to millions around the world and his name will become a household word. Far from meekly slinking away, defeated and unnoticed, he will leave this world in a blaze of horror and glory—just like in the movies.

Preventing violence

While there will always be a few unstable, psychopathologically violence-prone individuals in any large organization, the current emphasis on "offender profiling" obscures a greater contributor to workplace violence and general worker malaise, a set of factors that many companies might find far more difficult to address. These involve the twin evils of generally unfair management practices and lack of a specific workplace violence prevention and response plan.

While not every situation can be planned for, the absence of even the most rudimentary security measures and contingency plans in many organizations is appalling. The steps a firm takes to make its employees feel secure say a lot about corporate culture and workplace morale, and while no organization desires to operate under a fortress mentality, a few important measures can go a long way toward demonstrating concern for worker safety.

As deceptively simple as it sounds, the best way to avoid workplace violence is not to hire violent workers. Efforts in this regard include thorough application reviews and background checks, careful interviewing of prospective employees, and administering appropriate psychological screening measures.

Companies should have clear, strong, fair, and consistent written policies against violence and harassment, along with effective grievance procedures, efficient security programs, a reasonably supportive work environment, open channels of communication, and training in resolving conflicts through team building and negotiation skills. Plans should be in place that specify how threats are reported and to whom, as well as a protocol for investigating them.

The ideal goal of any disciplinary program is to strike a balance between an overly rigid and heavy-handed approach that presents management as hard and unreasonable, and a too-lax one that gives employees the impression of poor control in the organization. By identifying areas of agreement and disagreement, looking for alternatives, thinking creatively, and eventually finding solutions that have the support and commitment of all parties, a human resources manager is more likely to defuse the tension and resentment that may spark workplace violence. Discipline should occur in stages, with a clear policy and rationale, and with written documentation.

If it comes down to having no choice but to fire a worker, this should be done in a firm, but humane, manner. It should be made as clear as possible to the employee that the termination is for a specific reason, rather than for general "attitude" problems or personal reasons. The worker should understand that the termination action is final, and should be informed of any counseling or other services offered by the company for the transition period.

An example of this approach that has been successfully applied to violence occurring in health care facilities is Robert Flannery's Assaulted Staff Action Program (ASAP). It provides a range of services, including individual critical incident debriefings of assaulted staff members and entire wards, a staff victims' support group, employee victim family debriefing and counseling, and referrals for follow-up psychotherapy as needed. The ASAP team structure is comprised of 15 direct-care staff volunteers, three supervisors, and the team director, who is responsible for administering the entire program and for ensuring that the quality of the services is maintained.

The program's developers claim that ASAP has proven useful in reducing the traumatic impact of patient assaults on employee victims and in significantly lowering the overall level of violence in facilities where it has been applied. More germane to the bottom line, ASAP saves the previously mentioned costs of workplace violence.

When violence happens

Sometimes, despite the best efforts at prevention, a dangerous situation begins to brew and a violent incident becomes a distinct possibility, or an incident just erupts explosively and personnel have to respond immediately. The nature of the response will depend on how thorough the pre-incident planning and training have been.

Warning signs may be observed hours, days, or weeks prior to a violent incident, and may be preceded by a history of work-related problems. In all too many cases, the sparks of a potentially violent reaction have been fanned into flames by abusive discipline, clumsily executed termination, or failure of management to address employee–employee grievances, causing the worker to "take matters into his own hands."

Plans and training for defusing violent episodes must be developed, put in place, and reviewed periodically. These include initial actions to take when a violent episode appears to be threatening, codes and signals for summoning help, a chain of command for handling emergencies, appropriate use of verbal control tactics and body language, scene control and bystander containment, measures for dealing with weapons, and procedures for resolving hostage situations.

The crisis is not over when the police and TV crews leave. People may have been killed, others wounded, some held hostage, and many psychologically traumatized. Plans and policies for dealing with the aftermath of workplace violence are just as important as planning for the incident itself, and both may come under sharp scrutiny in later investigations, litigation, and corporate public relations. Companies should proactively set up policies and procedures for responding to the aftermath of a workplace violence incident. They should include mobilization of mental health services, media and public relations responses, family interventions, collaboration with law enforcement, physical security and cleanup, legal measures, postincident investigations, and plans for getting back to business. During the crisis and in its aftermath, the overriding question that will be asked by employees, their families, stakeholders and customers, the media, and the general public is: "What is this company doing to help its workers get through this?"

In this regard, commitment from the top of the management organization—"executive buy-in"—is crucial to determining how effectively such interventions will operate. In the worst case I can remember, a bank branch grudgingly arranged for a staff stress debriefing after a holdup, only because the service was mandated by their managed care contract. The branch managers clearly regarded the intervention as a waste of time that cut into employees' work hours. An uncomfortable backroom lunch and storage area was designated for the debriefing, which was frequently interrupted by people coming in and out to use the kitchen and bathroom. Some of those coworkers could be heard to make cracks about "free time." As a result, the participants wanted the whole thing over with as quickly as possible, and little therapeutic work was accomplished.

The best case I can remember (in terms of company support) involved a hostage and shooting crisis perpetrated by a disturbed customer of a medium-sized investment firm, resulting in two deaths and several injuries. The CEO immediately suspended business as usual, arranged for temps to cover the basic needs of the company, offered his home to be used for almost round-the-clock debriefings, and provided food, beverages, and, in a few cases, bed and board to employees who were too upset to drive home. He and the senior management staff offered help to survivors and their families, personally checked on proper funeral arrangements for the slain workers, frequently visited injured employees in the hospital, and generally shared in the grief and recovery of the members of their staff. Far more than any specific clinical services I could provide, this sincere and unselfish human response by senior management to tragedy within their ranks—a true expression of leadership—helped this firm to heal quickly and move on, always holding a place of respect for their slain comrades, but honoring their memories by productively continuing their work.

This brings us back to an earlier point: Bad things *do* happen to good companies—but they happen a lot less often than to bad ones. There will always be a few dangerously unstable people scattered among the workforce. However, businesses that treat their employees honorably, take the time and concern to implement safety measures, use firm but fair disciplinary procedures, and make it clear that harassment of its employees—by coworkers or management—will not be tolerated tend to have fewer violent incidents than less-well-run companies. Some workers may indeed have a short fuse, but fairly run and well-managed firms seem to know how to keep those fuses from being lit. This isn't just a safety issue—it's good business.

Laurence Miller, a psychologist in Boca Raton, Fla., specializing in neuropsychology, business psychology, and corporate counseling, is the author of Shocks to the System: Psychotherapy of Traumatic Disability Syndromes.

From USA Today magazine (Society for the Advancement of Education), March 2002. © 2002 by the Society for the Advancement of Education. Reprinted by permission.

Mail Preparation Total Quality Management

A candid conversation with John Wargo, U.S. Postal Service vice president, Service & Market Development, regarding the postal service's premier mail quality program.

by Richard W. Pavely, MSE

About 3.5 trillion letters ago, the U.S. Postal Service (USPS) embarked on the longest and most successful automation program in American business history, the Automation Plan for Business Mailers. That program, also known as Work Sharing, elevated the process by which the postal service sorted and distributed mail throughout the postal system by introducing POSTNET bar coding and other automation technology. Without it, it's estimated that a 1-ounce First Class letter would now require well over $2 in postage. Key to the success of that Herculean effort was the enlistment of the cooperation and support of the business mailers by offering deep discounts on postage for preparing and submitting automation-compatible mail.

Now, nearly two decades later, the postal service is again embarking on another arduous journey into deeper reaches of improved customer service by incorporating the best and the brightest features of three internationally recognized quality methodologies: the ISO 9000, the Malcolm Baldrige Performance Excellence criteria, and Total Quality Management.

The Mail Preparation Total Quality Management (MPTQM) program is designed to help businesses prepare letter mailings that meet or exceed postal service processing quality standards. Designed by industry mailers, it's a complete system of realistic quality control measures and standardized assessment procedures. It applies to all aspects of the mail preparation process, from the generation and bar coding of a letter to the final sorting and containerizing that takes place just prior to presenting the mailing to the postal service.

To assess the progress of the program and gain a better understanding of the benefits and requirements for participating, this author traveled to USPS Marketing Headquarters in Alexandria, Va. to interview John Wargo, vice president, Service and Management Development. Here are the highlights of that interview, followed by an assessment of the business consequences for participating in the MPTQM program.

OS: Why did the postal service choose to develop the MPTQM program to assure a quality process when other quality programs, such as the Malcolm Baldrige and ISO 9000 programs, already existed?

Wargo: Our initial action was to form an advisory group of postal service customers to help us define the quality program. We began by reviewing the specifications we require for mail and studying the processes the mailers use to produce it. This naturally drove us to a standards- and process management-based approach to quality. We then reviewed the other international methodologies, such as ISO, and decided our approach was more in depth and focused. We borrowed many ideas from those methodologies to strengthen MPTQM, however.

OS: What does the postal service hope to gain from the MPTQM program?

Wargo: Our goal is customer satisfaction. MPTQM will help ease the entry of business mail into our processing and distribution streams... Error free mail will sail through the mail acceptance process. High-quality mail also ensures timely delivery. The resulting customer satisfaction will drive increased use of the mail.

OS: Does the MPTQM program only apply to presort service bureaus and super high-volume mailers?

Wargo: We began MPTQM with presort service bureaus because of the complexity of their mailings. Many other large-volume mailers also have complicated mailings, and some of those mailers are now in the program. Improving quality first with these mailers is in line with our goals. All business mailers are welcome to participate.

OS: Who are list mailers?

Wargo: This is a term we use in the program for all but presort service bureaus. Most, but not all, of these mailers perform mail sortation from a computerized list versus an automated letter sorter or MLOCR (multi-line optical character reader). That's the origin of the term.

OS: Why would a list mailer benefit from becoming certified under the MPTQM program?

> "Our goal is customer satisfaction. MPTQM will help ease the entry of business mail into our processing and distribution streams... Error free mail will sail through the mail acceptance process."

Wargo: Program materials, including a training video and work aids, are free. Audits are free. Mail verifications are to be reduced, and fewer postage adjustments will be applied. There are a number of internal benefits mailers are seeing. Some are less down time on machines, fewer rejections of mail, fewer postage adjustments for poor quality, more employee pride in the company, an improved employee retention rate, reduced training costs.

OS: How long does it normally take to become certified in the program?

Wargo: About 12, months from the point of dedicated implementation.

OS: If a firm already has an existing quality program in place, can all or part of that program be incorporated into the MPTQM process? Or would they have to start from scratch with the MPTQM program?

Wargo: Mailers in this situation should contact Scott Hamel for guidance. He can be reached at 703/292-3824 or via the Internet at shamel@email.usps.gov. Following a telephone discussion and mailer registration, he will provide [them with] an MPTQM guidebook, which gives instructions on getting started and includes a "Gap Analysis" for mailers with existing quality programs to use.

OS: Would MPTQM certification be a useful procurement criterion for those firms who purchase production mail products and services from presort service bureaus or list mailers?

Wargo: Definitely. Our plans, in fact, are to move in that direction.

OS: How is the postal service organized to support the program? Are you using field personnel or contractors to conduct the audits?

Wargo: Scott Hamel, who works in the technical side of our headquarters marketing organization, is the program manager. He has a staff of 30 analysts who conduct mailer audits with the support of our district business mail entry offices. Most of his analysts now are Certified Quality Auditors through the American Society for Quality (ASQ). They lead the audits. A contractor was used to help establish this part of the program.

OS: How successful is the program?

Wargo: We are very excited with the results to date. The involved mailers continue to praise the value the process adds to their companies. Our relationships with these customers have improved. In terms of MPTQM's impact on mail quality, we will be building a performance measurement process this spring.

OS: How many service bureaus are certified?

Wargo: Twenty-eight service bureaus are certified.

OS: How many list mailers are certified?

Wargo: Five list mailers are certified.

OS: Do you have some advice for those who are considering investing in the rigors of certification?

Wargo: Interested mailers should contact Scott Hamel who can answer [their] questions and put them in touch with a few certified mailers who have processes most like theirs. Involved mailers have expressed great willingness to share their experiences with others. They recognize that the more MPTQM players we have, the healthier the entire mailing industry will be.

OS: What are your predictions for the MPTQM program?

Wargo: Within three years, all major-volume, and some lesser-volume, mailers will be installing the program. Large-volume postal customers will require their vendors, particularly lettershops and presort service bureaus, to be MPTQM certified.

OS Summary: From a business standpoint, the MPTQM program makes incredibly good sense. The cost to implement it is easy to justify. For starters, anytime you take an excellent program like Malcolm Baldrige and customize it to your unique situation, you raise the likelihood that the end result will be significantly improved. In addition to protecting the discounts that a mailer already enjoys, which can be measured in millions of dollars per year for a production mailer, certification under this program will result in less frequent verifications on the receiving dock, faster insertion into the system, and fewer of the new and nasty postage adjustments.

Furthermore, the routine application of quality standards within a production process will shorten the time for instituting corrective actions and reduce the cost of imbedded systemic problems, which would otherwise remain hidden in the turmoil of production activity.

Obviously, the postal service can't check everything it receives. By qualifying for MPTQM, the mailer positions his or her firm's mail as highly reliable and, therefore, not requiring further attention. That way, the postal service can concentrate its inspection efforts where serious problems are more likely to exist.

Richard W. Pavely, MSE, is president of Corporate Management & Marketing Consultants Inc. of Randolph, N.J. He's an active member of ASO, AQP, MSMA, and several Postal Customer Councils. He can be reached at 973/989-0229 or via the Internet at rpavely@cmmcinc.com.

From *Office Solutions*, April 2002, pp. 12-15. © 2002 by Quality Publishing, Inc.

Case: *Evaluation of Organizational Effectiveness*

The American Corporation, a $2.4 billion diversified conglomerate, acquired the $130 million Cordle Manufacturing Company. At a private luncheon with Sam Priest, American's chief executive officer, Carla Judson, a strategic planner with American's Division of Strategic Planning, learned that she was one of several persons being considered to replace, on an acting basis, Cordle Manufacturing Company's president, whose resignation was part of the acquisition agreement. Priest informed Judson that if the acting president could function effectively, the position would be permanent. He indicated, however, that one troublesome problem would have to be eliminated within six months. The problem had been revealed through a confidential survey conducted among 25 members of Cordle's middle management group. Judson was told that the survey results would be available to her and that a meeting of all officers would be held in two weeks to select the acting president. At that time, all candidates would be required to make a presentation outlining how problems revealed by the survey could best be handled.

In studying the survey results, Judson learned that each of the middle managers had been asked to evaluate other departments. The survey was designed to determine, if possible, the respect, cooperation, and goodwill generated between departments. Of the departments evaluated, all were rated satisfactory in efficiency, organization, work relationships, and cooperativeness, except for the sales department. From the 25 questionnaires returned, 18 participants said the sales department needed reorganizing. They said department members were difficult to work with and rarely cooperated with other departments.

As a strategic planner, Judson knew there were a number of feasible strategies she could present to American's officers. She knew that the survey results might be challenged as unreliable and invalid. On the other hand, she was aware that the distinct nature of the objectives, activities, and responsibilities associated with various departments often led to conflict between individuals in various areas. If she acknowledged the survey's validity, she would have to outline a plan for achieving efficient integration and coordination among departments and functional areas. Judson realized her future at American would be decided in the next few days by how her strategies would be perceived by American's officers and then by how effectively she could implement her strategies. What to decide on was her major task.

Using the Case on *Evaluation of Organizational Effectiveness*

Carla Judson is faced with the problem of trying to propose an organization for the new Cordle Manufacturing division of the American Corporation based upon the results of a study that was recently completed at the newly acquired business. The study indicates that most of the departments work well together with one major exception—sales. Ms. Judson's task is to develop a strategy to address and rectify this condition.

Discussion Questions

1. Should Ms. Judson challenge the validity and reliability of the study?
2. If Ms. Judson accepts the study, what are some of the possible strategies she could use to address this situation?

Exercise: *Win as Much as You Can!*

1. Divide the group into groups of eight and have each group (cluster) divide into teams of two (dyads).
2. The goal of this exercise is to win as much money as you can.
3. Using the chart at the top of the tally sheet, each dyad is to decide whether it will choose an "X" or a "Y" (with the hope of winning money). The dyads then write their choices on their tally sheets for round 1 while not letting any other dyads see their choices. No conversation among dyads should occur, except when provided for in rounds 5, 8, and 10.
4. After the allotted time for round 1 (2 minutes) has passed, each dyad will show its choice to the other dyads in the cluster. Using the chart on the tally sheet, each dyad should determine how much money it won or lost in round 1, and record this amount on the tally sheet. No comments among dyads are allowed. Proceed immediately to round 2, then 3, and so forth, as outlined on the tally sheet. Note that in rounds 5, 8, and 10, dyads can confer with each other at the beginning of the round. Note also that theamounts won or lost in these rounds are multiplied by three, five, and ten.

5. At the end of the exercise, determine which dyad won the most and which ended up furthest behind. Then compare clusters.

4 X's:	Lose $1.00 each
3 X's: 1 Y:	Win $1.00 each Lose $3.00
2 X's: 2 Y's:	Win $2.00 each Lose $2.00 each
1 X: 3 Y's:	Win $3.00 Lose $1.00 each
4 Y's:	Win $1.00 each

Strategy: You are to confer with your partner(s) on each round and make a joint decision. Before rounds 5, 8, and 10, you confer with the others in your cluster.

Questions for Discussion

1. How was the goal defined? What conflict did it create? (Do I win for my dyad or my cluster?)
2. Do people react differently in games than they do in real life? Do goals in life create conflict?
3. How does trust relate to influence? How many times can one person betray another and still retain his/her confidence? Did anyone stick to her/his word throughout?
4. What effect did communication have on the influence process?
5. What strategies were used to win? What conflict did these strategies create? What strategies were used to manage the conflict?

- The win/lose approach = self-oriented. (I win at your expense.)
- The lose/win approach = martyrdom. (You win at my expense.)
- The lose/lose approach = pride and revenge. (I may lose, but you do, too.)
- The win/win approach = trust. (We both win.)

6. Why is the win/win approach the most effective strategy in life?

Round	Time Allowed	Confer With	Your Choice Circle	Clusters Patterns of Choices	Payoff	Balance	
1	2 mins.	partner					
2	1 min.	partner					
3	1 min.	partner					
4	1 min.	partner					
5	3 mins. 1 min.	cluster partner					Bonus round payoff × 3
6	1 min.	partner					
7	1 min.	partner					
8	3 mins. 1 min.	cluster partner					Bonus round payoff × 5
9	1 min.	partner					
10	3 mins. 1 min.	cluster partner					Bonus round payoff × 10

Case: Evaluation of Organizational Effectiveness; Exercise: Win as Much as You Can!, Fred Maidment, McGraw-Hill/Dushkin, 2000.

UNIT 6
Staffing and Human Resources

Unit Selections

24. **Management Women and the New Facts of Life**, Felice N. Schwartz
25. **Who Are You Really Hiring?**, Shari Caudron
26. **Secrets of Finding and Keeping Good Employees**, Jim Sirbasku
27. **Pay It Forward**, Patricia K. Zingheim and Jay R. Schuster

    CASE VI. The "Homes" Is Where the Union Is; Exercise: Assumptions About People at Work

Key Points to Consider

- What do you think of the idea of a "Mommy Track"? What do you think of the idea of a "Daddy Track"? What do you think this does to people's careers in highly competitive organizations?

- For years women have talked about the networks that men have when developing their careers. Do you think women should develop their own? Does this exclude men? Is this fair? Why or why not?

- What are some of the workplace trends for this decade? How do you think organizations can find and keep good employees?

- What are some of the ways that companies can reward their employees that are different from what was done in the past? Do you think it is more effective?

 **Links: www.dushkin.com/online/**
These sites are annotated in the World Wide Web pages.

Electronic Frontier Foundation "Privacy" Archive
http://www.eff.org

School of Labor and Industrial Relations Hot Links
http://www.lir.msu.edu/hotlinks

U.S. Equal Employment Opportunity Commission
http://www.eeoc.gov

Managers of organizations get things done through people. Managers can plan, organize, direct, and control, but the central focus of all their efforts is people. People determine whether an organization is going to succeed, and the way that people perceive their treatment by management is often the key to that success. In today's world, it is necessary to recognize that people have different needs, wants, and desires. Women have different needs than men, which the organization is going to have to address if it wants to hold onto top performers. Some of these differences are discussed by Felice Schwartz in "Management Women and the New Facts of Life," the article that started the talk about the "Mommy Track," which soon led to talk about the "Daddy Track."

Since human resources are a key to the success of any organization, firms need to hire the very best people they can find, because it is people who make the plans, organize the operation, direct the processes to accomplish the organizational goals, and evaluate the results. But while people contribute directly to a firm's success, they also represent a significant cost to the organization. Not only salaries, but also the costs of benefits are rising at an alarming rate. Benefits cost proportionately more today than just a few years ago, and workers not only want to keep the benefits they have but seek to add others. Some of their demands include dental and eye care plans, child care, and senior care for their relatives. The Americans With Disabilities Act has established new criteria for employees with disabilities. Technology is changing the way people work, and management is going to have to deal with that, as seen in "Secrets of Finding and Keeping Good Employees."

The workforce is changing. It includes more minorities, women, and other groups with different needs, and if a corporation wants to hire these people, many of whom are outstanding, they are going to have to meet their needs. Otherwise, these potential employees will go elsewhere, frequently to the competition. No organization can afford to turn its back on such a large pool of potential talent.

Human resources often involve labor unions. While unions in North America have suffered in recent years from declining membership and plant closings, they have nevertheless served an important historical role as well as provided a balance for the potential excesses of management. American labor unions need to redefine their roles in industry, and their leaders must implement these changes. Unions will have to change the way they conduct business if they plan to survive.

Because of the increasing demand for qualified employees, organizations will have to do everything possible to retain good

workers, but they also need to be careful in whom they are hiring, as seen in "Who Are You Really Hiring?" Firms are responding to changes in the workforce in a variety of ways. To meet the needs of the future, management must recognize that people, organizations, and the environment will continue to evolve and that what motivates workers will change in the future. Maintaining an effective workforce will be an overarching goal for all organizations in the future, and keeping and finding new and creative ways of rewarding employees will be a major concern for all organizations, as discussed in "Pay It Forward."

Article 24

Management Women and the New Facts of Life

Felice N. Schwartz

The cost of employing women in management is greater than the cost of employing men. This is a jarring statement, partly because it is true, but mostly because it is something people are reluctant to talk about. A new study by one multinational corporation shows that the rate of turnover in management positions is 2 ½ times higher among top-performing women than it is among men. A large producer of consumer goods reports that one half of the women who take maternity leave return to their jobs late or not at all. And we know that women also have a greater tendency to plateau or to interrupt their careers in ways that limit their growth and development. But we have become so sensitive to charges of sexism and so afraid of confrontation, even litigation, that we rarely say what we know to be true. Unfortunately, our bottled-up awareness leaks out in misleading metaphors ("glass ceiling" is one notable example), veiled hostility, lowered expectations, distrust and reluctant adherence to Equal Employment Opportunity requirements.

Career interruptions, plateauing, and turnover are expensive. The money corporations invest in recruitment, training, and development is less likely to produce top executives among women than among men, and the invaluable company experience that developing executives acquire at every level as they move up through management ranks is more often lost.

The studies just mentioned are only the first of many, I'm quite sure. Demographic realities are going to force corporations all across the country to analyze the cost of employing women in managerial positions, and what they will discover is that women cost more.

But here is another startling truth: The greater cost of employing women is not a function of inescapable gender differences. Women *are* different from men, but what increases their cost to the corporation is principally the clash of their perceptions, attitudes, and behavior with those of men, which is to say, with the policies and practices of male-led corporations.

It is terribly important that employers draw the right conclusions from the studies now being done. The studies will be useless—or worse, harmful—if all they teach us is that women are expensive to employ. What we need to learn is how to reduce that expense, how to stop throwing away the investments we make in talented women, how to become more responsive to the needs of the women that corporations *must* employ if they are to have the best and the brightest of all those now entering the work force.

Two facts matter to business: only women have babies and only men make rules.

The gender differences relevant to business fall into two categories: those related to maternity and those related to the differing traditions and expectations of the sexes. Maternity is biological rather than cultural. We can't alter it but we can dramatically reduce its impact on the workplace and in many cases eliminate its negative effect on employee development. We can accomplish this by addressing the second set of differences, those between male and female socialization. Today, these differences exaggerate the real costs of maternity and can turn a relatively slight disruption in work schedule into a serious business problem and a career derailment for individual women. If we are to overcome the cost differential between male and female employees, we need to address the issues that arise when female socialization meets the male corporate culture and masculine rules of career development—issues of behavior and style, of expectation, of stereotypes and preconceptions, of sexual tension and harassment, of female mentoring, lateral mobility relocation, compensation, and early identification of top performers.

The one immutable, enduring difference between men and women is maternity. Maternity is not simply childbirth but a continuum that begins with an awareness of the ticking of the biological clock, proceeds to the anticipation of motherhood, includes pregnancy, childbirth, physical recuperation, psychological adjustment, and continues on to nursing, bonding, and child rearing. Not all women choose to become mothers, of course, and among those who do, the process varies from case to case depending on the health of the mother and baby, the values of the parents, and the availability, cost, and quality of child care.

In past centuries, the biological fact of maternity shaped the traditional roles of the sexes. Women performed the home-centered functions that related to the bearing and nurturing of children. Men did the work that required great physical strength. Over time, however, family size contracted, the community assumed greater responsibility for the care and education of children, packaged foods and household technology reduced the work load in the home, and technology eliminated much of the need for muscle power at the workplace. Today, in the developed world, the only role still uniquely gender related is childbearing. Yet men and women are still socialized to perform their traditional roles.

Men and women may or may not have some innate psychological disposition toward these traditional roles—men to be aggressive, competitive, self-reliant, risk taking; women to be supportive, nurturing, intuitive, sensitive, communicative—but certainly both men and women are capable of the full range of behavior. Indeed, the male and female roles have already begun to expand and merge. In the decades ahead, as the socialization of boys and girls and the experience and expectations of young men and women grow steadily more androgynous, the differences in workplace behavior will continue to fade. At the moment, however, we are still plagued by disparities in perception and behavior that make the integration of men and women in the workplace unnecessarily difficult and expensive.

Let me illustrate with a few broadbrush generalizations. Of course, these are only stereotypes, but I think they help to exemplify the kinds of preconceptions that muddy the corporate waters.

Women who compete like men are considered unfeminine. Women who emphasize family are considered uncommitted.

Men continue to perceive women as the rearers of their children, so they find it understandable, indeed appropriate, that women should renounce their careers to raise families. Edmund Pratt, CEO of Pfizer, once asked me in all sincerity, "Why would any woman choose to be a chief financial officer rather than a full-time mother?" By condoning and taking pleasure in women's traditional behavior, men reinforce it. Not only do they see parenting as fundamentally female, they see a career as fundamentally male—either an unbroken series of promotions and advancements toward CEOdom or stagnation and disappointment. This attitude serves to legitimize a woman's choice to extend maternity leave and even, for those who can afford it, to leave employment altogether for several years. By the same token, men who might want to take a leave after the birth of a child know that management will see such behavior as a lack of career commitment, even when company policy permits parental leave for men.

Women also bring counterproductive expectations and perceptions to the workplace. Ironically, although the feminist movement was an expression of women's quest for freedom from their home-based lives, most women were remarkably free already. They had many responsibilities, but they were autonomous and could be entrepreneurial in how and when they carried them out. And once their children grew up and left home, they were essentially free to do what they wanted with their lives. Women's traditional role also included freedom from responsibility for the financial support of their families. Many of us were socialized from girlhood to expect our husbands to take care of us, while our brothers were socialized from an equally early age to complete their educations, pursue careers, climb the ladder of success, and provide dependable financial support for their families. To the extent that this tradition of freedom lingers subliminally, women tend to bring to their employment a sense that they can choose to change jobs or careers at will, take time off, or reduce their hours.

Finally, women's traditional role encouraged particular attention to the quality and substance of what they did, specifically to the physical, psychological, and intellectual development of their children. This traditional focus may explain women's continuing tendency to search for more than monetary reward—intrinsic significance, social importance, meaning—in what they do. This too makes them more likely than men to leave the corporation in search of other values.

The misleading metaphor of the glass ceiling suggests an invisible barrier constructed by corporate leaders to impede the upward mobility of women beyond the middle levels. A more appropriate metaphor, I believe, is the kind of cross-sectional diagram used in geology. The barriers to women's leadership occur when potentially counterproductive layers of influence on women—maternity, tradition, socialization—meet management strata pervaded by the largely unconscious preconceptions, stereotypes, and expectations of men. Such interfaces do not exist for men and tend to be impermeable for women.

One result of these gender differences has been to convince some executives that women are simply not suited to top management. Other executives feel helpless. If they see even a few of their valued female employees fail to return to work from maternity leave on schedule or see one of their most promising women plateau in her career after the birth of a child, they begin to fear there is nothing they can do to infuse women with new energy and enthusiasm and persuade them to stay. At the same time, they know there is nothing they can do to stem the tide of women into management ranks.

Another result is to place every working woman on a continuum that runs from total dedication to career at one end to a balance between career and family at the other. What women discover is that the male corporate culture sees both extremes as unacceptable. Women who want the flexibility to balance their families and their careers are not adequately committed to the organization. Women who perform as aggressively and competitively as men are abrasive and unfeminine. But the fact is, business needs all the talented women it can get. Moreover, as I will explain, the women I call career-primary and those I call career-and-family each have particular value to the corporation.

With too few men to go around, women have moved from a buyer's to a seller's market.

Women in the corporation are about to move from a buyer's to a seller's market. The sudden, startling recognition that 80% of new entrants in the work force over the next decade will be women, minorities, and immigrants has stimulated a mushrooming incentive to "value diversity."

Women are no longer simply an enticing pool of occasional creative talent, a thorn in the side of the EEO officer, or a source of frustration to corporate leaders truly puzzled by the slowness of their upward trickle into executive positions. A real demographic change is taking place. The era of sudden population growth of the 1950s and 1960s is over. The birth rate has dropped about 40%, from a high of 25.3 live births per 1,000 population in 1957, at the peak of the baby boom, to a stable low of a little more than 15 per 1,000 over the last 16 years, and there is no indication of a return to a higher rate. The tidal wave of baby boomers that swelled the recruitment pool to overflowing seems to have been a one-time phenomenon. For 20 years, employers had the pick of a very large crop and were able to choose males almost exclusively for the executive track. But if future population remains fairly stable while the economy continues to expand, and if the new information society simultaneously creates a greater need for creative, educated managers, then the gap between supply and demand will grow dramatically and, with it, the competition for managerial talent.

The decrease in numbers has even greater implications if we look at the traditional source of corporate recruitment for leadership positions—white males from the top 10% of the country's best universities. Over the past decade, the increase in the number of women graduating from leading universities has been much greater than the increase in the total number of graduates, and these women are well represented in the top 10% of their classes.

The trend extends into business and professional programs as well. In the old days, virtually all MBAs were male. I remember addressing a meeting at the Harvard Business School as recently as the mid-1970s and looking out at a sea of exclusively male faces. Today, about 25% of that audience would be women. The pool of male MBAs from which corporations have traditionally drawn their leaders has shrunk significantly.

Of course, this reduction does not have to mean a shortage of talent. The top 10% is at least as smart as it always was—smarter, probably, since it's now drawn from a broader segment of the population. But it now consists increasingly of women. Companies that are determined to recruit the same number of men as before will have to dig much deeper into the male pool, while their competitors will have the opportunity to pick the best people from both the male and female graduates.

Under these circumstances, there is no question that the management ranks of business will include increasing numbers of women. There remains, however, the question of how these women will succeed—how long they will stay, how high they will climb, how completely they will fulfill their promise and potential, and what kind of return the corporation will realize on its investment in their training and development.

There is ample business reason for finding ways to make sure that as many of these women as possible will succeed. The first step in this process is to recognize that women are not all alike. Like men, they are individuals with differing talents, priorities, and motivations. For the sake of simplicity, let me focus on the two women I referred to earlier, on what I call the career-primary woman and the career-and-family woman.

It is absurd to put woman down for having the very qualities that would send a man to the top.

Like many men, some women put their careers first. They are ready to make the same trade-offs traditionally made by the men who seek leadership positions. They make a career decision to put in extra hours, to make sacrifices in their personal lives, to make the most of every opportunity for professional development. For women, of course, this decision also requires that they remain single or at least childless or, if they do have children, that they be satisfied to have others raise them. Some 90% of executive men but only 35% of executive women have children by the age of 40. The *automatic* association of all women with babies is clearly unjustified.

The secret to dealing with such women is to recognize them early, accept them, and clear artificial barriers from their path to the top. After all, the best of these women are among the best managerial talent you will ever see. And career-primary women have another important value to the company that men and other women lack. They can act as role models and mentors to younger women who put their careers first. Since upwardly mobile career-primary women still have few role models to motivate and inspire them, a company with women in its top echelon has a significant advantage in the competition for executive talent.

Men at the top of the organization—most of them over 55, with wives who tend to be traditional—often find career women "masculine" and difficult to accept as colleagues. Such men miss the point, which is not that these women are just like men but that they are just like the *best* men in the organization. And there is such a shortage of the best people that gender cannot be allowed to matter. It is clearly counterproductive to disparage in a woman with executive talent the very qualities that are most critical to the business and that might carry a man to the CEO's office.

Clearing a path to the top for career-primary women has four requirements:

1. Identify them early.
2. Give them the same opportunity you give to talented men to grow and develop and contribute to company profitability. Give them client and customer responsibility. Expect them to travel and relocate, to make the same commitment to the company as men aspiring to leadership positions.
3. Accept them as valued members of your management team. Include them in every kind of communication. Listen to them.
4. Recognize that the business environment is more difficult and stressful for them than for their male peers. They are always a minority, often the only woman. The male perception of talented, ambitious women is at best ambivalent, a mixture of admiration, resentment, confusion, competitiveness, attraction, skepticism, anxiety, pride, and animosity. Women can never feel secure about how they should dress and act, whether they should speak out or grin and bear it when they encounter discrimination, stereotyping, sexual harassment, and paternalism. Social interaction and travel with male colleagues and with male clients can be charged. As they move up, the normal increase in pressure and responsibility is compounded for women because they are women.

Stereotypical language and sexist day-to-day behavior do take their toll on women's career development. Few male executives realize how common it is to call women by their first names while men in the same group are greeted with surnames, how frequently female executives are assumed by men to be secretaries, how often women are excluded from all-male social events where business is being transacted. With notable exceptions, men are still generally more comfortable with other men, and as a result women miss many of the career and business opportunities that arise over lunch, on the golf course, or in the locker room.

The majority of women, however, are what I call career-and-family women, women who want to pursue serious careers while participating actively in the rearing of children. These women are a precious resource that has yet to be mined. Many of them are talented and creative. Most of them are willing to trade some career growth and compensation for freedom from the constant pressure to work long hours and weekends.

A policy that forces women to choose between family and career cuts hugely into profits and competitive advantage.

Most companies today are ambivalent at best about the career-and-family women in their management ranks. They would prefer that all employees were willing to give their all to the company. They believe it is in their best interests for all managers to compete for the top positions so the company will have the largest possible pool from which to draw its leaders.

"If you have both talent and motivation," many employers seem to say "we want to move you up. If you haven't got that motivation, if you want less pressure and greater flexibility, then you can leave and make room for a new generation." These companies lose on two counts. First, they fail to amortize the investment made in the early training and experience of management women who find themselves committed to family as well as to career. Second, they fail to recognize what these women could do for their middle management.

The ranks of middle managers are filled with people on their way up and people who have stalled. Many of them have simply reached their limits, achieved career growth commensurate with or exceeding their capabilities, and they cause problems because their performance is mediocre but they still want to move ahead. The career-and-family woman is willing to trade off the pressures and demands that go with promotion for the freedom to spend more time with her children. She's very smart, she's talented, she's committed to her career, and she's satisfied to stay at the middle level, at least during the early child-rearing years. Compare her with some of the people you have there now.

Consider a typical example, a woman who decides in college on a business career and enters management at age 22. For nine years, the company invests in her career as she gains experience and skills and steadily improves her performance. But at 31, just as the investment begins pay off in earnest, she decides to have a baby. Can the company afford to let her go home, take another job, or go into business for herself? The common perception now is yes, the corporation can afford to lose her unless, after six or eight weeks or even three months of disability and maternity leave, she returns to work on a full-time schedule with the same vigor, commitment, and ambition that she showed before.

But what if she doesn't? What if she wants or needs to go on leave for six months or a year or, heaven forbid, five years? In this worst-case scenario, she works full-time from age 22 to 31 and from 36 to 65—a total of 38 years as opposed to the typical male's 43 years. That's not a huge difference. Moreover, my typical example is willing to work part-time while her children are young, if only her employer will give her the opportunity. There are two rewards for companies responsive to this need: higher retention of their best people and greatly improved performance and satisfaction in their middle management.

The high-performing career-and-family woman can be a major player in your company. She can give you a significant business advantage as the competition for able people escalates. Sometimes too, if you can hold on to her, she will switch gears in mid-life and reenter the competition for the top. The price you must pay to retain these women is threefold: you must plan for and manage maternity, you must provide the flexibility that will allow them to be maximally productive, and you must take an active role in helping to make family supports and high-quality affordable child care available to all women.

The key to managing maternity is to recognize the value of high-performing women and the urgent need to retain them and keep them productive. The first step must be a genuine partnership between the woman and her boss. I know this partnership can seem difficult to forge. One of my own senior executives came to me recently to discuss plans for her maternity leave and subsequent return to work. She knew she wanted to come back. I wanted to make certain that she would. Still, we had a somewhat awkward conversation, because I knew that no woman can predict with certainty when she will be able to return to work or under what conditions. Physical problems can lengthen her leave. So can a demanding infant, a difficult family or personal adjustment, or problems with child care.

I still don't know when this valuable executive will be back on the job full-time, and her absence creates some genuine problems for our organization. But I do know that I can't simply replace her years of experience with a new recruit. Since our conversation, I also know that she wants to come back, and that she *will* come back—part-time at first—unless I make it impossible for her by, for example, setting an arbitrary date for her full-time return or resignation. In turn, she knows that the organization wants and needs her and, more to the point, that it will be responsive to her needs in terms of working hours and child-care arrangements.

In having this kind of conversation it's important to ask concrete questions that will help to move the discussion from uncertainty and anxiety to some level of predictability. Questions can touch on everything from family income and energy level to child care arrangements and career commitment. Of course you want your star manager to return to work as soon as possible but you want her to return permanently and productively. Her downtime on the job is a drain on her energies and a waste of your money.

For all the women who want to combine career and family—the women who want to participate actively in the rearing of their children and who also want to pursue their careers seriously—the key to retention is to provide the flexibility and family supports they need in order to function effectively.

Time spent in the office increases productivity if it is time well spent, but the fact that most women continue to take the primary responsibility for child care is a cause of distraction, diversion, anxiety, and absenteeism—to say nothing of the persistent guilt experienced by all working mothers. A great many women, perhaps most of all women who have always performed at the highest levels, are also frustrated by a sense that while their children are babies they cannot function at their best either at home or at work.

In its simplest form, flexibility is the freedom to take time off—a couple of hours, a day, a week—or to do some work at home and some at the office, an arrangement that communication technology makes increasingly feasible. At the complex end of the spectrum are alternative work schedules that permit the woman to work less than full-time and her employer to reap the benefits of her experience and, with careful planning, the top level of her abilities.

Incredibly, very few companies have ever studied the costs and statistics of maternity leave.

Part-time employment is the single greatest inducement to getting women back on the job expeditiously and the provision women themselves most desire. A part-time return to work enables them to maintain responsibility for critical aspects of their jobs, keeps them in touch with the changes constantly occurring at the workplace and in the job itself, reduces stress and fatigue, often eliminates the need for paid maternity leave by permitting a return to the office as soon as disability leave is over, and, not least, can greatly enhance company loyalty. The part-time solution works particularly well when a work load can be reduced for one individual in a department or when a full-time job can be broken down by skill levels and apportioned to two individuals at different levels of skill and pay.

I believe, however, that shared employment is the most promising and will be the most widespread form of flexible scheduling in the future. It is feasible at every level of the corporation except at the pinnacle, for both the short and the long term. It involves two people taking responsibility for one job.

Two red lights flash on as soon as most executives hear the words "job sharing": continuity and client-customer contact. The answer to the continuity question is to place responsibility entirely on the two individuals sharing the job to discuss everything that transpires—thoroughly, daily, and on their own time. The answer to the problem of client-customer contact is yes, job sharing requires re-education and a period of adjustment. But as both client and supervisor will quickly come to appreciate, two contacts means that the customer has continuous access to the company's representative, without interruptions for vacation, travel, or sick leave. The two people holding the job can simply cover for each other, and the uninterrupted, full-time coverage they provide together can be a stipulation of their arrangement.

Flexibility is costly in numerous ways. It requires more supervisory time to coordinate and manage, more office space, and somewhat greater benefits costs (though these can be contained with flexible benefits plans, prorated benefits, and, in two-paycheck families, elimination of duplicate benefits). But the advantages of reduced turnover and the greater productivity that results from higher energy levels and greater focus can outweigh the costs.

A few hints:

- Provide flexibility selectively. I'm not suggesting private arrangements subject to the suspicion of favoritism but rather a policy that makes flexible work schedules available only to high performers.
- Make it clear that in most instances (but not all) the rates of advancement and pay will be appropriately lower for those who take time off or who work part-time than for those who work full-time. Most career-and-family women are entirely willing to make that trade-off.
- Discuss costs as well as benefits. Be willing to risk accusations of bias. Insist, for example, that half time is half of whatever time it takes to do the job, not merely half of 35 or 40 hours.

The woman who is eager to get home to her child has a powerful incentive to use her time effectively at the office and to carry with her reading and other work that can be done at home. The talented professional who wants to have it all can be a high performer by carefully ordering her priorities and by focusing on objectives rather than on the legendary 15-hour day. By the time professional women have their first babies—at an average age of 32—they have already had nine years to work long hours at a desk, to travel and to relocate. In the case of high performers, the need for flexibility coincides with what has gradually become the goal-oriented nature of responsibility.

Family supports—in addition to maternity leave and flexibility—include the provision of parental leave for men, support for two-career and single-parent families during relocation, and flexible benefits. But the primary ingredient is child care. The capacity of working mothers to function effectively and without interruption depends on the availability of good, affordable child care. Now that women make up almost half the work force and the growing percentage of managers, the decision to become involved in the personal lives of employees is no longer a philosophical question but a practical one. To make matters worse, the quality of child care has almost no relation to technology, inventiveness, or profitability but is more or less a pure function of the quality of child care personnel and the ratio of adults to children. These costs are irreducible. Only by joining hands with government and the public sector can corporations hope to create the vast quantity and variety of child care that their employees need.

Until quite recently, the response of corporations to women has been largely symbolic and cosmetic, motivated in large part by the will to avoid litigation and legal penalties. In some cases, companies were also moved by a genuine sense of fairness and a vague discomfort and frustration at the absence of women above the middle of the corporate pyramid. The actions they took were mostly quick, easy, and highly visible—child care information services, a three-month parental leave available to men as well as women, a woman appointed to the board of directors.

When I first began to discuss these issues 26 years ago, I was sometimes able to get an appointment with the assistant to the assistant in personnel, but it was only a courtesy. Over the past decade, I have met with the CEOs of many large corporations and I've watched them become involved with ideas they had never previously thought much about. Until recently, however, the shelf life of that enhanced awareness was always short. Given pressing, short-term concerns, women were not a front-burner issue. In the past few months, I have seen yet another change. Some CEOs and top management groups now take the initiative. They call and ask us to show them how to shift gears from a responsive to a proactive approach to recruiting, developing, and retaining women.

I think this change is more probably a response to business needs—to concern for the quality of future profits and managerial talent—than to uneasiness about legal requirements, sympathy with the demands of women and minorities, or the desire to do what is right and fair. The nature of such business motivation varies. Some companies want to move women to their positions as role models for those below them and as beacons for talented young recruits. Some want to achieve a favorable image with employees, customers, clients, and stockholders. These are all legitimate motives. But I think the companies that stand to gain most are motivated as well by a desire to capture competitive advantage in an era when talent and competence will be in increasingly short supply. These companies are now ready to stop being defensive about their experience with women and to ask incisive questions without preconceptions.

Even so, incredibly, I don't know of more than one or two companies that have looked into their own records to study the absolutely critical issue of maternity leave—how many women took it, when and whether they returned, and how this behavior correlated with their rank, tenure, age, and performance. The unique drawback to the employment of women is the physical reality of maternity and the particular socializing influence maternity has had. Yet to make women equal to men in the workplace we have chosen on the whole not to discuss this single most significant difference between them. Unless we do, we cannot evaluate the cost of recruiting, developing, and moving women up.

Now that interest is replacing indifference, there are four steps every company can take to examine its own experience with women:

1. Gather quantitative data on the company's experience with management-level women regarding turnover rates, occurrence of and return from maternity leave, and organizational level attained in relation to tenure and performance.
2. Correlate this data with factors such as age, marital status, and presence and age of children, and attempt to identify and analyze why women respond the way they do.
3. Gather qualitative data on the experience of women in your company and on how women are perceived by both sexes.
4. Conduct a cost-benefit analysis of the return on your investment in high-performing women. Factor in the cost to the company of women's negative reactions to negative experience, as well as the probable cost of corrective measures and policies. If women's value to your company is greater than the cost to recruit, train, and develop them—and of course I believe it will be—then you will want to do everything you can to retain them.

We have come a tremendous distance since the days when the prevailing male wisdom saw women as lacking the kind of intelligence that would allow them to succeed in business. For decades, even women themselves have harbored an unspoken belief that they couldn't make it because they couldn't be just like men, and nothing else would do. But now that woman have shown themselves the equal of men in every area of organizational activity, now that they have demonstrated that they can be stars in every field of endeavor, now we can all venture to examine the fact that women and men are different.

On balance, employing women is more costly than employing men. Women can acknowledge this fact today because they know that their value to employers exceeds the additional cost and because they know that changing attitudes can reduce the additional cost dramatically. Women in management are no longer an idiosyncrasy of the arts and education. They have always matched men in natural ability. Within a very few years, they will equal men in numbers as well in every area of economic activity.

The demographic motivation to recruit and develop women is compelling. But an older question remains: Is society better for the change? Women's exit from the home and entry into the work force has certainty created problems—an urgent need for good, affordable child care; troubling questions about the kind of parenting children need; the costs and difficulties of diversity in the workplace; the stress and fatigue of combining work and family responsibilities. Wouldn't we all be happier if we could turn back the clock to an age when men were in the workplace and women in the home, when male and female roles were clearly differentiated and complementary?

Nostalgia, anxiety, and discouragement will urge many to say yes, but my answer is emphatically no. Two fundamental benefits that were unattainable in the past are now within our reach. For the individual, freedom of choice—in this case the freedom to choose career, family, or a combination of the two. For the corporation, access to the most gifted individuals in the country. These benefits are neither self-indulgent nor insubstantial. Freedom of choice and self-realization are too deeply American to be cast aside for some wistful vision of the past. And access to our most talented human resources is not a luxury in this age of explosive international competition but rather the barest minimum that prudence and national self-preservation require.

Felice N. Schwartz is president and founder of Catalyst, a not-for-profit research and advisory organization that works with corporations to foster the career and leadership development of women.

Reprinted by permission of *Harvard Business Review*, January/February 1989, pp. 65–76. Copyright © 1989 by the President and Fellows of Harvard College. All rights reserved.

Who Are You Really Hiring?

Companies often don't screen executive-level applicants. They should. High echelon crooks and cons can cost you fortunes. But there are ways to safeguard a firm from liars and cheats at the top.

By Shari Caudron

James Baughman was imprisoned for stealing money from student funds while he was a California high school principal. He lied about earning a doctorate at Stanford. He eventually became director of recruitment for Lucent Technologies.

Al Dunlap was fired in 1973 by Max Phillips & Son after just seven weeks of employment. Three years later, he was fired by Nitec Paper Corporation—which soon went broke—over allegations of financial fraud. Twenty years later, he surfaced as chairman and chief executive officer for Sunbeam Corporation.

George O'Leary lied on his résumé about earning a master's degree in education from New York University. He lied about lettering in football for three years at the University of New Hampshire. He later was hired as Notre Dame's football coach.

Lucent, Sunbeam, and Notre Dame were not aware—at the time—that they had hired a felon, an alleged books-cooker, and a liar to fill positions of authority. But these organizations *could* have learned about their employees' tainted backgrounds if they'd taken time to do a routine background check.

Open the help-wanted section of any major metropolitan daily and you'll see ads for front-desk clerks, delivery drivers, and salespeople warning that background checks are required. Drug tests, criminal-record checks, and employment and education verification are de rigueur for the rank and file in many companies. But when it comes to filling upper-level positions, there's a class system at work in corporate America. Instead of sifting through background data for the kind of debris that would prevent a clean hire, companies are all too willing to take executive-level applicants at their word.

"You'd think the logic would be that the higher the position, the more screening companies would do," says Les Rosen, attorney and president of Employment Screening Resources in Novato, California. "But from what we've seen, that's not true. Somehow, there is a sense of impropriety in challenging the credentials of people higher up."

Douglas Hahn, president of HRplus, a background-screening firm based in Evergreen, Colorado, agrees. "At some companies there is definitely a good ol' boy network that prevails," he says. "Executives tend to hire their friends, and they hold the integrity of those friends above that of anybody else in the company. Unfortunately, that sometimes backfires."

And those backfires can be devastating. While a low-level employee might manage to embezzle a few thousand dollars or steal some inventory, a single dishonest executive with the right influence and access to accounts can plunge a company into the depths of bankruptcy, taking scores of jobs and billions of dollars in retirement savings and shareholder investment along with it.

While it might be impossible to safeguard a company against every potential act of dishonesty, HR professionals can minimize the chances for unscrupulous behavior by understanding who it is they really are hiring. This means developing background-checking procedures that are utilized at all levels of the organization, including—and perhaps most especially—those at the very top.

Why checking execs is more important today

Up until two years ago, a go-go economy compelled a lot of companies to hire many employees quickly. The talent war was so brutal that businesses didn't have time to slow down and check every detail of an applicant's background. They had to find candidates, make an offer, and issue a company parking pass before the competition could steal that person away. As a result, corners were cut, guidelines were overlooked, and unscrupulous people slipped through the cracks.

Renee Svec, marketing manager of HireCheck, Inc., an employment-screening firm in St. Petersburg, Florida, tells the story of a *Fortune* 500 company that hired a new executive and decided to forgo the background check. "Not long after he was hired, the executive started coming on to a woman in his department," Svec says. "The woman reported his behavior to the corporate security department, which ran a background check and discovered that the executive had operated under several aliases and served more than one prison term for financial fraud."

Today, there's no reason why someone like this should be offered an executive-level position. The labor market has opened up considerably, and HR professionals now have time to check the background of each potential new hire. Furthermore, there's a lot more motivation to do so. The events of September 11 brought the threat of terrorism to the forefront. The scandals in the Catholic Church heightened awareness of sexual predators. Workplace violence is an ongoing concern, especially when unemployment rises. And the collapse of some of the country's largest corporations has shown the enormous potential for financial fraud at the executive level.

If none of these factors sway you to do more digging into a candidate's past, consider this startling fact: a full 44 percent of all resumes are inaccurate, according to Eric Boden, president and CEO of HireRight, a Web-based employment-screening company based in Irvine, California. The inaccuracies could be little white lies such as listing a volunteer position never held, or major whoppers such as lying about advanced degrees or former jobs. Regardless, with so many people being laid off and looking for work, the temptation to make one's resume more attractive is greater now than it has been in some time. And often, the people who pad their resumes are the people you'd least expect.

Two years ago, HireCheck was introducing its background-screening services to a management team at a hospital. The hospital administrator invited HireCheck to run some test searches on a few employees, and put her staff in charge of selecting the sample employees. Thinking it would be fun to run a check on their boss, the staff members chose the administrator as one of the test cases. In conducting the background search, HireCheck discovered that the administrator had falsified details of her educational background, which was grounds for immediate dismissal.

The administrator's termination—which was unwittingly effected by her own hand— would be laughable if the problem of résumé deception weren't so widespread. But even if lying weren't so commonplace, verifying an employee's background is something that all companies should be doing. After all, it doesn't take a parking lot full of dishonest employees to create havoc for an organization. A single well-placed unethical employee can plunder profits before anyone knows what's under way.

What's that, you say? Conducting extensive background checks on management employees is expensive? Better to save the $2,000 to $10,000 average cost and trust your gut? A Toronto-based trucking company thought it was saving money by not checking the background of a woman hired to manage its accounts department. The woman was impressive, after all, and seemed to have the right credentials. Over the course of two years, the employee siphoned $250,000 from the company's general accounts. Ultimately, she was prosecuted on criminal charges and sentenced to three years in jail. Had the trucking company taken the time to call her previous employer, they would have discovered she'd also defrauded that company to the tune of $100,000.

How to integrate background-checking at all levels

HR professionals have an obvious and important role to play in safeguarding company assets by hiring honest employees. But conducting a thorough background check on every employee is not easy, especially if it's not already an accepted part of the culture to do so. Here are some steps that HR people may want to consider:

1. Lobby for the fact that integrity is important. In many companies, HR gets involved in hiring lower-level workers, but executive recruitment is handled by those at the top, who tap into their own executive network. This is fine, but if the executive team wants to build and maintain a company that holds integrity and honesty in the highest regard, everyone should be subjected to the same level of background-checking once a job offer has been made—and it's HR's job to argue for this.

"HR has got to lobby for the fact that high integrity should be a requirement for every job," says Philip Sullivan, vice president of recruitment and placement at nSight, Inc., a staffing firm in Burlington, Massachusetts. One way to do this is to talk about the potential financial consequences of *not* conducting thorough checks.

For instance, if Sunbeam had done a more thorough background check on Al Dunlap, the company might have discovered the allegations of financial fraud in his background and declined to hire him. It's hard to say for sure, but if Dunlap had not been at the helm, Sunbeam might not have had to endure plummeting stock values, stockholder lawsuits, and eventual bankruptcy.

"If an executive wants to shortcut the process and hire a peer without consenting to a background check," Sullivan says, "HR has to make clear to the executive that, in doing so, he or she is putting his or her own integrity at stake."

2. Treat all employees fairly. All employees should be subject to a standard background-screening that includes a credit check; a review of motor vehicle and criminal records; reference checks; and verification of employment, education, professional licenses, and Social Security number. However, Rosen says, "it is perfectly acceptable to have different levels of screening for different positions as long as everyone is treated *fairly*." Someone on an assembly line, for example, would not necessarily receive the same level of scrutiny as a potential executive. But all assembly-line workers should be treated the same way and all executives should be treated the same way. "What you want to do is conduct the screenings that are appropriate for the position," he says.

3. Dig deeper with executive candidates. When hiring executives, Rosen suggests going beyond a standard security-screening and conducting something he calls an "integrity check." "The typical pre-employment screening is a low-cost risk-management tool that looks at verifiable, known factors," he says. An integrity check, however, is more investigative and entails looking at such things as involvement in lawsuits, the financial performance of the person's previous firm, and when and why the candidate might have appeared in local or national newspapers.

Detecting Employees Who Steal

Employee fraud is on the rise, soaring from $400 billion in lost revenue for U.S. businesses in 1996 to an estimated $600 billion in 2002. But there are preventive measures that HR executives can take to spot employees who might be stealing.

First, recognize that small businesses are most vulnerable to employee theft, says Dick Stackpool, a consultant with Aon Risk Services in Minneapolis. In a small firm, a single employee has more responsibility, and therefore often has more access to company information and finances than an employee in a large business.

There's also less managerial oversight in small companies and a more familial atmosphere. Many small-business owners refuse to believe that their employees, who have been treated as friends and family, would ever turn on the company, Stackpool says.

Aon and the Association of Certified Fraud Examiners, in Austin, Texas, have identified several trends that can help HR managers detect employees who might steal:

- The majority of employees who steal—68.6 percent, according to ACFE—have no prior criminal record.
- More of them are males—53.5 percent versus 46.5 percent females—who have a high school education or less. "Losses are strongly related to the perpetrator's position, and in many organizations, the vast majority of managerial and executive positions are still held by males" states ACFE's *2002 Report to the Nation*.
- As the employee's education level rises, the incidence of theft declines: 56.9 percent of thieves have a high school education or less, 32.7 percent have a bachelor's degree, and 10.4 percent have a postgraduate education.
- Watch for employees who are struggling financially or suddenly make large purchases far beyond their means. Stackpool poses this question: "Are they going through a difficult time in their lives—possibly a divorce, or their spouse is laid off—or do they have a mountain of debt?" Although most employees undergoing a personal or financial crisis don't steal, he says, "sometimes they find themselves in a situation where they are just taking some cash to get them over the short-term hump, and that short-term hump moves into a long-term hump… and gets out of hand for them."
- Also watch for an increase in fraud prior to, or in the midst of, merger and acquisition activity. "Employees get the 'I'm going to get mine while I can, I don't have a career here' attitude," he says. Most fraud and theft can be prevented with a few simple internal controls:
- Background checks, which could include criminal checks as well as double-checking of references, are a simple preventive measure. "At a minimum, I would think that checking the past employment would be obvious. Many companies never do reference checks or background checks," Stackpool says.
- The duties of employees should be segregated, so that one employee does not have all control and oversight over the finances and/or inventory. "Does the individual who makes bank deposits also reconcile the books, so they can hide the fact that the cash was not deposited?" he asks.
- An internal accounting system, or a system of checks and balances whereby transactions are reviewed and approved by managers, is essential.
- An internal anonymous hotline for employees to report fraud can also be helpful. "Tips from employees led to the highest percentage of cases being discovered (26 percent, according to ACFE)," Stackpool notes.
- Corporate kindness goes a long way "Share the wealth," he adds. Rewards can range from buying pizza for employees to giving them bonus checks. "It makes it more difficult for them to steal in a place where they're valued."

—*Christine Blank*

4. Don't rely solely on a candidate's former employer. Although a number of states have enacted legislation that protects employers in giving truthful information about a former employee, labor lawyers still counsel HR people to only verify facts of employment. Furthermore, in the age of consolidation and big business, the central HR departments of many companies typically have only sketchy records.

For these reasons, it is not enough to rely on a reference from a former employer. To do an in-depth search, HR people should ask the candidate's supplied references for the names of three other people who might know the candidate.

5. Don't rely solely on search firms. Search firms that don't conduct a thorough background check of candidates can be misled as easily as any employer. In March 1998, Robert Half International Inc. recruited T'Challa Ross as a temporary bookkeeper for Fox Associates Inc., a small advertising agency in Chicago. She performed so well at the job that the company hired her permanently 30 days later. Within months, Ross was taking blank checks from Fox and forging signatures. Within a year, she had embezzled more than $70,000. What makes the case especially disturbing is that the staffing firm had failed to uncover the fact that just two months earlier, Ross had pleaded guilty to stealing $192,873 from another employer and been sentenced to four years' probation and 100 hours of community service.

The problem with relying on staffing services is that they are typically not paid their contingency fee until a job candidate has been placed in the job. Thus, they have a vested interest in placing employees quickly. To ensure that staffing firms take the time to conduct thorough background checks, Eric Archer, president of Spherion Professional Recruiting Group, a professional services staffing firm based in Fort Lauderdale, suggests a pricing mechanism whereby the staffing firm is paid a fee based on two-thirds contingency and one-third retainer. "This shows sincerity on the part of the client who wants to hire someone, and it buys a commitment from the recruiting organization to conduct a more thorough search," he says. This way, if a firm uncovers troubling aspects of a candidate's background that prevent his being hired, the staffing firm still receives some compensation for the work involved.

6. Check everyone, including temps, part-timers, and contract employees. A few years ago, the Los Angeles-based National Academy of Recording Arts and Sciences was preparing for its annual Grammy Awards presentation. To help put together the labor-intensive show, the organization hired several temporary workers. One of them, unbeknownst to the academy's HR people, was a reporter who was posing as a temp in an effort to get inside the academy and gain information on the show's winners. According to HR manager Shonda Grant, the ruse was discovered before the reporter managed to get any privileged information. But ever since then, the academy has required thorough background checks on all employees, including temporary, part-time, and contract workers.

In this era of heightened concern about terrorism and theft, many organizations are choosing to screen the backgrounds of everyone who works for them. In the six months following September 11, for example, Eli Lilly and Company commissioned criminal-background checks of more than 7,000 employees of outside vendors, including construction workers and fast-food staffers.

"There is a clear trend and more genuine concern from companies about checking out all of their employees," Boden says. "Companies are no longer solely concerned with establishing a defense against negligent hiring. They want to be careful about who is being brought in to the business."

7. Don't have interviewers conduct background checks. As a former grocery-store owner and now president of a background-screening firm, Douglas Hahn has interviewed countless people for jobs, and what he's learned is this: you cannot trust your own instincts. "I've been nailed so many times," he says. "At the grocery store, one of my most charismatic, friendly managers was stealing me blind and I had no idea."

Because Hahn has learned to not trust his gut, he always makes it a point to have one person on his staff interview a candidate and another conduct the background check. "People become prejudiced," he says. "You ask questions differently if you've interviewed someone and liked them. For example, instead of asking a reference if there is anything in a person's history that would prevent you from giving him the keys to the vault, you might say, 'There are no problems with this person, right?'"

At HireCheck, Renee Svec confirms that likable and charismatic employees can be particularly challenging. "Recently, we were going to hire a key executive for our office," Svec says. The candidate had been referred by corporate higher-ups who believed she had potential. Svec's team met with the woman and thought she was terrific. The candidate had impressive credentials, an excellent employment history, and professional licensing.

HireCheck offered her the job, contingent on a clean background check. "Basically, everything this woman claimed turned out to be completely false, and we were amazed how she had the nerve to pursue a position with a background-checking company," Svec says. "Prior to that, she'd been our top candidate. She had everybody snookered."

Given the fact that few companies conduct thorough background-screenings on their top-level candidates, chances are good that many more employers are being duped. And sometimes the level of deceit isn't uncovered until it is too late. "We don't often do routine background checks on executives unless it's for a merger or joint venture," says Chris Mathers, vice president of KPMG Forensic, Inc., in Toronto. "But when we do do them, it's typically because a company is about to terminate a person for wrongdoing and they'd never checked that person out in the first place."

Mathers recently worked with an international company that had hired a Harvard graduate with "sterling" credentials. Almost immediately, the company started having problems with the employee, who would stay late at night and engage in bizarre behavior. Eventually, he was caught trying to steal software from the company for his own gain. "Before terminating him, we checked with three previous employers, and all three said the guy was bad news," Mathers says. "He was involved with substance abuse, had assaulted his wife, and had also been terminated at other jobs for stealing.

"Anyone who avoids checking employees does so at their own peril."

Thoroughly checking someone's background doesn't guarantee that you'll prevent the kind of fraud that brought down Enron, WorldCom, and the other corporate disgraces. But in the realm of human behavior, a little safeguarding can go a long way.

workforce.com

For more info on: **Hiring Right** Get 27 steps you can take during hiring to minimize any surprises about the background of one of your employees. workforce.com/02/11/feature1

Contributing editor Shari Caudron lives in Denver. E-mail editors @workforce.com to comment.

Secrets of Finding and Keeping GOOD EMPLOYEES

"To do the best job possible, it is important for America's hiring professionals to challenge their interview processes."

BY JIM SIRBASKU

EVERY JOB IN A COMPANY is important, or it wouldn't exist. In other words, there is a good job for everyone—one where each individual makes a valuable contribution, regardless of where that job is in a company's structure. Finding that person, though, requires a scientific process. That conviction comes from over 35 years experience recruiting, interviewing, and selecting nearly 10,000 salespeople.

Many people believe gut instinct works like magic in selecting key personnel. This is especially true when the person doing the hiring is also successful at doing the job. For example, a top sales producer may think that he or she is the best person to pick other people who will be able to sell successfully. In reality, that likelihood results in less than a 50% success ratio. With stats like that, a toss of the coin could save recruiters a lot of time, energy, and money.

In most job searches, those responsible for doing the hiring sell the job before they select a candidate. This approach is backwards. Why sell the job to someone who isn't a candidate? After all, a savvy applicant may be a good "interview"—well-groomed, friendly, professional, enthusiastic, interested, a good listener, etc. What happens in this case is the recruiter starts doing the talking, telling about the job requirements before the interview starts. It's the candidate who's doing the listening, learning how to appeal to the recruiter. The result is that,

"Teamwork means that each of you do exactly what I tell you to do."

since most individuals can mask their true tendencies for at least 45 minutes, the interviewer rarely gets an accurate picture of the job candidate. Alternatively, why not learn profiles of interviewees before taking the time to sell the job? Then, it may not be necessary to disclose job specifics once this information is gathered if the candidate doesn't represent a good fit.

By selling the job before selecting a candidate, the individuals responsible for hiring often fall prey to pre- and postselection variables. It's a sink-or-swim philosophy that says, "Recruit them in masses; train them in classes; and roll them out on their hockey skates." *That* is postselection. This method is not effective, so some people camouflage it to make it look different. Preselection is when one tries to learn about the candidates and gather information *before* putting them on the job. For instance, accountants typically have personalities that are relatively high-energy, usually indicate a good learning pace, and show an interest in working with numbers and data in general. Yet, these traits cannot be assumed simply because a person is interviewing for an accountant position. The only way to really determine, at the end of an interview, if a job candidate is a potential match is to take the time *up front* to learn about an interviewee.

The art of interviewing is and always has been highly underrated. Many people can ask good questions, but those aren't always as specific to the position as they could be. For example, if you are hiring an accountant, there are questions designed specifically for determining whether a person is capable of offering what an employer needs. By knowing the position requires conscientious behavior and discourages spontaneity, interviewers can design and ask more-targeted and appropriate lines of inquiry, such as: Describe what you've done in the past to make your job easier, or Explain the types of circumstances in which you have felt it necessary to overlook some policies or procedures because they got in the way of reaching a goal. The responses to such inquiries can help uncover whether a person believes that rules can be interpreted loosely.

Similarly, if the position requires an organized individual vs. a reactive one, questions should be asked to zero in on those behaviors, such as: What system do you use to ensure nothing is lost or overlooked?, or Typically, how much time do you spend on planning and handling the small details at your work? The answers here help clarify whether the person will react to situations as they develop instead of creating proactive, detailed plans. Moreover, they show whether the person would have to go against his or her nature to do well in a structured organization with many rules, tight deadlines, and strict codes of behavior.

To do the best job possible, it is important for America's hiring professionals to challenge their interview processes. This includes looking closely at steps that lead up to final hiring decisions and estimating the degree to which hiring decisions are riddled with personal biases. The more scientific the interview is, the less likely emotional decisions will direct the ensuing course of events.

Let's face it; the right job is the only one you have. It may not be the best job, but it's the right job. Recruiting and hiring the wrong person into the right job set[s] in motion a chain of events that can prove disastrous.

Imagine the interviews where emotional hiring decisions are made. The wrong people begin the right jobs and, after trying to perform them, the new hires begin to feel uncomfortable with their obvious lack of progress. Their inability to move forward within a reasonable amount of time naturally brings on stress. The ongoing stress that now burdens these new employees regularly begins to manifest itself negatively. For example, they start to focus on contrary, pessimistic points of view. This should come as no surprise, considering the overwhelming insecurity they feel at this stage.

It is something of an imposter phenomenon. Employees know that, if the hiring process had been based on scientific data alone, they wouldn't have been considered past the first interview. Employees feel out of their league, assume that they are unable to meet expectations, and, thus, a continually defeatist attitude is born.

Heightened feelings of stress become part of the mismatched employee's every workday. Although stress is a psychosomatic illness, it manifests itself in physiological problems, one of which is fatigue. Watch these victims, and notice they tend to speak with a breathy tone once they have reached this stage of stress. Whether aware of it or not, this depressed tone is primarily due to their oppressive sense of fatigue. The next symptom is an increase in absenteeism or increasing difficulty to make it through a full day of work.

Most managers want to reduce and eliminate poor performers by just firing them on the spot. However, that drastic step is far different than what actually should be done. Consider the fact that business moves at the speed of thought, yet relationships aren't given the time or attention necessary to develop. So what typically happens is managers get frustrated and angry with their people and choose to employ the KITA (kick-in-the-ankle) motivation technique.

Often, the boss feels better by going in and turning up the heat. While the big boss walks out like a magician exiting the stage from an applauding audience, the already stressed-out employee enters the meltdown stage. This is when the search for self-preservation begins. They seek out partners-in-crime, meaning others whom dislike the boss, and begin the conflict stage.

After recruiting the coworkers who share their same defeatist attitude toward the company, they spend (waste) time discussing how unjustified the boss' actions are.

Once the word gets around, he is compelled to find a solution before the wrongly hired employee recruits even more malcontents, which could spiral the war between employer and employee out of control. Hiring the wrong person for the right job can set off a chain of events that often does irreparable damage.

Barring some unforeseen miracle, a person's personality doesn't change significantly. People cannot be what they are not meant to be for very long, and that is a painful realization for individuals who run companies. Hiring professionals, trainers, and managers cannot perform magic. Simply telling employees what you want them to become doesn't mean they can internalize those requests and strive to match the profile they were given. The result is that so much time and money are spent on hiring and training the wrong people for the right jobs.

The mistake to avoid goes beyond just having hired the wrong type of person. The real error comes from not realizing that, by simply moving that individual into a more-appropriate position within the company, the problem could easily be fixed. Otherwise, it's very difficult to move the wrong people out of the right jobs—especially if they are putting forth great effort in an ongoing attempt to succeed at what they are not meant to be doing anyway.

This can become a vicious circle that inevitably results in a lose-lose situation for all parties involved. If at all possible, the sensible solution is to relocate a mismatched employee elsewhere in the company. As the saying goes, "For every pot, there's a cover." For every job, there's a person who will perform it with excellence.

What works, what doesn't

Group interviews don't work. They are superficial and more like a game of tag. Selections based on first impressions are flawed. Recruiters' personal biases get in the way. What does work is testing. To understand why, consider a brief chronology of the industry's progress with identifiable components of the hiring process:

Interviews. For far too long, the most important factor in deciding whom to hire was the interview. Experience has shown only a coincidental correlation between the ability to deliver well in an interview and to do so on the job. Studies have pegged this correlation at 14%, or one good employee out of every seven hires. This number increases to 26% if the candidate can pass a background check.

Personality characteristics assessments. The first assessments used to improve the selection process measured personality characteristics. They helped raise the hiring success percentage to 38%.

Abilities assessments. When applicants were assessed for abilities as well as personality, employers found they were hiring the right people approximately 54% of the time.

Interests assessments. Becoming more sophisticated, interests assessment was added to the mix, improving results to 66%.

Integrated assessments. Most impressive to date, these measure a combination of factors, as well as introduce the component of "job match." Cutting-edge technology coupled with empirical data evaluate "The Total Person" in such a way as to measure how much candidates are like the employees who are exemplary in performing their duties. These assessments have increased an employer's ability to identify potentially excellent employees better than 75% of the time.

Assessment vehicles dramatically facilitate the hiring process. The job-match function is the most valuable feature of this process. It refers to the assessment's approach to analyzing a person's job-related attributes and compares them to the qualities required to perform successfully in a given job. By measuring thinking styles, occupational interests, and behavioral traits, the combination allows for a visualization of "The Total Person."

In an interview capacity, people only let you see what they want you to see. Therefore, it's true that individuals can be compared to icebergs in that what you don't see is more significant than what you do. In typical interviews, employers see/scan resumes for work history and education. They observe the way prospects dress, accessorize, and how they carry and conduct themselves. On the other hand, there are significant blind spots for interviewers who choose to ignore assessment testing.

Take, for instance, thinking styles. Evaluating how quickly people can solve problems or absorb information and how capable they are at dealing with simple numbers or comprehending written language are examples of these thinking styles. Occupational interests, as they relate to a particular job or position, are a significant factor in the results and productivity achieved by an individual. Essentially, this part of assessing means learning what will stimulate excitement and commitment from workers. Finally, the assessment of behavior tendencies, as they relate to a particular position, is a significant factor in the results and productivity achieved by an individual:

- *Accommodating* measures a person's general tendency to be friendly, helpful, and agreeable, to be a team person.
- *Assertiveness* measures a tendency to take charge, to be a leader.
- *Attitude* measures a tendency to have a positive attitude.
- *Energy level* measures a tendency to be self-motivated, energetic, to show a high sense of urgency and a capacity for a fast pace.
- *Independence* measures a tendency to make decisions, be self-

reliant, and take independent action.

- *Objective judgment* measures a tendency to be objective in decisionmaking.
- *Sociability* measures a tendency to be people-oriented, to be socially active and outgoing.
- *Manageability* measures the tendency to follow policies, accept external controls and supervision, and work within the rules.
- *Decisiveness* measures the tendency to utilize available information to make decisions quickly.

For a general indication of what happens "behind the scenes" with assessment testing, consider a firm that needs to hire salespeople. A tool is created that matches current top producers from a pattern of their behavioral traits, occupational interests, and learning styles. The combined pattern created is called a Job Match Pattern.

Dig further into the job's requirements by interviewing the people who will be managing the new hires. Ask these managers questions that will uncover their true expectations of the position that needs to be filled. A Job Profile Survey is then filled out and the results are combined with the Job Match Pattern, which ultimately produces a profile of the characteristics required to do the task successfully. In cases where there isn't an incumbent, those who know the job best determine the traits required by the position.

A war for talent is currently under way. This includes a price war, which CEOs need to avoid at all costs. One positive alternative to salary hikes is to offer opportunities for personal growth. In addition, companies should create a culture where employee recognition and appreciation are built into it. These steps will keep worker retention rates high. Here are some effective tools for accomplishing these goals:

- Use a newsletter to recognize an employee-of-the-month. This motivates everyone to get involved. Whether a person is hoping to be nominated or doing the nominating, the process is exciting and meaningful. Consider giving each month's winner a monetary bonus.
- Create an ambience where staff is comfortable. If offices have large windows, plants, outdoor patios, a pleasant dining area, etc., people can take a break and relax.
- Give employees the day off on their birthdays, and celebrate those birthdays at the office with a cake and/or other refreshments.
- Conduct a weekly training session, one night per week. At these meetings, allow each company executive the opportunity to lead a 30-to-60-minute discussion on whatever subject he or she chooses. In some cases, these might be emotional/personal stories. They can be serious or fun. At other times, an executive might want to discuss a recently read book, an industry event, or leadership and management topics. In addition to the presentations, set aside time for exchanging ideas and always include a segment for bringing employees up to date and up to speed, which is when all important company information is announced.
- For computer programmers, consider giving them keys to the building so they can have control over their specific areas. Allow them to work any hours they select and dress however they choose. It works for them. Many like staying up all night and working in little conclaves.

Remember, though, that the value and success of these opportunities are dependent on selecting the right person for the position and creating the right corporate culture.

> *"The importance of hiring the right people for the job cannot be overstated. That's why CEOs and managers can't become lazy in the hiring process."*

As a company grows, CEOs have to be cautious about their span of control. It is very hard to know 100 people very well, but not so difficult to know 10 very well. This means knowing that group's spouses, children, birthdays, what makes them happy, and what discourages them. Most importantly, it means understanding the three key characteristics—occupational interests, thinking styles, and behavioral traits.

When these characteristics are known, it helps managers to learn how certain workers will respond to stress, frustration, and conflict very differently than others. Some react by leaping into action, while others fold like a cheap suitcase. Therefore, the answer to learning what rewards and incentives work best is getting to know employees. Some are motivated by time off, others by freedom to come and go as they please. There is no alternative to and no advantage like getting to know what makes employees tick.

The importance of hiring the right people for the job cannot be overstated. That's why CEOs and managers can't become lazy in the hiring process. As the saying goes, "there's fish in every pond," so a constant stream of applicants coming through the door should be maintained. Doing this requires using nontraditional avenues to find them. The reality is that the classified section isn't the prevailing starting point for hiring anyone. Getting the message

Article 26. Secrets of Finding and Keeping GOOD EMPLOYEES

out means advertising on radio, television, including local cable, and the Internet. Since it is estimated that well over 50% of people aren't happy with their current jobs, it is likely that they are looking at these media for a stab at self-improvement or upward mobility.

Once the likely candidates are gathered, the importance of using assessments in the hiring process is critical. Be sure that all the assessments utilized have job-match concepts and that any tool used has been tested for validity and reliability. Don't be afraid to ask applicants to take a test that runs as long as an hour. It's their time, and you are not paying them for it.

In the end, this process creates a win-win situation for everyone. People are happier, produce more, and experience less stress. Every company needs more individuals who are able to get up in the morning, go to work, and enjoy what they do all day long. People need to think of ways they can do things instead of reasons they cannot. They have to look to their strengths over their weaknesses and their power over their problems. When companies focus on a good job match, by finding the best human capital available for the job, the real benefit goes to the employees. Employers owe it to society to match the right people to the right jobs.

Jim Sirbasku is CEO, Profiles International, a Waco, Tex.-based employment evaluation firm.

From *USA Today* magazine (Society for the Advancement of Education), January 2002. © 2002 by the Society for the Advancement of Education. Reprinted by permission.

CIPD REWARD CONFERENCE

Pay it forward

Sophisticated reward systems are based on performance: not only by individuals but at company, business unit and team level too. If your organisation has not yet managed this, these tactics will show you how

PATRICIA ZINGHEIM AND JAY SCHUSTER

BRANDING TOTAL REWARD SCHEMES has become globally popular. But there is a problem. Too often, when companies talk about "total reward" they simply mean providing generous benefits and a positive place to work. This makes a company attractive to the workforce in general but perhaps not to those who will make your enterprise prosper. We believe companies need to fashion their workplace to be attractive to people who are dedicated to adding value to the business. This is a critical priority, especially during these competitive business times.

It is true that the best people work for more than pay. But our experience shows that there are four essential components which create an atmosphere in which the best people will want to work (*see panel, "Total Reward Components"*). Offer employees an opportunity to grow from a career perspective and a chance to commit to a future they can help make a reality. Make the workplace positive and supportive of high performance. And provide total pay comprised of base pay, variable pay (incentives and equity), benefits, and recognition. While companies' packages vary in emphasis, this combination—our model of total reward—is key to making a company attractive to those who are essential to its success.

Companies have always given lip service to "paying for performance". But if you can capture the hearts, minds and performance of your workforce through a total reward model, instead of merely "sloganising", your company will perform better. It brands your company as an enterprise that wants those who are willing to perform and add value to the business.

Changing rewards is a "hot" change, meaning one that quickly gets everybody's attention. Other tools, such as training and employment policies, are "cold"—they are slow to act and may not even affect current members of staff. Cold changes are much easier but far less effective at boosting performance.

We encourage HR to focus during competitive times on more action-oriented change tools and a total reward solution is the most powerful. But this requires courage and patience. It isn't a quick-fix solution. Even if the effects are fast, it can take time to put in place and may mean following best effective practice rather than just prevailing practice and sometimes breaking new ground in your industry or country.

We propose that your package aims to reward performance at a variety of levels including the company, business unit, small team and individual. Companies wanting to provide attractive total rewards must justify any extra cost in terms of both organisational and workforce outcomes. The workforce must also understand that providing total rewards is reliant upon a sustained level of measured outcomes for organisation growth. Growth is essential—the top organisations seldom shrink to greatness.

Guaranteeing jobs, supporting an attractive work-life balance, adding pay and incentives, encouraging personal development and making the workplace appealing all make poor business sense without an understanding of the need for high performance. Yet we feel most existing solutions ignore performance and encourage entitlement.

Creating such a performance culture requires a relationship between business results and rewards. This means developing an effective performance measurement system that allows the company to credibly reward performance. This isn't an easy job under any circumstances, and not one that can be undertaken without sponsorship from the organisation's leaders and workforce involvement. It needs close attention to the design of the systems and tools that will be needed and effective communication. It isn't as simple as just matching what other companies have done and hoping for the best relative to workforce performance.

Total Reward Components	
Individual Growth	Compelling Future
Total Pay	Positive Workplace

Getting serious about total rewards in the context of value added to the business is the only logical reason to change reward design and communicate a new cultural direction. Here are some tactics to gain lasting value from reward change:

1. **Build the business case and strategy.** Decide why you are changing rewards, what the company will get from it and how this relates to making the enterprise more effective. Set down a meaningful strategy and tactical plan and build a logical business case that justifies why doing this is a priority.

2. **Design measurement metrics and tools.** If you decide to focus total rewards on performance improvement (and we hope you do!), determine what, how, and where performance will be objectively and credibly measured. Then measure it. Do a cost/benefit analysis so you know whether total rewards are adding value to your business.

3. **Target workforce groups.** Focus on the people who are most important to your enterprise. Make total rewards highly attractive to employee groups who have skills and competencies closest to those your company needs and the essential short-supply talent necessary for your business model. Target workforce members who are willing to go the extra mile to get the rewards.

4. **Develop total reward components.** Using our four components of total rewards as a guide, develop your company's total reward solution, keeping the first three tactical suggestions above, in mind. Build a business logic for what you are offering, describe your expectations and identify which employee groups will be attracted to work in a company with this total reward structure.

5. **Solidify champions for longer haul.** Make sure leaders are willing to sponsor the initiative. Help them appreciate that changing rewards may be a "noisy" process and that they will need to get the company through this to make a new reward model work. Be certain they understand that this new reward model applies to them as well as everyone else. Reward role models are very important to making lasting cultural change.

6. **Get people involved.** Involve employees through focus groups or participation in the design process. People more readily accept change they help to create, so getting those to whom the total reward solution is directed into the design process, is critical. An involved workforce can make acceptance much easier.

7. **Address technical design.** Make the total reward design technically sound. Give details the attention they deserve. But remember that a reward solution that is technically excellent but has a poorly conceived strategy is unlikely to add value.

8. **Communicate, follow up and fine-tune.** Strong and consistent communication and follow-up are essential even when you would like to congratulate yourself for a job well done. Constant tuning will be needed to fill any gaps. While cultural change can get a boost from a reward change, this remains a long-term commitment of time and resources.

There's no going back to reward designs that make either the employee the only customer for the reward change or the company the only beneficiary of the reward design. We will increasingly see reward formulas that have something nearly all current pay and reward designs miss: meaningful performance solutions and reward solutions.

Patricia K Zingheim and Jay R Schuster are speaking at the CIPD's Annual Reward Conference on 12 February at the Novotel London West Hotel, Hammersmith. For further details, call 020 8263 3434 or visit www.cipd.co.uk/RewardConference. They are partners in Schuster-Zingheim and Associates, Inc., a Los Angeles-based international pay and rewards consultancy founded in 1985. They were selected as pay and motivation gurus in *The Guru Guide* and wrote *Pay People Right! Breakthrough Reward Strategies to Create Great Companies*, (Jossey-Bass, 2000), along with the all-time best selling book on workforce pay, *The New Pay: Linking Employee and Organizational Performance*, (Jossey-Bass, 1996). They are international speakers and authors of over 100 articles.

Patricia K. Zingheim and Jay R. Schuster, Shuster-Zingheim and Associates, Inc. 1541 Bel Air Road, Los Angeles, CA 90077, www.paypeopleright.com. Reprinted by permission.

Case: *The "Homes" Is Where the Union Is*

Recently 700 employees of a city nursing home and the city home for the aged (two facilities located on the same plot of land) voted overwhelmingly to be represented by a union. The bargaining unit includes a great variety of employees, from custodial and maintenance to social workers and professional nurses. When interviewed after the union had won bargaining rights, the employees claimed that arbitrary and inconsistent treatment by management, and the supervisors in particular, comprised the main reasons for their voting for the union. They charged discriminatory treatment and flagrant favoritism. They also charged that the supervisors made it a practice to discharge employees for trivial reasons or without adequate prior warnings. Employees were subjected to frequent criticism by their supervisors with regard to their job performance. Although many of the supervisors had been promoted from the "ranks," many of them seemed to abuse their authority in dealing with their subordinates.

Top managers in both locations were genuinely surprised when they first learned during negotiations about this serious and widespread employee discontent.

Using the Case on The *"Homes" Is Where the Union Is*

For this case you should consider yourself an arbitrator who has been presented with this case. After reading the case, what decision would you give, knowing that other people had had time off and that memos were only requested at varying intervals?

Go over the review questions at the end. How does the class feel about this as a group? Why?

Exercise: *Assumptions About People at Work*

Instructions

The purpose of this exercise is to help you better understand the assumptions you make about people and their work behaviors. On the following questionnaire, you will find 10 sets of questions. Assign a rank from 0 to 10 to each item in each pair. (0 indicates that you completely disagree with the statement, and 10 means that you completely agree with the statement.) Answer each question as honestly as you can. There are no correct answers, so don't give a response to a question that will sound good to others or that you think is the way you are supposed to answer.

Questions

1. It's only human nature for people to do as little work as they can get away with. ____ (a) When people avoid work, it's usually because their work has been deprived of its meaning. (b)
2. If employees have access to any information they want, they tend to have better attitudes and behave more responsibly. ,____(c) If employees have access to more information than they need to do their immediate tasks, they will usually misuse it. ____ (d)
3. One problem in asking for the ideas of employees is that their perspective is too limited for their suggestions to be of much practical value. ____ (e) Asking employees for their ideas broadens their perspective and results in the development of useful suggestions. ____ (f)
4. If people don't use much imagination and ingenuity on the job, it's probably because relatively few people have much of either. ____ (g) Most people are imaginative and creative but may not show it because of limitations imposed by supervision and the job. ____ (h)
5. People tend to raise their standards if they are accountable for their own behavior and for correcting their own mistakes. ____ (i) People tend to lower their standards if they are not punished for their misbehavior and mistakes. ____ (j)
6. It's better to give people both good and bad news because most employees want the whole story, no matter how painful. ____ (k) It's better to withhold unfavorable news about business because most employees really want to hear only the good news. ____(l)
7. Because supervisors are entitled to more respect than those below them in the organization, it weakens their prestige to admit that a subordinate was right and they were wrong. ____ (m) Because people at all levels are entitled to equal respect, a supervisor's prestige is increased when s/he supports this principle by admitting that a subordinate was right and s/he was wrong. ____ (n)
8. If you give people enough money, they are less likely to be concerned with such intangibles as responsibility and recognition. ____ (0) If you give people interesting and chal-

lenging work, they are less likely to complain about such things as pay and supplemental benefits. ____ (p)
9. If people are allowed to set their own goals and standards of performance, they tend to set them higher than the boss would. ____ (q) If people are allowed to set their own goals and standards of performance, they tend to set them lower than the boss would. ____ (r)
10. The more knowledge and freedom a person has regarding his job, the more controls are needed to keep him/her in line. ____ (s) The more knowledge and freedom a person has regarding his/her job, the fewer controls are needed to ensure satisfactory job performance. ____ (t)

After Completing the Questionnaire

When you have completed all of the questions, you may score the questionnaire in the following manner. Add together the scores of items: (a), (d), (e), (g), (j), (I), (in), (o), (r), and (s). The sum of these scores will provide you with your 'Theory X" score. Then add together the remaining scores: (b), (C), (f), (h), (i), (k), (n), (p), (q), and (t). The sum of these scores will give you your Theory Y" score.

In a group, discuss the relative strength of each of your scores. Is there a significant difference in the two scores? What might this mean? How do you believe your assumptions might affect your actions as a manager? Do your past experiences support the self-profile that has emerged from your discussion? Discuss with other members of your group how your scores may be related to the concepts of "espoused theory" and "theory-in-use."

Case: The "Homes" Is Where the Union Is; Exercise: Assumptions About People at Work, Fred Maidment, McGraw-Hill/Dushkin, 2000.

UNIT 7
Perspectives and Trends

Unit Selections

28. **The Discipline of Innovation**, Peter F. Drucker
29. **American Corporations: The New Sovereigns**, Lawrence E. Mitchell
30. **The Need for a Corporate Global Mind-Set**, Thomas M. Begley and David P. Boyd
31. **Helping Organizations Build Community**, Tracy Mauro
32. **Ensuring Ethical Effectiveness**, Randy Myers
33. **The Competitive Advantage of Corporate Philanthropy**, Michael E. Porter and Mark R. Kramer
34. **Who Cares Wins**, Stephen Cook
35. **Determining the Strategies and Tactics of Ownership Succession**, James Ahern
36. **Hearts, Minds, and the War Against Terror**, Joshua Muravchik
    CASE VII. The Trip to Denver; Exercise: The Resume--A Career Management Tool

Key Points to Consider

- In the future, organizations are going to have to take a more proactive role in the affairs of the communities around them. How do you see them being involved?

- Multinational corporations are growing in power and in influence. How do you see this affecting the economy both in the United States and abroad?

- Corporate culture is one of the most powerful forces in any organization. How do you see this as determining the course that organizations are likely to take in the future?

- Ethics are a primary concern of any organization. Is it OK to take home a pen or a pencil or to make personal copies on the office copier? Where do you draw the line? When do people cross it?

- How do you think the war on terror has changed the way managers conduct their businesses?

- Where do you think the largest and most important battlefield will be in the war on terror? Defend your answer.

 **Links: www.dushkin.com/online/**
These sites are annotated in the World Wide Web pages.

Institute for International Economics
http://www.iie.com

Small Business Management
http://management.tqn.com/msubs.htm

Terrorism Research Center
http://www.terrorism.com

World Trade Organization (WTO) Web Site
http://www.wto.org/index.htm

Managers are facing new challenges. While it is never possible to determine exactly what the future will hold, there are certain trends and movements that can be perceived by an aware and thoughtful manager. Innovation is always going to be an important feature for a society that depends on technology to remain ahead of its competition to maintain its standard of living and competitive edge. In "The Discipline of Innovation" Peter Drucker identifies seven kinds of opportunities that may be used to help develop innovation.

The multinational corporation is changing the way people do business. These corporate giants are coming to dominate the global economy in ways that have not been foreseen. Most of these companies started in the United States, but there are also organizations with European and Japanese roots that would fall into this category. These organizations are very powerful, and there is concern that they may come to dominate, not only in the economic and commercial arena, but in other ways as well, as shown by Lawrence Mitchell in "American Corporations: The New Sovereigns."

Another development in American society has been the rise of the small businessperson. Over the past decade, the number of people employed by Fortune 500 industrial companies has declined, while the size of the workforce has increased. Many of these new workers have entered small firms. Small businesses tend to be family businesses, and it is often difficult to determine where the business ends and the family begins. In addition, these businesses are entrepreneurial in nature. Entrepreneurs serve the highly creative function of creating new jobs and new businesses. They develop and market new products and services and are often on the cutting edge of the new technology of tomorrow, both technical and managerial. One of the major challenges facing these firms is succession planning, which is discussed in "Determining the Strategies and Tactics of Ownership Succession."

Corporate culture is an aspect of organizations that many people know about but few truly understand. Every organization has a culture, which to a certain degree is a reflection of the values and ethics of senior management, as well as the values and ethics of the society of which the organization is a part. Paying attention to the culture is a key element in developing the organization and achieving success. Organizations that have strong cultures tend to be more successful than organizations that do not, and ensuring the strength of the organizational culture is a primary concern of management because it is from the culture that so many other aspects of the organization flow as seen in "Helping Organizations Build Community."

Managers and their organizations have been criticized over the past several years for a lack of ethics and morality. A small and, when they are caught, highly publicized minority has indeed played fast and loose with the law and with ethics. Some continue to do so, especially in the global arena where it has sometimes been difficult to enforce the rules of the corporations themselves concerning illegal acts. These acts have caused all managers to look more closely at their own behavior and to develop ethical guidelines, as discussed in "Ensuring Ethical Effectiveness." The public and, therefore, courts are starting to take a dimmer view of white-collar crime, to the point of sending some executives to triqal, such as those from Adelphia, Enron, and WorldCom, who face substantial prison sentences. Taking ethical and principled behavior one step further, many executives are learning that doing good for their communities can lead to greater competitive strength and profitability, as demonstrated in "The Competitive Advantage of Corporate Philanthropy," and "Who Cares Wins."

Managers are also challenged to deal with the new environment that resulted from the September 11 attacks. These attacks ushered in a new era for Western democracies, as well as for the businesses and corporations that have flourished in the capitalist environment provided by these democracies. There are changes both in the United States and abroad, and managers are going to play an important role in those changes.

Finally, managers are starting to examine their careers in light of the new developments in the marketplace. In earlier generations, managers would work for the same firm for their entire working lives. That is no longer the case. Managers in today's environment must be flexible. They have to be responsible for their own careers, because the firms they join could go out of business or be purchased, and they could be left without a job. Managers must look after themselves and make career moves independently, if they hope to succeed.

Article 28

The Discipline of Innovation

*In business, innovation rarely springs from a flash of inspiration.
It arises from a cold-eyed analysis of seven kinds of opportunities.*

by Peter F. Drucker

How much of innovation is inspiration, and how much is hard work? If it's mainly the former, then management's role is limited: Hire the right people, and get out of their way. If it's largely the latter, management must play a more vigorous role: Establish the right roles and processes, set clear goals and relevant measures, and review progress at every step. Peter Drucker, with the masterly subtlety that is his trademark, comes down somewhere in the middle. Yes, he writes in this article, innovation is real work, and it can and should be managed like any other corporate function. But that doesn't mean it's the same as other business activities. Indeed, innovation is the work of *knowing* rather than *doing*.

Drucker argues that most innovative business ideas come from methodically analyzing seven areas of opportunity, some of which lie within particular companies or industries and some of which lie in broader social or demographic trends. Astute managers will ensure that their organizations maintain a clear focus on all seven. But analysis will take you only so far. Once you've identified an attractive opportunity, you still need a leap of imagination to arrive at the right response—call it "functional inspiration."

DESPITE much discussion these days of the "entrepreneurial personality," few of the entrepreneurs with whom I have worked during the past 30 years had such personalities. But I have known many people—salespeople, surgeons, journalists, scholars, even musicians—who did have them without being the least bit entrepreneurial. What all the successful entrepreneurs I have met have in common is not a certain kind of personality but a commitment to the systematic practice of innovation.

Innovation is the specific function of entrepreneurship, whether in an existing business, a public service institution, or a new venture started by a lone individual in the family kitchen. It is the means by which the entrepreneur either creates new wealth-producing resources or endows existing resources with enhanced potential for creating wealth.

Today, much confusion exists about the proper definition of entrepreneurship. Some observers use the term to refer to all small businesses; others, to all new businesses. In practice, however, a great many well-established businesses engage in highly successful entrepreneurship. The term, then, refers not to an enterprise's size or age but to a certain kind of activity. At the heart of that activity is innovation: the effort to create purposeful, focused change in an enterprise's economic or social potential.

Sources of Innovation

There are, of course, innovations that spring from a flash of genius. Most innovations, however, especially the successful ones, result from a conscious, purposeful search for innovation opportunities, which are found only in a few situations. Four such areas of opportunity exist within a company or industry: unexpected occurrences, incongruities, process needs, and industry and market changes.

Three additional sources of opportunity exist outside a company in its social and intellectual environment: demographic changes, changes in perception, and new knowledge.

True, these sources overlap, different as they may be in the nature of their risk, difficulty, and complexity, and the potential for innovation may well lie in more than one area at a time. But together, they account for the great majority of all innovation opportunities.

1 Unexpected Occurrences

Consider, first, the easiest and simplest source of innovation opportunity: the unexpected. In the early 1930s, IBM developed the first modern accounting machine, which was designed for banks. But banks in 1933 did not buy new equipment. What saved the company—according to

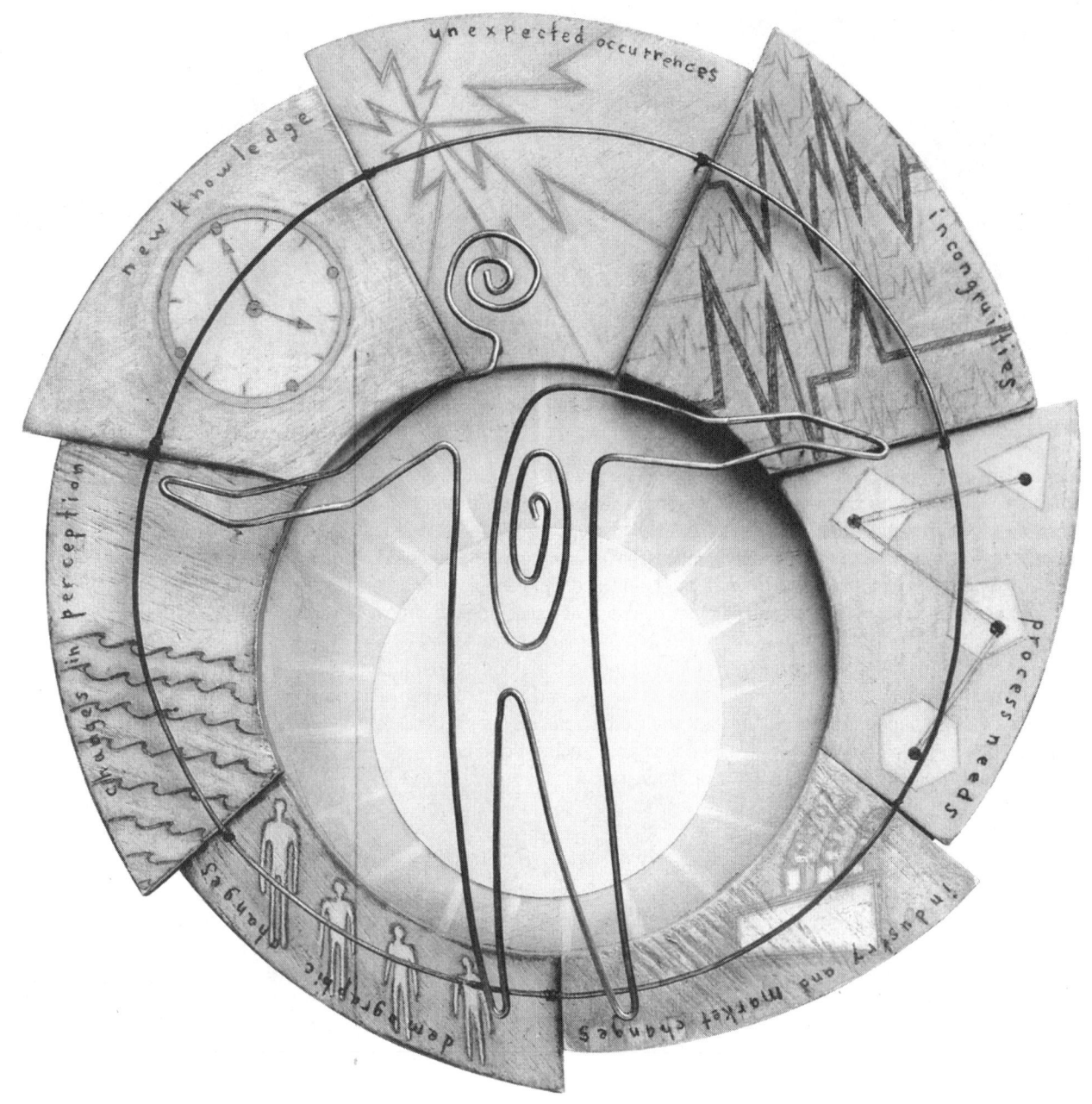

Illustration Maria Rendon

a story that Thomas Watson, Sr., the company's founder and long-term CEO, often told—was its exploitation of an unexpected success: The New York Public Library wanted to buy a machine. Unlike the banks, libraries in those early New Deal days had money, and Watson sold more than a hundred of his otherwise unsalable machines to libraries.

Fifteen years later, when everyone believed that computers were designed for advanced scientific work, business unexpectedly showed an interest in a machine that could do payroll. Univac, which had the most advanced machine, spurned business applications. But IBM immediately realized it faced a possible unexpected success, redesigned what was basically Univac's machine for such mundane applications as payroll, and within five years became a leader in the computer industry, a position it has maintained to this day.

The unexpected failure may be an equally important source of innovation opportunities. Everyone knows about the Ford Edsel as the biggest new-car failure in automotive history. What very few people seem to know, however, is that the Edsel's failure was the foundation for much of the company's later success. Ford planned the Edsel, the most carefully designed car to that point in American automotive history, to give the company a full product line with which to compete with General Motors. When it bombed, despite all the planning, market research, and design that had gone into it, Ford realized

166

that something was happening in the automobile market that ran counter to the basic assumptions on which GM and everyone else had been designing and marketing cars. No longer was the market segmented primarily by income groups; the new principle of segmentation was what we now call "lifestyles." Ford's response was the Mustang, a car that gave the company a distinct personality and reestablished it as an industry leader.

Unexpected successes and failures are such productive sources of innovation opportunities because most businesses dismiss them, disregard them, and even resent them. The German scientist who around 1905 synthesized novocaine, the first nonaddictive narcotic, had intended it to be used in major surgical procedures like amputation. Surgeons, however, preferred total anesthesia for such procedures; they still do. Instead, novocaine found a ready appeal among dentists. Its inventor spent the remaining years of his life traveling from dental school to dental school making speeches that forbade dentists from "misusing" his noble invention in applications for which he had not intended it.

This is a caricature, to be sure, but it illustrates the attitude managers often take to the unexpected: "It should not have happened." Corporate reporting systems further ingrain this reaction, for they draw attention away from unanticipated possibilities. The typical monthly or quarterly report has on its first page a list of problems—that is, the areas where results fall short of expectations. Such information is needed, of course, to help prevent deterioration of performance. But it also suppresses the recognition of new opportunities. The first acknowledgment of a possible opportunity usually applies to an area in which a company does better than budgeted. Thus genuinely entrepreneurial businesses have two "first pages"—a problem page and an opportunity page—and managers spend equal time on both.

2 Incongruities

Alcon Laboratories was one of the success stories of the 1960s because Bill Conner, the company's cofounder, exploited an incongruity in medical technology. The cataract operation is the world's third or fourth most common surgical procedure. During the past 300 years, doctors systematized it to the point that the only "old-fashioned" step left was the cutting of a ligament. Eye surgeons had learned to cut the ligament with complete success, but it was so different a procedure from the rest of the operation, and so incompatible with it, that they often dreaded it. It was incongruous.

Doctors had known for 50 years about an enzyme that could dissolve the ligament without cutting. All Conner did was to add a preservative to this enzyme that gave it a few months' shelf life. Eye surgeons immediately accepted the new compound, and Alcon found itself with a worldwide monopoly. Fifteen years later, Nestlé bought the company for a fancy price.

Such an incongruity within the logic or rhythm of a process is only one possibility out of which innovation opportunities may arise. Another source is incongruity between economic realities. For instance, whenever an industry has a steadily growing market but falling profit margins—as, say, in the steel industries of developed countries between 1950 and 1970—an incongruity exists. The innovative response: minimills.

An incongruity between expectations and results can also open up possibilities for innovation. For 50 years after the turn of the century, shipbuilders and shipping companies worked hard both to make ships faster and to lower their fuel consumption. Even so, the more successful they were in boosting speed and trimming their fuel needs, the worse the economics of ocean freighters became. By 1950 or so, the ocean freighter was dying, if not already dead.

All that was wrong, however, was an incongruity between the industry's assumptions and its realities. The real costs did not come from doing work (that is, being at sea) but from *not* doing work (that is, sitting idle in port). Once managers understood where costs truly lay, the innovations were obvious: the roll-on and roll-off ship and the container ship. These solutions, which involved old technology, simply applied to the ocean freighter what railroads and truckers had been using for 30 years. A shift in viewpoint, not in technology, totally changed the economics of ocean shipping and turned it into one of the major growth industries of the last 20 to 30 years.

3 Process Needs

Anyone who has ever driven in Japan knows that the country has no modern highway system. Its roads still follow the paths laid down for—or by—oxcarts in the tenth century. What makes the system work for automobiles and trucks is an adaptation of the reflector used on American highways since the early 1930s. The reflector lets each car see which other cars are approaching from any one of a half-dozen directions. This minor invention, which enables traffic to move smoothly and with a minimum of accidents, exploited a process need.

> *Knowledge-based innovations can be temperamental, capricious, and hard to direct.*

What we now call the media had its origin in two innovations developed around 1890 in response to process needs. One was Ottmar Mergenthaler's Linotype, which made it possible to produce newspapers quickly and in large volume. The other was a social innovation, modern advertising, invented by the first true newspaper publishers, Adolph Ochs of the *New York Times,* Joseph Pulitzer of the *New York World,* and William Randolph Hearst. Advertising made it possible for them to distribute news practically free of charge, with the profit coming from marketing.

4 Industry and Market Changes

Managers may believe that industry structures are ordained by the good Lord, but these structures can—and often do—change overnight. Such change creates tremendous opportunity for innovation.

One of American business's great success stories in recent decades is the brokerage firm of Donaldson, Lufkin & Jenrette, recently acquired by the Equitable Life Assurance Society. DL&J was founded in 1960 by three young men, all graduates of the Harvard Business School, who realized that the structure of the financial industry was changing as institutional investors became dominant. These young men had practically no capital and no connections. Still, within a few years, their firm had become a leader in the move to negotiated commissions and one of Wall Street's stellar performers. It was the first to be incorporated and go public.

In a similar fashion, changes in industry structure have created massive innovation opportunities for American health care providers. During the past ten or 15 years, independent surgical and psychiatric clinics, emergency centers, and HMOs have opened throughout the country. Comparable opportunities in telecommunications followed industry upheavals—in transmission (with the emergence of MCI and Sprint in long-distance service) and in equipment (with the emergence of such companies as Rolm in the manufacturing of private branch exchanges).

When an industry grows quickly—the critical figure seems to be in the neighborhood of 40% growth in ten years or less—its structure changes. Established companies, concentrating on defending what they already have, tend not to counterattack when a newcomer challenges them. Indeed, when market or industry structures change, traditional industry leaders again and again neglect the fastest growing market segments. New opportunities rarely fit the way the industry has always approached the market, defined it, or organized to serve it. Innovators therefore have a good chance of being left alone for a long time.

5 Demographic Changes

Of the outside sources of innovation opportunities, demographics are the most reliable. Demographic events have known lead times; for instance, every person who will be in the American labor force by the year 2000 has already been born. Yet because policy makers often neglect demographics, those who watch them and exploit them can reap great rewards.

The Japanese are ahead in robotics because they paid attention to demographics. Everyone in the developed countries around 1970 or so knew that there was both a baby bust and an education explosion going on; about half or more of the young people were staying in school beyond high school. Consequently, the number of people available for traditional blue-collar work in manufacturing was bound to decrease and become inadequate by 1990. Everyone knew this, but only the Japanese acted on it, and they now have a ten-year lead in robotics.

Much the same is true of Club Mediterranee's success in the travel and resort business. By 1970, thoughtful observers could have seen the emergence of large numbers of affluent and educated young adults in Europe and the United States. Not comfortable with the kind of vacations their working-class parents had enjoyed—the summer weeks at Brighton or Atlantic City—these young people were ideal customers for a new and exotic version of the "hangout" of their teen years.

Managers have known for a long time that demographics matter, but they have always believed that population statistics change slowly. In this century, however, they don't. Indeed, the innovation opportunities made possible by changes in the numbers of people—and in their age distribution, education, occupations, and geographic location—are among the most rewarding and least risky of entrepreneurial pursuits.

6 Changes in Perception

"The glass is half full" and "The glass is half empty" are descriptions of the same phenomenon but have vastly different meanings. Changing a manager's perception of a glass from half full to half empty opens up big innovation opportunities.

All factual evidence indicates, for instance, that in the last 20 years, Americans' health has improved with unprecedented speed—whether measured by mortality rates for the newborn, survival rates for the very old, the incidence of cancers (other than lung cancer), cancer cure rates, or other factors. Even so, collective hypochondria grips the nation. Never before has there been so much concern with or fear about health. Suddenly, everything seems to cause cancer or degenerative heart disease or premature loss of memory. The glass is clearly half empty.

Rather than rejoicing in great improvements in health, Americans seem to be emphasizing how far away they still are from immortality. This view of things has created many opportunities for innovations: markets for new health care magazines, for exercise classes and jogging equipment, and for all kinds of health foods. The fastest growing new U.S. business in 1983 was a company that makes indoor exercise equipment.

A change in perception does not alter facts. It changes their meaning, though—and very quickly. It took less than two years for the computer to change from being perceived as a threat and as something only big businesses would use to something one buys for doing income tax. Economics do not necessarily dictate such a change; in fact, they may be irrelevant. What determines whether people see a glass as half full or half empty is mood rather than fact, and a change in mood often defies quantification. But it is not exotic. It is concrete. It can be defined. It can be tested. And it can be exploited for innovation opportunity.

7 New Knowledge

Among history-making innovations, those that are based on new knowledge—whether scientific, technical, or social—rank high. They are the superstars of entrepreneurship; they get the publicity and the money. They are what people usually mean when they talk of innovation, although not all innovations based on knowledge are important.

Knowledge-based innovations differ from all others in the time they take, in their casualty rates, and in their predictability, as well as in the challenges they pose to entrepreneurs. Like most superstars, they can be temperamental, capricious, and hard to direct. They have, for instance, the longest lead time of all innovations. There is a protracted span between the emergence of new knowledge and its distillation into usable technology. Then there is another long period before this new technology appears in the marketplace in products, processes, or services. Overall, the lead time involved is something like 50 years, a figure that has not shortened appreciably throughout history.

To become effective, innovation of this sort usually demands not one kind of knowledge but many. Consider one of the most potent knowledge-based innovations: modern banking. The theory of the entrepreneurial bank—that is, of the purposeful use of capital to generate economic development—was formulated by the Comte de Saint-Simon during the era of Napoleon. Despite Saint-Simon's extraordinary prominence, it was not until 30 years after his death in 1825 that two of his disciples, the brothers Jacob and Isaac Pereire, established the first entrepreneurial bank, the Credit Mobilier, and ushered in what we now call finance capitalism.

The Pereires, however, did not know modern commercial banking, which developed at about the same time across the channel in England. The Credit Mobilier failed ignominiously. A few years later, two young men—one an American, J. P. Morgan, and one a German, Georg Siemens—put together the French theory of entrepreneurial banking and the English theory of commercial banking to create the first successful modern banks: J. P. Morgan & Company in New York, and the Deutsche Bank in Berlin. Ten years later, a young Japanese, Shibusawa Eiichi, adapted Siemens's concept to his country and thereby laid the foundation of Japan's modern economy. This is how knowledge-based innovation always works.

The computer, to cite another example, required no fewer than six separate strands of knowledge:

- binary arithmetic;
- Charles Babbage's conception of a calculating machine, in the first half of the nineteenth century;
- the punch card, invented by Herman Hollerith for the U.S. census of 1890;
- the audion tube, an electronic switch invented in 1906;
- symbolic logic, which was developed between 1910 and 1913 by Bertrand Russell and Alfred North Whitehead;
- and concepts of programming and feedback that came out of abortive attempts during World War I to develop effective antiaircraft guns.

Although all the necessary knowledge was available by 1918, the first operational digital computer did not appear until 1946.

Long lead times and the need for convergence among different kinds of knowledge explain the peculiar rhythm of knowledge-based innovation, its attractions, and its dangers. During a long gestation period, there is a lot of talk and little action. Then, when all the elements suddenly converge, there is tremendous excitement and activity and an enormous amount of speculation. Between 1880 and 1890, for example, almost 1,000 electric-apparatus companies were founded in developed countries. Then, as always, there was a crash and a shakeout. By 1914, only 25 were still alive. In the early 1920s, 300 to 500 automobile companies existed in the United States; by 1960, only four of them remained.

Innovation requires knowledge, ingenuity, and, above all else, focus.

It may be difficult, but knowledge-based innovation can be managed. Success requires careful analysis of the various kinds of knowledge needed to make an innovation possible. Both J. P. Morgan and Georg Siemens did this when they established their banking ventures. The Wright brothers did this when they developed the first operational airplane.

Careful analysis of the needs—and, above all, the capabilities—of the intended user is also essential. It may seem paradoxical, but knowledge-based innovation is more market dependent than any other kind of innovation. De Havilland, a British company, designed and built the first passenger jet, but it did not analyze what the market needed and therefore did not identify two key factors. One was configuration—that is, the right size with the right payload for the routes on which a jet would give an airline the greatest advantage. The other was equally mundane: How could the airlines finance the purchase of such an expensive plane? Because de Havilland failed to do an adequate user analysis, two American companies, Boeing and Douglas, took over the commercial jet-aircraft industry.

Principles of Innovation

Purposeful, systematic innovation begins with the analysis of the sources of new opportunities. Depending on the context, sources will have different importance at different times. Demographics, for instance, may be of little concern to innovators of fundamental industrial processes like steelmaking, although the Linotype machine became successful primarily because there were not enough skilled typesetters available to satisfy a mass market. By the same token, new knowledge may be of little relevance to someone innovating a social instrument to satisfy a need that changing demographics or tax laws have created. But whatever the situation, innovators must analyze all opportunity sources.

Because innovation is both conceptual and perceptual, would-be innovators must also go out and look, ask, and listen. Successful innovators use both the right and left sides of their brains. They work out analytically what the innovation has to be to satisfy an opportunity. Then they go out and look at potential users to study their expectations, their values, and their needs.

To be effective, an innovation has to be simple, and it has to be focused. It should do only one thing; otherwise it confuses people. Indeed, the greatest praise an innovation can receive is for people to say, "This is obvious! Why didn't I think of it? It's so simple!" Even the innovation that creates new users and new markets should be directed toward a specific, clear, and carefully designed application.

Effective innovations start small. They are not grandiose. It may be to enable a moving vehicle to draw electric power while it runs along rails, the innovation that made possible the electric streetcar. Or it may be the elementary idea of putting the same number of matches into a matchbox (it used to be 50). This simple notion made possible the automatic filling of matchboxes and gave the Swedes a world monopoly on matches for half a century. By contrast, grandiose ideas for things that will "revolutionize an industry" are unlikely to work.

In fact, no one can foretell whether a given innovation will end up a big business or a modest achievement. But even if the results are modest, the successful innovation aims from the beginning to become the standard setter, to determine the direction of a new technology or a new industry, to create the business that is—and remains—ahead of the pack. If an innovation does not aim at leadership from the beginning, it is unlikely to be innovative enough.

Above all, innovation is work rather than genius. It requires knowledge. It often requires ingenuity. And it requires focus. There are clearly people who are more talented innovators than others, but their talents lie in well-defined areas. Indeed, innovators rarely work in more than one area. For all his systematic innovative accomplishments, Thomas Edison worked only in the electrical field. An innovator in financial areas, Citibank for example, is not likely to embark on innovations in health care.

In innovation, as in any other endeavor, there is talent, there is ingenuity, and there is knowledge. But when all is said and done, what innovation requires is hard, focused, purposeful work. If diligence, persistence, and commitment are lacking, talent, ingenuity, and knowledge are of no avail.

There is, of course, far more to entrepreneurship than systematic innovation—distinct entrepreneurial strategies, for example, and the principles of entrepreneurial management, which are needed equally in the established enterprise, the public service organization, and the new venture. But the very foundation of entrepreneurship is the practice of systematic innovation.

Peter F. Drucker is the Marie Rankin Clarke Professor of Social Science and Management at Claremont Graduate University's Peter F. Drucker Graduate School of Management in Claremont, California. He has written more than two dozen articles for HBR. This article was originally adapted from his book Innovation and Entrepreneurship: Practice and Principles *(Harper & Row, 1985).*

Reprinted with permission from *Harvard Business Review*, August 2002, pp. 95-98, 100, 102. © 2002 by the Harvard School Publishing Corporation. All rights reserved.

American Corporations: the New Sovereigns

By Lawrence E. Mitchell

ONE of the most striking yet overlooked aspects of the current globalization debate is the quiet retreat of sovereign power—including that of the United States—in the face of imperial conquests by modern American corporations. At least until the recent downturns in the stock market—both the general one in 2000 and the sharper one following the attacks of September 11—a number of these companies, including Wal-Mart, Microsoft, Intel, General Electric, and Hewlett-Packard, have had market capitalizations larger than the gross national products of a number of developed and developing countries, including Spain, Kuwait, Argentina, Greece, Poland, and Thailand. The statistics overwhelmingly demonstrate that such corporations and American capital are increasingly dominant throughout the world. At last count, American institutional assets constituted an aggregate 66.8 percent of the total in five major foreign economies, including those of France and Germany.

Modern democracies are built to ensure the restraint of power and the pursuit of public will by forgoing efficiency for patience and consensus. In contrast, the modern American corporation, with its centralized control and absolute power in the board, is brilliantly and devastatingly built for economic efficiency—the ability to amass huge resources and deploy them instantly. No socialist economy has ever had the command-and-control capacities of the American corporation.

The scary thing is that we have come to see these corporations as built for a single purpose, to maximize stockholder wealth, and we have created them in a manner that exempts them from any of the normal moral constraints we expect from governments or individuals.

It has not always been so. Several factors led to the development of this new ethic over the last couple of decades. Among them were deregulation beginning during the Reagan era, together with an increased emphasis on wealth maximization as a social goal; the expectations created in stockholders by the quick money made in hostile takeovers, especially during the 1980s; and the charging bull market of the 1990s. Those phenomena have instilled stockholder expectations of large and immediate returns.

AMERICAN CORPORATIONS and their managers are thus increasingly driven by the faceless, soulless capital markets—markets composed of individuals with consciences but creating a collective that lacks one. Moreover, pressure on corporations to show higher stock prices fast has been increased by the enormous growth in institutional investors, which now own about half of the equity market in the United States.

They also dominate institutional investing in foreign markets like those of Western Europe. Institutional investors compensate their managers on the basis of their ability to raise the values of their portfolios immediately, so those managers have every incentive to push for short-term stock-price maximization over long-term gain and corporate stability.

In addition to the pressure of institutional investors, American investment banks, and consulting companies, markets are driven by nongovernmental organizations like the World Bank and the International Monetary Fund. Those players have implicitly, and sometimes explicitly, conditioned the supply of American capital (and in the case of the nongovernmental organizations, largely Western capital) to overseas markets on those markets' adoption of American-style, stockholder-centered, corporate capitalism.

To be sure, American corporations have brought the world great benefits: increased travel, communication, health, nutrition, and production capabilities. They have also brought Americans a higher material standard of living. But it is, in large part, the stockholder-centered nature of the corporation that leads it to behave in ways that no thoughtful person really wants, ways that most of us would consider to be irresponsible.

Although no legal doctrine requires it, American capitalist culture has adopted the view that maximizing stock price is the purpose of the corporation, its reason for being. Capital markets demand that maximization, and punish those corporations that fail to meet short-term expectations—just look at the stock price of any corporation that reports disappointing quarterly earnings. Corporate structure implies stock-price maximization: Only stockholders vote for directors, only stockholders have the right to sue, and only stockholders have the ability to sell the company out from under the directors.

Coupled with the maximization goal is the limited liability that shields the corporation. While corporations can be sued for causing harm, and sometimes even criminally prosecuted, the extent of their risk is finite. When a chemical plant in Bhopal, India, explodes because corners were cut, or Love Canal is poisoned because it is cheaper to pollute, or asbestos sickens thousands because the product is unsafe, the injured can recover only from the assets of the corporation. Directors and stockholders generally are not liable for its debts, and so many of the costs of maximizing stock price can be externalized onto all of those people and things, other than the stockholders, whom the corporation's behavior affects—workers, consumers, entire communities, the environment.

Layoffs are a fast way to cut costs and raise stock price. Saving a few dollars by placing a gas tank in not necessarily the safest spot, or by paying insufficient attention to tire safety, increases profit margins. Polluting entails limited risk of being caught and penalized, and the benefits, in terms of savings, sometimes exceed that risk. It's cheaper to shut down plants in areas of high labor cost and move them to other regions, no matter how dependent the community may be on the corporation.

Freed from the responsibilities of ownership, with surrogates directed to manage their corporations to maximize their wealth, American stockholders can, and for the most part do, wash their hands of responsibility for their corporations' behavior. Add to this the fact that most Americans tend to invest in corporations through intermediary institutions—mutual funds, pension funds, and the like—and yet another layer is placed between the stockholder and any feeling of responsibility.

WITH THESE CONDITIONS in place, American corporations have exported the dislocations they often cause at home through devices such as the leveraged, hostile takeover, and norms like stock-price maximization. *BusinessWeek* predicted (again, before the current recession) at least a $1-trillion mergers-and-acquisitions business in Europe, a region that has long celebrated its corporate stability. The profits drawn from such disruptions abroad go directly into the pockets of American stockholders, who demonstrate no concern with the effect of corporate behavior on anyone else. Arguments that transnational business helps the world's disadvantaged by raising their standard of living are disproved by the numbers. A recent United Nations report showed that American-style economic dominance has accelerated the widening gap between rich and poor throughout the world.

According to the UN's *Human Development Report 1999*, "the top fifth of the world's people in the richest countries enjoy 82 percent of the expanding export trade and 68 percent of foreign direct investment—the bottom fifth, barely more than 1 percent." That same wealthy population has 86 percent of the world's gross domestic product, and the income of that group was 74 times that of the bottom fifth in 1997, up from 60 times in 1990. And such data reflect only material wealth—not quality of life, leisure, education, or happiness.

> Because the goal of the corporation is to maximize stock price, managers use corporations narrowly and amorally as tools to achieve that end.

At least as dangerous as increasing inequality is the standard of behavior American corporate practices create for companies' managers. Because the goal of the corporation is to maximize stock price, managers use corporations narrowly and amorally as tools to achieve that end. When an ordinary human being with ordinary moral constraints walks into a board room or executive suite, he assumes those tunnel-visioned behaviors. That is, after all, his job. His own sensibilities can be left at the door—and even if they need not be, even if there is latitude (as there surely is) for good corporate behavior, he knows that the market will punish him unless his morality is reflected on the bottom line.

Like many social roles (that of a lawyer comes to mind), this one comes with a socially sanctioned set of expectations. But unlike most other roles, which exist and must interact in a wider social system, we so narrowly define the role of corporate actors as to give them a moral anonymity and a moral out. The corporate managerial role not only leads us to exculpate corporations for simply doing what we've created them to do, but it allows managers themselves to avoid feeling responsible, and being accountable, for their behavior. They have no personal contact with the people their decisions affect—those people are only numbers. The managers don't carry out the decisions themselves and witness the consequences, so they avoid the experiences that might help ensure empathy and restraint.

THE PROGRESS of the American corporation has been toward ever greater world dominance, not only in the products it sells and the services it provides, which export American culture throughout the world, but also in its exportation of American-style, stockholder-take-all capitalist practices. Given corporations' efficiency and speed in contrast to those of governments, corporations can establish strongholds and affect entire cultures long before those cultures have time to react. And once in place, corporate wealth and economic dominance allows them to remain firmly entrenched.

The problem is not only one of America against the developing world. American corporations, aided by the investment community, have also largely colonized the various forms of capitalism that used to distinguish Western European business from ours. Corporate behavior in Germany, France, Scandinavia, and Italy, for instance, was designed to provide for full employment, social stability, and social welfare. American companies, and American practices, have eroded those core values.

The European anger directed against President George W. Bush on his first visit there in June (somewhat abated since September 11 by a different anger, sympathy, and fear) is symptomatic of even the developed world's feelings of helplessness in the face of the continued onslaught by American-style corporate capitalism.

The recent terrorist attacks have been directed against sovereign governments. But to the extent that much of the unsettled state of the world derives from the increasing divide between haves and have-nots, to the extent that culture wars in America and abroad are driven at least in part by rearguard actions against disappearing ways of life, the cause lies less in the behavior of sovereign governments such as our own than it does in the collective behavior of corporate America and the American investment community.

Only government has the power, the resources, and the right to restrain corporate conduct and to demand corporate accountability. For far too long we've taken the attitude that business is business, as if that very mantra exempted corporations from the normal moral and responsible conduct that we expect from individual citizens. At the same time, we have granted our corporations almost all of the rights and freedoms of individual citizens. But unless we control our corporate goals and practices, unless our government regulates markets in a way that restrains our voracious drive for wealth, international strife and discord will only worsen.

Lawrence E. Mitchell, a law professor at George Washington University, is the author of Corporate Irresponsibility: America's Newest Export, *published recently by Yale University Press.*

The Need for a Corporate Global Mind-Set

It's not enough for a few executives at a multinational to have a global mind-set. All employees should excel at balancing global consistency with local responsiveness. That's why many organizations are testing ways to embed a *corporate* global mind-set in companywide policies. Research shows that managers universally recognize the imperative, but only a few are close to implementing it.

Thomas M. Begley and David P. Boyd

When a certain U.S. multinational corporation sought to adopt a global policy on employee mobility, it convened a yearlong symposium with representatives from units worldwide. Through a format that encouraged brainstorming and in-depth discussion, a consensus gradually emerged that enabled executives to reduce mobility classifications from eight to two. One category, the expatriate assignment package, encompassed managers who agreed to a company-requested posting of two or more years; it included 23 core elements that were standard. The other category, the international assignment package, covered employees who were assigned to a position for less than two years or requested an international posting; that had 13 core elements and left the other 10 adjustable to local situations. Both the policies themselves and the process used to develop them were well received abroad.

In another U.S. multinational, however, a task force of U.S. employees from different levels and functions drafted a major revision of work-force policies. The draft was discussed in several managerial forums, and a detailed questionnaire solicited the opinions of all U.S. personnel. Corporate executives considered the final product, which reduced the number of policies from 120 to 10, a notable success. Unfortunately, the process included little input from overseas. Instead, headquarters presented the results to all geographic units as a *fait accompli*. A company executive later commented, "International participation was an afterthought." The policies and the process were not well received abroad.

Both companies had progressive reputations. Why then did they approach international involvement in such different ways? A corporate global mind-set was the critical difference: The first company showed it, whereas the second did not. We define a global mind-set as the ability to develop and interpret criteria for business performance that are not dependent on the assumptions of a single country, culture or context and to implement those criteria appropriately in different countries, cultures and contexts.[1] The global mind-set is a critical component of globalization. And as often noted, the truly globalized corporation is more a mind-set than a structure.[2]

Getting to a corporate global mind-set requires individual managers to demonstrate a *glocal* mentality, which features three components.[3] First, think globally; recognize when it is beneficial to create a consistent global standard. Second, think locally: The process of becoming "truly global... means deepening the company's understanding of local and cultural differences."[4] Third, think globally and locally simultaneously; recognize situations in which demands from both global and local elements are compelling. Our research reveals that the corporate version of an individual manager's global mind-set emerges from policy development led by a core group. A core managerial group with a glocal mentality is an essential component of a corporate global mind-set.[5] However, such a mind-set will not become embedded in an organization until executives pull the structure, process and power levers to activate it. Then the newly globalized lower-level managers will pull *their* levers to convert employees in cascading fashion through critical parts of the company.

Formerly, it was possible for a close-knit network of leaders to handle organizational tensions through informal dialogue. But as businesses grew more complex, fast-paced and dispersed, a small group could no longer do everything, necessitating a broader base of managers to share in global decision making. Lacking globe-spanning experience, the broader group

About the Research

We began by conducting an in-depth examination of worldwide human-resources policy and program development in one high-technology multinational corporation. That pilot stage included more than 20 hours of interviews with the executive responsible for worldwide HR policies, interviews with six managers involved in the process, and questionnaire surveys of five additional HR executives in the Asia-Pacific region, Canada, Europe, Latin America and the United States. Fortified by a literature review, those sessions guided direction of subsequent interviews.

The interview set included 39 HR executives in 32 publicly traded high-technology multinational enterprises. All were headquartered in the United States. Of those interviewed, 21 were vice presidents, seven were directors, and 11 were managers. Executives were chosen through a combination of convenience (personal contacts) and snowball sampling (interviewing executives recommended by earlier interviewees). The fiscal year 2000 size of companies ranged from $1.4 billion to $85.9 billion in revenue and from 6,500 to 320,000 employees. The number of company employees working outside the United States varied from 100 to 160,000.

We followed a semistructured interview format. The average interview lasted 70 minutes. Both authors took extensive notes and audiotaped the sessions. Analysis followed the template approach.[1] After initially coding responses into thematic constructs, we continued categorical revision and refinement as we developed the data. We then qualitatively interpreted emergent patterns. Analysis focused on corporate culture, national culture, human-resources systems and the interactions among them.

Concentrating on the U.S. high-technology sector permitted us to limit the effects of cross-industry and cross-country variability. Targeting companies above a minimum threshold of $1 billion in annual revenue ensured that companies would have the capability to run substantial operations in several countries.

The companies studied included Advanced Micro Devices, Analog Devices, Apple Computer, AT&T, Bell Atlantic, Cisco Systems, Compaq Computer, EMC, Gateway, GTE, Honeywell, Hewlett-Packard, IBM, Intel, Lotus, Lucent Technologies, Media One, Microsoft, Motorola, NCR, Oracle, Polaroid, Qualcomm, SCI Systems, Seagate Technology, Sun Microsystems, Teradyne, Texas Instruments, 3Com, Unisys, Wang Global and Xerox.

1. The template approach was applied to organizational research by N. King, "The Qualitative Research Interview," in C. Cassell and G. Symon, eds., "Qualitative Methods in Organizational Research: A Practical Guide" (Thousand Oaks, California: Sage, 1994), 14–36.

---

often demonstrated a parochial view just when global expansion was tearing the fabric of home-country-bound corporate cultures. That's why the global mind-set is such a vital evolutionary adaptation, one that helps companies give recognition, respect and representation to all employees while improving agility and competitiveness.

On the Road to a Global Mind-Set

To increase its global presence, a company must manage its global work force. Geographic dispersion and cultural diversity create challenges in their own right. The prospect of uniting employees in pursuit of company prosperity is further daunting. Yet success depends on a corporation's ability to direct employee behavior toward collective goals. Thus, a company must optimize its relative emphasis on worldwide requirements and country variations.

Academics have long highlighted the need to adjudicate between global consistency and local responsiveness.[6] Ill-advised scope can have far-reaching implications: Companies that short-change global reach lose opportunities to maximize efficiencies and consolidate costs; companies that shortchange local responsiveness endanger market share and alienate employees.

For example, tensions surfaced at Sun Microsystems when local managers were accorded wide discretion in adopting employee stock-option plans. The longtime practice perturbed the central human-resources and finance executives, who wished to manage incentive compensation as a strategic tool. Conversely, Cisco Systems pushed for a global culture that encouraged employees to disregard hierarchy, upsetting Asian employees' tendency to look to higher levels for authority.

A grid can help crystallize the organizational parameters. (See "The Global Consistency/Local Responsiveness Grid.") Companies that emphasize global consistency seek cost advantages by maximizing world-scale systems. Those maximizing local responsiveness adjust for country differences by allowing local autonomy. Those combining both dimensions use mutually inclusive arrangements.

There are no pure types; all organizations must optimize the balance between two forces inherently at cross purposes. Variables such as industry sector, company strategy and organizational capability will pressure companies toward different points. Even within companies, functions have different grid locations. Marketing, for example, often must respond to local tastes, whereas finance pursues a globally unified approach. In addition to such complexities, work-force management decisions must take into account the cultural, govern-

The Global Consistency/Local Responsiveness Grid

To achieve success internationally, managers must balance global consistency vs. local responsiveness to varying degrees. Extreme global consistency seeks cost advantage by maximizing world-scale systems. Extreme local responsiveness adjusts for country differences by allowing local autonomy. Companies combining both dimensions use mutually inclusive arrangements.

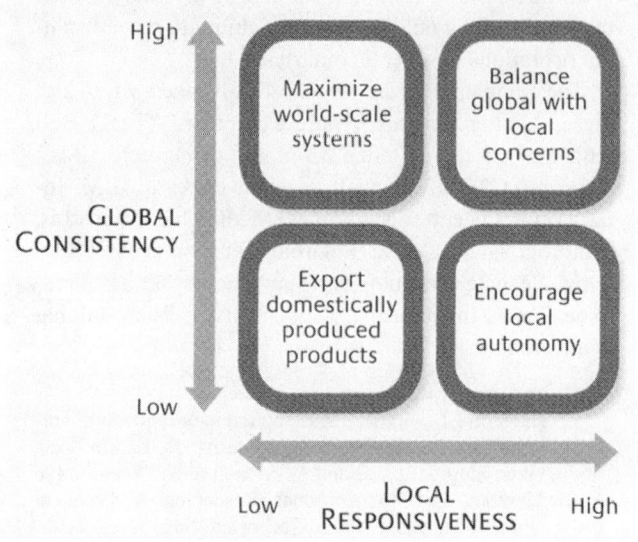

mental and social dimensions that affect human behavior and limit managerial discretion.[7]

To enact the particular work-force management approach that best fits their company's positioning on a consistency vs. responsiveness continuum, managers need tools. The two most often used criteria for evaluating management decision making have been effectiveness and efficiency. Effectiveness means extracting maximum gain from the external environment; efficiency is the ability to secure optimal use of internal resources. But work-force management policies also directly affect employee well-being, so recent studies accent the importance of a third criterion, fairness.[8] Policies judged as unfair will be resisted and hence will be neither efficient nor effective.

In our research, executives strove to deal with all three work-force management concerns amid the tensions of the competing forces. For effectiveness, they structured policies to channel employee behavior toward productive activity, asking, To what extent should policies be set as formal regulations or as flexible guidelines? For efficiency, they streamlined the process for policy enactment, framing the key question as, To what extent should policies be universally standardized or locally customized? And they sought to enhance fairness by locating the power to develop policy at the suitable level of organizational hierarchy, asking, To what extent should policies be centrally mandated or geographically delegated?

When the dimensions of each tension are placed in a grid, the resulting planes clarify options available to decision makers in formulating policies worldwide. (See "The Three Tensions of a Global Business.") Policy development challenges managers to enact the skill contours of a glocal mentality—that is, to recognize when global consistency, local responsiveness, or a balance of global and local tensions is best. By dealing with the tensions, companies can ensure that the glocal mentality of individual executives becomes embedded enterprisewide.

The Structure Tension: Global Formalization vs. Local Flexibility

The primary structural tension concerns the proper mix of rules vs. guidelines (and guidelines can be formal or informal). A case in point, U.S. companies continue to wrestle with enforcing the Foreign Corrupt Practices Act. The act prohibits bribery of foreign officials to procure business. Following a formal-rules approach, Intel strictly defined a bribe as "a thing of value given to someone with the intent of obtaining favorable treatment from the recipient." The company specifically proscribed payments to expedite a shipment through customs if the payments did not "follow applicable rules and regulations, and if the agent gives money or payment in kind to a government official for personal benefit."

Texas Instruments adopted the middle way, a formal-guidelines approach. It called on employees to "exercise good judgment" in questionable circumstances "by avoiding activities that could create even the appearance that our decisions could be compromised." TI further required employees to abide by the letter and spirit of the company's code of conduct as well as country laws. Analog Devices, following an informal-guidelines approach, set up a policy manager as a consultant to overseas operations. The policy manager helped callers think through the issues and informed them how the corporate office handled similar situations—but also emphasized that the decision was local management's.

The Process Tension: Global Standardization vs. Local Customization

The primary process tension concerns the appropriate blend of uniformity and uniqueness in worldwide processes. Companies deal with the tension when they ponder the development of processes for performance reviews, for example. Adopting a standardized-process approach, EMC identified 15 competencies required of all executives. The company initiated a process to evaluate managerial performance against the same competencies worldwide, using a standard form and a common set of defined steps. The executives in our study believed it provided a basis for evaluating talent and development managerial skills.

IBM sought to customize performance appraisal processes around a standard core. Dimensions that reflected its win/execute/team core values were mandatory. But the company allowed customization of particular steps in the process according to national, divisional or functional needs. The number of items rated and their effect on pay differed by country. Meanwhile, GTE opted for customized processes in its international units

Article 30. The Need for a Corporate Global Mind-Set

control the necessary levers, they must have a glocal mentality themselves as well as a vision for guiding the company toward a global mind-set. When a core group initiates a process to identity the optimal configuration of global and local elements, it can begin to establish its mind-set in the company. In the context of policy development, application of a global mind-set requires executives to recognize options presented by various locations in the grid. Then they can make decisions that maximize three important kinds of consistency: consistency across the structure, process and power dimensions within each policy; consistency between policies; and consistency of the policies with the values guiding the company's approach to global work-force management. Within-policy and between-policy consistency are virtues only if alignment occurs with values. So a corporate global mind-set also is demonstrated in the emphasis on the values that guide a company's orientation toward work-force management issues.

The Three Tensions of a Global Business

To achieve a corporate global mind-set, managers must balance global formalization vs. local flexibility, global standardization vs. local customization, and global dictate vs. local delegation.

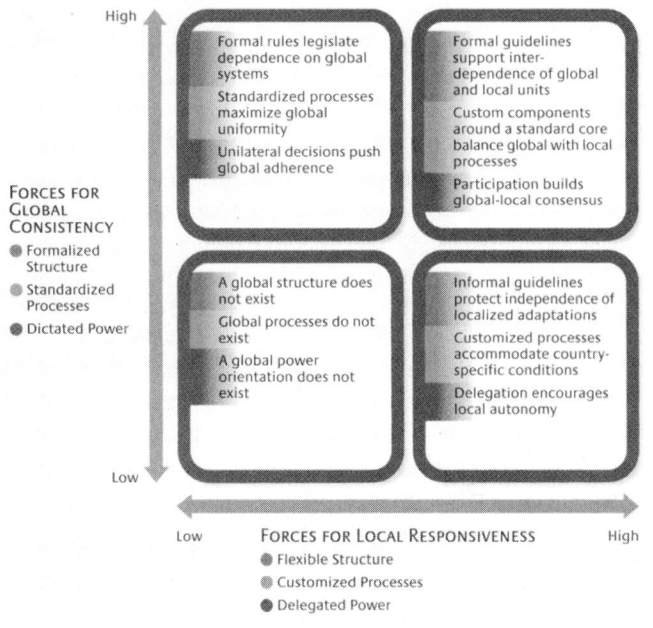

and encouraged (but did not require) overseas operations to tap the expertise of other units and headquarters.

The Power Tension: Global Dictate vs. Local Delegation

The primary fairness tension involves the locus of power in the exercise of worldwide decision making. Corporations address the tension as they consider how to design and implement incentive compensation schemes. Recently, companies have reacted differently to questions about who should decide the form and amounts of such incentives. The questions are particularly relevant to the power-orientation dimension.

SCI Systems, a company that globally enforced its unilateral policies, developed the same reward formula for top managers in each of its 35 plants worldwide. Sun Microsystems took a participative approach. In response to requests from country units, it sought to extend profit sharing worldwide. Negotiated agreements between country units and corporate headquarters ensured that both corporate requirements and local needs were accommodated. At Seagate Technology, control was delegated to local units, which were responsible for adapting incentive schemes to their needs.

Applying the Model

Use of the structure, process and power-orientation grid helps embed a corporate global mind-set. But because top managers

Within-Policy Consistency

Choices made on the structural, process and power-orientation questions are interdependent. Consistency across the grid is desirable; inconsistencies generate problems. For example, in the past, Hewlett-Packard's benefits managers tried to combine insurance coverage of many countries to get volume discounts. Following the company's consensus-oriented culture, a task force was formed that spanned national, divisional and hierarchical lines. After a lengthy process, member support was split among several alternative plans attempting to address concerns of all parties. Minimal cost advantage was obtained. The integrative task force's processes and the company's participative orientation combined to undermine the formal rules needed for cost savings. More recently, as part of a move toward accentuating the primacy of performance, a few executives at headquarters formally centralized the criteria for insurance vendor selection, identified substantial cost savings through worldwide pooling, and then communicated the selected vendors and rationale to benefits managers in various countries.

Between-Policy Consistency

Policy optimization occurs when a policy not only shows internal consistency but also fits with other company policies. The resulting alignment reduces friction and supports global efforts. More than one-third of the companies studied were in various stages of completely overhauling work-force management policies. A goal was to purge the policy set of inconsistencies and mixed messages. Compaq, for example, having acquired Digital Equipment and Tandem within a short period, sought to create unified work-force management policies. The task was rendered especially difficult by Digital's extensively detailed policies and by some idiosyncratic Tandem policies that reflected its Silicon Valley heritage. Hewlett-Packard's recent acquisition of Compaq has generated a new round of policy alignment to merge divergent corporate cultures.

Policies' Consistency With Values

A company can attempt to change its policies for global work-force management, but it also must align them with corporate values. By the same token, policies can be valuable in recasting company values.[9]

Companies that permit local autonomy forgo the benefits of global scale and cross-national learning.

For example, when Texas Instruments shifted from predictable competition for defense-related contracts to volatile markets for fast-changing, high-technology products, executives jettisoned the company's massive policy manual. To herald movement from the high consistency corner of the grid toward a position closer to the high consistency/high responsiveness corner, TI sought worldwide participation to identify a few values that embodied its evolving philosophy. It then developed formal guidelines to facilitate the interpretation of its major global policies. In the words of an executive, TI exchanged a strictly defined "Ten Commandments" for "Six Commandments and Four Suggestions." Supported by a succinct pamphlet communicating the revised values, the approach was a powerful stimulus to organizational change.

Choosing a Location on the Consistency/Responsiveness Grid

In choosing a position on the grid, companies should consider their particular situations. A need for global consistency would favor policies that accentuate formalization, standardization and global dictates, whereas a need for local responsiveness would favor flexibility, customization and delegation. U.S. companies operating abroad gravitate toward global consistency through heavy emphasis on formal rules, standardized processes and headquarters control, an approach that elicits charges of insensitivity and even colonialism.[10] However, companies that permit local autonomy forgo the benefits of global scale and cross-national learning. When companies need both dimensions, policies that allow balance are best.

In practice, relatively few companies have been able to move in the high consistency/high responsiveness direction, an increasingly attractive location that can modulate difficulties when strategic direction faces cross-cultural constraints. For example, the need for U.S. companies to enforce consistent behaviors for the Foreign Corrupt Practices Act may create a challenge for companies that favor locally responsive policies. However, the German requirement to consult employee representatives prior to major decisions necessitates that U.S. companies moderate any preference for consistency. When companies face both kinds of demands, a high consistency/high responsiveness pattern offers flexibility in handling pressures.

Several executives we interviewed maintained that work-force management policy decisions, in particular, require an increasingly high consistency/high responsiveness approach. They argue that a company's vision and values must show global consistency. However, a company's workplace practices, which translate policy guidelines into day-to-day procedures, should be locally determined. The only way to integrate philosophy and practice is through policy guidelines.[11] Further, in a multicultural work force, corporate values will inevitably clash with local cultural values. Solutions that are high in both consistency and responsiveness preserve a balance and avoid either forcing corporate values on the local culture or acquiescing counterproductively to local values.

Although there is progress in functions such as marketing and new-product development, our research indicates that a glocal mentality has yet to take hold with human-resources executives, the prime custodians of work-force management policies. Once labeled the most local of corporate functions, HR has shifted toward an emphasis on consistency in worldwide corporate culture and the policies and programs that support it. HR also must pay heed to national culture, government fiat and idiosyncratic social systems, but even as HR executives widely hail the glocal mentality as a key managerial competency, many remain uncertain how to move their own managers toward it.

HR can greatly influence a company's ability to inculcate a glocal mentality. Given the glocal mentality's increasing importance, what are the organizing principles that enable company executives to encourage it in work-force management issues? Academics in international management, organizational design and corporate culture have begun to identify ways to create opportunities for glocal thinking and to describe the activities of executives who have translated their glocal mentality into a corporate global mind-set.[12]

Developing a Global Mind-Set

Developing a global mind-set requires movement toward the high global/high local corner of the structure, process and power grid. That involves balancing formalization with flexibility through modular networks and communities of practice; balancing standardization with customization through distributive management, centers of excellence and corporate vision; and balancing global dictates with delegation through the application of procedural justice.

Balancing Formalization With Flexibility

Two approaches that managers can use to ease the inherent tension between global and local structure are modular networks and communities of practice.

Modular networks. In between the dependence that formal rules impose and the independence that informal guidelines encourage, the formal-guidelines approach fosters interdependence. Executives should seek avenues of mutual reliance and benefit, crystallized around modular networks. Instead of emphasizing formalized headquarters communication to divisional and regional units, the webs created by modular interaction underscore a more flexible give-and-take among the divisions and units themselves. Thus, in an effort to increase cross-unit communication, GTE and MediaOne emphasized serving as consultants to geographic units. GTE executives posed a challenge: "We have global talent; how can we use it globally?" They referred country units experiencing problems to other country units that had solutions. Soon the Puerto Rican unit, which had considerable experience with broadbanding, reached out to the Venezuelan unit, which had needed advice. Flexible adjustments to broadbanding, suggested by the Puerto Rican unit, enhanced the likelihood of successful implementation in Venezuela.

To integrate the network, executives must reinforce its use. A key requirement is to reward managers for synergistic cross-unit projects. At General Electric, where cross-unit collaboration is an integral component of the management culture, executives are recognized for using it.

Communities of practice. Another integrative device is communities of practice.[13] At NCR the first community consisted of a worldwide intranet site using proprietary technology called "Round Table," which let the company's compensation professionals resolve problems and share innovative approaches. Active contributors to the community were rewarded.

Balancing Standardization With Customization

Distributive management, centers of excellence and corporate vision assist managers in resolving process tension.

"Someone answering a phone in Iowa is not going to know what affects a caller in Europe or Asia."

Distributive management. Distributive management accords significant decision-making responsibilities to managers in dispersed locales and provides the resources to implement the decisions. Distributed resources enable integration of standardization with customization. But executives must ascertain a company's work-force capabilities worldwide. Many companies with a sophisticated U.S. skills-inventory system lack such systems overseas. Hence a software-services company encountered the perils of negotiating large worldwide contracts. Without a worldwide skills inventory, the company was flying blind. Whenever it was successful in the bidding process, the company had to scramble to find ways of servicing the contract. Consequently, management was sometimes immersed in last-minute efforts to build capabilities in new locales. That made it hard to provide good service and hampered cost control.

Centers of excellence. The next step is to determine how to distribute responsibilities and resources across geographic locations. Through centers of excellence around the globe, companies can effectively leverage capabilities by parlaying strategic knowledge to other units.[14] For example, strict employment laws and strong unions in France encourage expertise in manpower-planning systems. That knowledge can cascade across the company by means of a center of excellence. Although increasingly prominent in fields such as marketing, information systems and research and development, the notion of distributed centers is not yet ensconced in human-resources management.

By strengthening the role of regional headquarters, companies can counterbalance the current predominance of industry-based structures and worldwide divisions that push for standardization. Regional groups can become centers of excellence developing customized organizational capabilities. Most companies already have regional headquarters to represent, at least for administrative functions, Europe; the Middle East and Africa; the Asia-Pacific area; Latin America; and North America. SCI Systems executives believe that intraregional interests lend themselves to cross-unit meetings, whereas cross-regional assemblies share fewer problems. Oracle has focused its shared services at the regional level to attain high effectiveness at low cost, reasoning that "someone answering a phone in Iowa is not going to know much of what affects a caller in Europe or Asia." IBM is also retreating from global policies to focus more attention on regional centers. It believes direct movement to worldwide processes might be too great a leap, if even desirable. Regionwide policies carry potential because of cultural similarities within a group of countries.

Corporate vision. Integrated networks also allow managers latitude to develop a customized solution for their locale, based on awareness of alternatives used elsewhere in the organization. The challenge is to ensure that customization takes place within shared parameters. That means top management must stimulate a global mind-set by promoting a corporate vision that values glocal thinking. The process for inculcating the overarching vision is socialization.[15] Companies must provide opportunities for managers to interact in forums. Message dissemination can occur through worldwide conferences and meetings, electronic-communication technology, executive role modeling, measurement and reward systems, and worldwide rotating assignments. Such processes of "glue technology" promote trust and solidify bonding.[16] Corporate education centers serve the purpose well. Focused management-development programs are useful if a company wishes to signal changes in the vision. When Texas Instruments recast its core values, it instituted management development programs. The sessions underscored the need for a new vision, established parameters for desired changes and defined action steps.

Balancing Global Dictates With Delegation

Procedural justice can assist managers in resolving tension over power.

Global dictates often yield substantially uneven benefits, depending on locale, and thus impede distributive fairness. In such situations, attention to the psychological aspects of the decision-making process becomes essential. Participative decision making has proved effective in achieving procedural fairness. Two-way communication helps dispel perceptual inequity. Provision for feedback contributes to a climate of open exchange.

Moreover, engagement of overseas units pays dividends because employees who provide input into the decision-making process are more likely to support and implement the final results. Conversely, estrangement from the decision-making process can induce powerful resistance to change.[17] Participation at the country level also opens the possibility of more-creative solutions.

3Com has processes for systematic worldwide input into decisions bearing on work-force policies. If a policy change is under consideration, 3Com executives notify HR managers worldwide. As the policy statement evolves, the managers evaluate its potential fit in their respective countries and raise any red flags about problems that might attend implementation. A couple of people in a region may be designated as the unit's eyes and ears for a particular policy. For policies under development, 3Com designed an internal, password-protected Web site to facilitate dynamic and continuous dialogue. In evolving an inclusive process, the next logical step would be to assign primary responsibility for global-policy formulation to units outside the United States.

Clearly, a corporate global mind-set is not simply "all in the head." Rather it requires supporting policies and practices. To formulate appropriately consistent policies, executives must assess and align structure, process and power tensions. Although any point on the grid presents a possible salutary response, work force management polices appear to call increasingly for an approach high in both consistency and responsiveness.

A Competitive Advantage

Many respondents considered a global mind-set to be a desirable state, believing that competitive advantage ensues from actions consistent with it. The literature reinforces the view that such actions can improve financial performance, employee commitment and receptivity to organizational change.[18] Yet in every one of our sample companies, such a comprehensive perspective lagged the company's global expansion.

IBM seemed to have made the greatest strides toward a global mind-set. In the 1960s, so rigid was its emphasis on global consistency that every employee received the same benefits regardless of need. The company even funded medical benefits in countries that guaranteed their citizens universal health coverage. Then, shaken by its early 1990s crisis, IBM embraced a more flexible approach, including global policy-development teams, worldwide knowledge networks and the IBM performance management systems. In attempting to balance global with local concerns and inculcate a global mind-set, IBM executives have pushed many levers, but they report a gap they still need to close.

Because many U.S. executives regard globalization as the pursuit of standardized products through centralized decision making, they naturally favor global consistency over local responsiveness. Yet in their relentless rush toward consistency, they have not secured the cooperation of local constituents. Through a global mind-set, corporate decision-making processes become more permeable to ideas and influences from beyond the home country. As evidence of the mind-set, management must recognize when an issue calls for a locally adaptive response, a globally consistent response or a response featuring both elements. The third response is rapidly expanding its sphere. The corporate global mind-set is more than a catchphrase; it is a requirement for motivating a diverse and sprawling work force. The global mind-set offers the promise of a corporation energized and enhanced by all its employees.

REFERENCES

1. See M. L. Maznevski and H. W. Lane, "Shaping the Global Mind-Set: Designing Educational Experiences for Effective Global Thinking and Action" in N. Boyacigiller, R. Goodman and M. Phillips, eds., "Teaching and Experiencing Cross-Cultural Management: Lessons From Master Teachers" (London: Routledge, in press). We have slightly modified Maznevski and Lane's individual-level definition so that it refers instead to the company level.

2. See C. A. Bartlett and S. Ghoshal, "Managing Across Borders: The Transnational Solution," 2nd ed. (Boston: Harvard Business School Press, 1998), and "The Myth of the Generic Manager: New Personal Competencies for New Management Roles," California Management Review 40 (fall 1997): 92–116; V. Govindarajan and A. K. Gupta, "The Quest for Global Dominance: Transforming Global Presence Into Global Competitive Advantage" (San Francisco: Jossey-Bass, 2001); and T. P. Murtha, S. A. Lenway and R. P. Bagozzi, "Global Mind-Sets and Cognitive Shift in a Complex Multinational Corporation," Strategic Management Journal 19 (February 1998): 97–114.

3. G. Svensson, "'Glocalization' of Business Activities: A 'Glocal Strategy' Approach," Management Decision 39 (2001): 6–18.

4. R. M. Kanter and T. D. Dretler, "Global Strategy and Its Impact on Local Operations: Lessons from Gillette Singapore," Academy of Management Executive 12 (November 1998): 60–68.

5. N. Athanassiou and D. Nigh, "The Impact of the Top Management Team's International Business Experience on the Firm's Internationalization: Social Networks at Work," Management International Review 4 (spring 2002): 157–181.

6. For example, Y. L. Doz and C. K. Prahalad, "The Multinational Mission: Balancing Local Demands and Global Vision" (New York: Free Press, 1987); and C. K. Prahalad and K. Lieberthal, "The End of Corporate Imperialism," Harvard Business Review 76 (July–August 1998): 68–79.

7. In an attempt to limit the variation induced by multiple country and industrial sectors, the research focused on U.S.-based high-technology companies, including most of the major companies in computer hardware, software and services as well as the telecommunications industry. The momentum and magnitude of this sector make it an attractive domain for exploring how companies face the challenge of managing a worldwide work force. Moreover, many of these companies are regarded as management trendsetters.

8. For example, J. Greenberg and R. Cropanzano, eds., "Advances in Organizational Justice" (Stanford, California: Stanford University Press, 2001).

9. T. M. Begley and D. P. Boyd, "Articulating Corporate Values Through Human-Resource Policies," Business Horizons 43 (July–August 2000): 8–12.

10. E. Yuen and H. Kee, "Headquarters, Host-Culture and Organizational Influences on HRM Policies and Practices," Management International Review 33 (fall 1993): 361–383; and M. P. Kriger and E. E. Solomon, "Strategic Mind-Sets and Decision-Making Autonomy in U.S. and Japanese MNCs," Management International Review 32 (fall 1992): 327–343.

11. R. S. Shuler, P. J. Dowling and H. De Cieri, "An Integrative Framework of Strategic International Human-Resource Management," Journal of Management 19 (summer 1993): 419–460.

12. Bartlett, "Managing Across Borders"; R. E. Miles and C. C. Snow, "Fit, Failure and the Hall of Fame: How Companies Succeed or Fail" (New York: Free Press, 1994); J. C. Collins and J. I. Porras, "Built To Last: Successful Habits of Visionary Companies" (New York: HarperBusiness, 1994); and Greenberg, "Advances in Organizational Justice."

13. E. C. Wenger and W. M. Snyder, "Communities of Practice: The Organizational Frontier," Harvard Business Review 78 (January–February 2000): 139–145.

14. K. Moore and J. Birkinshaw, "Managing Knowledge in Global Service Firms: Centers of Excellence," Academy of Management Executive 12 (November 1998): 81–92.

15. Collins and Porras, "Built To Last."

16. P. A. L. Evans, "Management Development as Glue Technology," Human Resource Planning 15 (1992): 85–105.

17. See, for example, W. C. Kim and R. A. Mauborgne, "Making Global Strategies Work," Sloan Management Review 34 (spring 1993): 11–27.

18. K. L. Newman and S. D. Nollen, "Culture and Congruence: The Fit Between Management Practices and National Culture," Journal of International Business Studies 27 (fall 1996): 753–779; S. Taylor and S. Beechler, "Human Resource Management System Integration and Adaptation in Multinational Companies," in S. Prasad and R. Peterson, eds., "Advances in International Comparative Management" (Greenwich, Connecticut: JAI Press, 1993), 155–174; R. Gill and A. Wong, "The Cross-Cultural Transfer of Management Practices: The Case of Japanese Human Resource Management Practices in Singapore," International Journal of Human Resource Management 9 (February 1998): 116–135; and B. L. Kirkman and D. L. Shapiro, "The Impact of Current Values on Employee Resistance to Teams: Toward a Model of Globalized Self-Managing Work Team Effectiveness," Academy of Management Review 22 (July 1997): 730–757.

Thomas M. Begley *is an assistant professor and* ***David P. Boyd*** *a professor of human-resources management at Northeastern University's College of Business Administration in Boston. Contact them at t.begley@neu.edu and d.boyd@neu.edu.*

Reprinted from *MIT/Sloan Management Review*, Winter 2003, pp. 25-32, by permission of the publisher. © 2003 by Massachusetts Institute of Technology. All rights reserved.

Helping Organizations Build Community

A sense of community at work can make all the difference

September 11 changed how many employees view their jobs and workplace. People may find it difficult to focus on learning. Building a sense of community in organizations can help refocus people on shared values and create an environment of support in which employees are fully engaged.

by Tracy Mauro

I was introducing a group of managers to the concepts in James Autry's book *Love and Profit* when I heard about the World Trade Center and Pentagon attacks. The class had started at 8:30 a.m., just before the first plane hit. Managers who came to the session late shared fragmented updates of the situation they'd heard on television. People began talking and asking questions, none of which pertained to Autry's book. As our small, suburban Chicago office was evacuated, a senior manager canceled the session. I realized in that moment that everything would change—not just the onset of war or tightened security but the way people view their workplace, their co-workers, and even the meaning of their work.

Training professionals have a difficult job right now. We're trying to impart knowledge to employees who are at best distracted or apathetic and at worst scared and disillusioned. Abraham Maslow's hierarchy of needs proposes that people are motivated by unsatisfied needs and that "lower needs" such as safety and security have to be satisfied before attending to "higher needs" such as personal growth and development. How can learning professionals do their jobs and help organizations become successful when employees are wondering whether their mail is laced with anthrax? The answer may lie in helping to create an environment of support and belonging, in which employees have the opportunity to do their best. Economic downturn and massive layoffs make that a challenge, but not impossible. In fact, people might be especially receptive now to opportunities to shape and have more control over their surroundings. One way to encourage that is by building a sense of community.

Powering community in the workplace isn't new. The quality movement in the late 1970s touched on the idea of participative management as a way to bring groups of employees together around common principles, such as quality. In the early 1990s, Peter Senge and James Autry talked about the necessary elements of a productive community to produce learning organizations and caring leaders. Autry writes: "Community is the new metaphor for organizations," saying that before the industrial age, all values entered society through the church and stare.

People witness healthy and destructive values played out in the workplace. A community teaches values, and those values have the power to strengthen its members or divide them. Like it or not, the pillars of commerce have become a central place where people learn values. Organizations that want to survive cultivate healthy values that bring success to staff and shareholders.

The need to belong and feel supported in the workplace becomes more important as our world becomes more uncertain. Many people spend at least half of their waking hours during the week at work, making the workplace a home away from home. Think for a moment about the home where you live and the reasons you chose to live there. The community and people were probably major factors in your decision. It's no different in the workplace. In community-building exercises I lead, I ask participants to remember a time when they experienced a positive community and to list the characteristics that made it special. Later in the exercise, they usually discover that the characteristics they listed are the same attributes they seek in their workplace now.

Clifton Taulbert, in his book *Eight Habits of the Heart: The Timeless Values That Build Community Within Our Homes and Our Lives,* writes: "From the classroom to the... office cubicle, there are people who wait to hear someone say, 'Welcome.' No one really enjoys eating alone or having no one to talk with."

The profound effect of the events of September 11 and since offer organizations a new opportunity to create places of support and acceptance. Organizational leaders can stabilize their workforces by recognizing what Autry calls "the sudden, compulsive search for connection and a sense of community," in which the workplace is the neighborhood and co-workers are extended family.

A home by any other name

Training professionals must first have a clear definition of what community is before they can begin the process of helping an organization build one. Although there is no commonly accepted definition of community, most definitions include similar characteristics. Community seems to be categorized by either sharing a common space or common interests. The definitions in *Merriam-Webster's* combine both of those aspects: "an interacting population of various kinds of individuals in a common location" or "a body of persons of common and especially professional interests scattered through a larger society." Community researcher Carl Moore provides a simple definition appropriate for the workplace: "[where people] work together to bring the greatest good for the greatest number of people."

Many management experts think that shared values and goals are an important part of the definition of community within organizations. James Kouzes and Barry Posner, in their book *Credibility: How Leaders Gain and Lose It, Why People Demand It*, say that in order for people to perceive themselves as part of a community, they need to believe that their goals are cooperative and that they share a common purpose. Only then will people make their co-workers' problems their own and solve them together.

Regardless of how learning and workplace performance professionals define *community*, the word evokes unique images in the minds of participants. Many think of a physical place where they experienced a sense of *community*, such as the neighborhood where they grew up. Taulbert recalls the small town in the Mississippi Delta where he grew up amidst segregation in the years before Martin Luther King Jr.: "But I realize now that the place was just a set.... In other words, the real community I knew as a child was not held captive by geography, nor was it defined by the physical stuff that was part of our place." Rather, he says, community was defined by the actions and behavior of the members. Taulbert underscores that definition: "Community is an intangible that is so real that you miss it when it can't be found."

In May 1999, the National League of Cities held a conference to help representatives foster inclusion and belonging in their hometowns. When asked to finish the sentence "Community is...," participants mentioned working together and caring, having a sense of collective responsibility and ownership, and providing a safe environment for citizens to participate in. As any trainer knows, those are essential elements in fostering an environment for learning to take place.

The value of creating a sense of community in the workplace might be obvious to people in the learning and performance profession, but some powers-that-be will want an explanation of how that's useful to the company. Some executives may view community building as another soft-skills program that takes employees off the floor but doesn't produce immediate results. Taulbert, who teaches community building to executives, says he generates buy-in from his high-level audiences by showing that community makes a clear connection between employees' hearts and minds and improved job performance.

"You have to bring leaders back to the point of realizing that nothing can be built without people. People are still the key to building the business," says Taulbert. Most of the time, people aren't fully engaged and working at 100 percent capacity, especially when distracted by crises. Employees choose every day when and how much extra effort they will expend after meeting the minimum performance standards, which Kouzes and Posner refer to as discretionary effort. When companies create an environment in which employees want to be fully engaged, they "touch the soul," as Taulbert describes it, and people are more likely to expend their discretionary effort.

Once employees are fully engaged in their work, extraordinary things start to happen. The presence of positive community leads to tangible results. The advisory council for the NLC has found several benefits of building a sense of community in cities, which are readily applicable in organizations. Employees can be involved in every step of a community-building process, which when combined with the values a supportive community espouses, creates a sense of responsibility people feel towards other community members and their organizations. People are more likely to fulfill obligations and perform at their best when they feel committed to the organization and its members. An environment of mutual support also empowers teams themselves to solve their problems and leads to shared ownership of work results. In addition, problems are identified early when employees anticipate that they'll receive help from others and can openly discuss the issues.

Last, employees who perceive themselves as community members can be expected to interact more frequently than employees in other groups. The process of learning about each other can break down stereotypes. Though community can't be measured quantitatively, that doesn't take away from its real and powerful importance.

Getting started

The good news about beginning the process of building community in the workplace is that most organizations don't need to start from scratch. Elements of positive community are probably already apparent. Supportive and caring connections between people have been forming spontaneously in organizations as long as they've been around. Such relationships are often formed without the support—and, in some cases, the efforts—of management.

Says Autry, "In the new workplace, the bonds of family and neighborhood have emerged so strongly that managers, running to catch up, may arrive to find an environment the employees have already created." In other words, employees will create some form of community on their own. Workplace communities are like gardens that may grow wild when unattended or flourish when guided. Organizations can build on the best qualities of the community employees have already formed to help it develop in a positive direction.

An NLC 1998 report, "Building a Nation of Communities," recommends starting a conversation at all organizational levels about the need to create community. The focus should depend on the audience. Training professionals working with a group of executives will want to drive home the potential effect on productivity and give examples of other organizations that have reaped rewards from community building. Managers will want to know how strengthening community will make their jobs easier regarding their teams. Individual contributors will be interested in hearing how community building will benefit them and what the organization will do to support them in that endeavor.

Community building is an unstoppable process once it gets started.

One question to anticipate from management is how to deal with employees who don't buy into the community-building effort. Taulbert suggests asking managers to think of creating community in the same way as implementing any standard work process. "Suppose you had a process in place for how work was going to get done," he says "You would forge ahead."

As with any major organizational initiative, leaders should champion the effort to foster a healthy community and work with people who want to take part. That will drive momentum around the community, have a positive effect on relationships and the organization, and win over stragglers. "Community building is an unstoppable process once it gets started," says Taulbert.

Building and sustaining a community requires strong leadership. Taulbert cautions that "it isn't for the faint of heart and requires tough leadership in the presence of community. " Leaders must be fully committed and must maintain commitment from others even in difficult times. Although employees form positive communities in spite of unsupportive leadership, that's not the usual or best case.

Positive values

Two important components of a discussion around community are allowing people to explore what community means to them and educating employees about elements that might be found in a positive community. Participants can uncover their personal meaning of community by finishing the statement "Community is…." Unfortunately, some people have never experienced a healthy community, either at home or in the workplace, and will lack a model. Organizations need to make sure employees have a clear idea of what positive community values are so that the community can grow in a productive direction.

One way to educate employees about what a positive community looks like is to provide examples of how other organizations have successfully built communities or values found in productive communities. In his book, Taulbert describes these important values of any healthy community:

A nurturing attitude. Members care about each other and believe that the organization cares about them. For example, a manager might call a sick employee at home to see how that person is feeling. Autry talks about a group of employees at a municipal water plant who donated part of their vacation time so that a co-worker with cancer could extend his medical leave.

Dependability. Employees need to be able to rely on their co-workers, especially in times when they can't depend on the organization for support. Members of strong communities don't want to let co-workers down and will often fulfill their commitments despite challenging circumstances.

Responsibility. Employees who are part of a community care about their workplace and feel individually responsible for maintaining a productive environment. They realize that every act, no matter how small, has the power to build or break community.

Friendship. "When friendship is absent, people often live in envy and fear. " Taulbert's words highlight the importance of the often-overlooked element of friendship. People don't leap out of bed in the morning to be with co-workers they don't like and who don't care about them. Friendships at work help people get through the day and make them want to contribute to the team.

Brotherhood and sisterhood. A strong community is needed to bring together people with differing agendas so that they can work side-by-side as equals. Organizational boundaries can blur as technology enables global influences to permeate physical barriers. Taulbert alludes to the challenge of diversity by saying we've "entered a global community where we're challenged to reach beyond the comfort of our closest relationships to welcome others different from ourselves. " Leaders can model diversity acceptance by holding themselves accountable to the same expectations they have for their staff and by pitching in to help when needed.

High expectations. Expectations have power because people will rise to the level of high expectations or live down to low ones. Leaders who make a daily practice of telling employees that they're valuable and competent build a community in which people are encouraged to maximize their talents.

Courage. Creating a positive community will test the character of everyone involved. Says Taulbert,"It takes courage to keep your gaze on what's right when all around you, people are padding their expense accounts… or cheating customers…. " He adds, courage is "speaking out on behalf of others, and making a commitment to excellence in the face of adversity or the absence of support."

Employees need to see their leaders model ethical behavior at all costs to know what the organization values and expects.

Hope. Hope sustains people during the worst of times, and communities that pull together for the common good create an abundance of hope.

Once commitment to the process is secured and employees understand the concept of community, the next step is to engage employees by creating and encouraging activities that promote community. If community is defined partly by the behavior of its members, then it makes sense to establish a set of shared values and goals; that's where many experts suggest starting. Unless people know what they have in common and realize that their individual goals can be met only by cooperating with others, there's little reason for them to commit to building a community. It's important that the values upon which a community is based be shared among its members and leaders, because people won't support values, individually or as a group, if they can't identify with them. Shared values also strengthen commitment to the organization when employees find that their personal values match the values that their work community practices.

Identifying shared community values as a group can flow naturally from the initial discussion about what community means to each person. Team members will often mention similar aspects of community that can translate into defined team values. The leader of the community is responsible for structuring processes that reinforce the shared values and that create shared goals. Managers can give team members projects that require them to make recommendations or solve problems as a group. Kouzes and Posner say that most people are genuinely interested in helping others, as long it doesn't mean they'll lose if the other team wins. Leaders who reward team success as opposed to individual efforts will avoid power struggles.

If you build it, they will come.

Employees who have identified a set of shared community values and are engaged in cooperative projects should be encouraged to take their new community and run with it. Taulbert challenges his clients to become general contractors responsible for building the community. It's crucial to encourage people to think of their community at work in the same way as their community at home. Sometimes, physical transformations can facilitate the community-building process.

Some employees choose to make their workplace resemble a small town by giving aisles street names and setting up a coffee shop in a shared space. Employees also form birthday committees and organize team potluck lunches. Such activities might seem frivolous to some people, but they can go a long way towards creating a friendly, nurturing environment that promotes trust and strengthens commitment to team members. It's why most organizations hold holiday parties and employee picnics in the summer.

Community-building efforts that affect work directly shouldn't be ignored. Community members, either as a team or through a designated committee, should be guided to identify business-related challenges held by members of their community, to develop the means to address those issues, and to set goals and priorities for their community.

The final step in building a workplace community is to sustain the effort for the long term. Trainers can be especially helpful in this phase because if employees don't have the interpersonal skills that will help them build positive relationships, they'll need training. Ideally, training should start during the formation of the community-building initiative so that employees are prepared by that stage. Of course, people don't learn trust and respect in a classroom but by doing. In those instances, trainers can serve as coaches.

An organization's leaders play an important role in sustaining communities, which is similar to maintaining a house: The physical structure demands a continual process of upkeep. In the workplace, employees can't just grow community one time; they must cultivate it for as long as they're together. Leaders can nurture the community by establishing the strong expectations that employees will develop cooperative work relationships and deal openly with problems. Leaders should back up those expectations by rewarding employees who practice the community's values and by coaching those who don't. Managers can use hiring practices that find candidates who already share at least some of the key community values, and new-employee orientation can communicate the values.

Last, it's essential to review community values periodically so that teams can renew themselves as the environment changes. For example, a critical event such as those on September 11 may cause a team to focus more on a value such as connectedness—not only within the community, but also with neighboring teams and external communities.

A strong sense of community tends to correlate with exceptional company performance.

Ultimately, the community is responsible for its survival. Like all organization initiatives, communities will go through dormant and renewal phases. Fear not when you see the spirit of community wax and wane. Scott Peck, author of *A World Waiting to Be Born,* contends that a group doesn't have to be in a genuine state of community at all times to be healthy. "It's normal for groups to fall out of this genuine state and into temporary emptiness or even chaos. Truly healthy groups are determined by how quickly its members recognize that they have lost community and by their willingness to rapidly rebuild it."

The principles of positive community can reach far beyond the physical boundaries of a single office building. Organizations with employees who are located internationally, who telecommute, or who work in a virtual community can build strong communities that reach out to distant groups. Companies with offices in other parts of the world will find that, though the languages may differ, the yearning to belong is universal.

Creating community is especially important in virtual organizations, where employees may never meet their coworkers or customers. Developing relationships with members of the community can combat feelings of isolation.

A strong sense of community tends to correlate with exceptional company performance. Two popular examples are eBay and Southwest Airlines. Chat rooms, bulletin boards, and newsletters have made eBay a 24/7 forum for people who like to trade and collect. Some eBay community members hold picnics and take trips together.

At first, eBay founder and chairman Pierre Omidyar was surprised by the response. "I thought people would simply buy and sell things, but what they really enjoyed was meeting other people," he says in the February 2001 issue of *Inc.* Executives at eBay educate new employees during orientation about shared values, and those values are reinforced. President and CEO Meg Whitman strives to foster connections between employees and customers by encouraging staff to start collections of their own.

One of the few airlines that didn't seek a federal loan after September 11 was Southwest. It's no coincidence Southwest has done well financially even in hard times. The airline reinvented air travel with low fares, exceptional service, and a strong sense of identity. It found success by being courageous enough to create an environment in which people can love and care at work.

Several months have passed since the events on September 11, and life at work has returned to a new form of normalcy. I repeatedly hear from company leaders that we should "get back to business as usual" and "move on." They may not see that many employees are still glued to Internet news sites every time a plane crashes or when another person contracts anthrax. Executives may see training sessions packed with participants, but not their eyes staring through the instructor as they worry about not receiving raises this year because business is down. Letting employees remain disengaged is unhealthy for them and financially disastrous for an organization.

Leaders should be encouraged to take advantage of this present opportunity to unite people around common values that will create a place where people feel good about the work they do. Your company's survival may depend on it.

Tracy Mauro *is a management trainer at MCI WorldCom; tracy.mauro@wcom.com.*

From *Training & Development*, February 2002, pp. 52-58. © 2002 by ASTD Magazines. Reprinted by permission.

Ensuring Ethical Effectiveness

New rules mean virtually every company will need a code of ethics.

BY RANDY MYERS

Stung by the high-profile accounting scandals that drove some the nation's leading companies into bankruptcy court, Congress and other regulatory authorities have taken up their pens in an attempt to legislate business behavior. The Sarbanes-Oxley Act, which President Bush signed into law in July of 2002, requires publicly traded companies to disclose whether they have adopted a code of ethics for their senior financial officers, and if not, why. They also must report promptly any amendments to or waivers from the code.

The New York Stock Exchange, meanwhile, proposed new corporate governance standards which—if the SEC approves them—would require companies traded on that exchange to adopt corporate governance guidelines and a code of business conduct and ethics for *all* employees. CPAs can help employers or clients navigate these new rules and create a code of ethics that complies with all of the requirements.

NUTS AND BOLTS

For companies that choose to adopt a set of ethics guidelines in response to Sarbanes-Oxley—and few will run the risk of not doing so given the negative message it would send to investors, regulators and potential litigants—section 406 of the act says the code should seek to ensure that senior financial executives

• Conduct themselves honestly and ethically, particularly in handling actual or apparent conflicts of interest.

• Provide full, fair, accurate, timely and understandable disclosure in the periodic reports their employers file with the SEC.

• Comply with all applicable government laws, rules and regulations.

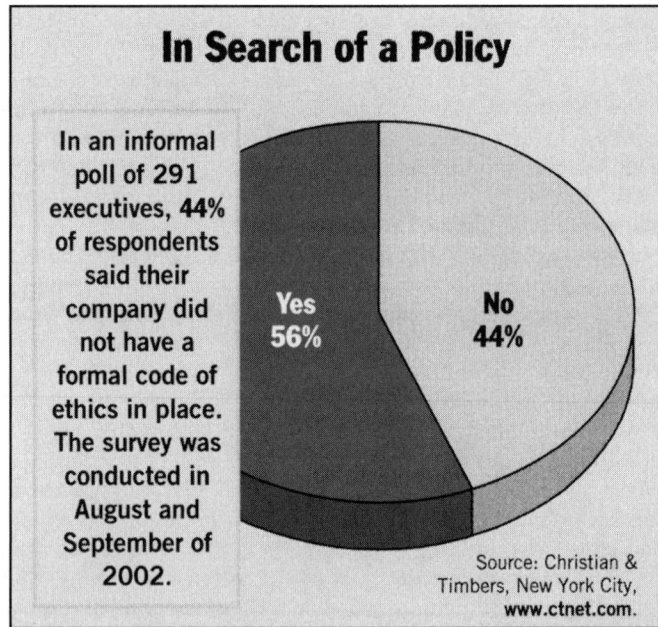

In Search of a Policy

In an informal poll of 291 executives, **44%** of respondents said their company did not have a formal code of ethics in place. The survey was conducted in August and September of 2002.

Yes 56% No 44%

Source: Christian & Timbers, New York City, www.ctnet.com

Even for CPAs who don't toil as principal financial officers, comptrollers or principal accounting officers—job titles Sarbanes-Oxley specifically targets—the new law introduces a raft of issues. As interpreted by the SEC in the proposed rulemaking notice it issued on October 16, 2002, Sarbanes-Oxley does more than suggest companies have a code of ethics for senior financial executives.

Once SEC rules are finalized, section 404 of the act will require publicly traded companies to file in their annual reports an "internal control report" that outlines what steps management has taken to establish and maintain adequate internal controls and financial reporting procedures, as well as management's conclusions about the effectiveness of those controls and procedures—a report CPAs and corporate finance departments likely will have a hand in drafting. The report must say the company's public accountant has attested to, and reported on, management's evaluation of the company's internal controls and financial reporting procedures. The company must include a copy of the auditor's attestation in its annual report.

The Sarbanes-Oxley Act now requires publicly traded companies to disclose whether they have adopted a code of ethics for senior financial officers. The New York Stock Exchange is considering new rules that would require listed companies to have a code of business conduct that applies to all employees.

What's not clear, says CPA Sherrie McAvoy, national director of corporate compliance and ethics services for Deloitte & Touche in Dallas, is whether an external auditor would be required to formally audit a client's compliance with its own code of ethics. While her initial suspicion is it would not, she says it won't be clear until the SEC issues final regulations. An SEC spokesman notes that Sarbanes-Oxley gave the agency 180 days from the date of the law's enactment, or roughly until the end of January 2003, to issue final rules.

CPA Richard Steinberg, head of the corporate governance practice for PricewaterhouseCoopers in Florham Park, New Jersey, takes a similar view. "As they look at internal controls, the external auditors are going to focus on this (the code of ethics)," he says. "Not that they're going to audit it, but they'll consider it as they assess the company's control environment."

INCREMENTAL CHANGE

Those counting on ethics codes to change corporate behavior may be surprised to learn that most public companies—at least those in the *Fortune* 1000—already have them. When the U.S. Federal Sentencing Guidelines became law in 1991, they listed seven elements of an effective corporate compliance program judges could take into consideration when sentencing corporations for federal offenses. Most large public companies quickly realized the value of incorporating these elements into their operations, if only as risk-management tools. Among them was establishing compliance standards and procedures—otherwise known as a code of conduct or ethics.

Today, says McAvoy, surveys her firm conducted show approximately 95% of *Fortune* 1000 companies have a code of conduct. Stuart C. Gilman, president of the nonprofit Ethics Resource Center in Washington, D.C., says many private companies have such guidelines as well; he estimates that altogether there are more than 3,000 ethics officers working in the United States.

What's different now that Sarbanes-Oxley is on the books? According to McAvoy, the new law puts more emphasis on financial reporting, particularly its accuracy. This could translate into more responsibility for CPAs. Section 301 also mandates that companies put in place a mechanism for employees to raise concerns about financial reporting matters—confidentially and anonymously. The SEC's proposed rules for implementing section 406 go on to say the code of ethics should identify the person or persons to whom employees should deliver those anonymous reports.

Establishing a process for rank-and-file employees to confidentially report code violations is a critical component of any ethics program, according to McAvoy. Most of the companies that already have established such procedures assign a case number to each complaint or tip an employee makes so he or she can track its progress. In addition, the person to whom employees report alleged violations is generally someone outside the ordinary chain of corporate command—an ethics or compliance officer, for example, or an ombudsman—who nonetheless has access to the company's top executives and its board of directors.

CPA Sherrie McAvoy says that while most companies already have ethics codes, Sarbanes-Oxley puts more emphasis on the financial reporting aspects

The WorldCom case amply illustrated the perils of having employees report complaints to a senior executive with routine corporate responsibilities. Internal auditors who uncovered the company's accounting fraud reported it to the company's then CFO Scott Sullivan. The federal government now alleges Sullivan instigated the fraud and attempted to block the internal investigation. According to an in-depth report *The Wall Street Journal* published in October of 2002, WorldCom didn't finally acknowledge, make public and address the fraud until its vice-president of internal audit, Cynthia Cooper, took damaging evidence to the company's audit committee.

Many CPAs will have a role in helping companies comply with Sarbanes-Oxley. Certainly, those in corporate finance departments can be expected to be involved in drafting or reviewing those portions of their company's code dealing with financial matters, says Nancy Wilgenbusch, president of Marylhurst University in Portland, Oregon, and a member of the AICPA ethics committee. The portions of the code CPAs might handle would range from insider trading to appropriate and accurate expense reporting, acting as good stewards of company assets, avoiding conflicts of interest and assuring accurate corporate communications with the public. To the extent the code of ethics includes quantifiable measures of accountability concerning items such as insider trading or entertainment expense reporting, for example, Wilgenbusch says CPAs are ideally suited, by virtue of their training and professional expertise, to evaluate or test the results.

EXECUTIVE SUMMARY

- **THE SARBANES-OXLEY ACT NOW REQUIRES PUBLICLY** traded companies to disclose whether they have adopted a code of ethics for senior financial officers. In addition, the New York Stock Exchange is considering new rules that would require listed companies to have a code of business conduct that applies to all employees.

- **UNDER THE ACT THE SEC REQUIRES COMPANIES** to file an internal control report with their annual report outlining management's responsibilities for establishing and maintaining adequate internal controls as well as its conclusions about the effectiveness of those controls. The company's auditor must attest to management's evaluation.

- **MANY COMPANIES ALREADY HAVE ETHICS CODES.** With the emphasis in Sarbanes-Oxley on financial reporting, CPAs may want to help employers and clients review these codes to make sure they comply with the new regulations. Companies will need to establish a process for rank-and-file employees to report code violations confidentially to someone outside the ordinary corporate chain of command.

- **THE BEST WAY TO DRAFT A CODE OF ETHICS** all employees will follow is to bring together a multidisciplinary team from all parts of the organization. Employees must then be trained in what the code means using real-life dilemmas they might encounter on the job. Regular refresher courses are important because ethics training is perishable—people forget.

- **COMPANIES WITH AN EXISTING ETHICS CODE UNLIKELY** will need a new one. Still, businesses may want to revisit the code to make sure they have a full-blown compliance program in place. Even though the act focuses on the CFO, the SEC expects the entire organization to comply with the law.

External auditors would also appear to have a role in assessing compliance with codes of ethics, if only in the context of a code's being part of a company's internal control process. Gilman encourages outside auditors to go a step further: For each client, the auditor should sign a statement noting that it understands and accepts the client's code of ethics. "This allows the outside auditing firm to comport with the company's internal environment," Gilman says. "It permits a level of independence and says, 'We're willing to obey and abide by the same set of standards the organization holds itself to.'"

DOING IT RIGHT

A number of companies—including Raytheon and Texas Instruments—have been widely recognized for the scope and quality of their ethics programs. Raytheon makes ethics training a requirement for every employee, all the way up to the CEO. Texas Instruments' employee ethics handbook dates to 1961 and the company has received three ethics awards for its leadership in the field. Texas Instruments also provides employees with a business-card-sized pamphlet that serves as a "quick test" for workers faced with an ethical dilemma.

- Is the action legal?
- Does it comply with our values?
- If you do it, will you feel bad?
- How will it look in the newspaper?
- If you know its wrong, don't do it.
- If you're not sure, ask.
- Keep asking until you get an answer.

Companies should put together a multidisciplinary team from all parts of the organization to draft a code and communicate it to employees.

While it's difficult to calculate a hard return on investment for drafting and implementing a code, Bruce Pfau, national practice leader for organization measurements at Watson Wyatt Worldwide has tried. A survey his consulting company conducted in 2000 found workers who believed their company operated with honesty and integrity showed higher levels of commitment to their employer in terms of job satisfaction and company pride than those who judged their employer to have low ethical values. Pfau also found companies highly rated by their employees for honesty and integrity produced, over the previous three years, a higher return to shareholders (112%) than poorly rated companies (76%).

PUTTING TOGETHER A CODE

With virtually all companies needing a code of ethics so they can avoid having to report they don't have one under Sarbanes-Oxley, the task of developing one from scratch need not be too involved. The Financial Executives Institute has drafted a one-page model code of ethics for senior financial executives it says conforms to the new law; it can be found on the organization's Web site at **www.fei.org**. Another code developed by Parson Consulting, a national consulting company specializing in finance, accounting and business systems is available at **www.parsongroup.com/sarbanes-market_position.asp**.

But most experts say it would be far better to create a code of ethics for the entire company, one that applies to all employees and builds on their input. Under the proposed changes to the NYSE listing requirements, such a policy would be required of all companies trading on the Big Board.

AICPA ethics committee member Nancy Wilgenbusch says CPAs will help draft ethics code provisions dealing with financial matters.

The challenge companies face—whether creating an entirely new code or reassessing and upgrading an existing one to reflect Sarbanes-Oxley—is to draft a document that isn't just decoration on the company bulletin board but instead helps employees live up to the ethical standards investors, legislators and regulators demand. "We're terrified here of what we call the three Ps—the print, post and pray syndrome," says Gilman. "You print a code of conduct, post it on the wall and pray people actually read it."

According to Gilman and other ethics professionals, the correct approach is to bring together a multidisciplinary team from all parts of the organization—finance, sales, human resources, operations, marketing, executive—to draft a code, communicate its importance to employees and then involve them in seminars to help understand how the code applies to them and their colleagues. Finally, says Minneapolis-based ethics trainer Nan DeMars, author of *You Want Me To Do What?* (Fireside, 1998), senior management must follow through and hold people accountable for complying with the code.

One way to make a code of ethics come alive for employees, DeMars says, is for human resources to plan training sessions that engage them in discussions about real-life or theoretical ethical dilemmas they might expect to handle on the job. The more specific the situations are to the particular company, the more valuable they will be. DeMars gives these examples of the types of questions she might pose in a seminar: "You are the assistant to David Duncan, lead auditor for Arthur Andersen. You know the firm is about to be subpoenaed. He asks you to shred documents. What would you do? Or, you are Sharon Watkin's assistant at Enron and you type her memo to Ken Lay warning him of the possibility Enron will implode if its current accounting practices continue. Now that you know the company is in trouble and your boss is aware of this, what do you do?"

"You've got to take the words as well as the legal requirements and translate them into understandable practices," agrees John J. Castellani, president of The Business Roundtable, an association of CEOs of leading corporations. "Ultimately, doing so gives you a very strong tool. When employees violate the policy, they are dismissed."

DeMars and others agree ethics programs don't achieve much when they are handed down by senior management with little input from other employees or when senior managers themselves fail to abide by the code or neglect to stress its importance. Enron had a rigorous code of ethics, for example, yet it fell victim to unethical behavior in part because its board of directors twice voted to suspend the code to allow the company's former CFO, Andrew Fastow, to launch business activities that created, for him, a conflict of interest. Ethics professionals warn against viewing educational programs as a once-and-done procedure. "Ethics training is perishable," Gilman says. "People forget." To deal with this problem, companies should schedule regular refresher courses for all employees.

FINDING HELP

While companies must enlist the cooperation of their own staff members to draft a code of ethics that will resonate with them, there's plenty of outside help available, too. Among the Big Four accounting firms, both Deloitte & Touche and PricewaterhouseCoopers offer ethics consulting services, says Gilman. So do some law firms and a number of nonprofit organizations and academic centers. Among the latter are Gilman's own Ethics Resource Center as well as the Ethics Officers Association in Belmont, Massachusetts; the Institute for Global Ethics in Camden, Maine; and the Markkula Center for Applied Ethics at Santa Clara University in California. (See box for information on how to contact these and other resources.)

Elsewhere, the nonprofit Practicing Law Institute in New York City offers programs on ethics and corporate compliance several times a year, says McAvoy, and has published a series of books on the topic. All that said, Gilman cautions companies against off-loading too much responsibility to outside consultants. "Ethics are one of those things where you don't want someone doing an assessment and charging you a lot of money to tell you what you want to hear," he explains. The best ethics code is one drafted in-house.

Resources

The following organizations can help accountants who are charged with developing, implementing or monitoring a corporation's code of ethics.

Ethics Officers Association
30 Church Street
Suite 331
Belmont, Massachusetts 02478
617-484-9400
www.eoa.org

Ethics Resource Center
1747 Pennsylvania Avenue, NW
Suite 400
Washington, D.C. 20006
202-737-2258
www.ethics.org

Institute for Global Ethics
P.O. Box 563
Camden, Maine 04843
207-236-6658
www.globalethics.com

Markkula Center for Applied Ethics
Santa Clara University
500 El Camino Real
Santa Clara, California 95053-0633
408-554-5319 **www.scu.edu/ethics**

Practicing Law Institute
810 Seventh Avenue
New York, New York 10019-5818
800-260-4PLI or 212-824-5710
www.pli.edu

While Sarbanes-Oxley specifically covers the CFO, the SEC has made it clear it's going to expect the entire organization to comply.

Many companies that already have a code of ethics are unlikely to need a new one to respond to Sarbanes-Oxley, says attorney Tom Patton, a partner with Tighe Patton Armstrong Teasdale PLLC in Washington, D.C. This is especially true since the new law doesn't require a company to publish its set of guidelines but merely to confirm it has one. "The statute defines a code of ethics in very broad terms, so you have to make sure your existing code meets all of them; assuming it does, you probably don't need to develop a new one," he says.

Stephen Hill Jr., a partner with the Kansas City, Missouri, law firm Blackwell Sanders Peper Martin LLP, concurs but adds companies may still want to review their code point by point to make sure it covers all of the provisions in the new law and that they have a "full-blown compliance program in place." The proposed SEC regulations under Sarbanes-Oxley make it clear the code should promote "compliance with applicable government laws, rules and regulations."

At many companies, such reviews are already under way. "A number of companies are taking a hard look at their codes and making sure they're current and sharing them with their boards of directors," says Deloitte & Touche's McAvoy. "They're also taking a look at the financial reporting aspects and making sure they are as robust as they can be." Meanwhile, the Ethics Officers Association reports that about 100 companies have hired ethics officers through October of 2002 alone.

Hill says his firm is telling clients their entire organization, not just the CFO, must be prepared to deal with compliance issues. "Sarbanes-Oxley covers the CFO, but in its October 16 statement, the SEC makes it clear it's going to expect the entire organization to comply with the law," Hill says. By way of example, the proposed SEC regulations mandate that a company's code of ethics apply not only to senior financial executives but also to the "principal executive officer," even though that position was not specified in the act.

Attorney Stephen Hill says most companies won't need new ethics codes but should review existing ones to make sure they cover all the new provisions.

According to the London-based Institute of Business Ethics (IBE) (www.ibe.org.uk) a code of ethics should include a preface, signed by the chairman or CEO, explaining what values are important to top management in conducting the business. It should then cover these key areas:

- The purpose of the business and its values.
- Employee relations including working conditions, recruiting, training, discrimination policies and use of company assets by employees.
- Customer relations guidelines.
- The importance of protecting the investment made by shareholders or other investors.
- Relationships with suppliers.
- How the company relates to society as well as to the wider business community.
- How the company will implement the code, including training.

The IBE also advises any company drafting a code to find a champion—hopefully the CEO—who is prepared to drive the introduction of a business ethics policy. Without this support, there is little chance the company will find the code a useful tool. The board of directors should also endorse the ethics policy.

WILL IT WORK?

Whether any of this will prevent unethical behavior is uncertain, although most experts say codes can make a difference when companies develop and implement them properly. "There's nothing we can do to prevent a crook from stealing if he or she wants to," says ethics committee member Wilgenbusch. "If people are greedy, a code won't prevent them from behaving unethically. But if the CEO gets the company's top 20 people in a room and says, 'We're going to adhere to both the spirit and letter of the law; we're going to play by the rules in every sense of the word and anybody who steps across that line of ethical behavior not only will be discharged immediately but prosecuted to the full extent of the law,' then you are going to avoid unethical behavior." That's a goal every accountant can endorse.

RANDY MYERS is a freelance financial writer who lives in Dover, Pennsylvania. His e-mail address is randy@randymyers.net.

Article 33

The Competitive Advantage of Corporate Philanthropy

by Michael E. Porter and Mark R. Kramer

CORPORATE PHILANTHROPY is in decline. Charitable contributions by U. S. companies fell 14.5% in real dollars last year, and over the last 15 years, corporate giving as a percentage of profits has dropped by 50%. The reasons are not hard to understand. Executives increasingly see themselves in a no-win situation, caught between critics demanding ever higher levels of "corporate social responsibility" and investors applying relentless pressure to maximize short-term profits. Giving more does not satisfy the critics—the more companies donate, the more is expected of them. And executives find it hard, if not impossible, to justify charitable expenditures in terms of bottom-line benefit.

This dilemma has led many companies to seek to be more strategic in their philanthropy. But what passes for "strategic philanthropy" today is almost never truly strategic, and often it isn't even particularly effective as philanthropy. Increasingly, philanthropy is used as a form of public relations or advertising, promoting a company's image or brand through cause-related marketing or other high-profile sponsorships. Although it still represents only a small proportion of overall corporate charitable expenditures, U.S. corporate spending on cause-related marketing jumped from $125 million in 1990 to an estimated $828 million in 2002. Arts sponsorships are growing, too—they accounted for an additional $589 million in 2001. While these campaigns do provide much-needed support to worthy causes, they are intended as much to increase company visibility and improve employee morale as to create social impact. Tobacco giant Philip Morris, for example, spent $75 million on its charitable contributions in 1999 and then launched a $100 million advertising campaign to publicize them. Not surprisingly, there are genuine doubts about whether such approaches actually work or just breed public cynicism about company motives. (See the sidebar "The Myth of Strategic Philanthropy.")

Most companies feel compelled to give to charity. **Few have figured out how to do it well.**

Given the current haziness surrounding corporate philanthropy, this seems an appropriate time to revisit the most basic of questions: Should corporations engage in philanthropy at all? The economist Milton Friedman laid down the gauntlet decades ago, arguing in a 1970 *New York Times Magazine* article that the only "social responsibility of business" is to "increase its profits." "The corporation," he wrote in his book *Capitalism and Freedom*, "is an instrument of the stockholders who own it. If the corporation makes a contribution, it prevents the individual stockholder from himself deciding how he should dispose of his funds." If charitable contributions are to be made, Friedman concluded, they should be made by individual stockholders—or, by extension, individual employees—and not by the corporation.

The way most corporate philanthropy is practiced today, Friedman is right. The majority of corporate contribution programs are diffuse and unfocused. Most consist of numerous small cash donations given to aid local civic causes or provide general operating support to universities and national charities in the hope of generating goodwill among employees, customers, and the local

The Myth of Strategic Philanthropy

Few phrases are as overused and poorly defined as "strategic philanthropy." The term is used to cover virtually any kind of charitable activity that has some definable theme, goal, approach, or focus. In the corporate context, it generally means that there is some connection, however vague or tenuous, between the charitable contribution and the company's business. Often this connection is only semantic, enabling the company to rationalize its contributions in public reports and press releases. In fact, most corporate giving programs have nothing to do with a company's strategy. They are primarily aimed at generating goodwill and positive publicity and boosting employee morale.

Cause-related marketing, through which a company concentrates its giving on a single cause or admired organization, was one of the earliest practices cited as "strategic philanthropy," and it is a step above diffuse corporate contributions. At its most sophisticated, cause-related marketing can improve the reputation of a company by linking its identity with the admired qualities of a chosen nonprofit partner or a popular cause. Companies that sponsor the Olympics, for example, gain not only wide exposure but also an association with the pursuit of excellence. And by concentrating funding through a deliberate selection process, cause-related marketing has the potential to create more impact than unfocused giving would provide.

However, cause-related marketing falls far short of truly strategic philanthropy. Its emphasis remains on publicity rather than social impact. The desired benefit is enhanced goodwill, not improvement in a company's ability to compete. True strategic giving, by contrast, addresses important social and economic goals simultaneously, targeting areas of competitive context where the company and society both benefit because the firm brings unique assets and expertise.

community. Rather than being tied to well-thought-out social or business objectives, the contributions often reflect the personal beliefs and values of executives or employees. Indeed, one of the most popular approaches—employee matching grants—explicitly leaves the choice of charity to the individual worker. Although aimed at enhancing morale, the same effect might be gained from an equal increase in wages that employees could then choose to donate to charity on a tax-deductible basis. It does indeed seem that many of the giving decisions companies make today would be better made by individuals donating their own money.

What about the programs that are at least superficially tied to business goals, such as cause-related marketing? Even the successful ones are hard to justify as charitable initiatives. Since all reasonable corporate expenditures are deductible, companies get no special tax advantage for spending on philanthropy as opposed to other corporate purposes. If cause-related marketing is good marketing, it is already deductible and does not benefit from being designated as charitable.

But does Friedman's argument always hold? Underlying it are two implicit assumptions. The first is that social and economic objectives are separate and distinct, so that a corporation's social spending comes at the expense of its economic results. The second is the assumption that corporations, when they address social objectives, provide no greater benefit than is provided by individual donors.

These assumptions hold true when corporate contributions are unfocused and piecemeal, as is typically the case today. But there is another, more truly strategic way to think about philanthropy. Corporations can use their charitable efforts to improve their *competitive context*—the quality of the business environment in the location or locations where they operate. Using philanthropy to enhance context brings social and economic goals into alignment and improves a company's long-term business prospects—thus contradicting Friedman's first assumption. In addition, addressing context enables a company not only to give money but also to leverage its capabilities and relationships in support of charitable causes. That produces social benefits far exceeding those provided by individual donors, foundations, or even governments. Context-focused giving thus contradicts Friedman's second assumption as well.

A handful of companies have begun to use context-focused philanthropy to achieve both social and economic gains. Cisco Systems, to take one example, has invested in an ambitious educational program—the Cisco Networking Academy—to train computer network administrators, thus alleviating a potential constraint on its growth while providing attractive job opportunities to high school graduates. By focusing on social needs that affect its corporate context and utilizing its unique attributes as a corporation to address them, Cisco has begun to demonstrate the unrealized potential of corporate philanthropy. Taking this new direction, however, requires fundamental changes in the way companies approach their contribution programs. Corporations need to rethink both *where* they focus their philanthropy and *how* they go about their giving.

Where to Focus

It is true that economic and social objectives have long been seen as distinct and often competing. But this is a false dichotomy; it represents an increasingly obsolete perspective in a world of open, knowledge-based compe-

Article 33. The Competitive Advantage of Corporate Philanthropy

tition. Companies do not function in isolation from the society around them. In fact, their ability to compete depends heavily on the circumstances of the locations where they operate. Improving education, for example, is generally seen as a social issue, but the educational level of the local workforce substantially affects a company's potential competitiveness. The more a social improvement relates to a company's business, the more it leads to economic benefits as well. In establishing its Networking Academy, for example, Cisco focused not on the educational system overall, but on the training needed to produce network administrators—the particular kind of education that made the most difference to Cisco's competitive context. (For a more detailed look at that program, see the sidebar "The Cisco Networking Academy.")

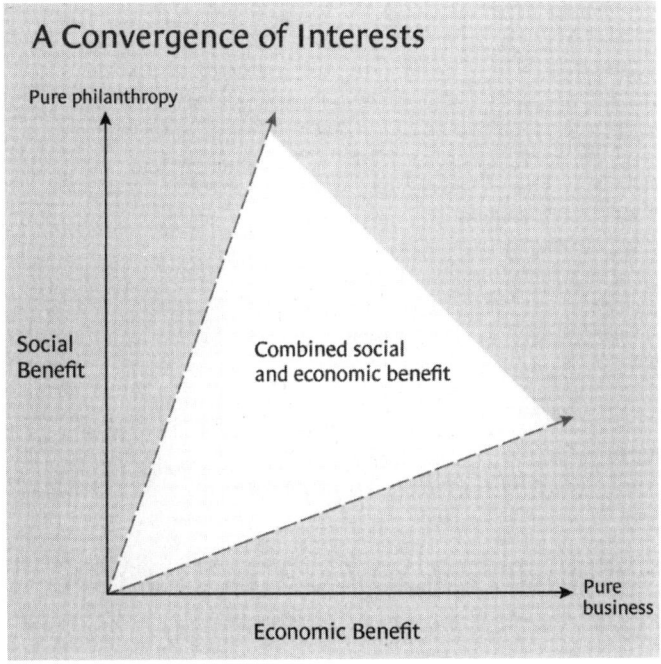

In the long run, then, social and economic goals are not inherently conflicting but integrally connected. Competitiveness today depends on the productivity with which companies can use labor, capital, and natural resources to produce high-quality goods and services. Productivity depends on having workers who are educated, safe, healthy, decently housed, and motivated by a sense of opportunity. Preserving the environment benefits not only society but companies too, because reducing pollution and waste can lead to a more productive use of resources and help produce goods that consumers value. Boosting social and economic conditions in developing countries can create more productive locations for a company's operations as well as new markets for its products. Indeed, we are learning that the most effective method of addressing many of the world's pressing problems is often to mobilize the corporate sector in ways that benefit both society and companies.

That does not mean that every corporate expenditure will bring a social benefit or that every social benefit will improve competitiveness. Most corporate expenditures produce benefits only for the business, and charitable contributions unrelated to the business generate only social benefits. It is only where corporate expenditures produce simultaneous social and economic gains that corporate philanthropy and shareholder interests converge, as illustrated in the exhibit "A Convergence of Interests." The highlighted area shows where corporate philanthropy has an important influence on a company's competitive context. It is here that philanthropy is truly strategic.

Competitive context has always been important to strategy. The availability of skilled and motivated employees; the efficiency of the local infrastructure, including roads and telecommunications; the size and sophistication of the local market; the extent of governmental regulations—such contextual variables have always influenced companies' ability to compete. But competitive context has become even more critical as the basis of competition has moved from cheap inputs to superior productivity. For one thing, modern knowledge- and technology-based competition hinges more and more on worker capabilities. For another, companies today depend more on local partnerships: They rely on outsourcing and collaboration with local suppliers and institutions rather than on vertical integration; they work more closely with customers; and they draw more on local universities and research institutes to conduct research and development. Finally, navigating increasingly complex local regulations and reducing approval times for new projects and products are becoming increasingly important to competition. As a result of these trends, companies' success has become more tightly intertwined with local institutions and other contextual conditions. And the globalization of production and marketing means that context is often important for a company not just in its home market but in multiple countries.

A company's competitive context consists of four interrelated elements of the local business environment that shape potential productivity: factor conditions, or the available inputs of production; demand conditions; the context for strategy and rivalry; and related and supporting industries. This framework is summarized in the exhibit "The Four Elements of Competitive Context" and described in detail in Michael E. Porter's *The Competitive Advantage of Nations*. Weakness in any part of this context can erode the competitiveness of a nation or region as a business location.

Some aspects of the business environment, such as road systems, corporate tax rates, and corporation laws, have effects that cut across all industries. These general conditions can be crucial to competitiveness in developing countries, and improving them through corporate philanthropy can bring enormous social gains to the world's poorest nations. But often just as decisive, if not

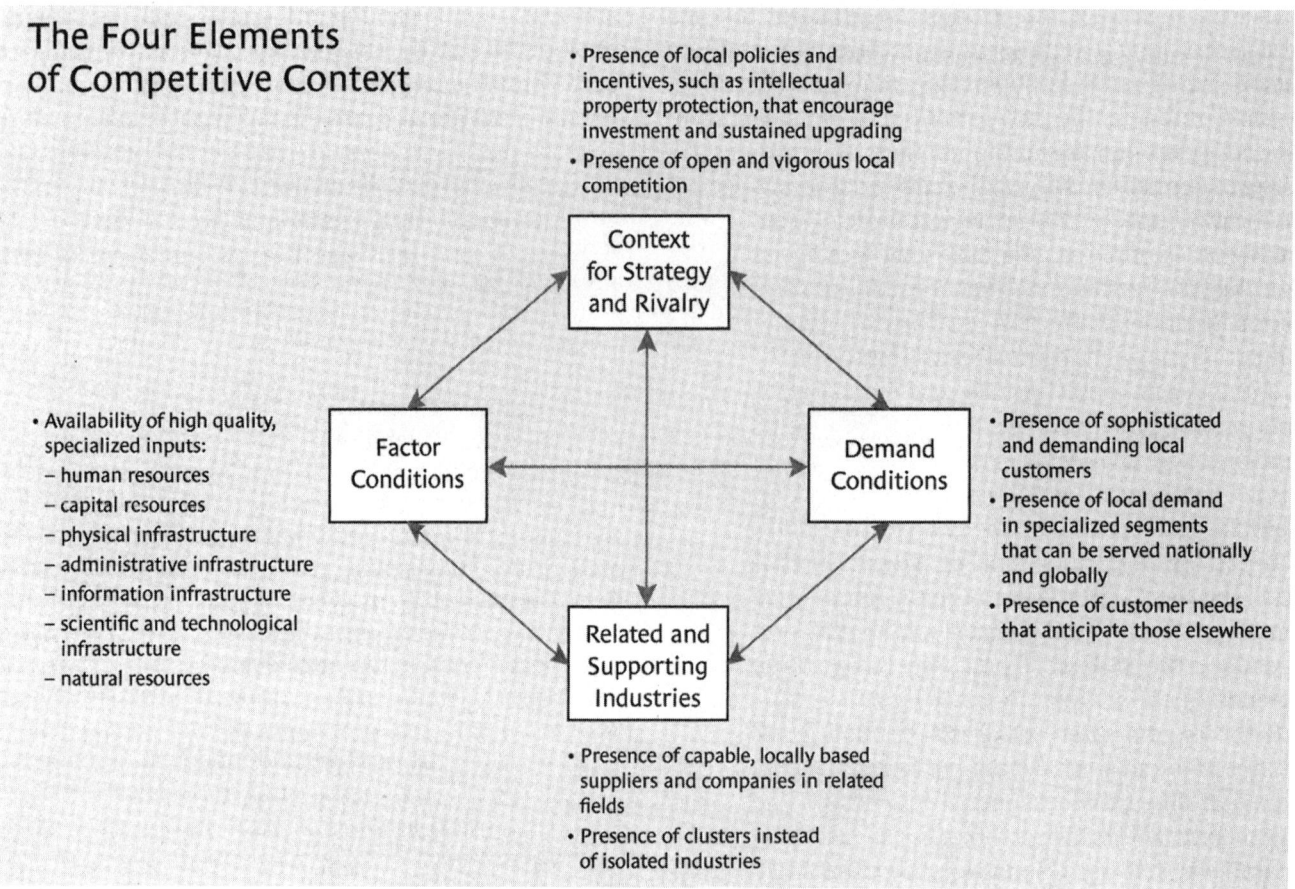

more, are aspects of context that are specific to a particular *cluster*—a geographic concentration of interconnected companies, suppliers, related industries, and specialized institutions in a particular field, such as high-performance cars in Germany or software in India. Clusters arise through the combined influence of all four elements of context. They are often prominent features of a region's economic landscape, and building them is essential to its development, allowing constituent firms to be more productive, making innovation easier, and fostering the formation of new businesses.

Philanthropic investments by members of a cluster, either individually or collectively, can have a powerful effect on the cluster's competitiveness and the performance of all of its constituent companies. Philanthropy can often be the most cost-effective way—and sometimes the only way—to improve competitive context. It enables companies to leverage not only their own resources but also the existing efforts and infrastructure of nonprofits and other institutions. Contributing to a university, for example, may be a far less expensive way to strengthen a local base of advanced skills in a company's field than developing training in-house. And philanthropy is amenable to collective corporate action, enabling costs to be spread over multiple companies. Finally, because of philanthropy's wide social benefits, companies are often able to forge partnerships with nonprofit organizations and governments that would be wary of collaborating on efforts that solely benefited a particular company.

> **Philanthropy can often be the most cost-effective way for a company to improve its competitive context, enabling companies to leverage the efforts and infrastructure of nonprofits and other institutions.**

Influencing Competitive Context

By carefully analyzing the elements of competitive context, a company can identify the areas of overlap between social and economic value that will most enhance its own and its cluster's competitiveness. Consider each of the four elements of context and how companies have influenced them through philanthropy in ways that have improved their long-term economic prospects.

Factor Conditions. Achieving high levels of productivity depends on the presence of trained workers, high-quality scientific and technological institutions, adequate physical infrastructure, transparent and efficient administrative processes (such as company registration or permit requirements), and available natural resources. All are areas that philanthropy can influence.

Charitable giving can, for example, improve education and training. DreamWorks SKG, the film production company, recently created a program to train low-income students in Los Angeles in skills needed to work in the entertainment industry. Each of the company's six divisions is working with the Los Angeles Community College District, local high schools, and after-school programs to create a specialized curriculum that combines classroom instruction with internships and mentoring. The social benefit is an improved educational system and better employment opportunities for low-income residents. The economic benefit is greater availability of specially trained graduates. Even though relatively few of them will join DreamWorks itself, the company also gains by strengthening the entertainment cluster it depends on.

Philanthropic initiatives can also improve the local quality of life, which benefits all citizens but is increasingly necessary to attract mobile employees with specialized talents. In 1996, SC Johnson, a manufacturer of cleaning and home-storage products, launched "Sustainable Racine," a project to make its home city in Wisconsin a better place in which to live and work. In partnership with local organizations, government, and residents, the company created a communitywide coalition focused on enhancing the local economy and the environment. One project, an agreement among four municipalities to coordinate water and sewer treatment, resulted in savings for residents and businesses while reducing pollution. Another project involved opening the community's first charter school, targeting at-risk students. Other efforts focused on economic revitalization: Commercial vacancy rates in downtown Racine have fallen from 46% to 18% as polluted sites have been reclaimed and jobs have returned for local residents.

Philanthropy can also improve inputs other than labor, through enhancements in, say, the quality of local research and development institutions, the effectiveness of administrative institutions such as the legal system, the quality of the physical infrastructure, or the sustainable development of natural resources. Exxon Mobil, for example, has devoted substantial resources to improving basic conditions such as roads and the rule of law in the developing countries where it operates.

Demand Conditions. Demand conditions in a nation or region include the size of the local market, the appropriateness of product standards, and the sophistication of local customers. Sophisticated local customers enhance the region's competitiveness by providing companies with insight into emerging customer needs and applying pressure for innovation. For example, the advanced state of medical practice in Boston has triggered a stream of innovation in Boston-based medical device companies.

Philanthropy can influence both the size and quality of the local market. The Cisco Networking Academy, for instance, improved demand conditions by helping customers obtain well-trained network administrators. In doing so, it increased the size of the market and the sophistication of users—and hence users' interest in more advanced solutions. Apple Computer has long donated computers to schools as a means of introducing its products to young people. This provides a clear social benefit to the schools while expanding Apple's potential market and turning students and teachers into more sophisticated purchasers. Safeco, an insurance and financial services firm, is working in partnership with nonprofits to expand affordable housing and enhance public safety. As home ownership and public safety increased in its four test markets, insurance sales did too, in some cases by up to 40%

Context for Strategy and Rivalry. The rules, incentives, and norms governing competition in a nation or region have a fundamental influence on productivity. Policies that encourage investment, protect intellectual property, open local markets to trade, break up or prevent the formation of cartels and monopolies, and reduce corruption make a location a more attractive place to do business.

Philanthropy can have a strong influence on creating a more productive and transparent environment for competition. For example, 26 U.S. corporations and 38 corporations from other countries have joined to support Transparency International in its work to disclose and deter corruption around the world. By measuring and focusing public attention on corruption, the organization helps to create an environment that rewards fair competition and enhances productivity. This benefits local citizens while providing sponsoring companies improved access to markets.

Another example is the International Corporate Governance Network (ICGN), a nonprofit organization formed by major institutional investors, including the College Retirement Equities Fund (TIAA-CREF) and the California Public Employees Retirement System, known as CalPERS, to promote improved standards of corporate governance and disclosure, especially in developing countries. ICGN encourages uniform global accounting standards and equitable shareholder voting procedures. Developing countries and their citizens benefit as improved governance and disclosure enhance local corporate practices, expose unscrupulous local competitors, and make regions more attractive for foreign investment. The institutional investors that support this project also gain better and fairer capital markets in which to invest.

Related and Supporting Industries. A company's productivity can be greatly enhanced by having high-quality supporting industries and services nearby. While outsourcing from distant suppliers is possible, it is not as efficient as using capable local suppliers of services, components, and machinery. Proximity enhances responsiveness, exchange of information, and innovation, in addition to lowering transportation and inventory costs.

Philanthropy can foster the development of clusters and strengthen supporting industries. American Express, for example, depends on travel-related spending for a large share of its credit card and travel agency revenues. Hence, it is part of the travel cluster in each of the countries in which it operates, and it depends on the success of these clusters in improving the quality of tourism and attracting travelers. Since 1986, American Express has funded Travel and Tourism Academies in secondary schools, training students not for the credit card business, its core business, nor for its own travel services, but for careers in other travel agencies as well as airlines, hotels, and restaurants. The program, which includes teacher training, curriculum support, summer internships, and industry mentors, now operates in ten countries and more than 3,000 schools, with more than 120,000 students enrolled. It provides the major social benefits of improved educational and job opportunities for local citizens. Within the United States, 80% of students in the program go on to college, and 25% take jobs in the travel industry after graduation. The economic gains are also substantial, as local travel clusters become more competitive and better able to grow. That translates into important benefits for American Express.

The Free Rider Problem

When corporate philanthropy improves competitive context, other companies in the cluster or region, including direct competitors, often share the benefits. That raises an important question: Does the ability of other companies to be free riders negate the strategic value of context-focused philanthropy? The answer is *no*. The competitive benefits reaped by the donor company remain substantial, for five reasons:

- Improving context mainly benefits companies based in a given location. Not all competitors will be based in the same area, so the company will still gain an edge over the competition in general.
- Corporate philanthropy is ripe for collective activity. By sharing the costs with other companies in its cluster, including competitors, a company can greatly diminish the free rider problem.
- Leading companies will be best positioned to make substantial contributions and will in turn reap a major share of the benefits. Cisco, for example, with a leading market share in networking equipment, will benefit most from a larger, more rapidly growing market.

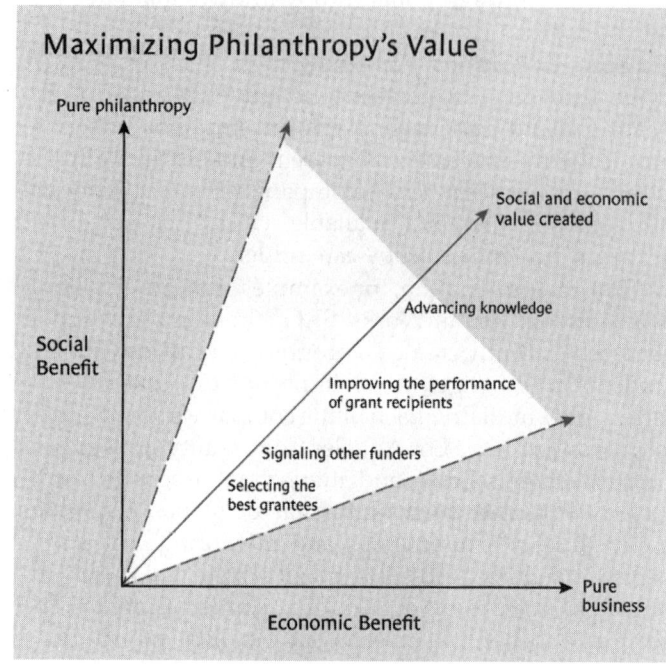

- Not all contextual advantages are of equal value to all competitors. The more tightly corporate philanthropy is aligned with a company's unique strategy—increasing skills, technology, or infrastructure on which the firm is especially reliant, say, or increasing demand within a specialized segment where the company is strongest—the more disproportionately the company will benefit through enhancing the context.
- The company that initiates corporate philanthropy in a particular area will often get disproportionate benefits because of the superior reputation and relationships it builds. In its campaign to fight malaria in African countries, for example, Exxon Mobil not only improves public health. It also improves the health of its workers and contractors and builds strong relationships with local governments and nonprofits, advancing its goal of becoming the preferred resource-development partner.

A good example of how a company can gain an edge even when its contributions also benefit competitors is provided by Grand Circle Travel. Grand Circle, the leading direct marketer of international travel for older Americans, has a strategy based on offering rich cultural and educational experiences for its customers. Since 1992, its corporate foundation has given more than $12 million to historical preservation projects in locations that its customers like to visit, such as the Foundation of Friends of the Museum and Ruins of Ephesus in Turkey and the State Museum of Auschwitz-Birkenau in Poland. Other tours travel the same routes and so benefit from Grand Circle's donations. Through its philanthropy, however,

Grand Circle has built close relationships with the organizations that maintain these sites and can provide its travelers with special opportunities to visit and learn about them. Grand Circle thus gains a unique competitive advantage that distinguishes it from other travel providers.

How to Contribute

Understanding the link between philanthropy and competitive context helps companies identify *where* they should focus their corporate giving. Understanding the ways in which philanthropy creates value highlights *how* they can achieve the greatest social and economic impact through their contributions. As we will see, the where and the how are mutually reinforcing.

In "Philanthropy's New Agenda: Creating Value" (HBR November-December 1999), we outlined four ways in which charitable foundations can create social value: selecting the best grantees, signaling other funders, improving the performance of grant recipients, and advancing knowledge and practice in the field. These efforts build on one another: Increasingly greater value is generated as a donor moves up the ladder from selecting the right grantees to advancing knowledge. (See the exhibit "Maximizing Philanthropy's Value.") The same principles apply to corporate giving, pointing the way to how corporate philanthropy can be most effective in enhancing competitive context. Focusing on the four principles also ensures that corporate donations have greater impact than donations of the same magnitude by individuals.

Selecting the Best Grantees. Most philanthropic activity involves giving money to other organizations that actually deliver the social benefits. The impact achieved by a donor, then, is largely determined by the effectiveness of the recipient. Selecting a more effective grantee or partner organization will lead to more social impact per dollar expended.

Selecting the most effective grantees in a given field is never easy. It may be obvious which nonprofit organizations raise the most money, have the greatest prestige, or manage the best development campaigns, but such factors may have little to do with how well the grantees use contributions. Extensive and disciplined research is usually required to select those recipients that will achieve the greatest social impact.

Individual donors rarely have the time or expertise to undertake such serious due diligence. Foundations are far more expert than individuals, but they have limited staff. Corporations, on the other hand, are well positioned to undertake such research if their philanthropy is connected to their business and they can tap into their internal capabilities, particularly the financial, managerial, and technical expertise of employees. Whether through their own operations or those of their suppliers and customers, corporations also often have a presence in many communities across a country or around the world. This can provide significant local knowledge and the ability to examine and compare the operation of nonprofits firsthand.

In some cases, a company can introduce and support a particularly effective nonprofit organization or program in many of the locations in which it operates. Grand Circle Travel, for example, uses its 15 overseas offices to identify historical preservation projects to fund. FleetBoston Financial assembles teams of employees with diverse management and financial skills to examine the inner-city economic development organizations that its foundation supports. The teams visit each nonprofit, interview management, review policies and procedures, and report to the corporate foundation on whether support should be continued and, if so, where it should be directed. This level of attention and expertise is substantially greater than most individual donors, foundations, or even government agencies can muster.

Signaling Other Funders. A donor can publicize the most effective nonprofit organizations and promote them to other donors, attracting greater funding and thus creating a more effective allocation of overall philanthropic spending.

Corporations bring uniquely valuable assets to this task. First, their reputations often command respect, becoming imprimaturs of credibility for grantees. Second, they are often able to influence a vast network of entities in their cluster, including customers, suppliers, and other partners. This gives them far greater reach than individual donors or even most nonprofits and foundations. Third, they often have access to communication channels and expertise that can be used to disseminate information widely, swiftly, and persuasively to other donors.

Signaling other funders is especially important in corporate philanthropy because it mitigates the free rider problem. Collective social investment by participants in a cluster can improve the context for all players, while reducing the cost borne by each one. By leveraging its relationships and brand identity to initiate social projects that are also funded by others, a corporation improves the cost-benefit ratio. The Cisco Networking Academy draws support from numerous technology companies in Cisco's cluster as well as educational systems and governments throughout the world, all of which benefit from the graduates' success. American Express's Travel and Tourism Academies depend on the help of more than 750 travel cluster partners who bear part of the cost and reap part of the benefit. Different companies will bring different strengths to a given philanthropic initiative. By tapping each company's distinctive expertise, the collective investment can be far more effective than a donation by any one company.

Improving the Performance of Grant Recipients. By improving the effectiveness of nonprofits, corporations create value for society, increasing the social impact achieved per dollar expended. While selecting the right grantee improves society's return on a single contribu-

The Cisco Networking Academy

Cisco Systems' Networking Academy exemplifies the powerful links that exist between a company's philanthropic strategy, its competitive context, and social benefits. Cisco, the leading producer of networking equipment and routers used to connect computers to the Internet, grew rapidly over the past decade. But as Internet use expanded, customers around the world encountered a chronic shortage of qualified network administrators, which became a limiting factor in Cisco's—and the entire IT industry's—continued growth. By one estimate, well over 1 million information technology jobs remained unfilled worldwide in the late 1990s. While Cisco was well aware of this constraint in its competitive context, it was only through philanthropy that the company found a way to address it.

The project began as a typical example of goodwill-based giving: Cisco contributed networking equipment to a high school near its headquarters, then expanded the program to other schools in the region. A Cisco engineer working with the schools realized, however, that the teachers and administrators lacked the training to manage the networks once they were installed. He and several other Cisco engineers volunteered to develop a program that would not only donate equipment but also train teachers how to build, design, and maintain computer networks. Students began attending these courses and were able to absorb the information successfully. As Cisco expanded the program, company executives began to realize that they could develop a Web-based distance-learning curriculum to train and certify secondary-and postsecondary-school students in network administration, a program that might have a much broader social and economic impact. The Networking Academy was born.

Because the social goal of the program was tightly linked to Cisco's specialized expertise, the company was able to create a high-quality curriculum rapidly and cost-effectively, creating far more social and economic value than if it had merely contributed cash and equipment to a worthy cause. At the suggestion of the U. S. Department of Education, the company began to target schools in "empowerment zones," designated by the federal government as among the most economically challenged communities in the country. The company also began to include community colleges and midcareer training in the program. More recently, it has worked with the United Nations to expand the effort to developing countries, where job opportunities are particularly scarce and networking skills particularly limited. Cisco has also organized a worldwide database of employment opportunities for academy graduates, creating a more efficient job market that benefits its cluster as well as the graduates and the regions in which they live.

Cisco has used its unique assets and expertise, along with its worldwide presence, to create a program that no other educational institution, government agency, foundation, or corporate donor could have designed as well or expanded as rapidly. And it has amplified the impact by signaling other corporations in its cluster. Other companies supplemented Cisco's contributions by donating or discounting products and services of their own, such as Internet access and computer hardware and software. Several leading technology companies also began to recognize the value of the global infrastructure Cisco had created, and, rather than create their own Web-based learning programs, they partnered with Cisco. Companies such as Sun Microsystems, Hewlett-Packard, Adobe Systems, and Panduit expanded the academy curriculum by sponsoring courses in programming, IT essentials, Web design, and cabling. Because the project was linked to Cisco's business, it could gain the support of other companies in its cluster and use their contributions effectively.

Although the program is only five years old, it now operates 9,900 academies in secondary schools, community colleges, and community-based organizations in all 50 states and in 147 countries. The social and economic value that has been created is enormous. Cisco estimates that it has invested a total of $150 million since the program began. With that investment, it has brought the possibility of technology careers, and the technology itself, to men and women in some of the most economically depressed regions in the United States and around the world. More than 115,000 students have already graduated from the two-year program, and 263,000 students are currently enrolled, half of them outside the United States. The program continues to expand rapidly, with 50 to 100 new academies opening every week. Cisco estimates that 50% of academy graduates have found jobs in the IT industry, where the average salary for a network administrator in the United States is $67,000. Over the span of their careers, the incremental earnings potential of those who have already joined the workforce may approach several billion dollars.

To be sure, the program has benefited many free riders—employers around the world who gain access to highly skilled academy graduates and even direct competitors. But as the market-leading provider of routers, Cisco stands to benefit the most from this improvement in the competitive context. Through actively engaging others, Cisco has not had to bear the full cost of the program. Not only has Cisco enlarged its market and strengthened its cluster, but it has increased the sophistication of its customers. Through these tangible improvements in competitive context, and not just by the act of giving, Cisco has attracted international recognition for this program, generating justified pride and enthusiasm among company employees, goodwill among its partners, and a reputation for leadership in philanthropy.

tion, and signaling other funders improves the return on multiple contributions, improving grantee performance can increase the return on the grantee's total budget.

Unlike many other donors, corporations have the ability to work directly with nonprofits and other partners to help them become more effective. They bring unique assets and expertise that individuals and foundations lack, enabling them to provide a wide range of nonmonetary assistance that is less costly and more sophisticated than the services most grantees could purchase for themselves. And because they typically make long-term commitments to the communities in which they operate, corporations can work closely with local nonprofits over the extended periods of time needed for meaningful organizational improvement. By operating in multiple geographical areas, moreover, companies are able to facilitate the transfer of knowledge and operational improvements among non-profits in different regions or countries. Contextual issues within a particular industry or cluster will often be similar across different locations, increasing a company's ability to add and derive value in multiple regions.

By tying corporate philanthropy to its business and strategy, a company can create even greater social value in improving grantee performance than other donors. Its specialized assets and expertise, after all, will be most useful in addressing problems related to its particular field. DreamWorks' film production expertise helped it design the educational curriculum necessary to help inner-city students in Los Angeles get jobs in the entertainment industry. The Cisco Networking Academy utilized the special expertise of Cisco employees.

FleetBoston Financial took similar advantage of its corporate expertise in launching its Community Renaissance Initiative. Recognizing that its major markets were in older East Coast cities, Fleet decided to focus on inner-city economic revitalization as perhaps the most important way to improve its context. Fleet combined its philanthropic contributions with its expertise in financial services, such as small business services, inner-city lending, home mortgages, and venture capital. The bank's foundation identified six communities where the bank had a presence, the economic need was great, and strong community-based organizations could be identified as reliable partners: Brooklyn and Buffalo, New York; Lawrence, Massachusetts; New Haven, Connecticut; and Camden and Jersey City, New Jersey. The foundation committed $725,000 to each city, building a coalition of local community, business, and government organizations to work on a set of issues identified by the community as central to its revitalization. Bank personnel provided technical advice and small business financing packages to local companies as well as home mortgages and homebuyer education programs. The foundation also attracted $6 million from private and municipal sources, greatly amplifying its own $4.5 million investment.

Another example is America Online, which has unique capabilities in managing Internet access and content. Working closely with educators, AOL developed AOL@School, a free, easy-to-use, noncommercial site tailored by grade level to students, administrators, and teachers. This service improves the classroom experience for hundreds of thousands of students nationally by giving them access to enrichment and reference tools while providing lesson plans and reference materials for teachers. Through this program, AOL has been able to leverage its specialized expertise, more than just its donations, to assist in improving secondary school performance more rapidly and cost-effectively than could most other organizations. In the process, it has improved both the long-term demand for its services and the talent needed to provide them.

Advancing Knowledge and Practice. Innovation drives productivity in the nonprofit sector as well as in the commercial sector. The greatest advances come not from incremental improvements in efficiency but from new and better approaches. The most powerful way to create social value, therefore, is by developing new means to address social problems and putting them into widespread practice.

The expertise, research capacity, and reach that companies bring to philanthropy can help nonprofits create new solutions that they could never afford to develop on their own. Since 1994, IBM has committed a total of $70 million to its Reinventing Education program, which now reaches 65,000 teachers and 6 million students. Working in partnership with urban school districts, state education departments, and colleges of education, IBM researched and developed a Web-based platform to support new instructional practices and strategies. The new curriculum is intended to redefine how teachers master their profession; it bridges the gap between teacher preparation and the classroom experience by providing a common platform that is used in the teachers' college courses and also supports their first years of teaching. Neither the colleges of education nor the school districts had the expertise or financial resources to develop such a program on their own. An independent evaluation in 2001 found that teachers in the Reinventing Education program were registering substantial gains in student performance.

Pfizer developed a cost-effective treatment for the prevention of trachoma, the leading cause of preventable blindness in developing countries. In addition to donating the drugs, Pfizer worked with the Edna McConnell Clark Foundation and world health organizations to create the infrastructure needed to prescribe and distribute them to populations that previously had little access to health care, much less modern pharmaceuticals. Within one year, the incidence of trachoma was reduced by 50% among target populations in Morocco and Tanzania. The program has since expanded aggressively, adding the Bill & Melinda Gates Foundation and the British government as partners, with the aim of reaching 30 million people worldwide. In addition to providing an important social benefit, Pfizer has enhanced its own long-term business prospects by helping build the infrastructure required to expand its markets.

Just as important as the creation of new knowledge is its adoption in practice. The know-how of corporate leaders, their clout and connections, and their presence in communities around the world create powerful networks for the dissemination of new ideas for addressing social problems. Corporations can facilitate global knowledge transfer and coordinated multisite implementation of new social initiatives with a proficiency that is unequaled by most other donors.

A Whole New Approach

When corporations support the right causes in the right ways—when they get the *where* and the *how* right—they set in motion a virtuous cycle. By focusing on the contextual conditions most important to their industries and strategies, companies ensure that their corporate capabilities will be particularly well suited to helping grantees create greater value. And by enhancing the value produced by philanthropic efforts in their fields, the companies gain a greater improvement in competitive context. Both the corporations and the causes they support reap important benefits.

> As long as companies remain focused on the **public relations** benefit of their contributions, they will sacrifice opportunities to create social value.

Adopting a context-focused approach, however, goes against the grain of current philanthropic practice. Many companies actively distance their philanthropy from the business, believing this will lead to greater goodwill in local communities. While it is true that a growing number of companies aim to make their giving "strategic," few have connected giving to areas that improve their long-term competitive potential. And even fewer systematically apply their distinctive strengths to maximize the social and economic value created by their philanthropy. Instead, companies are often distracted by the desire to publicize how much money and effort they are contributing in order to foster an image of social responsibility and caring. Avon Products, for example, recently mobilized its 400,000 independent sales representatives in a high-profile door-to-door campaign to raise more than $32 million to fund breast cancer prevention. Fighting breast cancer is a worthy cause and one that is very meaningful to Avon's target market of female consumers. It is not, however, a material factor in Avon's competitive context or an area in which Avon has any inherent expertise. As a result, Avon may have greatly augmented its own cash contribution through effective fund-raising—and generated favorable publicity—but it failed to realize the full potential of its philanthropy to create social and economic value. Avon has done much good, but it could do even better. As long as companies remain focused on the public relations benefit of their contributions instead of the impact achieved, they will sacrifice opportunities to create social value.

This does not mean that corporations cannot also gain goodwill and enhance their reputations through philanthropy. But goodwill alone is not a sufficient motivation. Given public skepticism about the ethics of business—skepticism that has intensified in the wake of the string of corporate scandals this year—corporations that can demonstrate a significant impact on a social problem will gain more credibility than those that are merely big givers. The acid test of good corporate philanthropy is whether the desired social change is so beneficial to the company that the organization would pursue the change even if no one ever knew about it. Cisco, for example, has achieved wide recognition for its good works, but it would have had sufficient reason to develop the Networking Academy even if no goodwill had been created.

Moving to context-focused philanthropy will require a far more rigorous approach than is prevalent today. It will mean tightly integrating the management of philanthropy with other company activities. Rather than delegating philanthropy entirely to a public relations department or the staff of a corporate foundation, the CEO must lead the entire management team through a disciplined process to identify and implement a corporate giving strategy focused on improving context. Business units, in particular, must play central roles in identifying areas for contextual investments.

The new process would involve five steps:

Examine the competitive context in each of the company's important geographic locations. Where could social investment improve the company's or cluster's competitive potential? What are the key constraints that limit productivity, innovation, growth, and competitiveness? A company should pay special attention to the particular constraints that have a disproportionate effect on its strategy relative to competitors; improvements in these areas of context will potentially reinforce competitive advantage. The more specifically a contextual initiative is defined, the more likely the company is to create value and achieve its objectives. A broad initiative such as Avon's efforts to improve the health of all women will not necessarily deliver contextual benefits, even if it helps some employees or customers. And a tightly targeted objective does not necessarily diminish the scale of impact. Narrowly focused initiatives, like Pfizer's trachoma program, IBM's Reinventing Education, or Cisco's Networking Academy, can potentially benefit millions of people or strengthen the global market for an entire industry.

Review the existing philanthropic portfolio to see how it fits this new paradigm. Current programs will likely fall into three categories:

- Communal obligation: support of civic, welfare, and educational organizations, motivated by the company's desire to be a good citizen.
- Goodwill building: contributions to support causes favored by employees, customers, or community leaders, often necessitated by the quid pro quo of business and the desire to improve the company's relationships.
- Strategic giving: philanthropy focused on enhancing competitive context, as outlined here.

Most corporate giving falls into the first two categories. While a certain percentage of giving in these categories may be necessary and desirable, the goal is to shift, as much as possible, a company's philanthropy into the third category. As for cause-related marketing, it is marketing, not philanthropy, and it must stand on its own merits.

Assess existing and potential corporate giving initiatives against the four forms of value creation. How can the company leverage its assets and expertise to select the most effective grantees, signal other funders, improve grantees' performance, and advance knowledge and practice? Given its strategy, where can the company create the greatest value through giving in ways that no other company could match?

Seek opportunities for collective action within a cluster and with other partners. Collective action will often be more effective than a solo effort in addressing context and enhancing the value created, and it helps mitigate the free rider problem by distributing costs broadly. Few companies today work together to achieve social objectives. This may be the result of a general reluctance to work with competitors, but clusters encompass many related partners and industries that do not compete directly. More likely, the tendency to view philanthropy as a form of public relations leads companies to invent their own contributions campaigns, which are branded with their own identities and therefore discourage partners. Focusing on the social change to be achieved, rather than the publicity to be gained, will expand the potential for partnerships and collective action.

Once a company has identified opportunities to improve the competitive context and determined the ways in which it can contribute by adding unique value, the search for partners becomes straightforward: Who else stands to benefit from this change in competitive context? And who has complementary expertise or resources? Conversely, what philanthropic initiatives by others are worth joining? Where can the company be a good partner to others by contributing in ways that will enhance value?

Rigorously track and evaluate results. Monitoring achievements is essential to continually improving the philanthropic strategy and its implementation. As with any other corporate activity, consistent improvement over time brings the greatest value. The most successful programs will not be short-term campaigns but long-term commitments that continue to grow in scale and sophistication.

The context-focused approach to philanthropy is not simple. One size does not fit all. Companies will differ in their comfort levels and time horizons for philanthropic activity, and individual firms will make different choices about how to implement our ideas. Philanthropy will never become an exact science—it is inherently an act of judgment and faith in the pursuit of long-term goals. However, the perspective and tools presented here will help any company make its philanthropic activities far more effective.

Were this approach to be widely adopted, the pattern of corporate contributions would shift significantly. The overall level of contributions would likely increase, and the social and economic value created would go up even more sharply. Companies would be more confident about the value of their philanthropy and more committed to it. They would be able to communicate their philanthropic strategies more effectively to the communities in which they operate. Their choices of areas to support would be clearly understandable and would not seem unpredictable or idiosyncratic. Finally, there would be a better division of labor between corporate givers and other types of funders, with corporations tackling the areas where they are uniquely able to create value.

Charities too would benefit. They would see an increased and more predictable flow of corporate resources into the nonprofit sector. Just as important, they would develop close, long-term corporate partnerships that would better apply the expertise and assets of the for-profit sector to achieve social objectives. Just as companies can build on the nonprofit infrastructure to achieve their objectives more cost-effectively, nonprofits can benefit from using the commercial infrastructure.

There is no inherent contradiction between improving competitive context and making a sincere commitment to bettering society.

To some corporate leaders, this new approach might seem too self-serving. They might argue that philanthropy is purely a matter of conscience and should not be adulterated by business objectives. In some industries, particularly those like petrochemicals and pharmaceuticals that are prone to public controversy, this view is so entrenched that many companies establish independent charitable foundations and entirely segregate giving from the business. In doing so, however, they give up tremendous opportunities to create greater value for society and themselves. Context-focused philanthropy does not just address a company's self-interest, it benefits many through broad social change. If a company's philanthropy only involved its own interests, after all, it would not qualify as a charitable deduction, and it might well threaten the company's reputation.

There is no inherent contradiction between improving competitive context and making a sincere commitment to bettering society. Indeed, as we've seen, the more closely a company's philanthropy is linked to its competitive context, the greater the company's contribution to society will be. Other areas, where the company neither creates added value nor derives benefit, should appropriately be left—as Friedman asserts—to individual donors following their own charitable impulses. If systematically pursued in a way that maximizes the value created, context-focused philanthropy can offer companies a new set of competitive tools that well justifies the investment of resources. At the same time, it can unlock a vastly more powerful way to make the world a better place.

Michael E. Porter is the Bishop William Lawrence University Professor at Harvard University; he is based at the Harvard Business School in Boston. He is a frequent contributor to HBR, and his most recent article, "Strategy and the Internet" (March 2001), won the McKinsey Award. *Mark R. Kramer* is the managing director of the Foundation Strategy Group, a consulting firm in Boston, and cofounder, with Porter, of the Center for Effective Philanthropy, a nonprofit research organization also located in Boston.

Reprinted with permission from *Harvard Business Review,* December 2002, pp. 57-68. © 2002 by the Harvard School Publishing Corporation. All rights reserved.

WHO CARES WINS

Boardrooms are abuzz with talk of corporate social responsibility. Yet attempting to establish a working definition of CSR is like nailing jelly to the ceiling. Get it right, though, and everyone could win—you, the company, society and the planet. **Stephen Cook** reports

Everyone cares these days. You can hardly walk through the door of a major company in the western world without tripping over stacks of glossy reports telling you how they care for the environment, their community, their stakeholders. They're all publishing their CO_2 emission targets, pledging themselves to international human rights and encouraging staff to go and bathe in baked beans for charity.

> 'It is not from the benevolence of the butcher, the brewer or the baker that we expect our dinner, but from their regard to their own self-interest...
> By pursuing his own interest, he frequently promotes that of society more effectually than when he really intends to promote it'
>
> Adam Smith (1776)

As we enter the new year, Corporate Social Responsibility is the phrase resounding around boardrooms and peppering the speeches of business leaders from Seattle to Sydney. CSR is the fresh acronym to cover what we used to call sustainability, diversity or good old-fashioned philanthropy. Everyone wants a piece. But remembering Bhopal, Enron and the sweatshops of the Far East, aren't we entitled to be a little bit sceptical?

Look at Enron's last CSR report. Sprinkled with images of sunlit foliage and smiling ethnic faces, it dwells on how the fraudulent energy giant conserved trees in Bolivia and told the security men at its Indian subsidiary to stop beating people up. Former chairman and CEO Kenneth Lay waxes lyrical about his firm's 'innovative practices'. For students of irony, the whole thing is a delight.

So as the CSR juggernaut gathers pace, is it really the big idea that will restore public faith in business and save the planet? Or is it a piece of nifty footwork and smart PR designed to spike the guns of the anti-globalisation campaigners, put the pressure groups off their stroke and persuade governments to go easy on regulation?

The question is put to Clive Mather, country chairman for Shell in the UK. To many, this is still the company that spectacularly mishandled the disposal of its Brent Spar oil rig in the mid 1990s and courted 10 kinds of pollution and human rights scandals in Nigeria. Since then, it has worked hard, with some success, to clean up and do the right thing wherever possible.

'This is for real,' says Mather. 'We can't escape it and there's no doubt about it. We are all going to have to apply ourselves to sustainable development if we're to succeed in ensuring the planet is as good a place in the future as in the last millennium. The demands of population and quality of life are going to stretch us all. No-one who thinks about it believes we can go on as we are.'

So he, and a whole cohort of leading businessmen, have moved a million miles from the strictures of Adam Smith and his followers, who continue to maintain that the business of business is business alone, and it is the elected government's job to regulate and decide what is good for society. It's a disconcerting, looking-glass world when a lifelong oilman starts talking renewables and sounding like Greenpeace.

This point was seized upon by pressure groups and non-governmental organisations at the 'greenwash awards', their spoof of the Oscars at the Earth Summit in Johannesburg last summer. 'Oil companies are presenting themselves as solar companies, and companies that promote giant agribusiness and oppose consumer information are claiming to be the solution to world hunger,' said Craig Bennett of Friends of the Earth.

Slick PR is certainly a big part of the burgeoning phenomenon, and specialist consultancies like Article 13 and ERM have noticed a sudden rush of competitors in one of the few areas where companies are willing to spend money right now. The PR industry, worried that CSR talk is taken with a large pinch of salt, is pondering how to make it ring true.

It would, however, be a mistake to take the cynical view that there's nothing going on but greenwash and PR. There are many out there 'putting something back'. A small example is the com-

'no-one who thinks about it believes we can go on as we are'
'we believe voluntarism has failed'

1776 THE 'INTELLECTUAL ANCESTOR OF MODERN ECONOMICS' AND CHAMPION OF THE ANTI-CSR LOBBY, **ADAM SMITH** LAYS FORTH HIS 'INVISIBLE HAND' THEORY: SELF-INTEREST IS THE WAY FORWARD—STICK TO RUNNING YOUR BUSINESS AND THE WORLD WILL TAKE CARE OF ITSELF.

1848 YORKSHIRE WOOL BARON AND PIONEER OF CARING CAPITALISM **TITUS SALT** ESCAPES BRADFORD—THEN OUR POOREST AND MOST POLLUTED TOWN—TO BUILD A NEW MILL JUST OUTSIDE. OVER 20 YEARS HE CREATES SALTAIRE, A MODEL COMMUNITY FOR HIS STAFF, WHERE EVERY HOME HAS RUNNING WATER.

1904 SWEET MANUFACTURER **JOSEPH ROWNTREE** BUILDS ROWNTREE VILLAGE IN YORK. HOUSES CENTRE AROUND A COMMUNITY HALL. IN 1906 HE SETS UP A PENSION FUND; IN 1916, A PROFIT-SHARING SCHEME; AND IN 1918, STAFF HOLIDAYS—A REVOLUTIONARY CONCEPT AT THE TIME.

1911 DAVID LLOYD GEORGE, THEN CHANCELLOR IN ASQUITH'S LIBERAL GOVERNMENT, LAYS THE FOUNDATIONS FOR STATE INVOLVEMENT IN CSR WITH HIS **NATIONAL INSURANCE ACT**. IT REQUIRES FIRMS TO MAKE CONTRIBUTIONS TO UNEMPLOYMENT AND SICKNESS INSURANCE FOR ALL STAFF.

1952 AN ANTICYCLONE SETTLES OVER LONDON ON 4 DECEMBER, CAUSING THE FIVE-DAY **GREAT LONDON SMOG**, WHICH CLAIMS 4,000 LIVES. THE GOVERNMENT SETS UP THE BEAVER COMMITTEE THE FOLLOWING YEAR TO TACKLE THE ISSUE OF INDUSTRIAL SMOKE. IN 1956, THE FIRST CLEAN AIR ACT IS PASSED.

1967 A HUGE SPILL FROM BP OIL TANKER **TORREY CANYON** OFF CORNWALL IS PERHAPS THE FIRST EVER MEDIA-LED ECO-DISASTER. IN 1980, THE **EXXON VALDEZ** SPILL OFF ALASKA PROMPTS THE US TO PHASE OUT SINGLE-HULLED TANKERS. LAST YEAR'S **PRESTIGE** SPILL OFF SPAIN LEADS THE EU TO CONSIDER SIMILAR NEW LAWS.

1969 **RALPH NADER** FOUNDS THE CENTER FOR RESPONSIVE LAW IN THE US TO EXPOSE CORPORATE ABUSES AND A LACK OF ENFORCED REGULATION. PREVIOUSLY, HIS INDICTMENT OF THE CAR INDUSTRY'S POOR SAFETY STANDARDS, 'UNSAFE AT ANY SPEED', LED TO THE 1966 MOTOR VEHICLE SAFETY ACT.

1971 **GREENPEACE** IS FOUNDED IN CANADA AS A RESPONSE TO US NUCLEAR TESTS. IT EXCELS IN HEADLINE-GRABBING DIRECT ACTION FOR ENVIRONMENTAL CAUSES. AFTER ITS FLAGSHIP, **RAINBOW WARRIOR**, IS SUNK IN AUCKLAND IN 1985, FRANCE ADMITS THAT ITS SECRET AGENTS WERE RESPONSIBLE.

1976 ANITA RODDICK OPENS THE FIRST **BODY SHOP** BRANCH IN BRIGHTON. THE COMPANY PLEDGES ITSELF 'TO THE PURSUIT OF SOCIAL AND ENVIRONMENTAL CHANGE'. WORKERS ARE VETTED TO ENSURE THEY LIVE UP TO THIS PHILOSOPHY, AND STAFF AT HQ SPEND A DAY A MONTH WORKING WITH DISADVANTAGED CHILDREN.

1977 **NESTLÉ** FEELS THE CHILL WIND OF PROTEST WHEN A GLOBAL BOYCOTT IS LAUNCHED IN THE US BY INFACT (INFANT FORMULA ACTION COALITION). IN 1980, A SIMILAR CAMPAIGN BEGINS IN THE UK, SLAMMING THE 'UNETHICAL MARKETING OF BREASTMILK SUBSTITUTES'. THE CAMPAIGN CONTINUES TODAY.

1982 SIR ALASTAIR PILKINGTON SETS UP **BUSINESS IN THE COMMUNITY** TO FORGE LINKS BETWEEN BUSINESS, TRADE UNIONS, GOVERNMENT, LOCAL AUTHORITIES AND COMMUNITIES. IN 1986, BIC LAUNCHES THE PER CENT CLUB, MADE UP OF FIRMS THAT INVEST AT LEAST 1% OF PRE-TAX PROFITS IN THE COMMUNITY.

1984 AN EXPLOSION AT A UNION CARBIDE PLANT IN **BHOPAL**, INDIA, KILLS 8,000 PEOPLE IN THE WORLD'S WORST INDUSTRIAL ACCIDENT. IN 1986 THE CASE FOR COMPENSATION IS MOVED FROM THE US TO INDIA. INDIA SETTLES OUT OF COURT FOR JUST $470M, HALF OF WHICH IS STILL IN GOVERNMENT COFFERS.

1992 CSR DOMINATES THE UN CONFERENCE ON ENVIRONMENT AND DEVELOPMENT—AKA 'THE EARTH SUMMIT'—IN **RIO DE JANEIRO**. MORE THAN 100 PRESIDENTS AND PRIME MINISTERS PRODUCE AGENDA 21, A BLUEPRINT FOR REVERSING ENVIRONMENTAL DAMAGE AND TACKLING WORLD POVERTY.

1993 TRANSPARENCY INTERNATIONAL, AN ANTI-CORRUPTION GROUP, IS FORMED IN BERLIN. CHAIRED BY EX-WORLD BANK OFFICIAL **PETER EIGEN**, TI TACKLES CORRUPTION IN DEVELOPING STATES AND THE G7. ITS 2002 CORRUPTION INDEX SHOWS A FALL IN THE HONESTY RATINGS OF THE UK AND US.

1995 GREENPEACE CALLS FOR A BOYCOTT OF SHELL OVER ITS PLANS TO SINK ITS OIL-STORAGE PLATFORM **BRENT SPAR**. SHELL'S SALES IN GERMANY PLUMMET, AND IT BACKS DOWN. HOWEVER, FEARS THAT THE NEW METHOD OF DISPOSAL COULD BE EVEN LESS ECO-FRIENDLY DAMAGE GREENPEACE'S CREDIBILITY.

1997 CSR GROWS UP AS THE **GLOBAL REPORT INITIATIVE** IS LAUNCHED AT THE UN IN NEW YORK. THIS INTENDS TO PUT SUSTAINABILITY REPORTING ON A PAR WITH FINANCIAL REPORTING AND HAS ESTABLISHED ITSELF AS AN INDUSTRY STANDARD USED BY MANY CORPORATIONS AS THEIR SUSTAINABILITY BENCHMARK.

1999 THE DOW JONES **SUSTAINABILITY INDEX** IS LAUNCHED IN THE US. THE INDEX IS RESTRICTED TO COMPANIES COMMITTED TO GREEN TECHNOLOGIES AND GOOD CORPORATE GOVERNANCE. IN JULY 2001, THE FTSE LAUNCHES ITS OWN UK SUSTAINABILITY INDEX, THE **FTSE4GOOD**.

2000 MARCH BRITAIN IS THE FIRST STATE IN EUROPE TO HAVE A MINISTER FOR CSR WHEN **KIM HOWELLS** IS APPOINTED. A YEAR LATER HE PUBLISHES THE FIRST EVER GOVERNMENT REPORT ON CSR, PLEDGING ITS COMMITMENT TO CSR AND EXHORTING GOOD PRACTICE. THE PRESENT CSR MINISTER IS **STEPHEN TIMMS**.

2000 OCTOBER CONTROVERSIAL BBC DOCUMENTARY, 'GAP & NIKE: NO SWEAT', REVEALS THAT CLOTHING FOR **NIKE** AND **GAP** IS BEING MADE IN CAMBODIAN SWEATSHOPS. DETAILS OF FORCED OVERTIME AND LOW WAGES SPARK A WORLDWIDE CAMPAIGN AGAINST NIKE THAT REMAINS ACTIVE TODAY.

2001 MARCH GEORGE W BUSH WITHDRAWS US SUPPORT FOR THE **KYOTO** ENVIRONMENTAL AGREEMENT, BREAKING ELECTION PROMISES TO IMPOSE LIMITS ON CO_2. BY MID 2002, THE EU AND JAPAN HAVE RATIFIED KYOTO BUT THE US—WHICH ACCOUNTS FOR 36% OF ALL CO_2 EMISSIONS—CONTINUES TO OPT OUT.

2002 JANUARY FORMER GREENPEACE BOSS **LORD MELCHETT** ASTOUNDS HIS EX-COLLEAGUES BY TAKING A JOB AT PR FIRM BURSON-MARSTELLER. BM'S CLIENTS OVER THE YEARS HAVE INCLUDED GM FOOD GIANT MONSANTO, THE INDONESIAN GOVERNMENT, BP AND UNION CARBIDE AFTER BHOPAL.

2002 JUDGING BY THE AMOUNT OF GOVERNMENT AND MEDIA ATTENTION IT GENERATES, CSR HAS ARRIVED. IN APRIL, MEPS REJECT MANDATORY COMPANY REPORTING ON CSR, BUT IN JULY A DTI WHITE PAPER RECOMMENDS THAT DIRECTORS OF 'ECONOMICALLY SIGNIFICANT' COMPANIES TAKE INTO ACCOUNT THE BROADER IMPACT OF THEIR BUSINESS ACTIVITIES ON SOCIETY. A MONTH LATER, THE 'RIO + 10' EARTH SUMMIT AT THE SANDTON CONVENTION CENTRE IN **JOHANNESBURG** MAKES HEADLINES AS MANY KEY POLITICAL FIGURES FAIL TO ATTEND—NOTABLY GEORGE W BUSH—AND PROTESTERS CLAIM IT HAS BEEN HIJACKED BY BIG BUSINESS. BY NOVEMBER, A PRIVATE MEMBERS' BILL ON CSR FALLS OFF THE COMMONS AGENDA. BUT THE YEAR ENDS ON A HIGH, WITH THE COPENHAGEN CENTRE'S CAMPAIGN REPORT ON EUROPEAN CSR EXCELLENCE 2002-03, THE FIRST EVER OVERVIEW OF CSR ACTIVITIES IN EUROPE. BRITAIN EMERGES AT THE HEAD OF THE FIELD, RANKING JOINT FIRST WITH THE NETHERLANDS. THE REPORT GOES ON TO CONCLUDE THAT MORE AND MORE BUSINESSES ARE ESTABLISHING CSR INITIATIVES AND THAT SOCIALLY RESPONSIBLE BUSINESS IS HERE TO STAY.

munity work done by lawyers at City solicitors Allen & Overy, one of whom is mentoring teenagers in Hackney School. And even the Enron report contains hard figures about the corporation's CO_2 emissions and an upfront account of an oil spill that shed 29,000 barrels of crude into a Brazilian river. The attempt may be patchy and in some cases not entirely sincere, but many companies—especially the big and influential ones—are genuinely trying to bring the idea of CSR to life.

We know this because they've concluded—along reassuringly Adam Smith lines—that their self-interest is involved. There may actually be more profit and competitive advantage for a company in behaving responsibly than in cutting corners. The environmental and human rights scandals of the past three decades have created consumers—and, just as importantly, employees—who prefer companies that are doing the right thing.

Recent Mori surveys indicate that 51% of people in the UK had recently chosen a product or service on social responsibility grounds, and that 74% thought industry did not pay enough attention to the communities where they operate. Other surveys show that 20% of people would be prepared to boycott a product on social grounds, and that there's been a 40% surge in UK purchases of 'fair trade' products giving a better deal to third world farmers.

OWNING UP: SCOTTISH POWER GAINS CREDIBILITY WITH HARD FACTS

One curious aspect of CSR is that many companies considered to be leaders in the field are ones that, by their very nature, damage the environment and pollute the planet—BP, Shell, Ford, and the electricity generator Scottish Power.

A top-level commitment to CSR, backed by a sustainability report that includes hard facts as well as trumpet-blowing, played a large [part] in winning the Business in the Community Company of the Year award last year (2002) for Scottish Power, which operates in the UK and the US.

It is a 30-page production that describes strategy, goals, 'stakeholder engagement' and 'environmental governance'. It also has figures for water use; emissions data for sulphur, nitrogen and carbon gases; cross-references to the Global Reporting Initiative guidelines; and a certificate from URS Verification Ltd.

'The golden rule is that even if we haven't achieved what we set out to achieve, we're open and transparent about it,' says Dominic Fry, corporate communications director. 'You get added credibility for owning up. Next year, we'll have a full-blown social and environmental report that will include all the things we do with the community.'

'Issues that many managers think are soft for business, such as environment, diversity, human rights and community, are now hard for business,' says David Grayson, a director of the charity Business in the Community (BIC), a big proponent of CSR that has just launched a new Corporate Responsibility Index with the support of the chancellor, Gordon Brown. 'They are hard to ignore, hard to manage, and very hard for businesses that get them wrong. Conversely, managed well, these issues can be a source of competitive advantage.'

Further pressure to improve CSR performance is coming from shareholders—and not just from ethically motivated private investors who have always avoided oil, tobacco and armaments. We now have the FTSE4Good list on the London Stock Exchange and the Dow Jones Sustainability Index in New York; some large fund managers in London are building CSR league tables and assessing the lending record of banks.

'They're driven less by moral purpose than by risk,' says Jenny Rayner of Abbey Consulting, which advises companies on CSR. 'They don't want banks lending money to environmentally doubtful projects, for example, which might bring huge clean-up costs and reputational damage.

'Another reason why CSR is no longer an optional extra is a change to the Pensions Act in July 2000, which now requires trustees of occupational pension funds to state the extent to which they take social, environmental and ethical issues into account when making investment decisions. It's forced them to sit up and take notice. So we've moved beyond the days when all you needed was corporate philanthropy and handouts of money to the community. If businesses don't take account of much wider responsibilities to society, they're unlikely to be sustainable in the long term. And the best companies are not just protecting their backside but exploring new opportunities.'

So what should companies do to get into shape? The problem is that there is not much agreement on definition of areas to be covered and targets to be met, so they have to work it out for themselves according to their own circumstances and the activities of their competitors. They can observe companies thought to be doing it well, such as BP, Ford and Scottish Power (see box), but essentially it is a free-for-all.

However, an increasing number of companies round the world are using a blueprint from the Global Reporting Initiative or GRI (www.globalreporting.org), which was set up five years ago by the Coalition for Environmentally Responsible Economies in partnership with the United Nations Environment Programme. The GRI has more than 100 pages of advice and would like CSR reporting to be 'as routine, rigorous, credible and verifiable as financial reporting'.

There are also guidelines from BIC, which divides the subject into four quadrants. The first is the workplace—are you treating your employees well, respecting human rights and employing minorities? Then there's the marketplace—are you responding to your customers' needs and concerns? Then, the environment—are you going for renewables, monitoring your emissions, setting targets to reduce them, and talking to the pressure groups? And finally, there is the community—are you communicating, helping, and giving something back?

The GRI says 2,000 companies around the world now report, but the information is 'generally inconsistent, incomplete and uncertified'. This is one reason why the Corporate Responsibility Coalition, composed of UK NGOs and trade unions, was recently able to persuade more than 230 MPs of all parties to back a Ten-Minute Rule Bill designed to make it mandatory for

> ### UNITED PARCEL SERVICES IS LATE IN DELIVERING THE FIGURES
>
> High on the list of sober and responsible US corporations comes United Parcel Service, which runs the world's 11th-largest airline and shunts nearly 14 million packages around the world every day. But its first CSR report won't come until later this year. 'Our company was founded on trust and it continues that way,' says Mike Esken, the chairman and chief executive officer. 'The staff have good pay and stock options, the directors pay themselves modestly and we've always been concerned about the environment.
>
> 'We've been experimenting since the 1940s in using electricity and natural gas to power our vans, and we installed new, quieter engines on all our aircraft rather than going for the cheaper option of fitting 'hush kits'. Our envelopes have an extra flap so you can use them twice.' But even if you're doing well, you need to be seen to be doing well, and so far UPS hasn't published figures or targets for CO_2 emissions. When its CSR report does appear, it will focus on the workforce (benefits, diversity, human rights); the environment (alternative fuels, reducing emissions); philanthropy (it has always done a good deal of this); and relations with its stakeholders (customers, communities and suppliers).

companies with an annual turnover of more than £5 million to produce social and environmental reports.

The Bill, a muscle-flexing exercise designed to influence the new Companies Bill expected before the next general election, proposed to require directors to minimise their companies' impact on society and the environment and set up a standards board to monitor CSR reports.

Another proposal contained in the Bill was to make it mandatory to consult stakeholders, and publish figures and targets on emissions and social performance.

'The requirement would cover only 2.6% of UK companies, but would account for 87% of business turnover,' says the coalition's Brian Shaad. 'We believe voluntarism has failed because there's no proper framework, companies only report what they want to report, and it's mostly greenwash and PR. Apart from anything else, the Bill would level the playing field for companies.'

Nearly three years ago, the prime minister challenged Britain's top 350 companies to produce CSR reports by the end of 2001, and only 79 managed it. Even so, the Government has stuck rigorously to a policy of voluntarism and exhortation, as has the European Community. 'The voluntary nature of CSR is its strength,' insists Stephen Timms, the CSR minister at the Department of Trade and Industry. 'Regulation would put a dead hand on innovation, creativity and imagination.'

Government and more progressive elements of industry are thus allied in a strategy of voluntary progress that continues to disturb right-wing commentators, who think companies that pursue social goals could be neglecting shareholder interests and usurping elected governments. One of the most cogent statements of their case came from Milton Friedman in 1962: 'If businessmen do have a social responsibility other than making maximum profits for stockholders, how are they to know what it is? Can self-selected private individuals decide what the social "interest" is?'

> ### BRITISH AMERICAN TOBACCO IS THE BUTT OF SCEPTICISM
>
> The news that BAT has produced a CSR report is often greeted with a loud guffaw, as if Genghis Khan had announced the appointment of a PR consultant. How can a company with a lethal product be socially responsible? The anti-smoking group ASH calls the whole idea laughable. BAT's social responsibility committee, chaired by the former chancellor and BAT deputy chairman Ken Clarke, is trawling for answers. BAT's CSR report last summer defined targets for reducing energy use, water consumption, CO_2 emissions and waste production. And the firm committed itself to enlightened employment practices. But only 34 out of 167 stakeholders invited to consult with BAT agreed to do so, and their main concerns were about BAT's enticement of children to smoke, and its ruthless marketing—it was caught on TV handing out packets of Benson & Hedges to teenage volleyball players in Gambia. BAT helped produce the International Tobacco Products Marketing Standards, intended to bring worldwide marketing in line with UK restrictions. But will it fund anti-smoking campaigns among the young? Er, not our job, it said. So it's hard to escape the incompatibility between its business interests and people's health.

Whether the progressive, anti-regulatory alliance of government and big business has public opinion on its side is a moot point: one survey by the PR firm Edelman last year showed that some 50% of opinion formers in Europe trust environmental campaigners more than governments. Other research has indicated that three-quarters of opinion formers think legislation is necessary to make companies act in a socially responsible way.

There is clearly a lot to play for in the CSR game, not least the possibility of reversing the decline in public trust of big business, which many think has been going on for 30 or 40 years. But, as in politics, the entire project is at the mercy of events—an Enron-type scandal in the UK, another blunder by a big oil company, and the green and virtuous credentials that progressive companies are nurturing could disappear in a puff of smoke.

Article 35

Determining The Strategies And Tactics Of Ownership Succession

By **James Ahern**

Roger Lockwood had two careers; his first was as a professional baseball player in the 1960s. After retiring from baseball, his second career started when he founded his own materials distribution company.

Roger was successful in attracting customers to his new business because of name recognition from his first career and because of his business smarts. His company grew, and by the mid-1990s, revenues approached $20 million.

> The deck is stacked against the entrepreneur; only one-third of companies successfully transition to a second generation of ownership

However, Roger had some concerns. His grown children were not interested in the business, and his wife wanted to spend more time with him, pursuing travel and hobbies. Personally, Roger decided he was tired of bearing the responsibility for his company and was at a crossroads—what path of ownership succession should he take?

Roger's situation (his profile has been changed to protect his privacy) parallels that of all successful entrepreneurs. Owners don't live forever, so strategies and tactics must be devised to execute a successful transition. Unfortunately, it seems the deck is stacked against the entrepreneur; it's estimated that only one-third of companies successfully transition to a second generation of ownership.

But, when business owners carefully evaluate the available exit strategies and work with experts in the field (lawyers, business valuators and insurance professionals), a successful transition can be made.

Before determining potential tactics of ownership succession, business owners need to do some soul searching and consider themselves, their family, money, employees, and taxes. These business owners must answer some difficult questions, such as:

1) Do you want out completely? Would you like to stay on as long as possible, but with reduced responsibility?

2) Do you want the company to be a legacy for your children? Are your heirs capable of running the firm, and if not, should they continue to own stock in the firm?

3) How much money do you need from the business to make personal retirement comfortable? Is that amount feasible if you want to walk away from the firm?

4) Is the management team capable of successfully running the firm? Should they be given the opportunity?

5) What will Uncle Sam take from any transaction? What tactics can help minimize the amount paid in taxes?

Business owners have a number of options to execute ownership transition, which we will consider here.

Outright Sale. Probably the most obvious choice is to sell the company, pay taxes on the sale of the business and move on. It should be noted that third-party sales can have some strings attached (usually an employment contract for one to three years, an escrow account for potential liabilities at closing, and potential pay-outs over time through a seller note), but they can represent the simplest exit route for an owner.

But third-party sales may not always be clean. Notes issued to the sellers may not be repaid on a timely basis, and in many instances, an owner can forget about having an enduring legacy when an acquirer takes over the company—it is often barely recognizable a year or two later.

Transition To Children. Another ownership transfer alternative is to transition the company to one's children. Some entrepreneurs have children who are active and want to see the business stay "in the family." This means the company retains all previous customer, employee and vendor relationships, including those with its insurers.

There are, however, roadblocks to this kind of transition, which can include deciding who among the active family members should lead the firm (management by committee is no way to run a business), and how to share the ownership among the second generation. Should the family members who do not work at the firm be eligible for a "free ride" based on the efforts of their sibling(s) leading the company?

And last but not least—the federal government assesses a tax on shares gifted from one generation to the next. Furthermore, in the event of an untimely death, the estate tax liability can be daunting. In this exit strategy, it is essential to look into the variety of insurance products available to ensure a smooth transition and to protect against unforeseen events.

Sale To Management. In a sale to management, the people who have worked closely with the entrepreneur buy out the owner and run the firm. Since they know the business very well, management teams can maintain important customer relationships and continue the prosperity of the company. Unfortunately, management teams also often lack the financial wherewithal to make a cash purchase for 100% of the stock, leaving the owner to take a note or retain an equity stake that would allow the owner a second chance to cash out more stock in future years.

In this kind of transition, sellers can retain a position with the firm. With diminished responsibilities, however, the former owner may lose interest in continuing to work for the company. In addition, unless some provisions have been made, capital gains taxes are payable in each sale, reducing net proceeds to the seller. Banks supporting a sale-to-management strategy will insist on corporate-owned life insurance policies on the buyers to protect against loan repayment problems that could arise due to a premature death.

Sale To Employees. For owners interested in deferring capital gains taxes on the sale of their stock, Employee Stock Ownership Plans, or ESOPs, are worth investigating. ESOPs are defined contribution employee benefit plans designed to hold employer stock. Congress chose to emphasize ESOPs as an ownership transition tool, and as a result, provided a capital gains tax deferral benefit to sellers.

The benefit to the ESOP as buyer is that it can repay the loan it used to acquire the seller's shares—both principal and interest-in pretax rather than after-tax dollars. This makes the ESOP exit strategy more favorable to the seller than the management buyout alternative because the principal repayment of the bank or seller note is not tax-deductible in a management buyout.

An owner selling to an ESOP can choose a staggered sale by first selling a minority interest to the ESOP and selling the remaining shares thereafter. This piecemeal approach allows the owner to take some cash off the table and diversify assets. Whether an owner sells all or a partial interest to an ESOP, insurance products once again become important because the bank or seller may require corporate-owned life insurance to support loan repayment in the event a tragedy befalls a key employee.

Close The Doors. Finally, an owner may choose to sell all assets, collect the receivables, pay all liabilities and close the business. Generally this option is exercised by firms that do not have an important role in their markets or are in a market that is rapidly declining. Profitable businesses with a talented workforce, a strong customer list, dedicated suppliers, and product or service proficiency lose all of that value if the business is closed.

An owner should be sure none of the company's intangible assets are salable before proceeding to shut the doors.

Owners planning for succession need to exercise introspection to determine what is important to them before choosing an exit strategy. Each approach to exiting a business has advantages and disadvantages. But, with a carefully structured and executed transition plan, a business owner can truly enjoy a blissful retirement.

James Ahern is a principal at Lakeshore Valuation, L.L.C. in Chicago, Ill. He can be reached at jahern@lakeshore-valuation.com

Hearts, Minds, and the War Against Terror

Joshua Muravchik

THE SCOOP appeared in the *New York Times* in February: as part of "a new effort to influence public sentiment and policy makers in both friendly and unfriendly countries," it revealed, the Pentagon was "developing plans to provide news items, *possibly even false ones*, to foreign media organizations" (emphasis added).

According to the *Times*, what had prompted the creation of this so-called Office of Strategic Influence (OSI) was the worry of "many administration officials" that "the United States was losing support in the Islamic world after American warplanes began bombing Afghanistan." And what had prompted the leak of the story? It seems that a number of people inside the Pentagon, whether for reasons of principle or for reasons of turf, were concerned that the new office, by combining the tasks of public relations with those of covert operations, would thereby taint the former. "It goes from the blackest of black programs to the whitest of white," an anonymous official was quoted, thus fueling the impression that the office would be peddling lies.

In fact, the U.S. has rarely done anything like this in its history. (The term "black operations" in this context properly refers to the practice of hiding the role of the government as the source of a given story rather than to the practice of spreading disinformation.) Nevertheless, the *Times* weighed in the very next day with an editorial denouncing the new office, which it called "Orwellian," while the columnist Maureen Dowd contributed her own broadside against what she dubbed the Office of Strategic Mendacity. In no time, scores of other newspapers around the country had registered their indignation, causing Defense Secretary Donald Rumsfeld to protest that "the Pentagon is not issuing disinformation to the foreign press or any other press."

But the die had been cast. Within a week of the first *Times* story, Rumsfeld announced he had closed the office down.

THIS ABORTED mission was not the only effort by the Bush administration to wage a battle for hearts and minds as part of its larger war against terrorism. The State Department had already brought in Charlotte Beers, formerly the head of the giant advertising agency Ogilvy & Mather, as undersecretary for "public diplomacy." According to Beers, her aim was to do for the United States what she had done for IBM in the 1990's—namely, to "rebrand" it. But her new job, she confessed, would be even tougher than her old one—indeed, "the most sophisticated brand assignment I have ever had." "It is almost," she added, "as though we have to redefine what America is."

If the goal sounded ambitious, she could at least count on the full backing of her formidable patron, the Secretary of State. For Colin Powell himself, it turns out, had been keen on the Madison Avenue approach to public diplomacy even before September 11, much preferring it to the more traditional and overly intellectual methods of the now-defunct United States Information Agency (USIA). In congressional testimony soon after taking office, Powell had declared: "I'm going to be bringing people into the public-diplomacy function of the department who are going to change from just selling us in the old USIA way to really branding foreign policy, branding the department, marketing the department, marketing American values to the world."

In the wake of September 11, and in line with the new spirit, Beers was reported to be considering "TV and radio spots in which sports stars and celebrities [would] talk up the U.S." Her office's major product was a shiny and colorful 25-page pamphlet, *The Network of Terrorism*, distributed in 36 languages and featuring vivid photographs of the September 11 destruction, harsh commentary on al Qaeda and the Taliban, and denunciations of terrorism by such world leaders as Kofi Annan, Tony Blair, and Jiang Zemin. By far the most prominent quotations, spread throughout the pamphlet in huge type, were by Muslims—three Arab sheiks, one Indonesian cleric, and the Council on American-Islamic Relations (CAIR)—repudiating the September 11 attacks and the taking of innocent life.

As the war began, the White House also created another agency, the Coalition Information Center (CIC), with offices in Washington, London, and Pakistan. Its purpose was (and remains) to publicize our side's war aims and to provide instantaneous rebuttal of enemy claims about civilian casualties or battlefield successes. Widening its writ, the CIC also gave impetus to the "Afghan women's initiative," which pressed for a role for women in post-Taliban power structures, thereby underscoring the humanly liberating aspect of a victory in Afghanistan.

More important than the work of any of these agencies, the hallmark of America's outreach efforts was the activity of George W. Bush himself. Three days after September 11, the President led an ecumenical service at the National Cathedral at which a spokesman for America's Muslims helped officiate. A few days later, the President visited the Islamic Center, a Washington mosque, where he proclaimed that "Islam is peace" and went on to castigate Americans who had made threatening gestures toward Muslims in the days since September 11. "Women who cover their head in this country must feel comfortable going outside," he declared. "Moms who wear cover must not be intimidated in America."

Bush's embrace extended beyond American Muslims to Muslims around the globe. In his address to Congress nine days after the attack, he enunciated several themes to which he has returned repeatedly in the months since:

> I also want to speak tonight directly to Muslims throughout the world. We respect your faith. It's practiced freely by many millions of Americans, and by millions more in countries that America counts as friends. Its teachings are good and peaceful, and those who commit evil in the name of Allah blaspheme the name of Allah. The terrorists are traitors to their own faith, trying, in effect, to hijack Islam itself. The enemy of America is not our many Muslim friends; it is not our many Arab friends.

To demonstrate his earnestness in this matter, the President invited a group of American Muslim spokesmen to breakfast at the White House in order "to discuss... what our country is going to do to make sure that everybody who is an American is respected." In November, he also invited the ambassadors of the member states of the Organization of the Islamic Conference (OIC) to pray and break the daylong Ramadan fast at the White House, expressing his esteem for Muslim "believers [who] built a culture of learning and literature and science" and with whom "we share the same hope for a future of peace." Secretary of State Powell held a similar dinner at the State Department, and U.S. ambassadors around the world were instructed to do likewise.

To REINFORCE Bush's message of openness to the faith whose teachings the September 11 terrorists had invoked in attacking us, Charlotte Beers's office printed up thousands of posters in a series called "Mosques of America," for distribution around the world. She herself declared that "We... have to be as good at listening as we are at proposing our point of view," so that our interlocutors will "understand... that they don't need to kill us to get our attention."

But if we had been better listeners, we might have been disconcerted by what we heard. Thus, the very same Islamic spokesmen whom the administration was celebrating for their anti-terrorist sentiments turned out to have, at best, mixed records on the issue. The first of the three sheiks featured in the State Department's pamphlet was Yussef al-Qaradawi of Qatar, who had praised suicide bombings—especially those directed against innocent Israeli civilians—as "martyrdom operations"; according to a columnist in the London Arabic newspaper *Al Hayat*, Qaradawi also endorsed a fatwa issued by another sheik supporting the killing of Americans. The pamphlet's second sheik, Mohammed Sayyed al-Tantawi of Egypt, had indeed criticized attacks on women and children, but subsequently qualified his position by stating that "whoever blows himself up among aggressors... who violate the dignity of our brothers in Palestine... is a martyr." The third sheik, Abdul Rahman al-Sudais of Mecca, although more outspoken than either of the other two in decrying violence, nonetheless was ambiguous when it came to the bottom line, appealing to Muslims "not to mix up the concepts of real terrorism and legitimate jihad."

The records of the American Muslims to whom the administration turned were no less clouded. CAIR, cited in large print in the State Department's publication and one of the hosts of the President's visit to the Islamic Center, is headed by Nihad Awad, who announced in the wake of the 1993 Oslo accords that he was shifting his support from the PLO to Hamas. Some of the guests at the White House breakfast for Islamic spokesmen likewise boasted histories of support for Hamas or Hizbullah, two groups that had done and continue to do much to earn their places on the United States list of terrorist organizations. And so forth.

IF THE only Muslim spokesmen we could find to second our message were themselves highly compromised, additional and devastating evidence was soon to emerge of how faintly that message was getting through. In March, the Gallup organization released the results of polling in nine predominantly Muslim countries. In only two of them did the proportion of respondents with a "very favorable" opinion of the United States exceed a tenth of the population: Lebanon, where the number was 18 percent, and Kuwait, where it was 11. But these pro-American respondents were themselves offset by the 30 percent of Lebanese and 23 percent of Kuwaitis who recorded their opinion of us as very *un*favorable. In Saudi Arabia, meanwhile, a mere 7 percent said they held a very favorable view of us, with seven times that number, or 49 percent, at the opposite end of the spectrum; in Pakistan, Gallup had to report an asterisk under "very favorable," signifying a response of less than 1 percent. With the exception of Turkey, the news was hardly any better elsewhere.

When asked specifically about the September 11 attacks, pluralities or bare majorities in most of the nine countries did say they found them "totally unjustifiable"—but much *higher* proportions condemned the U.S. military action in Afghanistan as itself totally unjustifiable. The most startling results were for Kuwait, where a mere 26 percent of respondents found the attacks on the World Trade Center and Pentagon totally unjustifiable, while over twice that number, 55 percent, applied this judgment to America's actions in Afghanistan. It would have been fascinating to see how Saudis assessed the September 11 attacks, but the presumptively pro-American Saudi government

Article 36. Hearts, Minds, and the War Against Terror

forbade Gallup to ask the question, as did the government of Jordan.

To make matters worse, even where substantial numbers found the September 11 attacks unjustifiable, there was widespread denial—except in Turkey—that they had been carried out by Arabs. In Pakistan, deniers outnumbered believers 86 percent to 4, in Kuwait 89 percent to 11—and this was *after* the release of the infamous videotape in which Osama bin Laden had boasted of having planned the attack. Some respondents who denied Arab involvement did (confusingly) name bin Laden or al Qaeda as the responsible party, but among Lebanese, Kuwaitis, and Moroccans the favored culprit was Israel, and for Iranians, America itself.

The import of these stark numbers was soon brought into question by news items challenging the methodology of the Gallup survey and the presentation of its findings. The main target of criticism was a press release, echoed by CNN and *USA Today*, that aggregated the data for the nine countries, thereby yielding numbers that were statistically meaningless since they ignored the wide disparities in the size of the various populations. But the flaw in Gallup's press release was quite irrelevant. However erroneous the procedure, the aggregated numbers did not make the data any more appalling than they would be if taken country by country, which is how I have cited them here.

Another complaint was that the group of nine—Indonesia, Turkey, Morocco, Iran, Kuwait, Saudi Arabia, Pakistan, Jordan, and Lebanon—do not necessarily represent the diversity of the Islamic world as a whole. This argument too is hard to credit. Not only does the list include a rather disparate array of polities, but the sample is hardly weighted toward the anti-American side. Within the Muslim Middle East, which is the focus of concern in the war against terrorism, one would be foolish to imagine more comforting results than these in, say, Syria, Iraq, Yemen, Libya, Algeria, or Egypt.

Finally, the government of Kuwait, a country liberated by American power from the clutches of Saddam Hussein only a decade ago, has looked for a way out of its embarrassment over the Gallup figures by complaining that the pollsters sampled residents at large rather than only citizens. (In Kuwait, noncitizens outnumber citizens.) But, as it happens, Gallup did ask respondents in that country to indicate their status; as between citizens and noncitizens, the answers differed hardly at all. In fact, if Kuwaiti citizens alone had been tallied, the percentage finding the September 11 attacks morally justified would have *risen*, from 36 to 40 percent.

Confronted with the Gallup figures, President Bush exclaimed, in a masterpiece of understatement: "We've got work to do."

How is the work to be done? Basically, public diplomacy comprises two broad functions, both of which have traditionally been carried out by specially trained foreign-service officers, mostly stationed in U.S. missions abroad. One is short-term public relations: explaining current U.S. policy, circulating speeches by the President and the Secretary of State, flacking for them on their visits. The other is long-term: academic exchanges, sustaining U.S. libraries and American-studies programs, cultivating relationships with writers and editors receptive to America and its values, even publishing intellectual magazines in local languages.

For decades, both of these functions were the responsibility of the United States Information Agency. Opinion differs as to how successfully they were performed—better in some eras and under some directors than in others, obviously—but in any case, as I have already noted, the USIA is no longer in existence. It was abolished in 1999, with its functions being putatively taken over by the State Department.

This "reorganization" was pushed through by Republican Senator Jesse Helms in order to streamline what he called the "outrageously costly foreign-policy apparatus." But it was first proposed not by Helms but by Bill Clinton's Secretary of State, Warren Christopher, and other former Secretaries of State hurried to endorse it. (USIA's $2-billion annual budget would make a large addition to State's funding.) George P. Shultz, who served under Ronald Reagan, called it "bold and constructive," and James Baker, who served the elder Bush, found it "breathtaking in its boldness and visionary in its sweep."

The consequences of the reorganization were as swift in coming as they were predictable. For one thing, the promised savings never materialized: in its official implementation report, the Clinton administration was soon explaining that the merger of the agencies had instead led to an *increase* in costs, and one that would continue "over the next several fiscal years." For another thing, the longterm side of public diplomacy was eviscerated. This too was predictable: in the State Department, the main focus is not on the long-term but on the immediate; what enhances the Secretary's image is public relations, not libraries or exchange programs. No wonder that, in unveiling his Madison Avenue approach to public diplomacy, Colin Powell had gone out of his way to deprecate the USIA.

There is a third side, or complement, to public diplomacy—namely, international broadcasting. But here, too, such meager instruments as were once in our hands have been diminished in recent times. Post-cold-war budget cuts have weakened the Voice of America to the point where its Arabic service has been broadcasting only seven hours a day in a single dialect (the Arab world is notable for wide variations in pronunciation), reaching an audience estimated at only 2 percent of the population.

But the paucity of our means is not the sole or even the major problem we face. Nor is a solution to that problem to be found in enhancing our technique, either through "rebranding" programs or through attempts to do "a better job of telling the compassionate side of the American story," as the President has also suggested.

The key underlying premise of our entire publicity effort is that we and the Muslim Middle East inhabit the same moral and cognitive universe, and that our task is therefore to demonstrate the congruence of our goals and actions with those shared values. Yet nothing in Middle Eastern politics—from the nearly universal obsessive hatred of Israel, to the brutal conduct of relations among Arab states themselves and among factions within them, to the pitiless way rulers treat their subjects—

suggests that there is any truth to that premise, let alone that compassion is a prized value in this part of the world.

Take the one principal theme of our outreach efforts—that our enemy is not Islam but terrorism. To judge by the Gallup poll and other evidence, this is another subject on which we speak a different moral language from those we wish to reach. The numbers who told Gallup they found our war against terrorism even "somewhat" justifiable amounted to 1 percent in Morocco, 2 percent in Indonesia, 4 percent in Pakistan, 9 in Iran, 17 in Kuwait, 19 in Turkey, and 20 in Lebanon; Saudi Arabia and Jordan once again refused to allow Gallup even to ask the question.

UN Secretary General Kofi Annan—no hawk, he—discovered all this for himself when he proposed a world treaty against terrorism in the aftermath of September 11. Appealing for "moral clarity," Annan condemned "the deliberate taking of innocent life, regardless of cause or grievance. If there is one principle that all peoples can agree on," he added, "surely it is this." So cautious and anodyne was the wording of the proposed treaty that North Korea itself proclaimed its support. Not so the Islamic Conference, which turned it down flat. Even when Annan "gambled his moral authority" (in the words of a UN diplomat) by a personal appeal to a meeting of the Conference, the Islamic states would not budge or accept any compromise unless a blanket exemption were included for terrorist actions against Israel. At its meeting in Malaysia in early April, the Conference reaffirmed its stance.

If there is "one principle that all peoples can agree on," in short, it is not this one. For most Muslim states (Turkey again excepted), "terrorism" is a concept defined not by the nature of the act but by the cause in whose name it is undertaken, or by the identities of the perpetrators and the victims. Almost any military action *by* Israel is considered terrorism, almost any violence *against* Israel is resistance. For some large number of Muslims, the same would seem to apply if the term "United States" is substituted for "Israel."

This widespread acceptance of terrorism is only one sign of a larger syndrome. The political culture of the Muslim Middle East is mired in tyranny, violence, fanaticism, bigotry, and fantasy. As Fouad Ajami showed in *The Dream Palace of the Arabs*, this is not just a matter of regimes and rulers. It is also a matter of thinkers—academics, journalists, intellectuals, writers and artists, professionals of every stripe: the very people whose hearts and minds we are seeking to address. The widespread denial that it was Arabs who were responsible for the September 11 attacks, the credence given to the preposterous rumor that 4,000 Jewish employees at the World Trade Center stayed home from work on September 11 because the Mossad slipped them the word that it was about to blow up the towers, is evidence of a deficiency not merely in information but in the skills of reality-testing.

Changing this, if it is within our power at all, is not a matter for the short or even the medium term, and it cannot be accomplished by public diplomacy conceived along Madison Avenue lines. If we are going to chip away at the solid wall of hostility that Gallup found, we will have to proceed less by polishing our image than by improving the Arab-Muslim way of looking at things. The problem is not our "brand"; it is their buying habits.

FIRST THINGS first, then. What is needful above all (as Norman Podhoretz argued in these pages last month) is to prosecute the war against terrorism relentlessly until it is won. Our victory need not await local political change; indeed, we dare not risk making it contingent on such change. Rather, the inverse applies: a triumph of arms may facilitate a triumph of ideas that could obviate future resort to military measures.

Contemporary Islamism arose as an idea in response to political rather than religious yearnings. It was not an answer to the question, "what does my faith demand of me?" but rather to the question, "how can I overcome my sense of national humiliation?" And it battened on the image of an America defeated by the Iran of the ayatollahs and of an America and Israel driven from Lebanon by Hizbullah.

It is a cliché that you cannot kill an idea. But the defeat of an *armed* idea can indeed lead to its death. That is what happened to fascism, and we can hope it will happen to Islamic extremism in its turn. Just as we succeeded in imbuing Japan and Germany with liberalism and democracy after we had defeated them decisively on the battlefield, so the defeat of terrorism, which in practice means the defeat of the various regimes that sponsor terror and of the Islamist movement, may open the way to new thinking in the Middle East. Although it is unlikely that we will occupy any countries as long or as thoroughly as we did at the end of World War II, our goal ought to be the same: liberalizing and democratizing cultures that have previously proved resistant to it.

It is here that public diplomacy properly should be brought in—for it is true that, in the long run, if we are to foment some betterment of the political culture of the Muslim Middle East, we will have need of it. In lieu of reprising General MacArthur's role in Japan as an ersatz emperor, we will have to rely on instruments of "soft power" to effect lasting change. Nor need we wait until the moment of military victory to begin deploying those instruments.

On this front, there is good news and bad. The good news lies in the area of broadcasting, where Congress has funded plans, already in the testing stages, for a new Middle Eastern Radio Network (MERN) that promises to repair many of the defects of our current operation. The plan calls for a mixture of public affairs and music (both Arabic and Western) to be broadcast 24 hours a day on AM and FM bands rather than only on short wave as at present, and in five different regional dialects of Arabic. The network is scheduled to begin full operation this summer.

Plans for revitalizing public diplomacy per se offer a less encouraging picture. The fiasco of the Pentagon's short-lived Office of Strategic Influence, and the embarrassment that was the State Department's pamphlet on terrorism or the President's breakfast with supporters of Hamas and Hizbullah—all give witness to a vacuum of coherent, long-range thought. During the very week of the OSI scandal, the White House confirmed that it was working on its own plan to transform the wartime

Coalition Information Center into a permanent office that would be oriented toward a more distant horizon. There is much value in such an idea—the presidency is a bullier pulpit by far than the State Department—but the political pressures that weigh on the State Department weigh even more heavily on the White House. The same purpose would be better served by reinventing a semi-independent agency like the old USIA.

No initiative of public diplomacy is likely to succeed, however, unless it is informed by a spirit of honesty, however politically incorrect, about the depth of the problem we face, and of unapologetic directness in confronting the sordid political culture that gave rise to the attacks of September 11. We need an effective capability for disseminating information and influence, but if its message is one of "anxious propitiation" (in the phrase of the eminent Islamic scholar Bernard Lewis), it will not only fail on its own terms but it will undercut and compromise the very different and necessary message being sent by our awesome military forces. On this front, not only do we have much work to do, we have not even begun.

JOSHUA MURAVCHIK, *a resident scholar at the American Enterprise Institute, is the author of* Exporting Democracy *and, most recently,* Heaven on Earth: The Rise and Fall of Socialism *(Encounter Books).*

Reprinted with permission from *Commentary*, May 2002, pp. 25-30. © 2002 by the American Enterprise Institute. All rights reserved.

Case: *The Trip to Denver: A Decision-Making Case* by Stan Bazan, Fred Maidment, and Fred Tesch

Thursday, September 6, 2001

Frank Smith joined Colonial two months ago to serve as Manager of Colonial's Purchasing and Supply Chain Management Group (PSCG). PSCG procures needed materials and services for Colonial Equipment in a timely and cost effective manner. Twenty-three people report directly to Frank. Colonial and the much larger National Diversified have moved toward a merger. National's Board of Directors meets November 1 to formally approve the merger with Colonial. Samantha Peterman, Vice-President of Corporate Services at National Diversified, has asked Frank to select two PSCG members to travel to Denver on October 8 to provide a detailed description and hands-on demonstration of Colonial's purchasing and supply chain management process and computer system. This visit is critical to National's final assessment of its pending merger with Colonial. Potential synergies or duplication must be identified. National believes Colonial's recently upgraded computer system is more advanced than theirs and has scheduled complex simulations to assess the system's compatibility and capabilities. The future of Colonial's Hartford-based purchasing group clearly depends on National's evaluation. Samantha wants the two people identified by Wednesday, September 26 to begin pre-visit coordination.

Tuesday, September 11, 2001

Two airplanes were deliberately crashed into the twin towers of the World Trade Center and another plane was crashed into the Pentagon. A fourth flight crashed near Shanksville, PA after an apparent struggle between the hijackers and passengers. The Federal Aviation Administration grounded all aircraft at 9:40 am.

Wednesday, September 12, 2001

President Bush called the attacks of September 11 "acts of war."

Thursday, September 13, 2001

Very limited flight schedules resumed under extraordinary security measures.

Thursday, September 20, 2001

President Bush addressed Congress and stated "Great harm has been done to us. We have suffered great loss. And in our grief and anger, we have found our mission and our moment. Freedom and fear are at war."

Friday, September 21, 2001

Frank spoke to Samantha Peterman several times during the preceding week. She acknowledged the issues surrounding Frank's decision. She stressed that she needed the two PSCG representatives at her site on October 8th and that she wanted them identified by Wednesday, September 26. Frank e-mailed Samantha that morning concerning alternatives to his people actually visiting Denver. Samantha's immediate reply was "The board will meet on November 1 so we need to stick with the original plan. I know that you will select the right people." Frank shared this e-mail with his vice-president at Colonial who responded "It seems like it is a go then, so book the flights early so there are no foul-ups."

Saturday, September 22, 2001

On Saturday morning, Frank retreated to his home office to consider his dilemma. Frank planned to review the facts, the decision process, and the implications. Before Frank began, he put aside his note pad and considered the business context of the decision and his own brief tenure at Colonial. Colonial had not done a merger before and was unclear on specifics of the process. Frank wished he knew more about the visit's agenda. Frank knew the frustration of having people make decisions without consulting him. He thought how quickly his two months at Colonial had passed and wished he knew his people's strengths and weaknesses better. At times some of his staff ignored his suggestions and requests for specific actions. He was surprised that most PSCG members ate at their desks or exercised at lunch and rarely socialized after work. When Frank consulted a fellow manager about this, he was told that PSCG people had a reputation for being professional but doing their own thing independently. Frank also learned several managers had rotated through his position just prior to their retirement. Frank was comfortable with the business processes but still struggled with the computer system.

Frank knew he had to select two individuals who are experts in business process and information technology. Frank determined that the following people were capable of doing the assignment.

- **Ruth Goldberg:** Age 35. Single mother with a 12-year-old daughter. Bachelor's degree in Business Administration. 13 years in the company. 11 years in purchasing. Served on four purchasing process improvement teams and led two. Served on three software testing teams. Reputed to be on the rise in the company.

- **Kelvin Johnson:** Age 26. Single. Bachelor's degree in MIS. Five years in the company and 4 in purchasing. Served on one process improvement team. Served on two software testing teams and led the most recent. Computer expert in the group. Very likable.

- **Beth LePage:** Age 42. Married to a successful engineer. A double-income, no-kids family. BS in Elementary Education. Ten years in the company and 6 in purchasing. Served on two process improvement teams and one software testing team. A former elementary school teacher. A steady performer and a pleasant personality.

- **Jorge Gomez:** Age 49. Single. Associate's degree in business. Twenty-nine years in the company, 3 years in purchasing. Served on numerous cross-functional process improvement teams in the company and one in purchasing. Provided significant input to software testing team during last upgrade. Popular in the company and a self-proclaimed bachelor. Was a quick study in learning his job in purchasing, especially the computer system.

- **Muhammad Bashir:** Age 33. Married with an 8-year-old and a 3-year-old son. Bachelor's degree in Business Administration. Completing MBA in Purchasing and Supply Chain Management. Nine years in the company and in purchasing. Served on three process improvement teams. Member of four computer testing teams and led two. A native of Pakistan. Lived in the United States since attending college.

- **David Johnson:** Age 38. Married with a 15-year-old son. Fourteen years in the company, 8 years in purchasing. Bachelor of Science degree. Served on two process improvement teams and two software testing teams. Reliable performer. Wife, known to be a rising star at Colonial, was recently promoted to Vice-President.

Frank considered other factors. PSCG people didn't typically travel so there was no existing travel assignments procedure. Frank's group knew the merger was moving forward, was likely inevitable and beneficial to both companies, and involved travel to National. Nobody in Frank's group made any specific comments about traveling but he sensed little enthusiasm for it. On the other hand, being PSCG's representative was a high visibility assignment. Frank knew Colonial had not developed new guidelines with respect to safe employee travel. Frank reviewed the facts at hand and revisited a number of questions: Should he make the decision on his own? Should he talk to people in his group and then make his decision? Should he call a meeting to decide? How would his people react to his decision? How would his actions affect his reputation with National? How would his actions affect his reputation with Colonial? Would or should he go himself?

Frank knew only one thing—by Wednesday he needed to identify the two representatives that will travel to Denver on October 8.

Instructor's Notes

Objective: To provide students with a relatively complex, topical, and engaging case study of decision making in organizational and social contexts.

Scenario: A department head, Frank Smith, is required to have two of his subordinates travel from Hartford, Connecticut, to Boulder, Colorado, in the weeks following the terrorist attacks of September 11, 2001.

Overt issue: What decision-making approach would best serve Frank Smith, his subordinates, his department, and his company, both immediately and in the future? The case can also be used as an exercise in applying Vroom & Yetton's decision-making model and decision tree.

Underlying issues and questions for discussion: The richness of the case permits discussions of four topical areas.

1. Decision making
    a. What decision-making process (individual, consultative, or group) is most appropriate in this situation? For Frank? For his subordinates? For his department?
    b. How do contextual factors affect how the decision must be made?
    c. How do the contextual factors affect the behavior of Frank and his staff?

2. Equitable Treatment
    a. How do stereotypes (e.g., gender, marital status) affect the staff's perceptions of the situation and of each other?
    b. In what ways can personal and family factors be balanced with work factors and organizational needs?

3. Ethics
    a. Is it reasonable or acceptable to put people at risk at the corporate level, at Frank's level, and at a personal level?
    b. What are some possible effects of this situation on future careers, both individual (going vs. not) and group (survival of Frank's unit after merger)?

4. Diversity
    a. When is diversity relevant to decision making? How should it be incorporated into decision making?
    b. While diversity is usually presented as an organizational resource, in what circumstances could it be a hindrance?

Notes

Index

A

Abilene Paradox, 98–107
Acceptance Priority Rule, managerial decision making and, 41
Acceptance Rule, managerial decision making and, 40
accountability, 84
accounting, rules-based versus principles-based, 128
Ackerman, Duane, 16
action anxiety, management of agreement, 101
agreement, management of, and Abilene Paradox, 98–107
alternative decisions, processes of, 39
Annan, Kofi, and proposed world treaty against terrorism, 212
Ansoff, Igor, 58
Arthur Andersen, failure of, 13, 17
Assaulted Staff Action Program, 134
Assumptions About People at Work exercise, of case VI, 160–161
Athens: model for corporate culture, 81–85; elements of democracy of, 82
audit: outside, relationship to audit committee of corporate boards of directors, 32, 33; internal, relationship of function to audit committee of corporate boards of directors, 32–33
audit committees of corporate boards of directors, 31, 32
auditor, outside, and performance of internal audit function, 33
Auditors' Oversight Board, 128
Automation Plan for Business Mailers, 135

B

background checks, and executive hiring, 149–152
Bad Men Do What Good Men Dream (Simon), 133
Baker, Howard, 100, 104
Beers, Charlotte, and "public diplomacy," 209, 210
BellSouth, 16
Benford's Law, 129
Birt, John, 20–21
"black operations," 209
Blair, Tony, 20
boards of directors: audit committee of, 31, 32; compensation committee of, 32; and corporate governance, 30; governance committee of, 31–32; nominating committees of, 31; outside directors as chairs of, 31; selection of, 31
Book of Leadership Wisdom, The (Bossidy), 108
Bossidy, Lawrence, 108
Branson, Richard, 20
Browne, Lord, 20
Buffet, Warren, 17, 21; on synergies, 114
Bush, George W., 21; European anger toward, 172; and "public diplomacy" post 9/11 toward Muslims, 210
business activity, types of, 58
Business in the Community, and CSR, 205
business intelligence systems, 128

C

Camus, Albert, 107
capital budgeting procedures, 9
Carlson, Sune, 5
Center for Creative Leadership (CCL) model, 88
centers of excellence, 179
CEOs: centralization of power in, 30–31; compensation of, 32; and corporate failures, 12–18; role of, 30–32
Chambers, John, 13
change management, 89
charisma: and awe, 109; and "carriers," 110; defined, 108; and leadership, 108–110
charitable foundations, and creating social value, 197–200
Cho, Fulio, 65, 66
Churchill, Winston, 108; and "Statistical Office," 16
Circuit City, 109
Cisco Networking Academy, 192, 193, 195, 198, 200
Cisco Systems, failure of, 13
Citigroup, 113
coaching, employee, 122, 123
Coalition for Environmentally Responsible Economies, and CSR, 205
Collins, Jim, 14, 84
collusion, management of agreement and, 103
communities of practice, 179
community within organizations: correlation to company performance, 185; defined, 183; process for building, in the workplace, 183–185; value in workplace of, 183; values of, 184
Compaq, merger with Hewlett-Packard, 64, 113
competitive context, 192; four elements of, 193–196
competitive forces, types of, 58–59
competitive paranoia, 15
Competitive Strategy (Porter), 58
conceptual basis model, of the decision-making process, 38–41
conflict, management of agreement and, 103, 104–105
Conflict Rule, managerial decision-making and, 40
conformity, management of agreement and, 103, 104–105
confrontation, management of agreement and, 103, 104, 105–106
control, as management function, 3–11
coordination, as management function, 3–11
Cordle Manufacturing Company, 138
corporate culture, 17, 64, 82
corporate governance, 29–33; and boards of directors, 30; British system of, 31; and the NYSE, 30
corporate infrastructure, 63
Corporate Library, 17
corporate oversight, 15
corporate philanthropy, 191–202
corporate social responsibility (CSR), 191, 203–206; Adam Smith on, 203; and British American Tobacco, 206; evolution timeline of, 204; and the Global Reporting Initiative, 205; and influence on consumer behavior, 204; and pressure groups, 203; and related legislation in Great Britain, 205–206; and shareholders, 205
corporate vision, 179
corporations, American: concept of limited liability of, 172; contrasted with European corporations, 172; economic magnitude of, 171; and effects of institutional investor holdings, 171; goal of, 171–172; and hostile takeovers, 171, 172
cost centers, in MAM context, 52
courage, management of agreement and, 103
CPAs, and compliance with Sarbanes-Oxley Act, 187–190
creative destruction, 12
Cub Scout Pack 81 exercise, of case IV, 118–119

D

Dean, John, 100–101
decisional roles, of managers, 7–10, 38–47
Dell Computer, 114
Department of Justice, 29
discretionary effort, 183
dissemination, management and, 7
distributive management, 179
disturbance handling, management and, 8
diversity, 91
"doom loop," 17
Drucker, Peter, 123
Duncan Paper Products Corporation, 94

E

E*Trade, 113
Ebbers, Bernard, 16
Ebitda, 15
Eckstein, Wendy, 68
Economy and Society (Weber), 108
education, on management, 11
effectiveness, defined, 176
efficiency, defined, 177
Eisenhower, Dwight D., managerial style of, 5
e-learning, 88
empirical basis model, of the decision-making process, 38–41
"employability contract," 83–84
employee fraud, trends related to, 151
employee matching grants, 192
empowerment, 81
engagement, practices of, 84
Enron, 12, 15, 17; audit committee of, 32; and corporate social responsibility, 203, 205; and ethics, 189; lapses by board of directors of, 31

Index

entrepreneurship: activity of, 165; elements of, 170; management and, 7, 8
ethics, codes of, for corporations: references for models of, 188; required by Sarbanes-Oxley Act, 186–187
Ethics Resource Center, and Sarbanes-Oxley Act, 187–189
Evaluation of Organizational Effectiveness exercise, of case V, 138–139
execution risk, 16
Executive Behaviour (Carlson), 5
executive hiring, and background checks, 149–152
Executive Role Constellation, The (Hodgson, Levinson, and Zaleznik), 5
executives: present-oriented, 90; future-oriented, 90

F

failure, corporate: defined, 13; magnitude of, 13; ten big mistakes leading to, 14; three quick fixes for, 15
Fairfax County Social Welfare Agency exercise, of case II, 68–69
Fairness Rule, managerial decision-making and, 41
Fastow, Andrew, 17
Fayol, Henri, 3
fear of separation, management of agreement and, 102
"feet of clay," 109
Ferguson, Sir Alex, 22
Fifth Discipline: The Art and Practice of the Learning Organization, The (Senge), 88
figureheads, managers as, 6
financial failure, 127–131; examples of, 127; and governance rules, 128; and IT systems to prevent, 128, 130; significance of Sarbanes-Oxley Act to, 128
financial reporting, complications in multinational corporations, 49
Fiorina, Carly, 113
Fisher Body, and General Motors, 113
flexibility programs, 147
fraud, against business: IT tools to protect against, 127, 128, 129, 130; magnitude of, 129, 151; trends regarding, 151
Friedman, Milton, on corporate goal, 191–192

G

General Motors and Fisher Body, 113
Generally Accepted Accounting Principles (GAAP), 48
glass ceiling, 143
global mind-set, corporate, 174–181; balancing global consistency with local responsiveness, 175–176, 178; defined, 174; developing in a company, 178–180; and the three tensions of global business, 176–177
Global Reporting Initiative for CSR, 205–206
Goal Congruence Rule, managerial decision-making and, 40
Good to Great (Collins), 109
governance committees of corporate boards of directors, 31–32
governance rules, 128; and protecting against fraud, 128–129, 130
Green, Philip, 21

Greenspan, Alan, 17
group consensus, as decision-making method, 69
groupthink, management of agreement and, 98–107
Grove, Andy, 14, 15
Guest, Robert H., 5, 6

H

Hale, Robert, 94
Hamlet, 101, 102
Harley-Davidson, and customer focus, 62–63
Hewlett-Packard, merger with Compaq, 64, 113
hiring, and background checking of prospective executives, 149–152
hiring process, 153–157; and the art of interviewing, 154; assessment vehicles, 155–156; components of, 155; and group interviews, 155; and mismatched employee behaviors, 154–155; and preselection, 154
Hodgson, Richard C., 5
Homans, George C., 5, 7
Home Depot, and customer focus, 62
"Homes," Is Where the Union Is exercise, of case VI, 160–161
Human Group, The (Homans), 5, 7

I

In Search of Excellence (Peters and Waterman), 8
information, managerial decision making and, 7, 39
infrastructure, 63
innovation, 165–171; and corporate reporting systems, 167; defined, 165; principles of, 170; seven areas of opportunity for, 165–169
institutional investors, 171–172
Intel, 14, 62
International Accounting Standards (IAS), 49
International Corporate Governance Network (ICGN), 195
International Monetary Fund (IMF), 171
interpersonal roles, of managers, 6–7
Iridium, 61, 62
Iridium Satellite LLC, 64
IT systems: and protection against fraud, 127, 128, 129, 130; and related rules-engine technologies, 129

J

Job Match Pattern, 156
Job Profile Survey, 156
Johnson & Johnson, and customer focus, 63
Judson, Carla, 138
jurisdiction practices, 84

K

Kennedy, John F., 102
knowledge: as competitive advantage, 90; benefits of managing, 90
knowledge management, 104; list of topical references, 92

L

leaders, charismatic, 108–110
leadership, 6; defined, 108; narcissistic, of Mullah Mohammad Omar, 109; new technology for development of, 46–47
Leahy, Sir Terry, 21
learning, motion study and, 79–80
learning organization, 86–88
learning orientation, 90
Levinson, Daniel J., 5
Linux, 64
liquidity risk, 16
list mailer, 136
listening exercise, of case IV, 118–119
local-center accounting model, 49, 50, 52
long-term models, of managerial decision-making, 43–44
LTV, and synergy, 113
Lucent, 16–17

M

Magruder, Jeb, 100–101, 104
Mail Preparation Total Quality Management (MPTQM), 135–137; benefits of, 136–137
management, implementing supervisor's decisions, 116–117
management accounting master (MAM): benefits of using, 51; characteristics of, 51; and cost centers, 52; globally harmonized, 48, 50–51; and integrated legal-entity reporting, 53–55; and profit centers, 52
management by objectives, 123
Managerial Behavior (Sayles), 5
managerial development, in Sherwood Forest, in case I, 34–35
managerial logjams, 10
maternity leave, 142–143
Mather, Clive, on corporate social responsibility, 203
McGinn, Rich, 16
men, versus women, in the corporate world, 142–148
mental toughness, values of, 20–22
mergers: and synergy, 113–114; Warren Buffet on, 114
merit, 84
Microsoft, 64, 114
Middle Eastern Radio Network (MERN), 212
Mitchell, John, 100–101
modular networks, 178–179
monitors, as managers, 7
moral reciprocity, 83
motion study, and work, 72–80
Motorola, 61, 63
Mozer, Paul, 17
Mulcahy, Anne, 14
Mullah Mohammad Omar, 109
multinational corporation accounting, 48–57; challenges to finance departments, 48
Murphy, Mike, 118

N

narcissists, attributes of, 108–109
NASA Exercise, of case II, 69

Index

National Institute of Occupational Safety and Health, on cause of death in the workplace, 132
National Safe Workplace Institute, 132
negative fantasies, management of agreement and, 102
negative synergy, 16
negotiation, management and, 9–10
Neustadt, Richard, 5, 7
New York Stock Exchange (NYSE), and corporate governance, 30
nursing homes, unions and, 160

O

Office of Strategic Influence, 209
Okuda, Hiroshi, 67
One Best Way to Do Work, The, Frank and Lillian Gilbreth's theory of, 72–80
O'Neill, Paul, 17, 18
organization: change capable, 89–93; qualities of, for capacity for change, 89
organization design, center-oriented, 51
organization exercise, of case III, 94–95
ownership succession planning, 207–208
Ozyx Corporation, management of agreement and, 99–100

P

pattern recognition: defined, 24; analogy to birding, 24–27; analogy to medical diagnosis, 25–26
performance appraisal, 111–112, 122–126; factors important in, 111; by groups, 123; guidelines for conducting, 111–112; problems of resistance regarding, 122–123; reasons for, 122; role of supervisors in, 123–124, 125; subordinate responsibility for, 123–124
philanthropy, corporate, 191–202; an approach to, 200–202; and the competitive context for, 192–202; and the free rider problem, 196–197; and goodwill, 200; as "strategic philanthropy," 191, 192
planning, as managerial task, 3–11
Polaroid, 13–14
Porter, Herbert, 100–101, 102, 103
Porter, Michael, 58–60
POST-NET, 135
Powell, Colin: and "public diplomacy," 209, 210; and USIA, 211
Pratt, Edmund, 143
Presidential Power (Neustadt), 5
profit centers, in MAM context, 52
Profit Patterns (Slywotzky and Morrison), 23
"public diplomacy," 209; in the Arab world, 212; missteps with Muslims, 210; short-term and long-term functions, 211

R

Rapaport, Robert, 101
real risk, management of agreement and, 102
reality, management of agreement and, 103, 104
resistance to change exercise, of case III, 94–95
resource allocation, 9
responsibility for problem-solving action, management of agreement and, 103–104

risk dashboard, 130
Robin Hood exercise, of case I, 34–35
Robinson, Gerry, 22
Roosevelt, Franklin Delano, managerial style of, 5, 6
rule-of-thumb method, 79
rules engine technologies, 129, 130
Rumsfeld, Donald, 209

S

Salomon Brothers, 17
Samsung, and automobile business, 15–16
Sarbanes-Oxley Act, 128, 186–190; assistance from CPAs for compliance with, 187–190; assistance resources for compliance with, 189; requirements of, for corporate codes of ethics, 186–187
Sayles, Leonard R., 5, 8–9
Schacht, Henry, 17
Sears, and synergy, 113
SEC. *See* Securities and Exchange Commission
Securities and Exchange Commission (SEC), 29, 48; and supervision of auditors of public companies, 33
September 11, 209, 210; Arab views on, 210–211
Simultaneous Motion Cycle Charts, 77
Sisyphus, myth of, and management of agreement, 107
Six Sigma, 61, 63
Slater, Philip, 103
Smale, John, 18; on board chairs, 31
SmithKline and Glaxo, and customer focus, 63
Snow, C. P., 102, 107
spokespeople, as managers, 7
standardization, motion study and, 79
Stewart, Rosemary, 5, 6
stock price, 17
strategic decision-making, six priorities of, 62–64
"strategic philanthropy," corporate, 191, 192
strategies: and the Internet, 60; new wave of, 59; three generic, 58
Street Corner Society (Whyte), 5
"structural observation" method, 5
structure, democratic, in contrast to corporate decision-making, 83
Sugar, Alan, 20
"Sustainable Racine," 195
Swatch, 90
SWOT analysis, 61
synergy: AOL-Time Warner as example of, 114; and media mergers, 113; and mergers, 113–114; the myth of, 114; unrealized expectations of, 113

T

Taliban, 109
Tannenbaum, Robert, 103
Target, and customer focus, 62
therbligs, 74–79
Ticking Bombs: Defusing Violence in the Workplace (Mantell and Allbrecht), 132
time and motion studies, work and, 72–80
Toffler, Alvin, 103
"total reward" compensation, 158; components of, 159; and value-added concept, 159; at multiple levels, 158–159
Toyoda, Kiichiro, 66

Toyota: aging customer base of, 67; the Americanization of, 65–67; relationship between Japan- and USA-based, management, 66–67
training: benefits of, 87–88; critical value of, 87–88; effective approaches to, 87; and employee retention, 88
Transparency International, 195
true elements, 72–80
Truman, Harry S., managerial style of, 5

U

United States Information Agency (USIA), 209, 211; absorption of, by Department of State, 211
Unstructured Problem Rule, managerial decision-making and, 40

V

value-chain activities, 58
Vandevelde, Luc, 21–22
victim and victimizer, management of agreement and, 103
violence, workplace, 132–134; actions to take post-incidents of, 134; annual cost of, 132; and changes in the workplace, 133; and dysfunctional workplaces, 133; prevention of, 133–134
Violence at Work: How to Make Your Company Safer (Kinney), 192
visualizing a classification, method of, 72–80

W

Wargo, John, 135–137
Watergate scandal, management of agreement and, 100–107
Watkins, Sharon, 15
Weber, Max, 108
Welch, Jack, 20
wheel of motion, 76
Whyte, William F., 5
Win As Much As You Can exercise, of case V, 138–139
women in management, 142–148; and the career-and-family woman, 144, 145–147; and the career-primary woman, 144–145; cost differential between males and, 142; and demographic change, 144; and maternity, 142–143; and the need for flexibility, 146–148; psychological predispositions of, 142; and shared employment, 147
worker disenfranchisement, 81
worker retention rates, 156–157
workforce attributes, 63–64
workplace violence. *See* violence, workplace
World Bank, 171
World Wide Web (www), 61
WorldCom, 12, 16; and violations of ethical standards, 187
Wurtzel, Alan, 109

X

Xerox, 14, 88

Z

Zara, 64

Test Your Knowledge Form

We encourage you to photocopy and use this page as a tool to assess how the articles in *Annual Editions* expand on the information in your textbook. By reflecting on the articles you will gain enhanced text information. You can also access this useful form on a product's book support Web site at *http://www.dushkin.com/online/*.

NAME: DATE:
_____

TITLE AND NUMBER OF ARTICLE:
_____

BRIEFLY STATE THE MAIN IDEA OF THIS ARTICLE:
_____

LIST THREE IMPORTANT FACTS THAT THE AUTHOR USES TO SUPPORT THE MAIN IDEA:
_____

WHAT INFORMATION OR IDEAS DISCUSSED IN THIS ARTICLE ARE ALSO DISCUSSED IN YOUR TEXTBOOK OR OTHER READINGS THAT YOU HAVE DONE? LIST THE TEXTBOOK CHAPTERS AND PAGE NUMBERS:
_____

LIST ANY EXAMPLES OF BIAS OR FAULTY REASONING THAT YOU FOUND IN THE ARTICLE:
_____

LIST ANY NEW TERMS/CONCEPTS THAT WERE DISCUSSED IN THE ARTICLE, AND WRITE A SHORT DEFINITION:

We Want Your Advice

ANNUAL EDITIONS revisions depend on two major opinion sources: one is our Advisory Board, listed in the front of this volume, which works with us in scanning the thousands of articles published in the public press each year; the other is you—the person actually using the book. Please help us and the users of the next edition by completing the prepaid article rating form on this page and returning it to us. Thank you for your help!

ANNUAL EDITIONS: Management 04/05

ARTICLE RATING FORM

Here is an opportunity for you to have direct input into the next revision of this volume.
We would like you to rate each of the articles listed below, using the following scale:

1. **Excellent: should definitely be retained**
2. **Above average: should probably be retained**
3. **Below average: should probably be deleted**
4. **Poor: should definitely be deleted**

Your ratings will play a vital part in the next revision.
Please mail this prepaid form to us as soon as possible.
Thanks for your help!

RATING	ARTICLE	RATING	ARTICLE
	1. The Manager's Job: Folklore and Fact		33. The Competitive Advantage of Corporate Philanthropy
	2. Why Companies Fail		34. Who Cares Wins
	3. If You Think You're Hard Enough		35. Determining the Strategies and Tactics of Ownership Succession
	4. Spotting Patterns on the Fly		36. Hearts, Minds, and the War Against Terror
	5. Restoring Public Confidence in American Business		
	6. A New Look at Managerial Decision Making		
	7. Management Accounting Master: Closing the Gap Between Managerial Accounting and External Reporting		
	8. Michael Porter: What Is Strategy?		
	9. Six Priorities That Make a Great Strategic Decision		
	10. The Americanization of Toyota		
	11. Classifying the Elements of Work		
	12. Beyond Empowerment: Building a Company of Citizens		
	13. Creating a Learning Organization		
	14. The Change-Capable Organization		
	15. The Abilene Paradox: The Management of Agreement		
	16. The Myth of Charismatic Leaders		
	17. Effective Performance Counseling		
	18. The Myth of Synergy		
	19. When You Disagree With the Boss's Order, Do You Tell Your Staff?		
	20. An Uneasy Look at Performance Appraisal		
	21. The Cost of Failure		
	22. How Safe Is Your Job? The Threat of Workplace Violence		
	23. Mail Preparation Total Quality Management		
	24. Management Women and the New Facts of Life		
	25. Who Are You Really Hiring?		
	26. Secrets of Finding and Keeping Good Employees		
	27. Pay It Forward		
	28. The Discipline of Innovation		
	29. American Corporations: The New Sovereigns		
	30. The Need for a Corporate Global Mind-Set		
	31. Helping Organizations Build Community		
	32. Ensuring Ethical Effectiveness		

(Continued on next page)

ANNUAL EDITIONS: MANAGEMENT 04/05

BUSINESS REPLY MAIL
FIRST-CLASS MAIL PERMIT NO. 84 GUILFORD CT
POSTAGE WILL BE PAID BY ADDRESSEE

**McGraw-Hill/Dushkin
530 Old Whitfield Street
Guilford, Ct 06437-9989**

ABOUT YOU

Name _____ Date _____

Are you a teacher? ☐   A student? ☐
Your school's name
_____

Department
_____

Address _____ City _____ State _____ Zip _____

School telephone #
_____

YOUR COMMENTS ARE IMPORTANT TO US!

Please fill in the following information:
For which course did you use this book?
_____

Did you use a text with this ANNUAL EDITION?   ☐ yes   ☐ no
What was the title of the text?
_____

What are your general reactions to the *Annual Editions* concept?
_____

Have you read any pertinent articles recently that you think should be included in the next edition? Explain.
_____

Are there any articles that you feel should be replaced in the next edition? Why?
_____

Are there any World Wide Web sites that you feel should be included in the next edition? Please annotate.
_____

May we contact you for editorial input?   ☐ yes   ☐ no
May we quote your comments?   ☐ yes   ☐ no